WAKING UP

WAKING UP

✦

Psychotherapy as Art, Spirituality, and Science

Keith Witt, Ph.D.

Santa Barbara Graduate Institute Publishing
iUniverse, Inc.
New York Bloomington Shanghai

WAKING UP
Psychotherapy as Art, Spirituality, and Science

iUniverse books may be ordered through booksellers or by contacting:

iUniverse
1663 Liberty Drive
Bloomington, IN 47403
www.iuniverse.com
1-800-Authors (1-800-288-4677)

Because of the dynamic nature of the Internet, any Web addresses or links contained in this book may have changed since publication and may no longer be valid.

The information, ideas, and suggestions in this book are not intended as a substitute for professional advice. Before following any suggestions contained in this book, you should consult your personal physician or mental health professional. Neither the author nor the publisher shall be liable or responsible for any loss or damage allegedly arising as a consequence of your use or application of any information or suggestions in this book.

ISBN: 978-0-595-51442-7 (pbk)
ISBN: 978-0-595-61902-3 (ebk)

Printed in the United States of America

The Waking

I wake to sleep, and take my waking slow.
I feel my fate in what I cannot fear.
I learn by going where I have to go.
We think by feeling. What is there to know?
I hear my being dance from ear to ear.
I wake to sleep, and take my waking slow.

O those so close beside me, which are you?
God bless the Ground! I shall walk softly there,
And learn by going where I have to go.

Light takes the Tree; but who can tell us how?
The lowly worm climbs up a winding stair;
I wake to sleep, and take my waking slow.

Great Nature has another thing to do
To you and me; so take the lively air,
And, lovely, learn by going where to go.

This shaking keeps me steady. I should know.
What falls away is always. And is near.
I wake to sleep, and take my waking slow.
I learn by going where I have to go.

~Theodore Roethke~

Contents

Section Four Cultivating compassion and depth of consciousness

Section Five Lines and Levels

Section Six States in Psychotherapy

Introduction

In 2002 my wife Becky listened to a tape of a lecture by David Deida[1] and we were especially loving with each other the following week. She was so impressed that I looked at one of his books but resisted the material, possibly because I unconsciously realized the vast changes that might occur if I really understood the teaching. Sometime later Becky and I went to one of his lectures and I was blown away. His descriptions of sexual polarity and masculine/feminine essences and aspects rang completely true. I realized later that the ideas that we are born on earth to serve each other and that masculine and feminine serve differently were beautiful, good, and true to me. They met the three great validity standards that Plato had written about, that Immanuel Kant had explored in his treatises, and that Ken Wilber had integrated into his elegant conceptualizations of the four quadrants.[2] The principles and practices were beautiful to me, they felt morally right, and I had observed external evidence of them every day of my life.

I immersed myself in the teaching. I listened to Deida's lectures, read his books, flew to New York to participate in a four-day workshop, and used his material in my work. My clients began developing much faster in their ability to grow and love. Work was more fun. My marriage, already great by my standards, blossomed.

How could it get better than this? Well, in Winter of 2003 I listened to Ken Wilber's tape series from his book, *A Brief History of Everything*, which introduced me to the Integral perspective.[3] The Integral perspective is the naturally occurring epistemology of knowledge, human development, and spiritual experience that Ken Wilber has discovered and developed in a lifetime of study and writing. I was mildly interested at first, but as I gradually moved more deeply into the system it captured my attention and imagination. I hungered for more. Wilber's books, *Sex, Ecology, and Spirituality,* and *Integral Psychology,*[4] were like rich chocolate. Each paragraph was a delicious morsel that released a new facet of understanding and expansion. I added his work to my ongoing reading list and immediately found that combining an Integrally informed perspective with David Deida's teachings about sacred sexuality created new dimensions in my individual and conjoint psychotherapy. I've since found that applying what Wilber now calls the Integral Operating System to any approach expands and enhances understanding and practical applications enormously.

We all have various combinations of masculine and feminine aspects in our basic natures as human beings. Almost all of us, when we're most relaxed and open, are more masculine or more feminine in our deepest heart. We suffer if we don't live a life that honors the truest expression of our deepest masculine or feminine sexual essence. We feel more at peace with ourselves and our world when we can discern and relax into whatever aspect of us the moment requires. When we are wide open, without restriction, and experience ourselves as serving love right now, our life tends to feel full and meaningful.

We all develop physically, emotionally, cognitively, spiritually, morally, interpersonally, and psychosexually from conception onward. These are a few of over twenty lines of development that all humans share. We grow on these lines through levels, each level including and transcending previous ones. At any moment we can inhabit a state of functioning at any level on any developmental line in our life. We can be immature, jealous, wise, dense, loving, or hurtful. An Integrally informed psychotherapeutic perspective helps pinpoint what types of person we and our clients are, how we are being influenced by internal and external sources, what our current levels and states of functioning are on what relevant developmental lines, and suggests what perspectives, states of consciousness, and focus of attention might be necessary to serve love and growth.

In 1979 I was in the front room of a beautiful old house in North Hollywood with Becky, a couple of friends, and a Taoist healer/martial artist named John Davidson. I had just ended my first healing session with him and was shaken physically and spiritually. His treatment style combined bodywork, psychotherapy, martial arts, and Chinese five-element theory, and was intrusive, physical, and demanding. After we finished the session I told him I intended to learn his system, and he said, "Sure."

We got to talking martial arts, and I told him I'd been training in several systems for fourteen years. He stood up and said, "Show me." I faced him, bowed, and attacked him with a classic Shotokan Karate technique, oi-zuki, lunge punch. It was a good attack. My focus was centered, my kiai was loud and startling, and my movement was quick and powerful. He felt me coming and, at the last moment, flicked out his right middle finger and struck me perfectly between the eyes with his fingertip. It stopped me cold, and afterwards I had a little indentation directly on my third eye.

That was a beautiful moment. One form of masculine bliss is loving challenge, and nothing is more challenging to a martial artist than being defeated by a fingertip. John's healing work and fighting style revealed exciting new possibilities, and I studied and practiced enthusiastically over the next two years resulting in paradigm shifts in my therapy, my martial arts, and my life.

David Deida's teachings on sacred sexuality, and Ken Wilber's teachings about the Integral approach have had a similar effect. They've awakened me to major new possibilities in understanding life, love, sexuality, and healing, resulting in paradigm shifts in my therapy, my relationships, and my life. Psychotherapy has become more fun and my clients get better faster and farther. I'm more confident helping them to be healthier and to love better. I have access to new perspectives that guide me to understand more deeply and intervene more gracefully.

Years after I finished the first draft of this book, I read in the last chapter of Wilber's *Integral Spirituality*[5] that he believed the Integral Operating System to be psychoactive in that internalizing it created an ongoing process of personal transformation. Since 1956, educators such as J. Bloom[6] have generally accepted that learning often progresses through six stages: knowledge, comprehension, application, analysis, synthesis, and evaluation. What has not been generally understood is that some bodies of learning, once processed through all six stages, create permanent changes in information processing, emotional response, and worldview. I believe the Integral Operating System, the principles of masculine, feminine, and sexual polarity, and a number of other perspectives presented in this book are potentially psychoactive forms of knowledge that can create and sustain ongoing awakenings in every aspect of our lives.

Though inspired by the teachings of Ken Wilber, David Deida, and many others, this book does not attempt to definitively represent any theoretical formulation, organization, or author other than myself. It is designed to synthesize a number of approaches in a comprehensive framework that honors and explores the art, spirituality, and science of psychotherapy. My hope is that this book will inspire you to expand your natural healing style, which is every therapist's personal gift to the world.

Psychotherapy is cocreative art.

Psychotherapy, like most art forms, develops and changes over the life of the artist. New systems, and new applications of old systems, intertwine with our personal development and our clients' offerings in the crucible of the therapy session. Over the life of the therapist/artist this cocreation unfolds in the classic include and transcend developmental rhythm of human growth, leading to exciting new possibilities.[7] I believe the process of personal/professional development is more important than any single aspect of content, so I encourage you to hold any facet of the material you encounter in this book lightly. Take what appeals to you and try it out in work and life to feel how it fits into your unique style as an artist and a healer.

I learn psychotherapeutic theory and practice best when I can understand the principles, have the applications described, and then see them in action. I've organized this book to generally follow that pattern. All the client examples are composites of individuals and couples I've worked with over the years. There are more segments from conjoint sessions because I believe conjoint work is in many ways more demanding than individual work, less understood than individual work, and because conjoint sessions often better reveal the dynamics of sexual polarity that are so important to human existence. Marriage and family difficulties account for about half of all visits to psychotherapists.[8] The transcripts of exchanges between clients and myself are presented in relatively short series because that's how psychotherapy often progresses: in series of exchanges, very much like foil fencing.

I've also included some of my interior experiences during the sessions in the form of perceptions, thoughts, feelings, judgments, and impulses. When studying with other therapists, I've found that such material helps me better understand and apply what I'm learning.

This book is fifty-two Chapters arranged in seven Sections:

- Section One, **Foundations** (Chapters 1–3), explores the process of therapy, introduces masculine and feminine types in therapy, and introduces the basic conceptual framework of the waking up approach to psychotherapy.

- Section Two, **The Integral Lens** (Chapters 4–6), gives an overview of Wilber's Integral approach including definitions and examples of quadrants, lines, levels, states, and types as they apply to psychotherapy.

- Section Three, **Polarity** (Chapters 7–11) explores the masculine and feminine theoretically, spiritually, practically, and especially from the perspectives of how the principles can apply to psychotherapy.

- Section Four, **Cultivating Compassion and Depth of Consciousness** (Chapters 12–23) explores psychotherapy first through two definitions.

    - Cultivating compassion and depth of consciousness to support healthy perspectives and actions.

- Co-creating a healing culture in which the client and the client's universe are cherished, each moment is experienced as a gift and an opportunity, and healthy perspectives and actions are considered beautiful, good, and true.

- Section Four continues with exploring the purpose of psychotherapy and the process of psychotherapy which are defined respectively as:

  - To remediate symptoms, enhance health, and support development.

  - To relate, teach, inspire, confront, interpret, and direct.

- Section Five, **Lines and Levels** (Chapters 24–34) explores the huge importance of thinking developmentally from a variety of perspectives including evolutionary psychology, parenting, psychopathology, the masculine and feminine, and psychotherapy with adults, children, adolescents, couples and families. In Section Four we also follow the developmental arc of a man and a woman (Allen and Evalyn) from conception to unity with all.

- Section Six, **States In Psychotherapy** (Chapters 35–45) begins with exploring waking, dreaming, and deep sleep states, and their applications and significance to psychotherapy. We then move to identifying **states of healthy response to the present moment** and **defensive states** of amplified or numbed emotion, distorted perceptions and thoughts, destructive impulses, and diminished capacities for empathy and self-reflection. These defensive states are further refined as manifestations of **neurotic, characterological, and relational defensive structures**, with corresponding indications for treatment and clinical examples.

- Section Seven, **Conjoint Therapy; Working With Lovers** (Chapters 46–52) explores the special characteristics and demands of the conjoint session, with Chapter 52 being a case study of one example of **sex therapy**, an important subcategory of conjoint treatment in general.

1. Deida (2006)

2. Wilber (1995)

3. Wilber (2000)

4. Wilber (1995, 2000)

5. Wilber (2007)

6. Bloom (1956)

7. Kegan (1982)

8. Harvard Mental Health Newsletter (V23, #9, 2007)

Section One

Foundations

1

Psychotherapy— How is it Possible?

As therapists we want to interact with our clients in ways that help them remediate symptoms, enhance health, and support development. To do this we relate, teach, inspire, confront, interpret, and direct throughout the session in a variety of ways depending on what we and our clients bring into the room.

In many ways this is an impossible task. Imagine you are a therapist in an initial session with a client. You have an hour. What relevant dimensions need attention?

Is your client physically comfortable, healthy, or in balance? How can you tell?

This client has consciousness, a sense of self. Are they comfortable or uncomfortable with their sense of self? How can you tell?

Your client is a social being, embedded in various social networks and relationships. Is there harmony or conflict in these social frameworks, and how can you tell?

Your client probably has both a masculine aspect of deep consciousness, hunger for purpose, and attraction to feminine radiance, and a feminine aspect of radiant love, yearning, and attraction to masculine presence. Your client almost certainly has predominantly a more masculine essence or a more feminine essence in their sexual relationships and in their social and professional networks, and can be more open or blocked in different areas in different circumstances.[1] Where is your client open and true to his/her deepest sexual essences, or blocked and constricted? How can you tell?

Your client is developing simultaneously on a variety of developmental lines such as self, cognitive, moral, spiritual, psychosexual, and relational.[2] What lines are most important to their current work? What levels of development are their centers of gravity (their current, most natural level of functioning) on those lines? What do they need to support development on those lines? How can you tell?

Your client remembers the past consciously, unconsciously, and in bodily tissues.[3] Is the past a peaceful place? Where do they feel liberated and strengthened by the past, and where do they feel shackled, wounded, or disabled by the past? How can you tell?

Your client anticipates and conceptualizes a future. Do they anticipate with pleasure or pain? Is there peacefulness with their path to inevitable death, or terror, anger, or numbness and dissociation? How can you tell?

Your client has a felt spirituality, a constellation of physical sensations and cognitive constructs that they identify as a sense of the sacred. This sense of the sacred can be associated with any number of things such as prayer, meditation, nature, love, family, communion with others, work, play, life, death, places, ceremony, or ideas. It is not an intellectual construct as much as an interior, visceral experience that identifies a spiritually charged area. This felt spirituality, either consciously and/or unconsciously, yearns both away from the body for oneness with transcendence beyond physical reality, and also into the body for feeling spirit in all of nature, sensation, pleasure, pain, and communion with others.[4] Where are these ascending and descending spiritual hungers being satisfactorily met, and where are they not? How can you tell?

Can your client effectively self-regulate and self-soothe in all environments and life circumstances, or does the environment sometimes intrude in the form of other peoples' attempts to regulate and/or soothe them, or in other life stressors such as illness, injury, or failure? How can you tell?

Your client has responsibilities to self, work, family, and relationships. Are these responsibilities powerfully and joyfully embraced, or are they experienced as burdens and constraints, perhaps even as miseries in response to perceived collapse and failure in felt duties (duties they have accepted on an emotional basis in areas such as profession or marriage)? How can you tell?

Your client needs a sense of personal meaning and/or deepest purpose. Are these needs identified and satisfactorily met, or does your client suffer from not knowing or being true to his or her deepest meaning or purpose? How can you tell?

Your client has a constellation of defensive states that can be cued by perceived threat. These states have characteristic amplified or numbed emotion, distorted perceptions and thoughts, destructive impulses, and diminished capacities for empathy and self-reflection.[5] How do you help this person cultivate awareness and abilities to shift into healthier states of consciousness, and how can you tell when they do?

You, as therapist, experience a wide array of perceptions, sensations, thoughts, feelings, judgments, and impulses during the session. How do you process and act on these to best help your client?

Now imagine that your client is joined in the session by his or her lover who also has all the above issues and concerns. This lover probably has a more masculine orientation if your client is more feminine or a more feminine orientation if your client is more masculine.[6] This lover has all the issues we just explored and shares with your client desires to love and be loved more, and to hurt and be hurt less. The complexity of the session has just increased by an order of magnitude. Relationships are living, intersubjective, energetic and behavioral systems that have their own patterns and demands, relational defensive structures, and strengths/weaknesses that involve varying degrees of self-awareness and varying abilities to self-regulate. Within this system there are two sets of individual characteristics, defensive structures, goals, and agendas, plus relationship issues. How do you prioritize and address all these new factors?

Good therapists cycle through multiple perspectives.

Let's face it. It is impossible to simultaneously address this overwhelming wealth of material in general, much less in one hour. What good therapists do is cycle (either consciously and/or unconsciously) through multiple perspectives during the session. These different perspectives enable therapists to identify issues, prioritize agendas, discern interventions, and maintain a healing culture in the session.

Most therapists develop an array of interconnected perspectives to guide them in understanding and nourishing their clients in the above domains. This array of perspectives serves to reveal each client's current functioning within frameworks that support remediating symptoms, enhancing health, and supporting development.

The Beautiful, the Good, and the True

Ken Wilber has written how each moment is experienced from multiple perspectives, many of which can be grouped into "I," "we," and "it."[7]

The "I" is our individual, inner subjective sense of who is looking out through our eyes, and who feels attraction or repulsion, positive or negative, toward most experiences. What "I" am subjectively drawn to or repulsed by involves the "beautiful" validity standard that each of us brings to bear on all that we sense. Something attracts us or repels us; it is more beautiful or more ugly. What "I" sense is subjective in that it varies according to my reactions and aesthetic values. Goat cheese might taste beautiful to me but taste ugly to you.

The "we" is our shared inter-subjective sense of unity with others in personally important social groups. These groups are characterized by shared understandings of what is right or wrong, moral or immoral, good or bad. "We" might agree that murder is bad, and altruism is good. "We" involves the "good" validity standard that is characterized by a sense of relative, inter-subjective texture to our experience. "We" is subjective in that it varies according to milieu and culture and reflects what we experience as shared inner validity standards that depend on a felt sense of right and wrong. A bikini is a morally acceptable garment on a California beach, but might evoke physical assault in Saudi Arabia.

"It" is an object. We can externally view people, places, things, thoughts, feelings, or beliefs as objects that can be externally represented through scientific, replicable observations. If we disagree on an observation, we can test it experimentally to resolve our differences, and our results can be verified through scientific method. This objective, externally observable, and scientifically verifiable validity standard can be referred to as the "true." An apple is tossed into the air and it falls. This experiment can be repeated and verified endlessly by anyone. The apple is always objectively an apple, and it always falls. The majority of students in any elementary school are under 12 years of age. We can verify this objectively through research and statistical representation. It is "true."[8]

You are a wife, in a therapy session with me, waiting for your husband to show up for the session.

Imagine you're a wife who has scheduled a conjoint therapy session with your husband and me, and he is fifteen minutes late. I see your breathing speed up and rise higher in your chest, your shoulders and jaw tense, and your hands tremble. Videotape would verify this "true" observation. Such behavioral information involves the "it," the externally observable, the "true" validity standard. Internally, you might be feeling angry with your husband. This involves both the "I," the "beautiful" validity standard that tends to be a function of your personal, subjective, "I" universe, and the "we," the "good" validity standard that tends to be a function of shared standards. To you it is clearly not beautiful for your husband to have failed to arrive on time. It does not attract you or open you; rather it repulses and closes you. Further, his lateness violates your moral "we" standard for punctuality. You have a belief that you experience as shared with important social groups that it is "wrong" to be late to therapy sessions.

We get a call from him and find out he was in a car accident that was not his fault. You continue to be angry at him for being late, and I bring my own felt "wrongness" of your current anger to your attention (after all, someone could have been killed), and you feel a little embarrassed or ashamed. You and I have a shared "we," moral sense of what is a good or bad, right or wrong, response to a husband being late to a session because of a car accident that was not his fault, and most people in our culture would agree with us.

I, we, and it: the individual, subjective interior, the shared inter-subjective interior, and the externally observable, scientifically verifiable exterior: the beautiful, the good, and the true.

The beautiful, the good, and the true in therapy.

To some extent, we bring the beautiful, good, and true validity standards to bear on each experience in every moment. Much of psychotherapy is opening up conflicted areas in our clients to shared awareness so they can sense felt truthfulness (a combination of all three validity standards), and have healing insights (awakenings) that pull them into healthier states of consciousness, healthier perspectives, and healthier actions. In the above example, your husband finally makes it to the session, and you hug and kiss him, glad to see him, grateful he is uninjured, and this feels good, moral, and right to all three of us. Your devotional love makes you beautiful to him. His presence with you, the fact that he accomplished his mission of making it to the session, and his added depth from being on the subjective edge of death in his car accident, makes him beautiful to you. I observe your energetic polarity through a variety of subjective, "I," internal mechanisms in my body and mind, and objective, "its," external cues of your expressions, your words, your tones, and your body language, and, knowing from externally verifiable social research that couples who can connect in this fashion have a better chance of being able to go deeper into love, I find what's going on beautiful, good, and true.

It can be useful to consciously attend to the beautiful, good, and true.

I suggest you evaluate everything presented in this book by these three validity standards. Does the material attract or repulse you? Does it feel good or bad, right or wrong, from a moral perspective? Is the material "true," consistent with scientific research and/or observable experience? You might notice in your life how you naturally bring these standards to bear in crucial situations or in casual everyday moments. If you are a therapist, you'll probably notice how central and important the beautiful and the good are in treatment. Much of your clients' decision making is dominated by what attracts or repels them in self and others, the beautiful. Most of your clients' experiences of emotion, thought, impulse, and behavior will have a flavor to them (and you) of moral or immoral, right or wrong, bad or good. Scientific, "it," "true," research has demonstrated that individuals and couples who generally feel positive about themselves and their lives ("beautiful"), and moral within their ethical frameworks ("good") are healthier people with fewer physical and emotional symptoms, and generally better relationships than individuals without these qualities.[9]

The beautiful, good, and true validity standards are invaluable in psychotherapy. An example of this is the following exchange between me and Mary and Dennis, a couple in their 50's (like all clinical examples in this book, Mary and Dennis are composites of people I've worked with over the years). Both are college graduates, professionally successful, and dedicated parents to their three teens. Under stress, Dennis tends to coerce and bully, while Mary tends to comply codependently and passive-aggressively. This is their seventh session:

Dennis: "All I did was ask her to go into the lingerie store."

Mary: "I went into the store."

Dennis: Sarcastically "Right, but you were completely not into it."

Keith: This is a familiar pattern. I want to encourage them to shift out of defensive states and off of critical judgments into more useful perspectives. "Mary, was it attractive or repulsive to you to go into the lingerie store?"

Mary: Hesitantly, fearing Dennis' critical judgment. "When you put it that way, it was repulsive."

Dennis: Distressed, and so he attacks. "I just wanted to add some spice to our marriage. God knows we need it."

Keith: Teaching, enticing them towards new perspectives. "There are three validity standards we bring to each moment. The first is what is externally observable and scientifically verifiable; what is true. The second is what attracts or repulses us individually; what is subjectively beautiful or not. The third is what feels right or wrong, moral or immoral; what is bad or good. These are the beautiful, the good, and the true validity standards. To you, Mary, it was not beautiful to walk into the store; it was repulsive. To you, Dennis, it was attractive to walk into the store; it was beautiful."

Mary: "He should know I wouldn't be interested."

Dennis: "I saw she was reluctant, but I thought it would help our marriage to do it."

Keith: "Did it?"

Dennis: "I guess not."

Keith: "So now you're trying to argue with her that what she finds repulsive should be beautiful. That's like telling her she should love a movie that she hated."

Mary: "It probably would be good for us to go to the lingerie store if we were getting along better."

Keith: "So you agree that it's not bad, or immoral, to shop in a lingerie store together?"

Both: "Yes."

Keith: "So this met the shared "good" standard for both of you, and, probably, couples that shop in lingerie stores do better, so it met the "true" standard for both of you, but it didn't meet the "beautiful" standard for you, Mary. For a shared decision to feel right, it needs to feel beautiful, good, and true to both of you."

Dennis: Interested, in a state of healthy response to the present moment. "How do you make that happen?"

Keith: "The way you make it happen, Dennis, is to stay connected to Mary's experience when you offer direction like that, and, if it's not beautiful to her, back off. That's one way for you to be a more trustable man."

Introducing the concepts of the beautiful, the good, and the true creates possibilities for consciously considering multiple new perspectives in their lives. These new perspectives support a language of non-critical evaluation that is crucial to one of the many paradoxical activities of psychotherapy, creating a sense of safety by communicating interest, love, and acceptance, while encouraging courageous exploration of threatening, destructive, and otherwise difficult to accept aspects of self and other.

1. Deida (1995)

2. Wilber (2000)

3. Siegel (1999)

4. Wilber (2003)

5. Witt (2007)

6. Deida (2004)

7. Wilber (2003)

8. *Ibid*

9. Gottman (1999)

2

Masculine And Feminine Types in Therapy

In the exchange with Mary and Dennis I was encouraging and instructing Dennis to be a more trustable man because that's often the number one thing feminine partners want in a masculine partner.[1] Part of my job as therapist is to teach men and women how to soothe and delight each other while being more aware and true to who they are. This reflects a largely unspoken central aspect of therapy, the often ignored elephant in the living room, that men and women are different types of human beings who live in largely different domains. The fundamental differences between masculine and feminine types is so deep and profound that it constitutes a ground upon which other types of person, such as introvert, extrovert, thrill seeking, shy, or risk adverse, manifest. I consider masculine and feminine types so central as to constitute meta-types upon which other types of personality are superimposed by the alchemy of temperament, attachment styles, and environment. An extroverted masculine person will be different from an extroverted feminine person, a thrill-seeking masculine person will be different from a thrill-seeking feminine person, and so on.

For Dennis and Mary to be happy, fulfilled, and giving their best gifts to each other and the world, a more masculine type like Dennis probably needs to cultivate a trustable presence, unrecoiling in the face of adversity, tuned into his own principles and to Mary's current states, committed to his own life's purpose, and embracing the responsibility of feeling into Mary and opening her with love, depth of consciousness, and humor. "Unrecoiling" means doing his best to stay open, connected, and caring, whether Mary is a gentle breeze or a raging storm. Mary, as a more feminine type, probably needs to cultivate her radiant feminine core, to be an open channel of emotion, to feel herself a wellspring of love, to be open in her body, to believe love is being served in her life, and to show Dennis pleasure through her body (her expression, voice, movement, breath, posture, and touch) at his integrity, and her suffering at his collapse.

Even though we all have masculine and feminine aspects, most men are primarily masculine types, and most women are primarily feminine types, though there are numerous exceptions of men and women, both gay and straight, being more masculine or more feminine in different moments and in different life circumstances, including their sexual relationships. How true we are to our deepest sexual essences is perhaps our single most important determinant of a happy, healthy, fulfilled life, and so is of central importance to the practice of psychotherapy.

David Deida: A Gold Standard of Perspectives on Masculine And Feminine

My favorite theoretical and practical teaching about masculine and feminine types, practices, and successful relating has been the work of David Deida. Deida suggested in one of his lectures (only half-humorously, I suspect) that most human existence revolves largely around obsessions with money and sex.[2] How we inhabit and express these obsessions is largely determined by our deepest masculine or feminine sexual essences. Further, independent of our deepest, most predominant masculine or feminine essence, we all have both of these principles in us to some degree and, if we are closed down in either, we suffer and cause suffering to others.

Whether celibate or sexually involved with another, gay or straight, being open in, and true to, our deepest masculine/feminine essences is a central feature of healthy and fulfilled human existence. It is mandated by the genetic imperatives to love, bond, create family, and have deep soul's purpose. These genetic imperatives are expressed through fundamental drives to create meaning, relate to others, and establish position on social hierarchies. Such drives tend to manifest differently in masculine and feminine types.

Helping each client identify and be true to their deepest sexual essence: a meta-agenda of many systems of psychotherapy.

Whether therapists are consciously aware of it or not, a meta-agenda of almost all psychotherapy is to help clients identify and be true to their deepest masculine and feminine sexual essences. In most therapy therapists are supporting a client's movement towards better *intrapersonal* relationships with various interior aspects of themselves and better *interpersonal* relationships with others. Both *inter*personal and *intra*personal relationships benefit from acceptance of self and optimal energetic polarities with others.

The drive to relate finds its deepest and most challenging expression in the ability to establish and maintain fulfilling relationships with lovers. Since I believe this area is particularly important in optimal health and development, I've chosen to emphasize relationships with lovers in clinical examples. A focus of much of the material will be applying the principles of masculine and feminine aspect, essence, practice, and polarity to the psychotherapeutic support of clients' movement towards identifying and honoring their deepest sexual essences, and creating and maintaining healthy and satisfying energetic polarities between themselves, their lovers, and other intimates in their lives.

The Integral Embrace.

Ken Wilber has postulated that five perspectives considered cumulatively tend to give us the most complete picture of a human's existence. These are quadrants, lines, levels, states, and types. Collectively they form the Integral Operating System which can be applied like a computer operating system to any branch of knowledge.

The four quadrants include the "I," "we," "it," and "its" perspectives that we briefly explored in examining the beautiful, the good, and the true validity standards.

We've just identified masculine/feminine types, and I've suggested that different temperamental predispositons such as introvert, extrovert, shy, thrill seeking, or risk adverse, are integrated with our masculine/feminine aspects and essence in helping to determine our unique individual natures.

Let's turn now to the additional perspectives of developmental lines and levels, and of different states of consciousness.

Developmental lines and levels.

Dennis and Mary, our couple who had the argument about the lingerie store, developed very much as all humans have for thousands of years. They entered the world as infants and matured in relationship with their genetic predispositions, caregivers, and environments to become unique adults. They learned language, developed self-aware consciousness, and were immersed in family, friend, and interior relationships. They gradually discovered strengths and vulnerabilities, likes and dislikes. Their development in a number of specific areas such as cognitive abilities, moral standards, values, interpersonal relating, and physical growth progressed in specific and universal sequences.

They were not born as adults and then encountered infancy later.

- They were born as infants and grew to toddlers, to children, to adolescents, to adults.

- Cognitively, they were born **sensorimotor** (literally relating to the environment through their sensory bodies) and grew to **preoperational** where they grew from being able to experience internal images, symbols, and beginning concepts, to acquiring language where they could manipulate and repress concepts, to **concrete operational** dealing with the environment in concrete, either/or, categorical ways that resisted being able to hold competing concepts simultaneously, to **formal operational** where they could inhabit "what if?" scenarios, and internally hold and compare conflicting perspectives.

- Morally, they were born egocentric and grew to caring for immediate others, to caring for others beyond their immediate purview.

"Physical, "cognitive", and "moral" constitute lines of development where growth proceeds through universal stages. There ten to twenty major lines that most humans are ebbing and flowing on constantly.

The self-line.

Some developmental lines (including cognitive, moral, masculine/feminine, and interpersonal) are intimately intertwined in the development of our self-aware consciousness, the "I" person who looks out of our eyes and experiences the world. These intertwining lines constitute the self-line of development like different strands constitute a rope.

Other specific developmental lines reflect talents or skills such as musical ability, mathematical ability, or some special kinesthetic abilities (Pele in soccer, for example) such as Howard Gardner observed in his work on multiple intelligences.[3] As is obvious from the above examples, we progress upward through different levels on each of these developmental lines. We can have peak experiences of enhanced functioning, or regression to more primitive functioning on any line at any time but, for enduring development, levels cannot be skipped on any line. We must be infants before we can be children, we must inhabit concrete operational cognition before we can inhabit formal operational cognition, and so on.[4]

States—We're always in them, but we don't always know which ones we're in.

Dennis and Mary, like humans of all ages, inhabit three great states of consciousness daily: waking, dreaming, and deep sleep. During their waking state they constantly shift emotions, perceptions, thoughts, and impulses in ways that are either healthy responses to the present moment, or defensive distortions unconsciously designed to resist change. In our example, Dennis and Mary moved from resenting, fearing, and attacking each other (defensive states), to caring for and connecting with each other (healthy responses to the present moment). Discerning and working with such shifting states of consciousness is much of the moment-to-moment work of psychotherapy.

Quadrants, lines, levels, states, and types.

An Integrally informed approach takes all the above into account when dealing with any aspect of human functioning. Integrally informed psychotherapy considers what levels each client inhabits on a variety of developmental lines, what states the client inhabits, and what type of person each client is; all from the "I" subjective beautiful, "we" inter-subjective good, and the "it(s)" objective true perspectives.

1. Deida (2006)
2. *Ibid*
3. Gardner (2003)
4. Wilber (2000)

3

Self As Healing Instrument

My clinical training involved a lot of lucky circumstances. Like many therapists, I discovered the healing power of psychotherapy in treatment as an adolescent with a gifted and charismatic psychologist named Joseph Erickson. Having decided to pursue clinical psychology as a profession, I entered the University of California at Santa Barbara for mostly the wrong reasons. I was attracted to the beautiful campus and the easy access to surf. After I arrived, I discovered that the Psychology Department was almost exclusively, even militantly, experimental rather than clinical. Figuring I needed grounding in psychology as a science, I pursued my studies, taking whatever clinical courses became available, and generally being fascinated with learning theory, brain and behavior, psychopathology, personality theories, and human development. My professors impressed me with their depth of knowledge and I could see clinical applications for most of the material they taught.

During my senior year and the first year of my MA program in Counseling Psychology I worked as a peer counselor at the University Counseling Center. There was a delightful diversity of clinical approaches represented by the staff therapists. Cognitive-behaviorists, Gestalt practitioners, Jungian approaches, Freudian orientations, Psychosynthesis, system's theory, and Rogerian Relationship approaches all coexisted in what now appears to me to be an Integral context of felt appreciation for multiple points of view. Everybody seemed to respect everybody else's clinical and theoretical gifts. I studied happily with all of them. It was clear to me that therapy was an art that was better learned from artists than from art historians. My more academic training was useful, but there was another dimension of understanding and application that clinicians brought to the experience that I found compelling. Over the subsequent years I've kept seeking out gifted clinicians and have arranged to both study with them and, if possible, enter treatment with them, to learn and integrate their styles.

All the therapists I've known have wanted to increase their own compassion and depth of consciousness, and to help their clients be happier and healthier. All have wanted their clients to have deeper and more compassionate understanding of themselves, their intimates, and their environments, with the duel agendas of supporting immediate improvements in functioning and encouraging growth and maturation. All have appreciated the power and unique nature of the therapy session as a culture, a world in itself, in which the client needs to feel safe, understood, and cared for, and all of these therapists instinctively cultivated and communicated compassionate understanding of their clients. In generating definitions of psychotherapy, my goal has been to offer constructs that might meet the validity standards of most experienced clinicians.

The following are two definitions of psychotherapy, followed by descriptions of the purpose of therapy and the process of therapy. The first definition emphasizes the personal focus of the therapist during the session on cultivating compassion and depth of consciousness in self and client, while the second emphasizes the shared activity of therapist and client of co-creating a healing culture.

- Psychotherapy is **cultivating compassion and depth of consciousness to support healthy perspectives and actions.**

- Psychotherapy is **co-creating a culture where the client and the client's universe is cherished, where every moment is experienced as a gift and an opportunity, and where healthy perspectives and actions are considered beautiful, good, and true.**

- The purpose of therapy is to **remediate symptoms**, **enhance health**, and **support development**.

- The manner therapists pursue these goals is by **relating, teaching, inspiring, confronting, interpreting**, and **directing**.

From primarily subjective and inter-subjective perspectives, the therapist, anchored in the purpose of cultivating compassion and depth of consciousness in self and client, energetically embraces the client into the unique culture of the session and, utilizing training, experience, personality, and loving intent, guides the process by relating, teaching, inspiring, confronting, interpreting, and directing into co-creating a healing environment.

This artistic co-creation soothes and challenges the client to access compassionate and deep aspects of self to consider and embrace healthy perspectives and actions in the session, and supports including those perspectives and actions into the client's universe to create a healthier, happier life.

Body work, group work, energy work, movement, and the panoply of healing traditions.

The above definitions can be applied to a wide variety of healing activities including body work, group work, family therapy, energy work, movement (for example dance therapy and the Alexander technique), twelve step programs, and other healing traditions. I'm not specifically including many of these in this volume for several reasons. Practically, there is just not room to include the plethora of techniques and disciplines that are relevant to psychotherapy in one volume, and I don't have what I feel to be the requisite training and experience to adequately represent many of these traditions, though I believe that all of them fit into the wide embrace of psychotherapy.

Also, many who read this will be licensed psychotherapists, or are aspiring to be licensed psychotherapists. Licensed psychotherapists are all accountable to licensing boards in the states or countries they practice in, and to the ethical standards of their professional organizations. Licensing boards and professional organizations are designed to protect consumers and support professional development and, from my experience in California, they function admirably in those two roles. The material in this book is designed to meet the legal and ethical validity standards of licensing boards and professional organizations. When dealing with traditionally esoteric aspects of healing such as subtle energies and spirituality, I've tried to use language and constructs that fit within the legal and ethical parameters of licensure and my current understanding of widely accepted terms and perspectives in the practice of psychotherapy.

Self as healing instrument in psychotherapy.

What are you feeling in your body at this moment? Are you relaxed or tense, hot or cold? Is your breath high in your chest, or low in your belly? What emotion are you feeling at this moment? Are you happy or sad, anxious or secure, angry or compassionate? What impulses do you have at this moment? Are you drawn to reading further or to put this book aside? Do you want to be alone or with another? Do you want to be still or in motion? What thoughts are you experiencing at this moment? Are you thinking about self as healing instrument, something related to self as healing instrument, or something else entirely? What judgments are you currently experiencing? Do various aspects of this material feel right to you, or wrong? Are you comfortable with having and discerning judgments, or uncomfortable discovering that you frequently are making moral evaluations?

If you are with another person, you and that person are constantly co-creating intersubjective fields that influence and direct all of the above. As therapists, our perceptions, sensations, emotions, thoughts, judgments, and impulses are all regularly being influenced and directed by the intersubjective fields we are co-creating with our client; intersubjective fields we experience in our body/mind system in the form of sensations, emotions, perceptions, thoughts, memories, anticipations, intuitions, judgments, and impulses. Attending to these experiences and using them as guides to co-create a healing culture is much of the craft and art of psychotherapy. A relaxed, satisfied feeling can indicate a productive area and a good alliance with a client. A flash of anxiety or irritation can indicate the appearance of a defensive state in our client and/or in us. An impulse to ask a certain question can indicate an intuitive, post-formal-operational (a combination of intuition and formal-operational logic; what Ken Wilber calls "vision logic"[1]) insight into a productive area of exploration. All these feelings, reactions, intuitions, and impulses are coming to us from the instrument our body/mind/spirit system, and can be read by us, as therapists, to guide us to better relate, teach, inspire, confront, interpret, and direct in the session to help clients remediate symptoms, enhance health, and support development. This is self as healing instrument.

Throughout each section of this book, and especially in the clinical examples, I've included internal, subjective experiences and sensations as components of the work. Your body/mind/spirit system will have different calibrations and indicators than mine, but allowing yourself to be aware of, accept, and examine sensations, feelings, thoughts, impulses, and judgments will help you develop your self as a healing instrument in psychotherapy.

Developing your self as an instrument of healing.

There are a number of ways to develop ourselves as healing instruments. Not surprisingly, most of these involve practicing the healthy perspectives and actions that we support in our clients. Most systems of psychotherapeutic training advocate various combinations of study, training, supervision, and healthy diet, exercise, rest, and relationships. Less obvious, but equally central, are:

- Ascending and descending spiritual practices.
- Cultivating and feeling appreciation for the contributions and validity of all worldviews.
- Cultivating the abilities to discern whether or not you are closing or opening the moment, and to adjust from closing to opening.

The rest of this chapter will briefly explore these three core methods for developing self as a healing instrument.

Psychotherapy and Spiritual Practice.

In each of the forty-five thousand plus therapy sessions I've conducted over the last thirty-five years, there has been some sense of the sacred. My internal experience of the sacred is often a profound feeling of joy and peace, combined with a sense in my heart of a loving, healing connection with my client. Further, there is always a desire, a hunger, in me to help my client feel the transcendent qualities of existence in each moment. Many of the most profoundly satisfying peak experiences I've had as a therapist involve supporting my client waking up to a new experience of, a new perspective of, more deeply loving self, others, and/or the world. These awakenings are peak experiences elicited by the culture of the session, and my clients frequently report that they are accompanied by a subjective sense of the sacred. Such peak experiences, or awakenings, stretch the worldview of clients and give them direction, motivation, inspiration, and hope for growth and positive change. In conjoint therapy, these moments often arise from experiences of deep love and hot sexual polarity between partners.

Ascending Spirituality: the many into one.

Ascending spirituality is the many into one, agency, hierarchical, more masculine, often involves solitary practice, and moves away from the body towards God.[2] "Many into one" refers to being drawn to organize and simplify spiritual orientation and practice into purer and more elegant constructs that eventually lead to a single experience of oneness with the divine. "Agency" is needing to create solutions to problems; to turn somethings into nothings as David Deida describes it.[3] "Hierarchical" refers to the human drive to compete for, and orient to, positions on social hierarchies. Ascending spiritual traditions usually involve hierarchical spiritual, social, and power structures. "More masculine" because the masculine craves the bliss of complete emptiness, and tends to delight in the other aspects of ascending practice. "Solitary practice" is the pleasure ascending practitioners generally feel in complete self-reliance on meeting the divine through releasing all attachment. "Away from the body towards God" refers to either regarding physical existence and sensory pleasure as of secondary importance compared to divine rewards after death (such as going to heaven or earning freedom from the wheel of karma), or to relax awareness through the body/mind/sensations/emotions to the deeper, ever present, unrecoiling witness that observes all objects but is itself not an object.

Most major religions have arisen from patriarchal, agrarian societies which emphasize masculine deities and spiritual practice (the Gods of foraging societies are approximately fifty percent masculine and fifty percent feminine, while agrarian societies tend to have overwhelmingly masculine deities). These more masculine spiritual orientations are ascending, and emphasize transcendence, or reward, after death, while de-emphasizing, even pathologizing, sensual pleasure in the moment. Zen meditation, vision quest, ordeal, and solitary prayer are all examples of ascending practices. These practices seek to reach through the distractions of the flesh and the attachments to the world to abiding as pure spirit. This drive towards transcendence, non-attachment, or nirvana, is at heart a pure expression of masculine agency, the drive to solve progressive problems in climbing the spiritual pyramid to God.[4] My favorite expression of ascending practice is the last few lines in *The Book of the Void*, the final section of Myamoto Musashi's *A Book of Five Rings*: "In the void is virtue and no evil. Wisdom has existence, principle has existence, the Way has existence. Spirit is nothingness."[5]

The signature psychopathology, or distortion, of the ascending traditions is repression, since the demands of the flesh and the material world are often considered at best second class, or, at worst, sinful.

Descending Spirituality: the one into many.

Descending spirituality is the one into many, communion, non-hierarchical, more feminine, often involves communal practice, and moves into the body, into pleasure, identifying with all life, all nature, all sensation, and everything that is arising in the present moment.[6] Dance, loving community, children, family, food, color, texture, sex, and pleasure take us progressively deeper into the physical world, eventually leading to a oneness with the luminosity of spirit that radiates constantly up through nature. This drive towards universal love, sensual oneness with all people and all of nature is at heart a pure expression of feminine communion.

The signature psychopathology, or distortion, of the descending traditions is regression, where egocentric stimulus hunger in pursuit of pleasure, or avoidance of pain or change, is mistaken for finding spirit in the sensual pleasures of the moment.

Sexual bliss between couples is a naturally occurring descending shared practice, and is thus a huge potential spiritual resource for lovers.

Psychotherapy supports ascending and descending spiritual practice.

Most psychotherapy embraces, and is enhanced by, both ascending and descending spiritual practice. Psychotherapy identifies blocks and distortions and moves to open and resolve them. Psychotherapy celebrates the liberation of human potential to move both away from the body towards oneness with emptiness, and into the body towards oneness with the overflowing fullness of everything that is arising in the material world. Personally, I've found it necessary to have ongoing ascending and descending practices to support my own development, help identify and address my own blocks, and to comprehensively understand and support my clients' needs. Thus ascending and descending spiritual practices, by enhancing compassion and deepening consciousness, support self as healing instrument in therapy.

All worldviews contribute.

Developmental psychologists have discovered that, as humans progress up different lines, there is a point in adult maturation where a dramatic shift in perspective appears for some people. Abraham Maslow, in his research on needs, found that the "deficiency needs" for food, shelter, and security (motivated largely by a sense of lack), shifted to "being needs" for actualization and transcendence (motivated largely by a sense of fullness) as individuals pursuing truth and growth in relatively stable environments.[7] Clare Graves observed that different worldviews always included critical judgments of other worldviews until, with some individuals, there was a shift to dramatically reduced fear and a felt appreciation for all worldviews. "Felt appreciation" is just that—feeling an interest in, and appreciation for, all points of view. Graves called this new territory "the second tier" and identified all worldviews that preceded it as "the first tier."

David Deida has observed that relationships develop from first stage egocentricism where individuals relate primarily to meet their own needs, to second stage egalitarianism where they negotiate deals that support 50/50 fairness, to third stage openness where the individual and couple primarily organize their lives to serve love.[8]

Wilber calls the first step into Graves' second tier where there is a dramatic reduction of fear and a felt appreciation for all worldviews "Integral." Much effective psychotherapy comes from the therapist occupying Integrally informed perspectives.

A useful corollary to this (in service of self as healing instrument) is that when the therapist experiences a critical judgment of anyone or anything, it is a cue to look inward to a possible defensive state that may be generating the judgment, and then resolve into a state of healthy response by adjusting back to felt appreciation. This is utilizing a defensive state to cultivate compassion and depth of consciousness. An example of this occurs in the following exchange with Dennis and Mary:

Mary: "First he blew up at our son, and then he just walked out and didn't come back for two days."

Dennis: "What do you expect? I was stressed. You've been nothing but cold for months. It hardly ever happens. You ..."

Mary: Trying to soothe him while pleading with him. "But you don't understand how it effects Seth when his father just ..."

Dennis: Interrupting, defensive. "He should know by now that I don't mean anything by it. He's just too sensitive. He ..."

Keith: At this point I'm feeling angry at Dennis and thinking how egocentric and selfish he's being. I'm making a critical judgment. I feel an impulse to attack him, to argue with him and tell him the suffering he's caused in his family by deserting them for two days. My hostile defensive state has been evoked by his defensive state. I notice this, remind myself of his suffering, and remind myself further that one of the best first steps towards addressing narcissistic defenses is mirroring pain.[9] As I do this I begin to feel compassion for him, interest in his worldview, and thus more trust in my own instincts. "Dennis, stop for a moment and feel how hurt you are inside. Feel how much you want Mary to understand that you felt driven to explode, that you know your desertion hurt them and you're sorry for causing that suffering."

Dennis: Less vehement, still defensive. "You have no idea how stressed I was."

Mary: Still angry at his rationalizations. "That's no excuse for being an asshole."

Keith: I feel a little bloom of irritation at Mary. Dennis was shifting into a healthier state and now I see his face hardening again as she attacks him. I remind myself that she's been the victim of his attacks and subsequent rationalizations hundreds of times, and needs new ways of addressing her pain. I begin to feel more compassion and empathy for her difficult situation. I decide to keep confronting Dennis by empowering her. "Mary, you're completely right that there are no excuses for emotional violence. You need to take a stand against it in your family, but not by being violent yourself. You will always be repulsed by Dennis' lashing out or deserting the family, and that repulsion should be enough for him to wake up, soothe himself, and open you and Seth with love rather than close you down with attacks, desertions, or excuses."

Mary: More relaxed. "I wish it was enough."

Dennis: Softening now that he's being confronted rather than pathologized. "I'd like to be able to do that."

Keith: Feeling affection and compassion for both of them. "I'll help you learn, Dennis."

Felt appreciation for all worldviews is my personal standard for attitudinal orientation in the session. Attending to my moment to moment reactions and using them to guide me to do the inner work necessary to feel that appreciation is one of the main processes that helps me maintain and develop my self as a healing instrument. The difference between this and hypocrisy or codependence is that the standard is not *pretending* to feel, but actually *arranging to feel*, an appreciation for the valid components of different worldviews.

Opening and closing the moment.

Opening the moment is discerning and mobilizing perspectives and actions that serve health and love right now. Closing the moment is indulging perspectives and actions that interfere with or block health and love right now. The world is constantly informing us of our influences on each environment we inhabit, and mirroring back to us whether we are effective or ineffective, attractive or repulsive, moral or immoral by immediate group standards. Other people are often the best mirrors, in that any behavior in an intersubjective field informs us of the nature of that field. I yell, you tense up; I smile, you relax.

Most healing systems support people monitoring and adjusting themselves to open themselves and others. This often involves taking on the responsibility to open the moment with love, generosity, and honesty, rather than close the moment with fear, lies, or selfishness. Most defensive states involve reflexive blocking of self-reflection and empathy, and often the unconscious rationalization that it's acceptable to get temporary relief by hurting self and/or another in some fashion. As we will explore more deeply in Section Six, discerning and managing these defensive states is one of the central components of psychotherapy.

The therapist's mission is to open the moment. If a client is closing down (usually indicating that they're entering a defensive state), they communicate their closure in many ways. They will look away, tense up, attack, defend, or otherwise separate from their most mature and compassionate self.

Therapists' sensations, emotions, thoughts, and impulses will shift accordingly in the intersubjective dance of the session. If we, as therapists, take on the responsibility of discerning whether we are opening or closing the moment, and then take on the responsibility to open it, we develop our selves as therapeutic instruments. In the previous exchange with Dennis and Mary, my initial impulses were to meet their defenses with my own, which would probably have closed the moment down. I might have compromised my status as a trustable man and reliable support source, and they might have constricted and closed in response. By anchoring myself in appreciation for the valid aspects of their worldviews, my love for them, and my desire to help them, I supported them relaxing and opening to their less defensive, more caring selves.

One of the best ways to enhance these abilities is to invite honest feedback from our friends and lovers to teach us whether we are personally opening or closing, whether we are being true to our purpose or kidding ourselves, or whether we are radiant with love or sucking energy from the environment. This feedback can guide us and help us open to be our best selves.[10] It is the foundation of clinical supervision. If we can welcome such feedback and act on it courageously, it speeds our development and hones our self as an instrument of healing. We discern when we're closing ourselves or the moment and we adjust to opening. We discern when we're opening ourselves and the moment and trust our instincts.

The next two sections are relatively brief summaries of Ken Wilber's Integral perspective, and David Deida's and others' teaching on the masculine and feminine. These sections will introduce language and concepts necessary to understand how to apply this material to psychotherapy. Together, these two men have written dozens of books, and recorded dozens of teaching sessions. I encourage you to read their books, listen to their recordings, visit their websites, and study with them in person if you have the opportunity. I've done all these things and am still being surprised and delighted by new perspectives and practices. Applied to psychotherapy, this material can result in awakenings—paradigm shifts in how you experience your self and your clients in treatment. It has the potential to be psychoactive catalysts to accelerate your own development. Perhaps more importantly, I'm reminded of what Becky suggested that I say about the material, "Tell them how much fun it is to learn these things and then see the world so differently."

1. *Ibid*

2. Wilber (2003)

3. Dieda (2004)

4. Wilber (2003)

5. Musashi (1974)

6. Wilber (2003)

7. Maslow (1962)

8. Deida (2006)

9. Kernberg (1975)

10. Deida (2004)

Section Two

The Integral Lens

4

Integral Psychology

The first ever Integral Psychotherapy conference took place near Denver in August of 2004. Fifty psychologists and students of psychology from fourteen countries gathered for six days to study and explore Integral psychotherapy. It was an exhilarating, inspiring, and exhausting experience.

The beauty of the integral operating system (I.O.S.) is that it can create startling insights and new perspectives when applied to any field of study or practice. Wilber and his friends, associates, and students have applied the I.O.S. to areas such as government, law, business, medicine, ecology, and spiritual practice, as well as psychology and psychotherapy.

Wilber's book, *Integral Psychology*[1], is a rich application of the integral model to a number of psychological disciplines. At the conference I observed this happening with all the presenters and practitioners. They took what they were expert in, reexamined that material from an Integrally informed perspective (quadrants, lines, levels, states, and types), and in the process uncovered new and deeper meanings and applications.

This section offers limited definitions of the core concepts of the Integral model, quadrants, lines, levels, states, and types, as I've found them to apply to psychotherapy with individuals and couples. Some aspects of this material, such as the astounding perspectives offered by Beck and Cowen in *Spiral Dynamics*, will be woefully simplified. A book could (and should) be written just on the applications of Spiral Dynamics to psychotherapy. If any part of the material that I must cover so briefly has special magic or appeal to you, I encourage you to study the source materials to expand your understanding. The beauty of the Integral model is that, no matter where your studies lead, you will be on a multidimensional map that connects to all knowledge and experience.

THE FOUR QUADRANTS

UPPER LEFT	UPPER RIGHT
INTERIOR/INDIVIDUAL	EXTERIOR/INDIVIDUAL
Intentional	Behavioral

Validity Standards:
  Felt Truthfulness
  Internally experienced
  Subjective
	Validity Standards:
	  Truth
	  Externally Observable
	  Objective

Self & Consciousness	Brain & Organism
BEAUTIFUL **I**	**TRUE** **IT**
LOWER LEFT	LOWER RIGHT
INTERIOR/COLLECTIVE	EXTERIOR/COLLECTIVE
Cultural	Social

Validity Standards:
  Mutual Understanding
  Internally experienced
  Intersubjective
  Moral
	Validity Standards:
	  Functional Fit
	  Externally Observable
	  Interobjective

	Soc. System & Environment Statistical Representations
Culture & Worldview	
GOOD **WE**	**TRUE** **ITS**

THE FOUR QUADRANTS
I, WE, IT, AND ITS
THE BEAUTIFUL, THE GOOD, AND THE TRUE

The chart on the opposite page presents the four quadrants which reflect four inter-related but distinct perspectives of the present moment. It will be helpful to keep referring to the chart as I explain the quadrants. You'll already recognize "I," "we," "it," and "its," and the "beautiful," the "good," and the "true" from Section One. Observe how both the upper left and lower left quadrants (the beautiful and the good) represent interiorly verifiable, subjective perspectives, and both the upper right and lower right quadrants (the true) represent scientifically (exteriorly) verifiable, objective perspectives. "Interiorly verifiable" means that we validate by observing what we feel inside ourselves, while "exteriorly verifiable" means that we validate by external observation. The upper left and upper right quadrants (the beautiful and the true applied to individuals) represent individual interior and individual exterior perspectives respectively, and the lower left and lower right quadrants (the good and the true applied to systems) represent group collective interior, and group collective exterior perspectives respectively.

The upper right quadrant; the "it" true, individual perspective

The upper right quadrant informs us about everything we can externally observe about an individual as an object and as interlocking systems of objects. Your eye color, weight, height, current brain waves, vocal register, cholesterol level, and high school SAT scores are all examples of upper right quadrant data. The validity standard for the upper right quadrant is the scientific, externally verifiable; the "true."

The upper left quadrant; the "I" beautiful perspective

The upper left quadrant informs us about all that is subjectively discernable to the individual. I can feel fear, love, attraction, repulsion, pain, or pleasure. All these experiences have objective correlates in brain waves, facial expression, muscle tension, and observable behaviors, but none of these measurements captures the subjective flavor of fear, love, attraction, repulsion, pain, or pleasure. Only "I", subjectively, can discern these upper left quadrant qualities. The validity standard for the upper left quadrant is internal, subjective, attractive or repulsive: the "beautiful."

The lower left quadrant; the "we" good perspective

The lower left quadrant informs us about all that is subjectively discernable in the shared intersubjective fields we occupy with others. We agree something feels right or wrong, good or bad (which often feels validating), or we don't agree, noticing that we have different morals in a particular situation (which is often disturbing). This is a subjective, moral standard. "We" believe that stealing cars is bad, and that helping someone who is injured is good. The social compact involves thousands of such mutual understandings. Robert Thurman was giving a lecture in May of 2005 at UCSB on Buddhism and his fly was unzipped. There was a palpable discomfort in the audience that resulted in hurried conversations and the eventually intervention of a moderator to direct Dr. Thurman to zip up. It did not meet the group's lower left quadrant, "we" good validity standards to be lectured to by Dr. Thurman with an unzipped fly. The validity standard for the lower left quadrant is shared, internal, subjective "we," moral or immoral: the "good."

The lower right quadrant; the "it's" true systems perspective.

The lower right quadrant informs us about all that is scientifically verifiable about groups or systems. Where the lower left quadrant, "we," good perspective is inter-subjective, the lower right quadrant is inter-objective. Social science and systems theory provide externally verifiable, statistical representations of different aspects of groups and systems. Thirty adults gather for a class. Sixty percent of them are therapists. One hundred percent answered "yes" when asked if they'd ever broken the speed limit driving a car, and eighty percent said "yes" when asked if they'd ever had a transcendent experience. You'll notice that a highly subjective "transcendent experience" can be studied and quantified by lower right quadrant statistical representation, but such statistical representation cannot capture the beauty or goodness of an experience; beauty and goodness remain in the subjective and inter-subjective realms. Similarly, we can mathematically represent the behavior of systems on any number of continua. Examples are group behavior after catastrophe, dissemination patterns of information in business communities, the distribution of fourth grade reading scores on a scatter diagram, and chaos theory applied to complex systems. These statistical representations deal with groups of anything (even self-reported subjective experiences) as objects to be viewed externally.

Helping people love through the quadrants

Remember the last time that you helped a person love themselves and/or some-one else better. Imagine yourself in this person's presence, see them in front of you, hear what you say and they say, and remember how you felt, what you thought, and what you did. I'm thinking of a session I had with a seventy-five-year-old alcoholic man named Ted who is in his fourth month of sobriety. Let's examine this kind of encounter from the perspectives of four quadrants.

Help them love from the upper right quadrant

From an objective perspective, what can you observe externally about yourself or this person? Are either of you smiling, crying, laughing, or frowning, and how are you breathing? Are you sitting or standing, erect or slouched? Are you speaking or silent, and, if speaking, what is each of you saying? I'm sitting with Ted, listening to him talk about his panic attacks and loneliness. I'm maintaining steady eye contact, my body is still and visibly relaxed in my armchair, and Ted's voice keeps shifting to more or less volume and higher and lower pitch. This is all externally verifiable data. If we both were hooked up to sensors, our basal resis-tance levels, brain waves, muscle tension, pulse, and respiration rates would cor-relate with our visibly observable behaviors. Sensors would probably reveal more alpha and theta, and less beta brain waves, more muscle relaxation and less ten-sion, and so on through externally observable phenomena. These hypotheses could be tested scientifically by anyone observing each of us.

The externally objective perspective is invaluable in psychotherapy. In Gestalt therapy, where pointing out the obvious and making the implicit explicit are the foundation practices, it is essential. The following exchange is an example of using such data in an individual session with Mary from Chapter One:

Mary: "Dennis blew up at me again yesterday."

Keith: Pointing out the obvious. "Your voice drops to a whisper when you say this."

Mary: "I'm scared he'll be angry at me for telling you."

Keith: "You're scared to tell me about Dennis' blow up."

Mary: "I've got to talk to somebody."

Keith: "Now your voice is loud and forceful."

Mary: "I'm angry. I shouldn't have to be afraid to tell the truth."

Keith: "You looked me straight in the eye, your voice was louder, and you didn't pause or hesitate as you talked."

Mary: "It feels good to tell the truth without being scared."

All my verbal content in this exchange is upper right quadrant data; externally observable and verifiable information. My non-verbal feedback (eye-contact, facial expression, body posture, gestures, voice tone, and timing and intensity of response) could be observed and quantified as objective (recordings, EEG or fMRI data, neural firing patterns, or other objective measures), but will be generated from, and felt as, subjective experiences by Mary and me in the intersubjective web of the session. This demonstrates how all four quadrants are always operating simultaneously, but our focus can be on any part of any one of them.

Helping them love from the upper left quadrant

Now, let's get back to your memory of helping another person love themselves or somebody else better, and my memory of Ted's and my session. From a subjective perspective, what can we internally observe about ourselves and this other person? You might have felt love, satisfaction, care, and/or interest. I certainly felt compassion, concern, interest, and periodic frustration as Ted and I talked about his alcoholism, his sense of confusion when considering his life's path, and his conflicted family relationships. Helping another person love better always evokes subjective experiences in the helper. The person you helped had their own subjective experiences during this activity, as did Ted. Helping someone love better is usually enjoyable to them to some extent. Ted, a hard driving warrior type, said, in a somewhat embarrassed tone, that he felt a pleasurable sense of "intimacy" with me. These reactions are interior and subjective. They can be studied exteriorly with instrumentation or statistical analysis, but the subjective experiences of embarrassment, intimacy, and pleasure are interior and only subjectively available to the individual having the experience.

Most therapy involves heavily subjective "I" components. As Mary and I continue our session, we mostly stay in the interior subjective:

Mary: "I don't know what to do."

Keith: Sharing my subjective emotional response. "I feel concerned as you talk."

Mary: "I'm sick of Dennis blowing up all the time. I'm worried that I made the wrong decision to stay."

Keith: This is a familiar theme with feminine people. Is love being served in my relationship? Do I love or am I loved? "You sound like you're repulsed by him right now."

Mary: "I am repulsed. I'm worried, though, that leaving is a mistake."

Keith: Feeling affection and concern for her. Having the impulse to provide a relaxed atmosphere where she can explore her confusing feelings and thoughts. "What worries you?"

Mary: "Well, I do love so much about him. He's a good provider, and he's funny when he's not angry. We've been through so much and he's been dealing with so much."

Keith: Feeling warmth, finding her compassion beautiful. "You sound compassionate as you talk about what you love about him."

Mary: "I do feel compassion for him. He works so hard. I just hate it when he goes off."

Keith: Feeling a subjective tingle of irritation and fear—she seems harder somehow. "Your voice just hardened and sounded angry again when you said you hate it when he goes off."

Mary: Sighs. "I guess I'm confused."

This is mostly subjective "I" material. "Angry," "confused," "repulsed," and "love" are all subjective experiences that involve varying degrees of attraction and repulsion. Many therapy sessions are spent in this manner, patiently exploring subjective, interior experiences, and encouraging the client to bring their validity standards to bear on the emerging material to help them confront and sooth amplified emotion, clarify and adjust distorted perceptions and beliefs, discern and turn away from destructive impulses, and discern and risk healthy action.

Help them love from the lower left quadrant

Let's return again to your memory of helping someone love better, and my memory of Ted and me. As you were present with, talked with, and/or touched this person in cherishing ways, you two had a shared experience. The intersubjective, cultural standard resides in the shared understandings between people. We tend to mostly agree as to what is right or wrong, good or bad. I certainly had the subjective sense that Ted and I shared a multitude of core values. We had a shared understanding that what we were doing in the session was "good." Supporting loving self and/or another better is usually considered moral in American culture, and especially so in the culture of the therapy session. If, suddenly, I had said to Ted, "We're making a big mistake. I think you should hate more right now. You should hate yourself for your years of alcoholism and hate your family for deserting you," it would probably feel wrong or immoral to both of us, as well as to most members of our cultural environments.

Moral, intersubjective perspectives figure prominently in psychotherapy. To seriously consider new beliefs and actions, people need to feel them as moral and good. To trust a therapist, a client needs to feel that the therapist is moral and good. As I continue the previous exchange with Mary, notice how being congruent with the "good" becomes a focus of the session:

Mary: "I want to leave but I can't."

Keith: Wanting to support her stand for "good", while helping her explore the moral complexities of her situation. I'll often tell clients in this process that, as we mature, we don't change our moral principles as much as we refine them. "What's wrong about divorce to you?"

Mary: "You're supposed to keep your family together and be true to your marriage vows. It's bad for kids when parents divorce."

Keith: "I think there's lots of validity in those principles. Are there ever exceptions?"

Mary: "Of course. When there's abuse, no love, or children are in danger."

Keith: "Are you experiencing any of these?"

Mary: "Dennis would never hurt me or the kids physically."

Keith: "Yet you often don't say what you truly feel or want because you fear Dennis' anger. That's one of the characteristics of an abusive relationship."

Mary: Addressing the central feminine issue of relationships "I just haven't loved him for so many years, and I don't love him. It's wrong to stay when there is no love."

This is mostly "we" material. Notice how there is a shared atmosphere between Mary and me of interest in, and commitment to, moral behavior. A therapist can disagree with a client on a variety of moral issues as long as there is the experience in the client that both are committed to complementary moral foundations. When a client is directly, or indirectly, seeking permission from a therapist (as Mary is in discussing the potentially "immoral" behavior of seeking divorce), the therapist is occupying the historical minister/priest/shaman position of moral arbiter. I believe it's in the client's interest for a therapist to relax into this role, be aware of both personal principles and biases, and the client's moral principles and biases, and understand that the client needs new perspectives and actions to feel moral, or "good," to be willing to risk inhabiting them.

Help them love from the lower right quadrant

Returning to you and the person you were cherishing, imagine that you were part of a great sociological research project that some persuasive psychologist had convinced the National Institute of Mental Health to fund. This research project was designed to explore the health benefits of helping people love better. This obviously involves objective systems data. It is inter-objective in that it represents scientifically verifiable relationships within groups (whereas the lower left quadrant is inter-subjective, representing interiorly observable subjective relationships). As it turns out, there is already lots of research that has been done in this area. As a group, individuals who work at loving themselves and/or others better tend to have less disease, more happiness, and enhanced well-being. Also, people who routinely help others tend to be physically and psychologically healthier than people who don't. Much of John Gottman's research on couples[2], and Seligman's work on positive psychology[3] supports this. In my session with Ted I quoted some of this data to encourage him to risk different perspectives and behaviors to create more love and health in his life.

In the session with Mary, systems input can potentially help her with struggles to find deeper truth and resolve. I, like most therapists, maintain a reservoir of data through study and practice that I bring to bear as one of my responsibilities as a psychologist—the responsibility to be a resource of objective, scientifically verifiable information from both right quadrants:

Mary: "What about the kids?"

Keith: "Statistically, studies quoted in *The Good Divorce* indicate that kids from intact families have a ten percent incidence of diagnosed emotional/behavioral problems, and kids from divorced families have a twenty percent incidence. The percentage of kids with problems after divorce went down with couples that interacted more reasonably and respectfully after separating.[4] Of course, these are just statistics and you and your family are unique individuals, but they do fit with my clinical experience and are helpful guides."

Mary: "This helps a little, but I'm worried about my parents' and sister's reactions."

Keith: "I've found, with almost all the single mothers I've worked with, that families rally to support them and their kids. If you decide to separate from Dennis, you might have to deal with some critical judgments, but mostly you'll probably get support. From what you've told me about your extended family, I'm almost certain of it."

Systems data such as this is often soothing to clients facing the uncertainties of life and change. In this example you can see how, in therapy, objective systems feedback can come both from external scientific sources on systems theory and statistical representations, and from the therapist's own data base of experience.

Balancing the Quadrants

Wilber suggests that one definition of health is balancing the quadrants. This involves attending to your life from all four quadrant's perspectives. What might balancing the quadrants look like in your life?

From the upper right quadrant, is your body observably healthy and functional? Is your blood work good? Do you exercise well, eat well, sleep adequately, relate in mature and honest ways, and work competently?

From the upper left quadrant, do you feel at peace with your life, satisfied with you affiliations, accepting of yourself, able to productively self-reflect, self-soothe, and deal constructively with defensive states? Are you comfortable with your means and progress in personal nourishment and development?

From the lower left quadrant, do you believe you live your life according to your principles, and do you feel in moral harmony with the various social groups you are a member of?

From the lower right quadrant, are your behaviors, practices, and participation in social networks consistent with social and medical research findings about healthy, happy existence conducted on groups of people that are representative of you and the cultures in which you are embedded?

Wilber calls balancing the quadrants "horizontal health" because such balancing involves arranging to maximize and harmonize our lives at this instant, relative to what our current worldview defines as health on all quadrants.[5]

Similarly, Wilber refers to optimizing development on different developmental lines as "vertical health," and we will explore this in Chapter Five, and then again in much more detail in Section Five.

1. Wilber (2000)

2. Gottman (1999, 2001)

3. Seligman (2002)

4. Ahrons (1994)

5. Wilber (2006)

5

Lines and Levels

We are always developing on many developmental Lines, but not always at the same rate.

Humans develop physically into a fetus from a sperm's eager masculine penetration of the welcoming feminine ovum, and then into an infant, into a toddler, into a child, into an adolescent, into an adult, into an older adult.

Drawing from the extensive research of Jean Piaget on cognitive development (his work has been extensively validated up to the formal operational level across numerous cultures and socioeconomic levels) and others, humans develop cognitively in the following universal sequence:

- Sensorimotor: processing the world through our senses.

- Pre-operational: having a separate physical and emotional self and developing language with capacities for internalized images, symbols, concepts, and repression.

- Concrete operational: having enhanced capacities for language, manipulating concepts, repression, and understanding the world in non-abstract, concrete ways.

- Formal operational: being able to hold competing concepts simultaneously, to inhabit "what if" scenarios, and to more easily understand abstract principles.

- Post-formal operational: being able to integrate logic and intuition in what Wilber calls "vision logic.

- Post-post-formal operational: where transrational, psychic experience is integrated into cognitive functioning.[1]

According to Carol Gilligan's research, women develop morally from egocentric selfish ("What's in it for me?"), to care (wanting to care for people in immediate cultural groups), to universal care (caring for all people). Men develop morally from egocentric selfish, to rights (the people in my family/group/tribe deserve the same rights), to universal rights (there are human rights that all should share). Interestingly, as men and women mature on the moral line, they tend to develop an integrated embrace of both universal rights and universal care.[2]

Physical, cognitive, and moral are three central developmental lines among a number of developmental lines that all humans share.

On each line, development in every human starts at the same level and moves in the same direction through the same sequence of levels, through as many levels as that individual eventually grows. Each level includes and transcends all previous levels, and we do not skip levels. No one is born formal operational or caring. No one who becomes formal operational or caring loses their capacity to be concrete operational or selfish. Each day we inhabit a variety of different levels on different lines.[3] As David Deida maintains in his three stage system of relationship development (moving from egocentric, to egalitarian, to serving love in the moment), at any time we can inhabit a first stage moment, second stage moment, or third stage moment.[4]

Our center of gravity is our most "at home" place on any line.

In the glop and slop of development we progress and regress daily. What changes over time is our center of gravity, the point that is our most natural position on each line. The more moments we spend in higher levels of functioning, the more natural those levels become, until we have a new, higher center of gravity. We can regress, usually under stress, to previous levels at any moment, or have peak experiences that give us glimpses of more mature functioning, but the developmental trajectory of starting at conception and moving through the same levels in an include-and-transcend process remains universal across cultures, ethnicities, socio-economic levels, and gender. Since we cannot skip levels, no one grows directly from pre-operational to formal operational, or from toddler straight to adolescent. Each level must be inhabited, integrated, differentiated from, and reintegrated into the next level on each developmental line.

The self-line and the specific abilities lines.

Wilber postulates over twenty lines of development falling into two broad categories; the self-line, and specific talent or ability lines. The self-line includes the cognitive, moral, values, sexual/interpersonal, and spiritual lines the way a rope includes its various strands, and figures heavily in who we experience ourselves to be as individuals. The specific talent or ability lines emphasize areas like Howard

Gardner's multiple intelligences[5], and include musical ability, sports ability, mathematical ability, mechanical ability, and similar constellations of gifts and interests with a specific focus.

Masculine and feminine types develop differently.

Masculine and feminine types (largely men and women, though a man can be a more feminine type, or a woman a more masculine type) develop identically on some lines, similarly on some lines, and differently on some lines.

Physically, men and women develop almost identically in their digestive systems (men and women have slightly different constellations of digestive enzymes), and differently in their reproductive systems.

Morally, Carol Gilligan has found that women develop from selfish, to care, to universal care, to integrated universal care and universal rights, while men develop from selfish, to rights, to universal rights, to universal rights and universal care. Men and women are similar in starting out selfish and decentering to including larger groups. They are different in that women tend to emphasize care over rights, and men tend to emphasize rights over care.[6]

Thinking developmentally makes therapy more effective and more fun.

Observing where clients are developmentally on different lines makes therapy more effective and more fun. A concrete operational client (or a more mature client in a concrete operational moment) will have difficulty comprehending formal operational insights, and a client in an egocentric moment might be indifferent to—even irritated by—altruistic motivational systems. Further, a common characteristic of defensive states in therapy is the sudden regression of the client to more egocentric, less empathetic, and less formal operational levels of functioning. What levels of functioning the client regresses from—and what levels they regress to—are indicators to the therapist of what language style to use, what motivational systems the client might respond to, and what forms of intervention might be optimal.

Section Five explores lines and levels in depth and details clinical indications, interventions, and case examples. In this chapter I will focus more narrowly on development on the constellation of lines that constitute the self line and the correlations of that self development with characteristic life conditions, worldviews, social patterns, and response sets as detailed by Beck and Cowen in their ground breaking book, *Spiral Dynamics*[7], and further elaborated by the Integral Institute in their adaptation of the spiral dynamics systems.

Spiral Dynamics: It will blow your mind.

Building on the work of Clare Graves[8], Beck and Cowan have described eight worldviews, or MEMEs, that dominate human cultures. They define "MEME" as "A cultural unit (an idea or value or pattern of behavior) that is passed from one generation to another by nongenetic means (as by imitation), or as "An idea, behavior, style, or usage that spreads from person to person within a culture." According to Beck and Cowan, each MEME "reflects a worldview, a valuing system, a level of psychological existence, a belief structure, an organizing principle, a way of thinking or a mode of adjustment."[9]

Each MEME can manifest in healthy and unhealthy ways. They have arisen in human history as human societies have evolved. They are designated as different colors to de-emphasize ethnicity and to emphasize the primacy of worldview over race. The colors progress from BEIGE, to PURPLE, to RED, to BLUE, to ORANGE, to GREEN, to YELLOW, to TURQUOISE. The following chart draws selectively from *Spiral Dynamics* and lists characteristics I've found to be especially relevant to psychotherapy:

- **BEIGE:** Surviving through the senses and instinct in nature. Primitive survival consciousness. Little awareness of self as a distinct being. A bridge condition between animal existence and tribal culture. Normal in infants. Wants survival.

- **PURPLE:** Tribal. Safe clans and nests. Ethnocentric and ruled by elders. Bloodlines are important and protected. Paternalistic, passive learning through rituals, customs, and routines. Strictly defined roles, rites of passage, and relational structures. Magical, mystical spiritual orientation anchored in nature mysticism with some mythological deity mysticism. Subsistence orientation. Normal in toddlers. Wants safety.

- **RED:** Power-God orientation. Might makes right. Immediate gratification, no guilt, and the powerful deserve power. "Us vs. them" consciousness leads to gang-like battles and tests of worthiness. Naturally forms feudal fiefdoms, turf wars, and vendettas. Seeks attention and dominance. Winning is moral, losing is weak. Normal in preschoolers. Wants power.

- **BLUE:** Conformist. Authority dictates one right way that obeys the "book" and the rules. Guilt in not conforming, and it is moral and beautiful to sacrifice for the honor of what is "right." Moralistic lessons and punishment for breaking the rules. Hierarchical steps of advancement, but only for those who are born into the group and/or abide by the "book." Ascending spirituality involving rewards in the afterlife for conformity now. Order and stability are moral and in keeping with the divine plan. Normal in elementary schoolers. Wants truth.

- **ORANGE:** Competes for success on merit-based hierarchies. Scientific, rational, material goal-oriented. Plays to win and enjoys competition. Mentors and guides teach skills that give a competitive edge in moving upward in hierarchies. Immediate material prosperity is beautiful and good, creating entrance to, and security in, elite societies. Normal in high schoolers. Wants prosperity.

- **GREEN:** Egalitarian, multicultural, seeking inner peace and harmony with all. Cooperation, feelings, shared experience, consensus, and social development are beautiful and good. Is communitarian. Spiritually inclusive and seeking, while unconsciously intolerant of other points of view. Normal in college society. Wants belonging, acceptance, justice, community, equality, and security for all.

- **YELLOW:** Integral. Enjoys the big picture, accepts the inevitability of change, uncertainty, and chaos. Highly principled, knowledge-centered, and the most competent deserve to address the problems and enjoy the solutions. Focus on functionality; what works best. Self-directed, non-rigid, with appreciation for all other worldviews, and a desire to operate in open systems. Reduced fear. Appreciation, enjoyment, and participation in ascending and descending spiritual orientations. Is systemic. Wants learning, freedom to grow, and service to the whole.

- **TURQUOISE:** Holistic, has felt appreciation for synergy and oneness of all life and spirit. Committed to the promise of harmony and a safe, orderly world. Plans for the long range. Global awareness, highly diversified, blending feelings and intuition with technology and science. Seeks outreach into interconnected systems designed to serve all. Is holistic. Wants interconnection, to fit into the chain of being, to maximize growth and consciousness for all.

Beck and Cowen include CORAL beyond TURQUOISE, which I'm not including because it represents a fraction of a percent of the human population (on the other hand, since CORAL integrates deep spiritual awakening with world service, those individuals tend to have a disproportionate effect on the collective). Aficionados of Spiral Dynamics postulate continuing MEMES, or levels, that exist as possibilities, waiting to be occupied as humans learn how to live longer and better accelerate and support development.

BEIGE through GREEN constitutes the first tier.

BEIGE through GREEN constitutes the first tier where people are driven primarily by what Maslow called "deficiency needs;" needs arising from a felt lack of food, shelter, affiliation, security, or achievement. Individuals from these first six MEMEs at best irritate, and at worst despise, each other.

YELLOW, TURQUOISE, and beyond represent the second tier where people have a felt appreciation for all perspectives and dramatic reductions of fear, and are driven by "being needs" coming from a sense of fullness and desire to serve and create. The Integral Institute describes a third tier where individuals have a stable relationship with unity of spirit and are drawn to join in like-minded groups to serve.

How are these MEMEs relevant to developmental lines and levels? Let's briefly follow the development of human culture and the (very) approximate emergence of these MEMEs, and then follow the development of a single human being from birth onward, and observe how human development naturally recapitulates these worldviews.

The emergence of the MEMEs.

Homo Sapiens were once family groups of **BEIGE** animals roaming on partially forested plains in Africa, who experienced the birth of consciousness, possibly through a mutation on the human FOXP2 gene two hundred thousand years ago that created enhanced abilities for grammar and symbolic communication.[10]

Human consciousness, manifested through interior and interpersonal capacities for symbolic language and multiple perspectives in the past/present/future, was a radiant seed that flourished through the human species to form **PURPLE** hunter-gatherer tribes which spread all over the world. There must have been great wisdom, mythic quests, and grand dramas as people expanded into the possibilities of tribe, consciousness, and multiple natural environments. Eventually some of these **PURPLE** tribes developed horticulture and then draft animal/plow aided agrarian cultures.

Between fifteen and twenty thousand years ago, along the Indus, the Nile, the Tigress Euphrates, the Hwang Ho rivers, and in Central and South America, **RED** warrior kings (who, functionally, became power-Gods ruling what they could hold by force) began the process that continues to this day of creating empires and dynasties. As concentrations of wealth, power, and relative stability occurred, cultures produced stable advances in writing, construction, book keeping, the arts, enhanced transportation, and advanced weapons systems. These developments inevitably resulted in progress in record keeping, geometry, materials sciences, road building, ship building, mathematics, aesthetics, politics, and written language. Written language and stable societies requiring organizational systems led to **BLUE** traditions, castes, standards, and rules dominating moral codes. The "Book" became the ultimate authority and moral arbiter in many cultures in which religion, science, and art were culturally fused. Priest castes became the arbiters of the Book and intermediaries with the Gods, and Power-God rulers who wanted divine rights of kings found that they needed to share power with conformist religious hierarchies.

The written word created the capacity for cumulative knowledge and wisdom beyond what an individual could develop and retain throughout a lifetime. As a result of this—and the fact that agriculture accelerated human *genetic* evolution by up to *one hundred* times the rate it had been previously[11]—all aspects of human culture exploded with BLUE moral imperatives driving religion, hunger to create beauty driving art, and hunger to understand, build, and dominate driving science. All this time **RED** power-Gods kept arising, creating dynasties which were consolidated as **BLUE** conformist hierarchies which were eventually supplanted or otherwise overthrown. The first documented peaceful transfer of power from one distinct group to another occurred in the 1800 U.S. election between Adams and Jefferson.

Wilber has observed that the enlightenment, beginning in the Renaissance and cascading into the Industrial Revolution, differentiated religion (morals, the "good"), art (the "beautiful"), and science (the "true"), leading to the domination of **ORANGE**, technological, capitalist, hierarchical, achievement oriented, merit-based societies.[12] The telegraph, telephone, widespread literacy, political stability, an expansion of the middle classes through technologically driven wealth creation, and progressively easier travel led to an upsurge of **GREEN** egalitarian, multicultural, anti-hierarchical, ecologically sensitive enclaves and political movements.

Freed by the technological revolution from the agrarian restraints of slavery and male physical strength dominating economic power, women and other disenfranchised groups successfully pursued equal rights and opportunity. Some children coming of age in **GREEN** societies had more access to spirituality outside of the rigid boundaries of **BLUE** fundamentalism, purpose outside the boundaries **ORANGE** profit-driven, rational, science-based capitalism, and hierarchies outside the bounds of **GREEN** egalitarianism, leading to more second tier

YELLOW individuals with a felt appreciation for all worldviews, dramatic decreases in fear, and hunger to serve the world arising from a sense of fullness. Occasionally, **YELLOW**'s hunger to grow and serve has lead to **TURQUOISE** systems, organized by individuals yearning to serve with like-minded others to solve specific problems, meet specific needs, fulfill specific purposes while honoring and utilizing the healthy expression of all worldviews.

All these MEMEs currently exist in the world, and will always be manifested in human societies. The percentages of people and cultures with different worldviews as their centers of gravity continually shift in response to changed life conditions. For example, Wilber, in 2003, estimated that three percent of American society was currently YELLOW—Integral—in their most central worldview; a percentage that might shift to as much as ten percent in the five to ten years.[13]

James grows from BEIGE to TURQUOISE.

Now, imagine an infant boy named James, born into an American middle class family. At birth, James exists in a **BEIGE** world of simple survival needs for food, contact, warmth, and stimulation.

As James develops language and differentiates emotionally from his mother, he integrates into a **PURPLE** world of magic ability to manipulate the physical environment, surrounded by huge forces that can manipulate him with God-like power.

With toddlerhood, James discovers he has no, or dramatically diminished, magic powers, but his parents are **RED** power-Gods who seem to be able to control the world. James himself can become a **RED** power-God for brief periods through play, by dominating the environment with narcissistic demands, or with extravagant displays of emotion.

As James matures into a boy of six or seven, he increasingly values belonging to his family, inhabiting the roles assigned to him, and obeying the rules of fairness, which lead him into **BLUE** conformity where rules often take precedence over the comfort or unique needs of the individual.

Maturing at around eleven or twelve into formal operational cognitive abilities where he can hold opposing viewpoints simultaneously, and explore "as if" scenarios, and being indoctrinated in school with the primacy of objective scientific knowledge, James begins to look for deeper principles in dogma and, feeling his emergent physical, emotional, and cognitive powers, strives for **ORANGE** achievement in sports, academics, and social status.

Idealism, multiple perspectives presented through life experience and formal education, an expanding sense of wider ranges of "we" perspectives being important, and increasing security in principles and adult identity lead James to **GREEN** multiculturalism, anti-hierarchy, and eco-consciousness (a common worldview of American higher education).

Dissatisfied with the paradox of obvious different levels in anti-hierarchical social structures, and hungry for a deeper spirituality that supports his increasing awareness that he is more than his thoughts, feelings, and body, and stretching his intuitive and psychic potentialities into wider perspectives, James crosses into the second tier and develops a **YELLOW**, integral appreciation for all world-views, a diminishment of fear, and an understanding that different perspectives are superior for different problems.

Frustrated by his limited individual capacity to serve, and feeling so full he is hungry to share his fullness, he seeks out and/or creates **TURQUOISE** systems to help the world and actualize his inner drive for deep soul's purpose.

James' development includes and transcends on each of his developmental lines. He retains the capacity to inhabit all levels on all his developmental lines, just as he's always had the capacity to have peak experiences in, and develop into, levels he has not experienced. He can do this in healthy ways or unhealthy ways.

Life conditions evoke MEMEs.

Community life conditions evoke cultural MEMEs. Perceived life conditions evoke individual developmental levels. A GREEN college professor, when mugged in an alley, might react with RED power-God violence to oppose his attackers. A BLUE fundamentalist might react with some GREEN multicultural-ism when her daughter announces that she is gay.

The unhealthy expressions of these worldviews, cued by perceived threats in the environment, constitute defensive states with characteristic distorted percep-tions and beliefs, amplified or numbed emotions, destructive impulses, and reduced capacities for self-reflection and empathy. The healthy expression of any worldview is that worldview's best response to the present moment.

The similarities between the vast unfolding of human history and the individ-ual unfolding of one human's journey from conception through dedication to second tier (YELLOW, TURQUOISE, and beyond) world service reflect a real-ity much broader than ontogeny recapitulating phylogeny. Beck and Cowan understand the MEMEs to be meta-genes in the species homo sapiens. Like our biochemical genes and chromosomes, these meta-genes are the seeds and blue-prints for the levels and stages that are currently expressed, and exist as potentials, waiting to be grown into—given the right life conditions—in individuals, collec-tives, the human race, all sentient beings, all life, and all of creation.

The Integral Institute (II) changed some of the colors and use them to reflect specific altitude on different developmental lines.

Recognizing that we can be at different altitudes on different developmental lines, the Integral Institute changed the color sequence *from*:

Spiral Dynamics referring to *worldview*:

- First tier: Beige, purple, red, blue, orange, green.

- Second tier: Yellow, turquoise, coral.

To:

The Integral Institute referring to *altitude* on a given developmental line:

- First tier: Infrared, magenta, red, amber, orange, green.

- Second tier: teal, turquoise.

- Third tier: indigo, violet, ultraviolet, and clear light.[14]

I find it useful to include the color designations as referring to altitudes on different developmental lines, but, to avoid confusion, I've chosen to mostly use the Spiral Dynamics designations throughout the rest of this book. Occasionally, the reference will be to an individual's characteristic worldview, their center of gravity, as in the BLUE Baptist preacher (AMBER altitude on the spirituality line in the II system), the ORANGE CEO (still ORANGE altitude in II), the GREEN eco-activist (still GREEN altitude in II), or the YELLOW spiritual seeker (TEAL altitude on the spirituality line in the II system).

All these individuals could be operating from other worldviews at any time (or different altitudes on various lines), given the right immediate life conditions. For simplicity's sake I will continue to use the Spiral Dynamics colors to refer to both worldview and altitude on various lines. Sometimes I'll refer to a regressive defensive state, as in "He bullied her with RED fury," or a progressive peak experience, as in "She was transported into a transcendent state of YELLOW acceptance and love for all." Sometimes I'll use the Spiral Dynamics colors to designate altitude on a given developmental line, as in he was TURQUOISE cognitively and YELLOW morally, though the idea of evaluating individuals as having different altitudes on various lines is an Integral Institute contribution.[15]

Psychotherapists support the health of the spiral in their clients and cultures by supporting the health of the spiral in themselves.

Each MEME is important and necessary to the whole spiral. Each child must successfully and fully inhabit current and previous MEME's to fully grow to new levels. Each individual is responsible for, either more or less artfully, dealing with the regular regressions that are inevitable concomitants of defensive states. All MEMEs need to be honored for therapy to be a safe place for clients. I believe therapists are social agents responsible for the health of the spiral. As we co-create healing cultures we support the ontogenetic development of our clients and the phylogenetic development of the cultures our clients are embedded in.

The way to support the health of the spiral in our clients and in the cultures we're embedded in is to support the health of the spiral in ourselves. Do we embrace, with affection and humor, our PURPLE tribal selves, our RED power-God selves, our BLUE conformist selves, our ORANGE competitive, scientific selves, our GREEN egalitarian, non-hierarchical selves, our YELLOW integral selves, and our TURQUOISE world service, networking selves? When the moment calls for one of these aspects, can we open fully to it? When we regress into egocentric defensive states, can we empower our deeper, more mature selves to contain, heal, and direct our regressed selves into healthy responses to the present moment with compassion and humor?

As we develop these attributes with skillful means, we naturally become spiral wizards who support both horizontal health (balancing the quadrants) and vertical health (ontogenetic/phylogenetic development) in our clients and cultures. We become more effective agents of attending to and balancing the health of the spiral.

We have examined the form of development as individuals grow through different levels on different developmental lines, but what about the process of development? What are the inner forces that drive individuals, and thus cultures, to grow?

Robert Kegan and the evolutionary truces between subject and object.

The importance of the interplay between individual development and cultural MEMEs is reflected in our underlying biological drives, literally instinctual imperatives that propel our development. Robert Kegan, in *The Evolving Self,* postulates that the instinct to create meaning between the subjective "I" and the objective universe is the fundamental driving force in human development.[16] This instinct to create meaning results in a series of "evolutionary truces" that we progressively make between ourselves (subject) and the world (object) in the include and transcend rhythm of human development. We fuse with a current worldview, differentiate from it as we grow and expand our knowledge and understanding, and reintegrate into a new worldview more consistent with our emerging discoveries of what is beautiful, good, and true.

The instincts to relate, to inhabit positions on social hierarchies, and to be true to our deepest sexual essences.

Each developing child's universe is dominated by the worldviews of the people surrounding him or her, and the cultures surrounding those people. In a slight departure from Kegan, I believe that, in addition to the instinct to create meaning, each of us also has profound and demanding instincts to relate to others, to love and be loved by others, to strive for and value positions on subjectively important social hierarchies, and to be true to our deepest masculine and feminine essences. How these instincts are felt and expressed in cultural contexts determine our worldviews, relationships, professional associations, communication styles, development, self-esteem, and spirituality.

The evidence of these instinctual drives is overwhelming. Every human society, without exception, is characterized by constant relating between individuals, omnipresent hierarchies in which each individual more or less generally knows—and often either values or laments—his or her position, and different gender roles for men and women. Each infant begins relating biologically at conception, starts relating socially at birth, and begins positioning on social hierarchies as soon as there is awareness of others in the social environment. As we have already examined, men and women develop differently in a variety of ways. As we will explore in more detail in Section Three, our relative relationships with and acceptance of our deepest masculine or feminine essences are huge determinants of relative happiness and self-esteem throughout life.

Applications of Spiral Dynamics to psychotherapy: different language styles appeal to different worldviews.

Appealing to an achievement oriented ORANGE marketing executive in the language of GREEN egalitarian, anti-hierarchical, eco-consciousness will probably irritate and alienate him. To help him consider new perspectives and actions, language and motivation for change need to be in harmony with his worldview, that is, need to be expressed in the language of ORANGE rationality, science, and the assumed central importance of personal and institutional success and profit.

Knowing what soothes and motivates each MEME's worldview provides a map to direct a therapist to optimally relate, teach, inspire, confront, interpret, and direct each client to maximize the cultivation of compassion and depth of consciousness to cultivate healthy perspectives and actions. What constitutes healthy perspectives and actions at any given moment will be relative to the worldview that each client generally and situationally inhabits.

Good therapy often comes from the second tier: YELLOW and above.

My personal conviction is that good therapy often comes from an Integral (YELLOW in Spiral Dynamics, TEAL altitude on the psychotherapy line) worldview in the therapist. Without a felt appreciation for all perspectives, therapists can fall into the trap of being irritated by, and then conflicting with, worldviews and language styles that are not their own. I believe this vulnerability has led to some of the stereotypes of therapists as GREEN elitists who have no PURPLE tribal heart, no RED warrior spirit, no BLUE moral center, no ORANGE ability to compete and achieve, and no YELLOW spiritual depth of consciousness.

Therapy from the second tier involves a therapist having felt appreciation for the security of PURPLE tribal clan consciousness, the pleasures of RED power hierarchies, the satisfaction of BLUE mythic membership in like-minded conformist groups, the thrill of competing on ORANGE merit based hierarchies, and the social responsibility of GREEN pluralistic multiculturalism.

1. Wilber (2000)

2. Gilligan (1993)

3. Wilber (2000)

4. Deida (2006)

5. Gardner (2003)

6. Gilligan (1993)

7. Beck (1996)

8. Graves (1970)

9. *Ibid*

10. Enard (2004)

11. Kaplan (2007)

12. Wilber (1995)

13. Wilber (2004)

14. Wilber (2006)

15. *Ibid*

16. Kegan (1982)

6

States: The Subjective Kaleidoscope of Existence

Gross, subtle, and causal: the three foundation states.

We are always inhabiting one of three, great states of consciousness; gross, subtle, or causal. In deep, dreamless sleep, (the formless, causal state) only the most accomplished meditators and enlightened sages have any conscious awareness at all. Most of us have no conscious awareness in deep, dreamless sleep. There is no form, no identity other than the deepest ever-present witness, and no objects arise. Some sects of Buddhism and Vedanta maintain that here, in deep, dreamless sleep, our "capital S" Self always resides.[1] This is our deepest consciousness which, according to David Deida, is our purest masculine essence.[2]

When we dream (the subtle state), we have awareness, but again, all but the most accomplished spiritual practitioners have no conscious awareness that they are dreaming. Consistent lucid dreaming (knowing in a dream that we are dreaming) is considered a sign of having ascended to higher spiritual levels in some spiritual traditions[3], and this makes sense. If we are consciously aware in a dream that we are dreaming, our identity has probably deepened to a point where we don't need our body, gender, profession, or relationships to help define our self. We are more likely to experience our self as a deeper witness who can more consistently observe objects in the same way we observe dream identities and figures while identifying exclusively with none of them.

We awake and enter the gross state of conscious awareness of the material world and our physical body. We see, smell, touch, taste, and hear the world. We inhabit our physical body, and we identify with whom we consciously experience ourselves to be. I awake from a dream where I might have been a child, an animal, or a disembodied observer, to re-encounter the physical world where I have my adult body, and my various identities as man, husband, father, therapist, friend, and soul.

Gross, subtle, causal; waking, dreaming, and deep dreamless sleep. The three great states all humans inhabit daily from birth to death.

Spiritual practices can extend conscious awareness of the gross, waking state into the subtle and even the formless, causal realms. Such practices have been shown to accelerate growth through the developmental levels. For example, Charles Alexander has demonstrated that a daily Transcendental Meditation practice for at least four years results in deepening an average of two developmental levels on the self and other lines, while other activities such as therapy result in an average movement of, at most, one half of a level.[4] This is especially significant since, in the absence of spiritual practice, people generally don't deepen significantly on these lines from age twenty-five (interestingly, the age our brain reaches full maturity) to our mid-fifties.

Gross, subtle, and causal in spiritual practice.

The gross, subtle, and causal states are also associated with various forms of spiritual practice. Nature mysticism is feeling one with what is arising in the gross realm, from a blade of grass, to an ocean. Deity mysticism is feeling infused by God, or a God-like presence, very much like the huge, mythic entities that we occasionally encounter in the subtle, dreaming state. Formless mysticism is extending depth of consciousness beneath/beyond mind, body, emotion, and time, to the formless, ever present ocean of consciousness that we have always been and always will be; the place we naturally inhabit in deep, dreamless sleep. The more aspects of self and world we comprehend and hold as objects of a larger, wider self, the deeper our consciousness.

Psychotherapy is all about states of consciousness. Throughout our waking life we shift into countless altered states of consciousness depending upon our biology, psychology, developmental levels on various lines, and a huge array of objective and subjective influences.

In psychotherapy, I've found it enormously useful to conceptualize these myriad states of consciousness as falling into two broad categories: healthy responses to the present moment, and defensive states.

Healthy responses to the present moment.

David Deida asserts that, most of the time, we are either opening or closing the moment.

"Opening the moment" is bringing our best gifts to bear through our deepest, truest essences in ways that optimize love, health, and the highest good for all. "Closing the moment" is engaging in some behavior or habit that blunts our gifts, obscures and/or distorts our deepest essences, and does not best serve love, health, and the highest good for all.[5]

Healthy responses to the present moment reflect our natural inclinations to open, love, and serve self and others. We're hungry, we eat healthy food; work demands, we give our best effort; our lover needs our attention, we provide loving attention. Healthy responses to the present moment reflect a graceful dance between inner drives and needs, compassion and depth of consciousness, and the parameters of our shifting environments. As the environment gives us feedback, we act on it in healthy ways. We become replete, we stop eating; we fail at solving a problem, we seek out a new approach; our lover closes in response to our attention, we offer an alternate form of attention. Healthy responses to the present moment usually reflect this homeostatic, flexible, interplay between our experience and our own and the world's responses to our experience.

Psychotherapy of all forms seeks to maximize moments of healthy response to the present moment. The main obstacle to this is our natural capacity, when we feel threatened, to activate defensive states of consciousness.

Defensive states.

When the healthy homeostatic interplay between our offerings and the world's responses is interrupted (usually when we perceive a threat or fail to discern a destructive impulse), and we are unable and/or unwilling to make necessary adjustments, we risk constellating some form of defensive state. These defensive states arise out of our habitual responses to perceived threat, and tend to have characteristic distorted perceptions and beliefs, amplified or numbed emotions, destructive impulses, and diminished capacities for self-reflection and empathy. Identifying, addressing, and transforming defensive states forms much of the foundation of psychotherapeutic practice.

Carl Jung recognized the idiosyncratic character—almost personality—of different defensive states and called them complexes.[6] Fritz Perls noticed the similarities between defensive states and distressed historic figures such as hostile fathers or rejecting mothers and called them introjects; pathological historic figures we had swallowed whole and never integrated, or psychologically digested properly.[7] Roberto Assagioli, founder of Psychosynthesis, preferred the construct of subpersonalities; little dissociated pieces of arrested development that manifest as irritating neurotic to psychotic entities depending on level of pathology and depth of developmental arrest.[8]

I've found all these conceptualizations to be valid and beneficial in therapy. The construct of a defensive state as an injured entity that is part of our larger self is especially useful when teaching clients how to set boundaries for, care for, and love repulsive, pathological aspects of self that can be conceptualized as hurt children compulsively exercising inappropriate power, when what they need is to be parented by a deeper, more mature executive ego of the client.

I often refer to the defensive states construct in therapy because it's easy to explain to clients, suggests that healthy states are just a change of perspective around the corner, firmly establishes defensive states as not representing the deeper, truer core identities of my clients, and helps me teach how to discern healthy and unhealthy functioning with a specific agenda of disidentifying with unhealthy defensive states and identifying with healthy responses to the present moment.

The following exchange is between Martin and Sally. Martin is a thirty-nine year old physician, and Sally is a forty-one year old accountant. She has a history of being physically abused, and he of being neglected by caregivers. They have three children, girls eleven and fourteen, and a sixteen year old son, and have been married nineteen years. This is their tenth session:

> Martin: Complaining, as he often does when yearning for something. "Why can't you be more adventurous sexually?"

> Sally: Instantly shifting into a defensive state, visibly closing and recoiling. "You're disgusting."

> Martin: Entering a complementary defensive state of his own, as lovers are prone to do when under perceived attack. Speaking in a contemptuous, morally superior tone. "You need to work through your sexual material. Until you do, you'll never be a whole woman."

> Sally: Going into defensive high gear in response to Martin's complementary provocation. "You have to be a whole man to know what a whole woman is, Martin!"

> Keith: I could stay with this process until they explode, sometimes a good idea since explosion can motivate new perspectives and change,[9] but I also realize that these aggressive patterns can do great damage if allowed to cycle out of control. I decide to take a stand for safety in the session, modeling for them how it's good to insist on non-violence in conflict. "If you two don't

switch channels, this is going to continue to be a contest of who can hurt whom the most."

Martin: Still in a defensive state, but shifting slightly in response to my intervention. "I'm just trying to tell it like it is."

Keith: "That's what you consciously intend, which is a good thing. Unconsciously, you're attacking Sally and refusing to take any real responsibility to change."

Sally: Sarcastic. Feeling supported by me and thus more free to indulge her amplified fear and anger, her distorted beliefs of Martin's sick, selfish nature, and her impulses to attack to get relief. "That's right, it's never your fault."

Keith: Feeling how her defensive state is protecting a sense of fragility, which she avoids by attacking. Agreeing with David Deida that the feminine grows best in the presence of loving praise while the masculine grows best in the presence of loving challenge.[10] Perceiving her RED egocentric state that listens best to egocentric motivational language. "Sally, you attack because you yearn so much to be safe loving and being loved by Martin. Stop attacking for a moment and feel how much you wish he could somehow make you feel safe."

Sally: Shifting to a more healthy response to the present moment, she begins to cry. "I never feel safe."

Martin: Feeling an impulse to shift to a complementary, more healthy state. "I want to make you feel safe."

While they are in their defensive states, Martin and Sally's worldviews are RED power-God and BLUE fundamentalist. They both have irresistible impulses to dominate and/or morally condemn each other and, if their struggle is not interrupted, they will keep trading off dominating and being dominated, condemning and being condemned. While in healthy responses to the present moment, their worldviews tend to be GREEN egalitarian. They want to be equal, fair, and each responsible for their own work. Almost every psychotherapy session, and especially conjoint sessions where couples frequently stimulate and restimulate defensive states in one another, are such roller coaster rides from healthy responses to the present moment to defensive states, and from worldview to worldview.

From an Integrally informed perspective, States are the crucial expressions of how quadrants, lines, levels, and types are manifesting together in the present moment. Further, they are central determinants of—and vehicles toward or away from—spiritual growth. In psychotherapy, they are the fabric of each session.

The art of being a therapist is in perceiving these shifting states and working with them to cocreate a culture in which the client and the client's universe is cherished, each moment is perceived as a gift and an opportunity, and healthy perspectives and actions are considered beautiful, good, and true. In Section Six we will explore this material and a variety of clinical applications in much more detail.

States and types.

Carol Gilligan has found that men tend to think hierarchically.[11] Organizational systems, classes, orders, and categories have dominated science since the time of Aristotle, when people were described as being influenced by the four humors; black bile, yellow bile, blood, and phlegm.

It was inevitable that (mostly) male theorists and researchers in the emergent field of psychology would observe different types of people. Their findings have been translated into the vast field of personality theory. Type refers to endogenous, enduring constellations of traits in individuals that are characteristic of groups, or types, of people. Freud described oral, anal, and genital types.[12] Sheldon described endomorphs, mesomorphs, and ectomorphs.[13] Jungian researchers produced the popular Myers-Briggs categories of extrovert, introvert, thinking feeling, sensing, and intuiting; that, in combination, describe myriad types of individuals.[14] Tomas Hartmann, in *The Edison Gene*, explores hunter types and farmer types.[15] My current favorite is the enneagram which describes nine enneatypes that, in various combinations, reflect our essence, personality, fixations, relational styles, and optimal developmental paths.[16]

I have never met a personality theory I didn't like. They all have been intriguing, informative, and clinically useful in a variety of ways.

The 800-pound gorilla of types, the category that I believe underlies all other categories, a meta-type, is sexual essence. Most people are primarily either a masculine or feminine type of person. Section Three is devoted to exploring these two types, especially as interpreted and taught by David Deida who maintains that we all have both masculine and feminine aspects, but that generally each of us has a more masculine or a more feminine sexual essence. So central to our experience that we rarely consciously notice it is the fact that men and women live in different domains.

The states of consciousness that we are constantly morphing into and out of are driven by what types of individuals we are. In psychotherapy, how to appropriately respond to a specific state of consciousness, especially a defensive state, is influenced by what type of person our client is, and especially if they are a more masculine or more feminine type.

One foundation aspect of health is accepting all of who you are and being increasingly true to your deepest, most authentic self. Consider the following exchange with Julia, a radiant, extremely feminine type in her late twenties:

Julia: "He's hitting on me and he's married. He won't stop. I'm cold and distant, but he just doesn't get the message."

Keith: With typical masculine direction. This is a problem that is easily solved. "Sounds like he won't stop until you give him an unambiguous 'no'."

Julia: "I just can't. I know I should, but I just can't."

Keith: Waking up to the fact that this is a feminine-type person. "What feels right to you?"

Julia: "I'll write him a note."

Two weeks pass and Julia and I have another session.

Keith: "Did you write that note to Dick?"

Julia: "No, it didn't feel right. I did ask about his wife every time we worked together. Now everything feels much better."

Women tend to think relationally and non-hierarchically. A masculine type would probably have felt a sense of failure at not following through on his "mission" of giving an unambiguous boundary to unwelcome advances. Julia, a feminine type, had no problem whatsoever in changing her mind and exploring alternatives that felt more right relationally. It would have been a disservice to her feminine sexual essence in this situation for me to challenge her to be more assertive and direct when she had arrived at a course of action that met her validity standards in another, less hierarchical and more relational, fashion.

When clients quote the homily, "People don't change," I often say to them, "I don't think therapy is as much about change, as it is about becoming more purely your self." Central to being more purely your self is moving toward accepting and balancing all the states you are capable of manifesting, and identifying and honoring the unique type of person you are which includes your deepest masculine/feminine sexual aspects and essence.

A beautiful quality of growth is that as we develop, especially on our self and spiritual lines, we tend to keep identifying with wider and wider groups until, ultimately, we can feel ourselves to be the Self that feels one with everything that is and ever was. This reflects an apparent paradox of therapy and growth; the fact that therapy helps us develop healthy egos, while continuing spiritual practice encourages us to disidentify with those egos and identify with larger entities like nature, mankind, or pure spirit. As Wilber explains to Tammy Simon in *Kosmic Consciousness*, the paradox is only apparent because, in the arc of development, a stronger, deeper, fuller sense of self naturally leads to disidentifying with smaller parts of self such as body, feelings, habits, consciousness, and mental thoughts, and identifying with larger entities such as humanity, life, nature, the ever-present witness, and all existence.[17] Still, no matter how much we are one with all spirit, that spirit is expressed thorough a body/mind system that is usually either more deeply masculine or feminine.

1. Wilber (2003)

2. Deida (2004)

3. Wilber (2003)

4. Alexander (1990)

5. Deida (2006)

6. Jung (1961)

7. Perls (1969)

8. Assagioli (1965)

9. Schnarch (1997)

10. Deida (2006)

11. Gilligan (1993)

12. Freud (1949)

13. Sheldon (1940)

14. Jung (1965)

15. Hartmann (2003)

16. Riso (1999)

17. Wilber (2003)

Section Three

Polarity

7

Health is Supported by Satisfying Erotic Polarity

Sixty percent of the books sold in America are romances bought almost exclusively by women. The feminine form is the most widely used marketing tool in every visual media. Ask any adolescent or young adult what their top three concerns are and romantic/sexual relationships will be on the list. Open any magazine and somewhere on the page or in the advertisements there will be a reference to eroticism, attractiveness, or relationship. Sexual polarity permeates our existence and we can be more or less healthy in how we deal with it.

When I first read Dolores Curran's book, *Traits of a Healthy Family*, I was surprised to find it more useful in psychotherapy than many academic psychology books on clinical theory and technique. Her research helped create a language of health that I could add to my therapy to complement the languages of functionality, pathology, and healing that had figured more prominently in my traditional training. For example, she found that in healthy families everyone interrupted each other, but interrupted equally. In healthy families mothers and fathers when presented with an opportunity for pleasure or play tended to go for fun in the moment. Fathers in healthy families were rarely the hard-driving top dog in their professional hierarchy, a position that involved too much sacrifice of family pleasures.[1] Her work anticipated the happiness research, and positive psychology principles and data (as researched and reported by Kahneman[2] and Seligman[3] among others) that has become so popular in current psychotherapy. The happy families in her study generally had parents with a satisfying love affair as part of their relationship. These parents had somehow been able to maintain their sexual polarity through the life cycles of their family. In previous work, I've maintained that conscious attention to optimal parenting and erotic polarity are organizing principles of healthy families.[4]

Masculine bliss.

Myamoto Musashi, the preeminent sword fencer in seventeenth centruy Japan, identified the positive defining characteristics of the warrior. After a lifetime of astounding and well documented individual and collective victories on many battlefields, he retired to a cave in the mountains and wrote *A Book of Five Rings*, his version of the Way of the Warrior. When I first read *A Book of five Rings*, Mushahi's visions of superior functioning as a warrior and martial artist rang true all the way from 1645. For example, his descriptions of "the warrior's twofold gaze, sight and perception," the warrior's stance, expression, and breath, and the warrior's monomaniacal focus on his mission ("Think always of the cutting")[5], reflect some ot the best contemporatry instruction of both martial arts and masculine practice. Many of my men clients yearn to feel true to their warrior nature. Confusion about sexual essence, ambivalence around relational responsibilities, and lack of resolve in intimate relationships all compromise the clarity of the warrior's gaze and compromise his mision.

Feminine bliss.

Regena Thomashauer in *Mama Gena's School of the Womanly Arts* creates similar visions of a woman who is joyful in her self, body, relationships, and life.[6] Her unabashed enthusiasm for pleasure in the body, sexual bliss, community with loving women, and devotional love for men, validates the deep yearning for feminine identity, knowledge, and practice that I have often felt from feminine clients.

In the area of relational heath and satisfaction, I've noticed that couples who regularly enjoy hot sex with each other seem to do significantly better than couples who are unable or unwilling to create this form of personal/relational nourishment. This is certainly supported by research. More frequent orgasms in men are associated with reduced risk of prostate cancer and, in one study quoted by the Wall Street Journal, the happiness-enhancing effect of weekly sex with a partner was the equivalent of an additional fifty thousand dollars a year in income. Self reported happy couples are more likely to be sexually active, feel more sexually fulfilled, and be more physically healthy.

Energetic polarity between masculine and feminine is present in most hot sex.

I invite you to participate in the following experiment. Remember the last time you had hot sex with another person. Who was your partner and what were you feeling for them? What was the environment? What was your partner like or what did they do to support the passionate encounter? What were you like and what did you do to support this passionate encounter?

At any given moment while you were making love, one of you was probably more of a trustable presence, feeling into your partner, opening them with pleasure, and hungering to penetrate and release into ecstatic explosion, and then sweet emptiness. If your lovemaking were a dance, you would be the leader.

At the same moment, one of you was probably more focused on opening, expressing love through your body, voice, and movement; yearning for fullness, and feeling trust and devotional love for your partner. If your lovemaking were a dance, you would be the follower.

Some version of the above description seems to fit most versions of hot sex. There are two poles of an energetic polarity that laser back and forth, creating progressively more energy, until there is release and resolution. David Deida calls these poles the masculine and feminine, and teaches how understanding and enhancing the polarity between them supports personal meaning and fulfillment, relational health, passionate sexuality, and spiritual growth.[7]

Masculine types of people suffer when they are not true to their deepest masculine needs and responsibilities, and cannot inhabit satisfying polarities with feminine partners. Feminine types of people suffer when they are not true to their deepest feminine needs and responsibilities, and cannot inhabit satisfying polarities with masculine partners.

We all have both masculine and feminine aspects in us.

We all have both masculine and feminine aspects in us. A wide open, unconflicted individual can fully inhabit any point on the masculine/feminine continuum. This continuum ranges from deepest, ever-present witness consciousness on the extreme masculine pole (the unchanging "I" that remains subjectively the same from birth to death), to being fully in the flow of life, love, change, nature, and sensation on the extreme feminine pole. A more masculine type person, when fully relaxed and open, tends to more frequently inhabit the masculine side of this continuum. A more feminine person, when fully relaxed and open, tends to more frequently inhabit the feminine side of this continuum.

Men and women can be either more masculine or more feminine in their deepest essences, and masculine and feminine people usually have areas of their lives where they benefit from activating different sides. One example could be a man who is hard driving, on a mission, and goal oriented at work, but sexually prefers to more often be the "bottom" where he receives direction, opens with pleasure to a trustable presence, and expresses devotional love through his body. Another example could be an American mother who enjoys being a radiant wellspring of love who is opened erotically farther than she can open herself by a trustable man, but who has to animate her goal oriented, hierarchical, structured masculine self to organize her household, get her children to school and appointments consistently, and engage in disciplined self-care in exercise, diet, medical treatment, and social organization.

Masculine and feminine are lines of development as well as types of individual.

Masculine and feminine types develop similarly but differently in significant ways, and thus appear to constitute different lines of development as well as types of person.

Carol Gilligan has shown that, morally, women develop from selfish, to care for intimate others and immediate social networks, to universal care, to both universal care and universal rights, while men develop from selfish, to rights for intimate others and immediate social networks, to universal rights, to both universal rights and universal care.[8]

Deida has observed how a man can develop relationally from a first stage egocentric who is mostly in relationship to gratify his own needs, to a second stage 50/50 egalitarian who can be sexually tepid, dedicated to pleasure in the moment, unwilling to commit too deeply, but sold on the idea of fairness and clear communication, to third stage presence serving his deepest purpose, his feminine partner, and the world in each moment as best he can.

Similarly, Deida observes how a woman can develop from first stage radiance for egocentric strokes, to second stage 50/50 egalitarian career girl (often sexually tepid, not relying on a man, and considering fairness and clear communication the answer to relationship problems), to third stage erotic radiance, devotional love, and free flow of emotion (giving her best gifts of radiant love to the world).

Since we have both a masculine and feminine principle in each of us, both masculine and feminine lines develop in each person to some extent throughout life. This echoes Carl Jung's conviction that human adult development, or "individuation," involves the gradual integration of animus (the masculine), anima (the feminine), and shadow (all those parts of us such as our violent selves, selfish selves, irrational selves, or our transcendent and beautiful selves, which we might resist perceiving and acknowledging).[9]

POLARITY

MASCULINE	FEMININE
Trustable Presence	Trusting, Devotional Love
Deep Soul's Purpose	Wellspring of Love
True to Principles	Love through the Body
Deepening Consciousness	Clear Channel of Emotion
Penetrating	Opening, Yearning
Seeks Emptiness	Seeks Fullness
	Wants to be seen as light

HOT SEX

DEEPENING SPIRITUALITY

His mission to open her to pleasure, love, deeper spirituality	Open me farther than I can open myself
	Show pleasure in his integrity
Unrecoiling in the face of anything	Show suffering in his collapse
Resolute acceptance of death	

As the chart on the opposite page illustrates, hot sex is often the outcome of two partners supporting erotic polarity by embracing and fully inhabiting the various aspects of their masculine/feminine aspects and essences. People can shift from masculine to feminine poles in life and in lovemaking. In love making, as long as both partners are artfully inhabiting complementary poles, erotic polarity tends to be maintained and enhanced.

Love, romantic infatuation, and sexual polarity.

Deida suggests that the relationship between lovers is largely determined by love, romantic infatuation, and sexual polarity.[10]

Love: feeling one with.

Love is a function of our ability to feel one with. We can love people, animals, plants, nature, objects, ideas, or processes. We can feel one with the mountain and love it. We can feel one with the ocean and love it. We can feel one with our dog and love her. We can feel one with our friends and love them. We can feel one with our lover and love him or her. Love can include, but is not limited to, romantic infatuation and erotic polarity.

Romantic infatuation: a biochemical joyride.

Romantic infatuation is the roller coaster ride into passionate connection. Usually it is a function of our wounds and desires interfacing with another's wounds and desires, creating an alchemy of erotic fascination and urgent sexual polarity. Research suggests that romantic infatuation is mediated by norepinephrine and dopamine systems in our brain, while loving attachment after infatuation is mediated by brain systems driven by oxytocin in women and vasopressin and oxytocin in men. Norepinephrine and dopamine are excitatory neurotransmitters associated with spikes of pleasure. Oxytocin and vasopressin are more bonding neurotransmitters associated with the easy familiarity of longer term intimacy.[11]

Romantic infatuation constitutes a biochemical vacation from defenses. People experiencing this state tend to naturally conceal their less attractive sides from themselves and their lover, and be naturally forgiving of their lover's less attractive sides. As most of us discover, the romantic infatuation stage of relationship fades after hours, months, or years, giving way to the more challenging demands of life, work, and family, where reliable erotic polarity between partners usually requires more conscious practice and commitment, and where individual and relational defenses naturally arise.

Sexual polarity: the arc of energy between the masculine and feminine.

Erotic polarity is the energy arc between masculine and feminine that is naturally amplified during romantic infatuation. When infatuation fades, love plus conscious evocation of erotic polarity can keep the sexual romantic core of a couple's intimate relationship alive and growing.

Effective psychotherapy often teaches, inspires, confronts, interprets, and directs clients to explore their deepest sexual essences, and be true to the needs and responsibilities that are revealed. In our lover relationships we tend to feel more fulfilled with reliable erotic polarity, and we tend to suffer when we feel helpless to support and develop it.

1. Curran (1983)

2. Kahneman (1999)

3. Seligman (2002)

4. Witt (2007)

5. Musashi (1974)

6. Thomashauer (2002)

7. Deida (2004)

8. Gilligan (1993)

9. Jung (1961)

10. Deida (2004)

11. Brizendine (2006)

8

Sacred Sexuality

I first heard David Deida lecture in Los Angeles in 2003.[1] I'd been to enough classes and workshops to appreciate how this one was designed and implemented to run like a fine watch. Clearly Deida and his group had been refining this work for a long time. This was impressive, but what was much more impressive was the content. Deida was speaking from a series of perspectives on men, women, and sex that seemed to take everything I had previously discovered to be valid, and elevate it to a new level of understanding and practical use. As I heard him discuss masculine and feminine aspects, essence, and practice, it resonated with my own felt sense of truthfulness and spoke to the regular absence of depth that has often irritated me about traditional scientific teaching. Wilber has the opinion that the "true" validity standard "colonized" the "beautiful" and the "good" in the modern era.[2] Almost anyone who has written an MA thesis or a doctoral dissertation has experienced some aspect of this bias in interchanges with his or her committee ("Take out this part; it's just an entertaining story" was something I heard regularly from my doctoral committee). Scientific bias has been reflected in much of academic culture's pluralistic, egalitarian, anti-hierarchical, politically correct perspectives through the modern and post-modern eras. An exclusively rational perspective can literally squeeze the juice out of knowledge.

Listening to Deida, it was staggeringly clear to me that some of my formal education had influenced me to subtly resist teaching masculine clients central practices that develop the warrior and the man of wisdom, and feminine clients central practices that support women as embodiments of the Goddess and wellsprings of love and primary emotion. I had learned to resist taking a principled position that we are here on earth to serve each other. I had regularly been unclear as to my responsibilities as a masculine person to open each moment with my presence and depth of consciousness, and to help my partner open each moment with her love and radiance. I had not systematically included in my work the masculine/feminine polarity that is at the heart of sexual charge and love in marriage.

Talk about your paradigm shifts.

As I immersed myself in Deida's teaching, new perspectives kept opening up. When Becky and I flew to New York to attend one of a series of workshops Deida has been refining for years, I found the experience to be spiritually charged, and reminiscent of the traditional Japanese Shotokan Karate dojos (schools) I had studied in, but also like listening to a series of wonderful, illuminating stories relevant to you and your friends from a good storyteller at a party. Deida's teaching has been a catalyst that has spread transformative insights throughout the systems I've studied, and has changed my understanding of all of them. When talking to friends and colleagues, I've found myself describing David Deida's teaching as the high note in the chord of the healing systems I've studied; observing that when that note was ringing true, everything else sounded better.

Polarity is omnipresent.

There is an arc of intersubjective energy between all creatures and who and what they interface with.[3] In humans the most central source of this arc is our deepest masculine or feminine essence. The arc of polarity between the masculine and feminine partners in a relationship is the central determinant of their eroticism. Learning to feel this polarity and adjusting your deepest essences to support hot sexual polarities between you and your partner is one organizing principle of sex therapy.

This arc of polarity is not confined to sexual relationships. There is an arc of energetic connection between us and any object, creature, or being we attend to or connect with. How we manage these intersubjective arcs of energy is a huge determinant of how we live our lives.

How do we know our deepest sexual essence?

How do we know our sexual essence? Pure consciousness, the ever-present, unchanging witness that resides deeper than our body, mind, and emotions, is our most masculine essence. Everything else, the world of the senses, relationships, objects, love, and luminosity, is the feminine. Healthy individuals exist on a continuum between extreme masculine and extreme feminine and can function from any point at any moment. There is a spot on this continuum where we feel most at home; a center of gravity we naturally relax into when we are open with no blocks, defenses, or kinks. This home spot is our sexual essence which is almost always either more masculine or more feminine. My clients tend to find this teaching validating and soothing, and it inspires them to want to know their sexual essences and support them.

Cathy and Robert.

Cathy and Robert were a couple in their early forties who came to me complaining of angry beliefs about each other, lack of sexual interest, secondary impotence, and chronic conflict. Cathy had no insight when she was angry with Robert and would compulsively criticize and demean him. Robert had no insight when he was threatened by Cathy and would engage in repetitive, passive-aggressive behaviors that would drive her crazy. He accepted no real responsibility for these attacks because he never consciously knew till after the fact that they had occurred, and even then he secretly rationalized them, attributing Cathy's distress to over-reaction. Both also had internalized conflicts around sexual and aggressive impulses, and anxieties about adequately fulfilling their roles as spouses, parents, and active members in their religious community. Neither had any consistent sense of what it was to be a masculine or feminine partner in a relationship. Both lost their sense of humor regularly when discussing their marriage. Neither had much conscious sense of the potential for erotic polarity that existed at the core of their relationship. Like many couples, they described hot sex and romantic infatuation when they first became lovers and had reconciled themselves to an inevitable cooling off as they aged, had children, and took on more adult responsibilities.

As I gathered information and began addressing their many complaints, I gradually explored and explained their masculine and feminine essences to them. Cathy had a deep, sexy femininity that had been squashed by a critical, judgmental family-of-origin, religious bias against open eroticism, and American puritan culture in general. She loved the idea of being a wellspring of love, a radiant source of light for her husband, family, and culture. She wanted to be ravished by a trustable man, and longed for Robert to be that man. She also had a masculine aspect that took charge of family business and was a mover and shaker in her community. She felt guilty and resentful at these responsibilities and was relieved to hear that, when they were authentic expressions of herself in the moment, she served love in taking charge in certain situations.

Robert was a dedicated M.D. who was adored by his patients and staff (since his passive-aggressive side rarely showed up at work where he felt an unconflicted mission—a deep soul's purpose—to serve as best he could). His sense of masculine power was regularly devastated in the face of Cathy's attacks and his repeated collapses both sexually and otherwise. He loved hearing about the Way of the Warrior. He warmed to the challenge of taking on the responsibility of standing present in the face of Cathy's emotional storm and being an advocate for passion and love when she hurled invective and critical, pseudo-psychological analysis at him. Robert had become hesitant and anxious sexually since he rarely finished a sexual encounter without Cathy having found some fault in his demeanor, behavior, or general performance, but he loved Cathy and regularly felt fierce desire for her. Robert liked the idea of approaching Cathy sexually for her sake, and Cathy tended to get sexy and romantic when she was discerning if Robert was trustable, and enjoyed opening to him when she felt trust. Further, it was relaxing for Robert to feel and acknowledge his occasional more feminine essence at home when Cathy had a clear, clean purpose with the kids, him, or their respective families. In these situations he could feel how it served love in his family to surrender to her direction.

In our sessions, all the above exploration, instruction, and work on masculine practice, feminine practice and sexuality happened simultaneously with addressing Robert and Cathy's other issues. Their individual and relational defensive structures and states still needed boundaries and direction and regularly required uncovering in the face of their developing sense of interior truthfulness. When they could not agree, they needed to be supported and held by me in their disagreement until they could break through to more mature relating and new solutions.

A multi-dimensional, fluid psychotherapeutic approach monitors each clinical moment from a variety of perspectives, and flows to the interventions (relating, teaching, inspiring, confronting, interpreting, and directing adjusted to each client's current functioning) that seem most needed to support health, love, and growth. The following is an exchange from our eighth session:

Cathy: "I went away for two days and Rob screwed everything up."

Robert: Hurt, defensive, and angry at her unfairness. "I did everything the kids needed. I got them to their games, I fed them, and I dealt with whatever came up. You're never satisfied."

Keith: Realizing he's both right and passive-aggressively attacking her for hurting him. I decide to confront and teach both of them through addressing him. "Robert, the feminine is never satisfied. Things can always be done better. Love can always be better served. You need to anchor yourself in the good work and service you provide to your family, and then love Cathy, even when she focuses on the negative."

Cathy: Defensive, but accessible. "I'm not focusing on the negative. The house was dirty, the kids got to bed late, and the wash hadn't even been started."

Keith: "All true, and what stuff did Robert follow through on?"

Cathy: "All the easy stuff."

Robert: "It's not easy to take care of three kids, schlep them around, feed them, and make sure they do homework."

Cathy: "Welcome to my life."

Keith: "So, Cathy, don't you feel some pleasure that the kids were safe, fed, and on time to their appointments?"

Cathy: Reluctantly, but more relaxed and warmer. "Well of course. I always know the kids are safe with Robert."

Keith: Again confronting both through him. Teaching him masculine practice, to stand unrecoiling and offer praise. "Robert, doesn't Cathy become more attractive when she relaxes, warms, and enjoys your offerings?"

Robert: Smiling. "Yes, she does."

Keith: Confronting both through her. "Cathy, isn't Robert more attractive when he stands unrecoiling, doesn't get defensive at your critical judgments, and loves you anyway?"

Cathy: Smiling. "I like you better this way Robert."

We all have masculine and feminine aspects.

It's helpful to remember that we all have both masculine and feminine aspects, any of which can be our deepest resting place at a given moment. In lovemaking, either partner can inhabit the masculine pole of feeling into themselves and their partner and then generously opening their partner into deeper pleasure. Conversely, either partner can inhabit the feminine pole of feeling into themselves and their partner and, if their partner is trustable, surrendering and opening into pleasure further than they can open themselves, and expressing that pleasure through the body in breath, sound, movement, and touch. Partners often switch polarities during lovemaking as the rhythms of their own essences and the specific encounter develop. Further, a woman may have a more masculine practice at work (for instance if she's a police officer, or CEO), and then switch to a more feminine practice when she comes home to her family. A man may be an artist, dancer, pre-school teacher, therapist, or musician inhabiting a more feminine essence at work, and then switch to a more masculine self when he comes home to his lover. When I believe my wife is more dialed into what's right in a situation, I embrace the more feminine pole and surrender to her direction. When I believe that I know what's best for her in a particular situation, I embrace the more masculine pole and offer her direction while detaching from whether she receives it or not (the more attached I am to her following my direction, the more coerced she'll feel and the less she'll find me trustable).

In general, when we relax, breathe deeply, and are most open, we inhabit a more masculine or more feminine essence. If we are not generally true to that deepest essence in the way we live our lives, we suffer. Robert, sexually, was mostly a masculine person who got off on opening Cathy to ecstatic sexual pleasure. Cathy, sexually, was a more feminine person who got off on feeling erotically magnetic, surrendering to deeper passion, and, eventually, feeling that she was showing Robert her pleasure as erotic devotion to his integrity.

What is your deepest sexual essence?

- Do you prefer action movies or relationship movies?
- Do you prefer talking and relating or competing and striving?
- Are you more attracted to standing firm in the face of any catastrophe or being a clear channel of emotion?
- Are you more excited by the idea of committing to deep soul's purpose, or committing to love in your lover relationship and family?
- Are you more delighted by being known and claimed by a partner, or by feeling your partner's pleasure as you know and claim them?
- Is it more erotic for you to open your partner into ecstatic passion or to surrender to your partner opening you deeper into pleasure than you can open yourself?
- Do you prefer shopping to watching or playing sports?
- Are you more inspired by courage at the edge of death or by being seen as a radiant wellspring of love and light?
- Are you more attracted to a spiritual practice of music, dance, pleasure of the body, fellowship, and delicious communal sharing, or a spiritual prac-

tice of being on a mission, steady in the face of anything, martial arts, deepest consciousness, and silent meditation in the exquisite emptiness of the void.

- Are you more inspired by fullness or emptiness?

First of all, you might notice that it was not necessary for me to delineate which of the above aspects reflect the feminine and which aspects reflect the masculine. You probably already have standards of what constitutes the masculine and feminine poles of the masculine/feminine continuum, and they probably generally agree with the above distinctions.

In answering the questions, you might say, "I like all those things," and be right, but, when you are relaxed and feeling most open, which descriptions most attract you? That set probably reflects your deepest sexual essence.

Becky collected two sets of terms that were associated with masculine and feminine in her studies. Which set speaks most deeply to you?

FEMININE:

- YEARN FOR LOVE
- LOVE THROUGH THE BODY
- FULLNESS, FILL ME WITH LIFE
- WAY IS SURRENDER, TRUST
- DEVOTION
- YEARNING
- EXPRESSION OF PRIMARY EMOTION, IMMEDIATE SOUNDS
- WILD
- KALI
- MOMENT-TO-MOMENT RESPONSE TO MEN
- RADIATING DEVOTION, ALLY TO THE WORLD
- WELLSPRING OF LIGHT AND LOVE
- MAGNETIC
- FLOW, SPONTANEITY, FLEXIBLE
- CHAOS

- OPENNESS, RECEPTIVE, SURRENDER, TRUST
- PLEASURE THROUGH THE BODY
- SENSORY, CELEBRATORY, DANCE, MOVEMENT
- STUFF, ADORNMENT

MASCULINE:

- PRESENCE
- HUNGER FOR FREEDOM
- DOING, TAKE ACTION, RIGHT AWAY
- LIVING ON THE EDGE OF DEATH
- DEDICATION, DIRECTION, STRUCTURE, MISSION
- WORDS
- FOCUS: WILLING TO PENETRATE THE FEMININE
- CONSCIOUS PURPOSE
- DEPTH, PROFUNDITY, PENETRATION
- EMPTY VESSEL
- FOCUSED ATTENTION, STEADY EYE CONTACT
- HUNTER'S EYES
- WARRIOR
- DIVINE DISCIPLINE
- KNOW AND LIVE YOUR DEEPEST PURPOSE IN EACH MOMENT
- STILLNESS MEDITATION
- DEPTH OF CONSCIOUSNESS

Some people seem equally moved and inspired by both sets, Deida believes as much as ten percent of people have some form of an equally balanced sexual essence. That hasn't been my experience. I've rarely encountered anyone who didn't seem to have a more predominantly masculine or feminine essence in his or her sexual relationships. Most of us identify more deeply with a masculine or feminine essence. Sexually, the masculine reaches from his heart, his principles, and his integrity into the feminine heart and opens her with his presence, humor, shadow, voice, body, and love. Sexually the feminine feels from her heart into the masculine heart and, if he is trustable, opens to him and shows him her pleasure through her body, breath, voice, and devotion and, if he is not trustable, shows him her suffering until he shifts back into integrity.

- The central question of the feminine, "Is love being served in this moment?"
- The central question of the masculine, "Am I committed to my deepest soul's purpose in this moment; am I on my path?"
- Masculine bliss is freedom, deep soul's purpose, meaning at the edge of death, and feminine erotic radiance.
- Masculine threat/anger is perceived loss of freedom.
- Feminine bliss includes being light, a wellspring of love, and devotional surrender to masculine presence and integrity.
- Feminine threat is perceived loss of love.
- Masculine spiritual practice is emptiness, Zen, solitary, ordeal, nothingness, deep. The masculine feels his purpose in his lower belly and offers his deepest consciousness to open each moment.
- Feminine spiritual practice is music, dance, pleasure through the body, family, fellowship with other women, communal, wide. She allows so much energy to flow through her body that she opens up to the full spectrum of the rainbow.
- Life tends to be delicious to the feminine; life tends to be a burden to the masculine.

We all have both sexual aspects that we express at different times, but …

Our basic nature is predominantly one or the other, and that nature is expressed differently at different levels of development. How we progress on masculine and feminine lines of development profoundly influences our sense of self, our relationships, and our emergent worldviews.

1. Deida (2003)

2. Wilber (2003)

3. Wilber (2007)

9

Living the Third Stage

First, second, and third stage levels of development and practice.

Deida acknowledges many developmental systems (he and Wilber are good friends), but he teaches from three broad stages of development, similar to Carol Gilligan's three stages of moral development (selfish, to care, to universal care), each one progressing to the next, including and transcending, moving towards deeper spirituality. Third stage sexuality is giving our gift of love to the world through our partner in the shared practice of sacred sexuality. Like all developmental systems, each stage includes and transcends the previous stages, though, in peak or regressive moments, anyone can inhabit any stage.

I've found this first, second, and third stage system accessible and widely applicable. This is great in therapy since it can be easily understood and utilized by clients and is a shorthand tool to determine current levels of your client's—and your own—functioning, both of which help guide interventions.

First stage is all about me.

The first stage is all about me. A first stage masculine person uses his presence and power to get what he wants, or collapses regularly in the face of life's tests. A dark version of this is the macho jerk. A light version is the young seeker, caught up in his own path and too immature to have consistent empathy for others. A first stage feminine person uses her radiance to get what she wants. The light version is the ingénue, luminescent but immature and full of herself. The dark is the selfish, self-centric who would rather destroy than grow; would rather seduce than love. Our egocentric moments are our first stage moments, where our personal feelings, needs, biases, and impulses are more important to us than fairness (second stage), or serving love (third stage).

First stage relationships tend toward high egocentricism and low mature self-reflection. Sex can be hot, but the individuals are into their own needs and have difficulty feeling into the other's experience. When self-reflection is less present, pain is more likely to be expressed in symptoms which are often addressed without conscious awareness of any potential developmental arrest that may be causing them. First stage men with sexual problems often seek medical solutions or technical advice which will improve sex without threatening them with self-reflective insight or intrapsychic change. First stage women with sexual problems often yearn for their husbands to stop harassing them and give them the attention or space they feel entitled to, and/or fantasize about idealized men to whom their husbands compare unfavorably.

In therapy, it's soothing to clients in first stage moments to honor the legitimate aspects of their feelings and desires, and work with them towards solutions that are designed to meet their personal needs. As people with a first stage center of gravity develop and consciously decide to grow, they take up self-help, therapy, spiritual practice, or applied study and move toward spending more and more moments in the second stage. We don't skip levels. Much of therapy is noticing egocentric first stage moments and helping clients move toward more moments of second stage fairness and clear communication. The following is an exchange with Robert and Cathy illustrating typical first stage issues:

Robert: "You're always critical. You never see anything good I do. Why should I bother trying to be nice to you? You never give me any credit. What's in it for me?"

Cathy: "You're so selfish. It's always you, you, you. You weren't there when my mother got sick, and you weren't there when I had my surgery, and you …"

Keith: Interrupting, knowing people don't skip levels, and wanting to support both of them moving from more sadistic first stage power orientations to second stage fairness under mutually agreed upon rules. "When you two get angry you tend to forget all the rules and guidelines you like so much when you feel better. Both of you agree it is a bad idea to attack and criticize when you're angry, and a good idea to talk when you're aware of your responsibilities."

Cathy: "I deserve better than him."

Robert: Lashing back, competing to see who can be the meanest power-God. "Well, leave and find someone better."

Keith: I feel attuned and have an impulse to wake them up out of their relational defensive structure and defensive states by confronting. "Both of you are seeking relief by sadistically attacking the other."

Cathy: Outraged. "I'm not sadistic."

Keith: Laughing. "If it looks like a duck, swims like a duck, and quacks like a duck, it's a …?"

Robert: Laughing. "OK, I'm a duck. I'm sorry Cathy, I was whining."

Cathy: Smiling. "We did agree to not criticize each other when we were mad."

They are now in a second stage moment and more available to establish the second stage safety that is a necessary platform for creating consistent third stage bliss.

Second stage is all about we.

The second stage is all about fairness, communication, negotiation, and balance. The foundation principles of the second stage are egalitarianism, clear boundaries, and personal integration of masculine and feminine. Fifty/fifty relationships are the standard of this stage, a conformist "we" moral certainty that leads Deida to say that, "Communication is the religion of the second stage". A second stage masculine person insists on clarity of expression and understanding, and strives to respect others' boundaries. A second stage feminine person believes in her independence, equal power, and equal authority. She might believe she should not "need a man" to have a happy or fulfilling life. She resists both her yearning for a trustable man to know her and claim her, and opening in erotic devotion to a trustable man.

You see how second stage relationships which have so many social "shoulds" might involve conformist acceptance problems such as fear of social condemnation that might threaten valued positions within the tribe. None of us is ever complying with *all* the "shoulds." This drive for acceptance can involve suffering caused by denying or neglecting an inner sense of felt truthfulness that might vary from social convention—suffering perhaps exacerbated by a disconnection with deepest masculine or feminine essence. Cathy and Robert were mostly second stage ("We're here to work on communication problems"), with regular first stage moments of selfish, sadistic, or passive-aggressive disregard for their partner's pleasure or suffering, and occasional third stage moments of altruism, care, and spiritual transcendence.

A fundamental assumption of much second stage intimacy is that the best way to solve couples' problems is always through better communication, with therapy being a favored last resort. As with Cathy and Robert, "We need communication skills," and "We have communication problems" are generally what second stage couples announce when they enter treatment. Others' needs are important in the second stage and are addressed in the quid pro quo of negotiation. "I go to your mother's house tonight, and you give me oral sex tomorrow morning." Sex can be viewed as a commodity to be traded on or negotiated with. This may be fair, but it is rarely sexy. The following is a typical second stage therapeutic exchange. You'll notice I make references to deeper, more third stage perspectives. This is to encourage peak experiences of serving love in the moment and to inspire them to strive for more mature personal standards. Much of therapy is helping people who get locked in first stage defensive states move toward second stage functioning while encouraging third stage peak experiences to inspire growth and transcendence:

> Keith: "It would be helpful for you, Cathy, to notice and remark on a least two things Robert does right each day. This would encourage you to notice and enjoy his offerings."
>
> Cathy: "I can try that."
>
> Keith: Hearing the hook, and challenging her masculine side to commit to change. "Often when you say, 'try,' you mean you'll do it until Robert irritates you and then you feel entitled to stop trying."
>
> Cathy: "OK, I'll do it whether he irritates me or not."
>
> Robert: "I'll do the same. You do lots that I appreciate."
>
> Cathy: "But we need to talk more. You just don't want to talk problems through with me."
>
> Keith: Robert has a confused expression. He doesn't like to "talk problems through" because it often means listening to a litany of Cathy's emasculating, distorted defensive beliefs, enduring her amplified hurt and anger, and encountering his own dense, passive-aggressive responses. I reach to inspire them. "You two make the same mistake most couples do; you think you can talk your way back to love while you're closed off from each other. It's always best to reach through your hurt and anger first with generous thought and

action, and then, after you're connected in love, to talk. Cathy, you truly yearn to be deeply loved by Robert. Show him that yearning for love through your body. Reaching through to love first is always more enjoyable and productive."

Robert: He's genuinely curious, and, like most men, wants specifics in how to solve problems. "How do we do that?"

Keith: "What you do, Robert, is to stand unrecoiling in the face of her storm, and to love her no matter what she says or does. To do this you have to be centered in your worth as a man and your willingness to die for your principles."

Cathy: Smiling more warmly. "I like the way that sounds."

Keith: Speaking to her feminine heart, which tends to grows best in the presence of loving praise. "And you, Cathy, need to do exactly what you just did. When he's trustable and in his integrity, give him a clear 'yum' through your smile, your tone, your words, and your body. When he collapses, or attacks, show him your suffering and yearning, but stay connected and current and avoid the angry talk. Notice when he adjusts back to being present, loving you, and then allow yourself to feel the pleasure of his presence, and show him your 'yum.'"

Second stage relationships are respectful, fair, and communicative.

Healthy second stage relationships involve partners who are willing to discuss difficult subjects and compromise in the interests of fairness. Unfortunately, an emphasis on "I hear you, can you hear me?" communication can make erotic ravishment and deep humor difficult. Safety in clear boundaries, conformity to cultural norms, and egalitarian principles are sometimes bought at the price of passion, the guilty knowledge of individual sexual variation from perceived community standards, and a lack of commitment to deep soul's purpose in the masculine, and surrender to receiving and offering the love of the universe through her body in the feminine. Because of these factors, second stage marriages often encounter problems of diminished sexual charge. On the other hand, second stage safety, clean boundaries, and clear communication is a necessary staging point for third stage erotic ravishment and commitment to opening the moment with our deepest gifts.

Third stage: giving your best gifts to the world.

The third stage is all about giving your gifts to the world through the medium of your purest essence. The assumption is that we are born to serve each other; to open each other to expanding consciousness and radiance in the best ways we can. Masculine third stage practice is seeking, finding, and committing to deep soul's purpose in every instant of existence. Feminine third stage practice is being a clear channel of emotion, love, and light that illuminates the world. For both men and women, the third stage often involves being able to inhabit any point on the masculine/feminine continuum if it serves to open the moment.

In a third stage sexual relationship, the masculine partner centers in his own purpose and integrity, and expresses it through his body. He feels into the heart of his partner, and opens her for her sake with his presence, humor, and shadow. The third stage feminine partner opens her heart and body, feels into her lover's heart, and, if he is trustable, lets him open her farther into bliss than she can open herself, and shows him her erotic devotion through her body, her face, her voice, and her pleasure. If he is not trustable, she shows him her suffering until he recovers from whatever collapse he's involved in and regains his presence, whereupon she shows him her pleasure through her body at his recovery.

Many of my clients are, like Robert and Cathy, second stage individuals experiencing first stage periods of suffering and occasional third stage peak experiences that inspire and illuminate. Second stage clients are hungry for growth and frustrated at their blocks. Couples often blame these blocks on each other and can be unaware that they have probably chosen a partner at a similar level of development as themselves, and have co-created a relationship that has thrown their blocks right in their face. Sexually and intimately, partners often continue to be blocked until they discover and honor their sexual essences. Honoring your sexual essences means taking responsibility to be fully who you are. A masculine partner true to his masculine essence does his best to stand unrecoiling in the face of anything, to find and give his best gifts to his partner and the world, and to open rather than close each moment with his presence. A feminine partner true to her feminine essence does her best to be a wellspring of love, a clear channel of emotion, and to open rather than close each moment with her love and warmth.

If people don't honor their sexual essences, the hypocrisy inherent in living a life in which central aspects of their nature are persistently being denied and frustrated effectively stops them from growing into the authenticity that is necessary for third stage functioning, especially in the area of passionate sexual engagement.

Passionate sexual engagement as a spiritual practice keeps challenging us to open to deeper truths about self, other, world, and spirit. This deepening of consciousness and devotional surrender paired with courageous self-examination is consistent with YELLOW (TEAL altitude in II), second tier functioning. When Robert was so connected with his love and integrity that he could sometimes stand present in the face of Cathy's attacks, he began to feel the power of living a third stage moment. He didn't always collapse into attacking her or himself, but sometimes instead firmly persisted in reaching through to love. When Cathy was so connected to her heart and power as a wellspring of love that she could sometimes reach through Robert's passive-aggressive defenses with warmth, humor, and eroticism, or show him her suffering non-aggressively in ways that touched his heart, she began to feel the real power of third stage feminine practice.

The above is why a multiple perspective approach to psychotherapy is appealing. Helping your client discover their sexual aspects and essence and how to develop and express them in ways that work for them, recognizing how various developmental lines and levels are currently manifesting, and helping them grow with the understanding that much human development involves increasing spirituality, creates a rich therapeutic environment. Attending to the perspectives of all quadrants on different levels of a variety of developmental lines helps us mobilize our clients' strengths and address their vulnerabilities to help them discern and address defensive states, and support healthy states. I always supported and praised Cathy's involvement with her service work while gently pointing out the archaic and destructive programming that her parents and teachers had inadvertently included from their cultural biases that pathologized sexuality, yearning, and devotional love.

I once saw a 25-year-old man named Ben who had plenty of deep soul's purpose (he was a scientist, passionately committed to his field of study), but who was depressed, lonely, and cynically angry at the world. He clearly had a deep, passionate masculine essence. I suggested physical training, healthy routine and diet, and a variety of masculine practices including breath, stance, gaze, and the commitment to opening each moment, especially with women whom he generally alienated with his arrogance and insensitivity. When I also suggested a spiritual practice of some kind, he asked, "Why?" Because his developmental center of gravity hovered primarily around second stage, conformist/rational, I knew my most acceptable language probably needed to be anchored in moral conformity (reassurance he was normal) and empirical science, and so I quoted the biological and sociological data that support the prevalence of, and externally observable benefits of, spiritual practice. I pointed out moral biases (supported by statistical data on relationships and sexuality) that had influenced his development, especially his sexual and relational development.

Having piqued his scientific self with observable data and the fact that there were even more data (defensive blind spots) that he had lived his life unconsciously avoiding, I began to refer to inner transformations that could only be experienced reliably by cultivating phenominological tools (such as contemplative practices), and seeing for himself whether there was merit in the activity. This served as a bridge to help Ben move from the second stage rational, empirical world he'd spent his academic years mastering, to understanding a third stage reality where he could experience himself as an energy system connecting constantly to other energy systems, and experiment with self-reflective practices that could support his further deepening.

To this lonely man, the idea that these endeavors would not only help him grow, but, if expressed through his body, would attract a reciprocally minded woman seemed both beautiful and reassuring. His inner sense of truthfulness resonated strongly with the principles that we attract our reciprocal, and that masculine and feminine practices were complementary but different. Maturing out of adolescence, he had pursued women like himself, fiercely dedicated to academic pursuits, separated from their bodies, and relatively indifferent to intimate relationships. Sexual relationships with these women always ended in frustration and blame since, after some romantic infatuation, polarity was impossible to maintain. The following exchange was from our second session.

> Keith: In response to Ben describing a breakup with his lover several months earlier, while making vague references to conflicts in his department at school. Ben has a typical masculine defense of denying pain, and so I mirror some of the emotional after-effects of losing his girlfriend. "You've been lonely."
>
> Ben: "I've been fine. I've been working."
>
> Keith: "You have a lot of meaning, deep soul's purpose, in your research and writing. That's one of the main sources of masculine bliss."
>
> Ben: Relaxing, comfortable talking about his work, but also in emotional pain. "If only I didn't have to deal with the politics of the department."
>
> Keith: "Politics?"
>
> Ben: "A thing happened with a professor. We didn't get along."

Keith: This piques my curiosity so, trusting my body as an instrument, I gently inquire further. "You didn't get along."

Ben: "He published some of my findings and didn't give me any authorship on the paper."

Keith: "How did you handle it?"

Ben: "I talked to him and then to the Department Chair."

Keith: "That's courage; challenging a professor to the Department Chair is scary stuff. Those guys tend to stick together."

Ben: "It wouldn't have been so bad if I hadn't just broken up with Lucy."

Keith: Asking a question that therapists are often inhibited by cultural conditioning to risk. "How was sex with her?"

Ben: "Good in the beginning, but her work took her away."

Keith: "Her work?"

Ben: Shifting in his chair uncomfortably, looking out the window. "She's finishing her Ph.D. in physics. We fought too much."

Keith: "How did you fight?"

Ben: "Mostly got mad and didn't talk to each other. Withdrew into our work, I guess."

Keith: "How come you didn't fix it?"

Ben: Surprised, confused. "What do you mean?"

Keith: Teaching; introducing the idea that he has a responsibility to his lover to maintain an alive, passionate relationship. I appeal to all three validity standards beginning with the "true" because his center of gravity is so often rational/scientific. "John Gottman, one of the preeminent researchers on couples, said once that happy couples are often characterized by the man's ability to sooth his partner when she is upset. It's a beautiful thing when a man can do this, and it always feels right to both partners to bring your relationship back to love."

Ben: Engaged. Not fidgeting or looking away, but—typically for most partners in conflicted relationships—he'd rather talk about her issues than his own. "She would never talk. I tried, but she wouldn't. That's why I left."

Keith: "So you want a woman who will embrace the responsibility of maintaining love; a woman who won't walk away."

Ben: "Yes, but why is it my responsibility to reach through to her? Isn't it hers, too?"

Keith: "Of course. David Deida, one of my favorite teachers about love and sex, says the two things you need most with a lover are sexual polarity and the willingness to practice love on the same level[1]."

Ben: Like most masculine people, he wants the formula. "How can you tell those things?"

Keith: "You feel sexual polarity in your desire for her, and her desire for you. You discern your different levels of practicing love by taking on the responsibilities of making her feel safe and loved, being true to your principles, and opening her to erotic bliss regularly."

Ben: "What do you mean, 'opening'?"

Keith: Demonstrating with my voice and demeanor. "You open her with your steady gaze, relaxed and confident stance, your integrity, humor, and shadow. Your shadow is all the things you hide from and are unaware of in your self; like your violence, anger, fear, primal lust, selfishness, and pride, but also great things like your generosity, yearning for love, and tenderness. If you deny and avoid these things, you become more driven unconsciously by them and more repulsive to others. If you acknowledge them, take responsibility for them, and resolve to do your best to not let these aspects of yourself hurt you or others, but instead to use them to inform you to better love and serve, you become more attractive to others. As you open her with all these things, you watch and feel if she's relaxing and opening, or recoiling, tensing, attacking, or constricting."

Ben: Laughing. "Lucy always got mad and stayed mad."

Keith: "You might want to choose a woman that becomes more warm and loving when you are your best self, even when she's mad."

Ben: Interested, engaged."How do you find a woman like that?"

Keith: Remembering the masculine grows best in the presence of loving challenge. "You take on the responsibility of being your best self around all women, especially those you feel sexual polarity with, and especially when you are angry. You open them and, as you do, you ask yourself, 'Can this woman practice love on the same level that I want to practice love?"

Living the third stage.

Living the third stage is staying open to what most serves the moment. Third stage sexual intimacy is especially difficult to establish and maintain for those of us who have blocks, or blind spots, in how we understand and express our masculine and feminine essences. Ben, for instance, had defensive structures that, when evoked by perceived threat, resulted in defensive states where he resisted being appropriately vulnerable and compassionate, and unconsciously indulged impulses to get relief through emotional violence to himself and others. Living the third stage is deciding to organize our lives to offer our best gifts of love through whatever the world and our blocks put in our way. The world won't stop offering blocks, demands, and challenges, and we will always have our defensive tendencies to some extent, but we can grow in our resolve and skill in offering love through the storms of existence. This is living the third stage.

Shells.

Deida teaches development and psychopathology using the concept of our deepest self defended by concentric rings of defensive shells that we created in response to pain. We are born with a mostly masculine or feminine sexual essence. As we develop and naturally express that essence we are either supported or blocked. Each parent will tend to block their child in those places where the parent is conflicted themselves (guided by subjective standards of what is ugly and wrong, and by defensive structures and states that involve blind spots). A parent who minimizes their own hunger for sexual fulfillment will naturally discourage their child's enthusiasm in that area. Each culture will tend to block in children what is taboo in that culture.

Science tends to adapt to culture's financial and social constraints, though scientists often deny that they are profoundly influenced by the subjective, interior validity standards of morality and aesthetics. Research that violates cultural norms has difficulty getting funded and published. In families, children will not get adequate permission and instruction in areas that are blocked in their parents. Judith Levine in her book, *Harmful to Minors*, summarizes a body of research showing that only a small percentage of parents actually talk directly to their children about a range of important sexual issues.[2] Internalized cultural blocks lead to not being able to maximally support development in conflicted areas.

An example of such a block could be a father conditioned by culture to be conflicted about his own warrior nature who either indulges his son's destructive violence ("If he pushes you, kick his ass!"), or suppresses his son's natural inclination to find meaning at the edge of death ("What you did to that beetle was disgusting!"). Instead of explaining to his son that the masculine often tends to seek out—actually find bliss in—the edge between life and death, or success and failure, the father pathologizes his son's explorations. The boy fears this censure and creates a protective feminine shell of sensitivity to others around his masculine essence. This is not a genuine expression of his radiant feminine self (we all have both aspects) but a defensive shell designed to hide his basic masculine essence in a form that will protect him from the dangers of his environment.

Another example of a parental block injuring a child could be a mother, conflicted about her own erotic radiance, either indulging her daughter's narcissistic self involvement ("You need to look perfect for the party"), or attacking her daughter's natural affinity to erotic light ("You look like a slut in that outfit!"). Instead of normalizing and supporting her daughter's desire to be appropriately erotically radiant ("It's great to want the boys to be attracted to you, and it's also great to dress in a way that feels just right for you"), she pathologizes her. The girl fears this censure and might create a masculine shell of pathologizing erotic radiance and possibly cultivate "acceptable" behaviors such as academic and/or athletic success in response to distress rather than from deep interest.

When our natural expression of our deepest sexual essence is blocked, we create protective adaptive shells. The boy might become a bully or a wimp. The girl might use her radiance to manipulate, or hide it behind a shell of masculine success in academics, sports, or intellectual debate, not because these things delight her spirit, but because they're successes and identities she feels capable of and supported in.

We enter adolescence acutely aware of our roles and social standing in group contexts and, being mature enough to consciously direct much of our own development, we are more or less satisfied with who we are. If we have shells around our basic essences, we yearn for deeper expression and look for models in our environment. The dedicated student girl sees the radiant MTV sex-goddesses and begins to copy them without resolving the conflicts present in the masculine shell she already has. This creates a feminine shell around the masculine shell around her basic feminine essence. The wimp sees the macho jocks (or the budding rock stars) who seem to have masculine power (they appear to impress the boys and attract the girls) and begins to copy them, creating a masculine shell around the feminine shell around his basic masculine essence.

We attract our reciprocal.

Her most public shell attracts his most public shell and, sensing similar desires for love and capacities to enact complementary defensive patterns of conflict, they feel at home with each other and fall in love, often with accompanying romantic infatuation that temporarily neutralizes defensive patterns and supports erotic charge. Since their true natures are hidden behind layers of shells (which block wide open, heart to heart intimacy) their relationship is programmed to fail unless they grow. If they both grow and resolve the barriers to expressing their deepest essences, they can learn to support each other in an ongoing developmental spiral that has endless possibilities for beauty and goodness. If they are unable or unwilling to do this work, their connection fades as their shells grind against one another in increasing frustration at the lack of real connection. This lack of connection is often most obvious sexually, because, after romantic infatuation fades, it is difficult to maintain and expand a vibrant, growing sexual polarity from one shell to another.

Sometimes, in despair, somebody decides to divorce. She might decide to give up on trusting men and be independent, in essence to be her own man, and embrace second stage thinking and functioning, perhaps choosing a career (not out of deep soul's purpose but because she finds men untrustable). He might give up on committed masculine responsibility and true warrior consciousness and decide to "Go with the flow," dedicated to pleasure in the moment, unwilling to commit too deeply to anything, especially to a woman whom he associates with loss of freedom. At any point in this sequence one or both of them might decide to try therapy. How do we help?

Waking up.

Traditional psychotherapeutic systems provide us with many tools for diagnosing, treating, and following up with our clients from the biological, psychological, behavioral, and systems perspectives. The principles of erotic polarity provide us with direction on how to determine our clients' deepest sexual essences, and teach them practices that will support both the authentic expression of their deepest essences, and also the ability to perceive and enhance the sexual polarity at the heart of their intimate relationships. The concepts of first, second, and third stage functioning help us conceptualize, explain, and direct our clients through blocks and developmental arrests toward serving love in the moment. The Integral map helps us determine current influences from relevant quadrants, lines, levels, states, and types and what language and motivational systems might most likely inspire growth, health, and passion.

Multiple genders.

A significant amount of our suffering is caused by a lack of knowledge of how to inhabit our masculine and feminine essences. Indigenous peoples have had traditions, roles, ceremonies, and rituals that have instructed and guided their members through developmental stages. Many cultures have had provisions for more than one gender choice sexually, reflecting the wide range of "home base" on the masculine/feminine continuum. The pre-colonial Navajo had an official third gender for those men who had a more feminine essence; third gender men who had practices and work that were a normal part of the community, existing largely with the women of the tribe, wearing women's cloths, and bonding sexually with more masculine men.

Our society seems to be growing in knowledge and maturity around sexual matters, but historically has been hamstrung by cultural taboos when it comes to conscious development of sexuality and sexual essence. David Deida, Sophia Diaz, Myamoto Mushashi, and Regena Thomashauer, among others, have generated perspectives and practices that identify and cultivate our deepest masculine and feminine essences to support love and passionate polarity. In the rest of this Section we will explore a variety of these perspectives and practices that I have found to be incredibly useful in psychotherapy.

1. Deida (2004)

2. Levine (2002)

10

Masculine Practice

Everything is perfect right now, and practices help us open the moment and grow.

Two major aspects of practice are accepting things as perfect in the moment, and having a growth mindset that involves the idea that we are always growing and developing.[1]

Most spiritual traditions have some principle of each moment being a perfect expression and manifestation of the divine. The sense of unity and complete acceptance that many have reported accompanying the subjective experience of spiritual awakening often includes some version of this moment being perfect. To me, the significance in training of considering this moment perfect is that there is a difference between training from continuing dissatisfaction with the present moment, and training from a deepening surrender to allowing spirit to manifest through me into the world. This is reminiscent of Maslow's observation that development leads us from organizing our behavior to satisfy *deficiency* needs (needs coming from perceived lack) to organizing our behavior to satisfy *being* needs (needs coming from feelings of fullness).[2] Dissatisfaction as a life position limits growth, pleasure, and depth, and thus limits the benefits of practice. Practice from the position of each moment being perfect supports a sense of being part of all that is arising, and encourages resolute acceptance of everything.

A second major aspect of practice is knowing that there are benefits from practices designed to open body, mind, spirit, and relationship to growth, love, and service. Recognizing responsibilities that are inherent in healthy human existence (for example, being responsible for everything we experience and do[3]) we commit to those practices that serve us and others. Sexually, we especially benefit from practices that challenge us to inhabit and develop aspects we resist or deny. Our violent selves, our lustful selves, our vulnerable selves, and our shadow in general (the parts of us we resist perceiving) are all resources that can support us in moving from first stage selfishness and second stage safety to third stage ravishment, passion, and service to the world.

Finding effort and progress more important and attractive than outcome is a central feature of what Carol Dweck calls "growth mindsets." Individuals with growth mindsets like challenge because it leads to increased discovery and mastery, and believe intelligence is a function of effort. Growth mindset individuals like talented people around them because new perspectives enrich current perspectives. They enjoy current success, but believe there are always superior practices and perspectives that can be discovered and perfected through openness and effort.

Dweck contrasts "growth mindsets," with "fixed mindsets," where individuals believe intelligence is innate, effort is a sign of diminished ability, challenge is to be avoided because it might lead to failure, failure is unbearable, and other talented people are threats to our basic worth. She has conducted endless studies showing the superiority of growth mindsets over fixed mindsets in education, business, and relationships.[4]

Accepting that each moment is perfect, but that we are fluid beings who are constantly changing in response to our values and intention, and that it is optimal to direct our intention and behavior to cultivating practices that support ongoing growth and development reflects a growth mindset. This perspective harnesses our consciousness to support increasing health, success, and satisfying intimacy.[5]

Love through habits of closure.

Most of us have experienced pleasure in growth and insight, and have felt resolve to deepen consciousness and strengthen our ability to love. We need resolve to translate insight into enduring change. As we age, we either love through or surrender to habits of closure that shut us down, especially in threatening moments. "Habits of closure" is how Deida refers to the architecture of defensive states.[6] Loving through habits of closure supports development.

Examples of habits of closure are habits of thought such as, "I am unable or unworthy," or "He/she is wrong or bad," or habits of behavior such as breathing higher in the chest instead of lower in the belly, compulsively fleeing from or attacking perceived threat, or compulsively tensing your body in reaction to perceived threat. Healthy practices support the depth of consciousness to discern when we are closing down, and the specific thoughts and behaviors we can cultivate to become more open.

Conscious practice is one way of addressing the conundrum that the more closed we are, the less inclined we are to engage in healthy behavior. Practice involves disciplining ourselves to consciously turn to alternatives that serve love in the face of our defensive resistance. If we do this on a regular basis we develop new habits that we increasingly turn to as we feel ourselves closing down into defensive states and becoming less inclined to risk alternative thoughts and behaviors. Just as states of peak experiences can eventually become stable traits in the include and transcend rhythm of development up various lines, healthy practices can eventually become more natural than habits of closure if we commit ourselves to doing them regularly, and, especially, if we do them when we most resist.

I'm going to present a variety of masculine and feminine practices that I've found useful, and I encourage you to experiment with them in your life and work.

In the therapy session the therapist does more than transmit information and practices that he or she has learned. The alchemy of intersubjective fields, the therapist's healing intent, the client's intent to heal and grow, both individual's worldviews, and the therapist's training and experience open up healing channels of information and technique. Practices often arise from these channels informed by previous knowledge, but altered by circumstances and the unique demands of the moment.

For example, one Friday night my wife Becky and I were hanging out in the living room, and our daughter Zoe (who was sixteen at the time) walked in after having a session with a health practitioner. She described her session, one part of which concerned her yearning to have a boyfriend. This resulted in the following exchange:

> Keith: "Would you like to know what I suggest to my single women clients who yearn for a good man?"
>
> Zoe: "Yeah, sure."
>
> Keith: "I suggest to them that they ask themselves the following questions about every man they meet, from teens to old men:
>
> - Is there sexual polarity between you and him?
> - Does he successfully self-regulate his physical and emotional health?
> - In conflict, would he be able and willing to do what it takes to get back to love with you?

[handwritten note: what about a woman's soul's purpose?]

- Would he be a superior parent?
- Does he have deep soul's purpose?

If the answer is 'yes', or, 'possibly' to all those questions, then that man is more likely to be a candidate for a life partnership with a woman with the feminine equivalent of those qualities, maybe you if he's available and in the right age cohort. In that case you might feel a sense of devotional love in your heart, and can let that love shine through your body, mind, voice, and spirit as an offering to masculine presence and depth of consciousness. If the answer to any one of the questions is 'no,' then why bother going deeper? This helps you learn how to both discern trustable men, and to offer devotional love appropriately."

Zoe: Intensely interested, which in itself is a great thing in a teen. "Could you write those down?"

Keith: "Sure, I'd love to."

Becky: Like most good mothers, she wants to know how this would be good for our son Ethan as well. "What are the qualities a man should look for to have a good relationship?"

Keith: "I suggest to single men that they ask themselves the same five questions about any woman they meet, with the exception of, in the fifth one, it changes from 'Does she have deep soul's purpose?' to, 'Would she admire, appreciate, and support my deep soul's purpose?' If the answer is 'yes' or 'possibly' to all five questions, then that woman might be a candidate for a life partnership with a man with the equivalent masculine qualities, possibly you if she's available and in the right age cohort. In that case you might feel drawn to her, and can open her, for her sake, with focused attention, depth of consciousness, humor, and shadow. If the answer to any one of those questions is 'no', then why bother going deeper? This helps you discern radiant feminine candidates and better offer depth of consciousness appropriately."

Becky wrote down these masculine and feminine practices and put them on the refrigerator door. I don't know if Deida, Myamoto Mushashi, or Regina Thomashauer would agree to all of them or not. These happened to be the perspectives and practices that flowed into the intersubjective fields of our family that Friday night.

As you explore the following principles and practices, it's useful to think of them cumulatively as a language that you might want to speak in supporting your own and other's health and development. As you do this you'll tend to develop your own voice, your own healing channel, to transmit this knowledge and help your clients and others heal and grow.

Masculine practice: being consciousness.

The masculine in us hungers for freedom, deep soul's purpose, meaning at the edge of death, and feminine erotic radiance. Masculine practice supports, evokes, and enhances these qualities in a number of ways. Early in my training with my Taoist teacher in Los Angeles, he introduced me to the Overlook Press edition of Myamoto Musashi's *A Book of Five Rings*, which I've already discussed briefly. Musashi, also known as "The Sword Saint" in Japan, was the preeminent samurai warrior of early seventeenth century Japan. He fought over sixty duels before he was thirty, winning them all, and progressed to become the most widely acclaimed warrior of his era. He retired to a cave at the age of fifty-nine to write *A Book of Five Rings*, his version of the Way of the Warrior. I felt enormous affinity for his system and included many of his technical and spiritual principles in my own training. Twenty-three years later when I heard Deida lecturing on masculine practice it was point for point in line with Musashi's Ni Ten Ichi Ryu system.

Musashi said that the first thing in the Way of the Warrior is the resolute acceptance of death. He had nine principles for his school of strategy:

- Do not think dishonestly.
- The Way is in training.
- Become acquainted with every art.
- Know the Ways of all professions.
- Distinguish between gain and loss in worldly matters.
- Develop intuitive judgment and understanding for everything.
- Perceive those things which cannot be seen.
- Pay attention even to trifles.
- Do nothing which is of no use.[7]

Not much in it about women, though it has everything to do with how attractive you are as a man. Standing firm in your principles, resolutely accepting any outcome, commitment to your life's purpose, and feeling into the moment is exactly what more feminine people often find most attractive. His principles also support the second tier standards of felt appreciation for all perspectives and reduced fear.

Man of wisdom.

When my son Ethan was seventeen, we had an opportunity to spend some days camping next to the Green River in Arizona with a group of men headed by a local Shaman, Jade Wah'oo. We did ceremony and told stories and generally had a great time. Half the group were young men like my son, just coming into their power as warriors. The rest of us were mostly in our fifties, entering the Man of Wisdom stage of masculine development. As Jade taught us and led us through ceremony, the developmental shift from Warrior to Man of Wisdom became progressively clearer. Around the campfire we older guys often ended up telling stories of our most conspicuous, usually hilarious, mistakes, while the young men listened respectfully and laughed with us.

This trip was especially poignant for me since it was the last year my son would live full time at home before college and, due to a herniated disc in my back, Ethan had to take care of me in many of the ways that I had been taking care of him for the previous seventeen years.

Jade maintained that the transition into Man of Wisdom happens as the Warrior no longer is primarily drawn to testing his strength and courage in battle, but instead comes to understand that it serves Spirit to share his hard won lessons; especially with the young Warriors seeking out their meaning, purpose, and ordeals. This mirrors Erik Erikson's generativity stage of psychosocial development, where older people are drawn to wisdom and yearn to share it with the collective.[8]

Jade told the young men to follow their hearts and make many mistakes—to plunge forward with courage toward whatever they found deeply meaningful. He encouraged us older men to access our wisdom and experience, and to trust the voices that we had spent decades of spiritual practice cultivating and surrendering to. He told us it was our responsibility to pass on our understanding to the young Warriors.

The Way of the Warrior and the Man of Wisdom; what do these paths entail, and how can we teach them?

Circular breathing.

Every yogic tradition teaches how to breathe. Deida calls his version "circular breathing."[9] Like many spiritual techniques, it's easy to learn and hard to practice consistently. Balance your weight over the center of your body, breathe in down your front all the way through your genitals with the inner feeling of "yes" to life in this moment. Feel your abdomen soften, become round, and rise as you breathe in. As you breathe out, imagine exhaling up your spine and over the top of your head. Mostly keep the tip of your tongue on the roof of your mouth. Lightly tighten your anal muscles on the exhale (sometimes called "the bounce.") As you do this breathing practice, feel how energy follows your breath down the front and up the back. It often helps to look down as you inhale and up as you exhale. Allow each breath to relax you and support you in this moment. Cultivate a faint smile on your lips, and continue the practice until you can feel the smile in your heart even when it is not on your lips, and your "yes" to life has become habitual and reflexive.

Circular breathing can be done standing, with your feet shoulder width apart, knees slightly bent, sitting in any position, or lying down. It's especially nice to hold your lover and do this together, softening your bodies into each other and eventually feeling that you are breathing energy down your lover's front and exhaling it up your lover's back.

I teach circular breathing to many of my clients and encourage them to practice it in lots of different situations. As it becomes reflexive, this breathing promotes focus, humor (remember the smile), relaxation, and dramatically reduced anxiety. Deep focused breathing is a central part of most yogic practices, as well as most stress reduction systems.

On your mission.

Your mission is your deepest gift to the world. With many masculine people their mission is their work. Most masculine people who are happy in their work have the sense that they are contributing something meaningful to the collective, the community, or mankind. This sense of mission also extends into your life. The standard is Mushashi's, "Do nothing that is of no use." When you're with your feminine partner, your mission is usually to feel into her and support her opening.

Resolute acceptance of death.

Death tends to fascinate masculine people. The masculine is drawn to nothingness, and death is the ultimate nothingness. Meaning at the edge of death is beautiful to most masculine people. Musashi says that resolute acceptance of death is the first thing in the Way of the Warrior. Deida suggests that you live your life as if you are already dead, or as if each moment was your last.[10]

Resolute acceptance of death means resolute acceptance of *everything*. The masculine ability to stand unrecoiling in the face of anything is both central to masculine practice, and soothing and attractive to the feminine.

Why do men watch and play sports? What is the appeal of hunting, fishing, skiing, surfing, action movies, and extreme activities? All these things give the masculine the sense of meaning at the edge of death. This is frequently a blissful place for masculine people. It is a beautiful thing to the masculine to go to the edge of death and retain presence, to be willing to resolutely accept anything that comes, even death itself. *avoidance of intimacy?*

Presence.

Presence is expressed through balanced stance and posture, deep breath, steady eye contact, no nervous habits, energy in your lower belly, being anchored in your purpose and principles, and being focused on opening the moment. If you are with someone else, you focus on helping that person become more open right now with your humor, your attention, your shadow, and your deepest understanding. If you are with your intimate partner, you focus on opening her as far as you can, *for her sake*. You are trustable because you are committed to being courageously self-reflective, ready to resolutely accept when you collapse, and to do your best to adjust back to presence when you discover yourself collapsing. Presence is depth of consciousness, deep soul's purpose, and integrity expressed through your body.

Deep soul's purpose.

Deep soul's purpose is the feeling of giving your best gifts to the world, being on your mission, in a way that feels profoundly significant. A man without deep soul's purpose is like a ship with no rudder, he is distressed with himself at his core and is often not fully trustable to a feminine partner. This last is huge because often the quality a feminine person yearns for most from a masculine partner is for him to be trustable.

The form deep soul's purpose takes is largely irrelevant. It could be any profession from tile setter to brain surgeon to claims adjuster. It could be any project from making a garden to writing a song. It could be serving people as husband, father, teacher, manager, coworker, or opponent. The central feature of deep soul's purpose is the felt sense of meaning that accompanies the activity.

You discover deep soul's purpose by pursuing activities that feel meaningful to you. I tell my clients that there is an easier way and a harder way to discover and pursue deep soul's purpose. The easier way is remaining present in each moment and pursuing those activities that have interest, meaning, and fascination for you. These activities can be service activities like jobs or professions, recreational activities like sports or hobbies, relational activities like certain kinds of time with friends or family, or spiritual activities like meditation or prayer. The harder way is to feel the suffering inherent in lack of purpose, and stay connected to that suffering until you are moved towards meaningful activity. Once a direction manifests, pursue it until you find deep soul's purpose, or discover you're on the wrong path. One form of masculine bliss is to have each moment of each day informed by deep soul's purpose. As Musashi said, "Do nothing which is of no use."

When you are with your feminine partner your deep soul's purpose is usually to open her farther than she can open herself. If you can't do this, your work is to do what it takes to be able to open her as much as you can.

Collapse.

Collapse is not living the moment according to your principles. It can be as minor as being rude to a telemarketer, or as major as cheating on your wife. All men collapse regularly. You become distracted from your path by defensive states (habits of closure), temptations of the world, your partner's irritating behavior, or any of countless other distractions and stresses. Shifting from appropriately serving others to egocentric or selfish activities constitutes many of the collapses men normally experience. Attacking others emotionally, avoiding right action, and attacking self are common examples of collapse.

Part of feminine pleasure in relationship is unconsciously creating situations which can evoke her masculine partner's collapse, and then feel his integrity with pleasure as he resists collapse and stands present, true to his principles and serving love with her.

A man in a first stage moment might deny collapse and attack his partner's suffering—suffering that is often a result of his own lack of presence.

A man in a second stage moment might acknowledge collapse, but try to negotiate his way out of it with quid pro quo bargaining and psychological rationalization. Often when a feminine partner gathers the courage in therapy to tell her second stage spouse how repulsive he is in some particular way, his first response is to argue or defend his behavior. This never results in the feminine partner becoming more attracted, but does provide a great opportunity for loving confrontation in psychotherapy; "You can argue all you want, she'll just find you more repulsive. Try finding what's valid in her feedback and using it to be a better man; now that's attractive." I had many such conversations with Robert when he attempted to deny or rationalize his passive-aggressive collapses with Cathy.

A man in a third stage moment cultivates depth of consciousness to discern when he collapses, take responsibility for everything he experiences and does, and then do his best to regain his presence and give his best gifts to open the world.

Presence with his lover.

A masculine person in a third stage moment with his lover feels into his heart and her heart courageously. He feels her open and he supports her opening to deeper pleasure in her body; he feels her close and he opens her with his presence, his humor, and his shadow. This is the foundation practice for the masculine in intimate relationships.

Stand unrecoiling in the face of her emotional storm.

Breathe in her emotion, let her storm teach you how to be a better man, and open her with your presence, understanding, humor, and compassion. Most feminine people yearn to be known and claimed by a trustable masculine partner. Standing unrecoiling in the face of her emotional storm, breathing in her energy, and looking for wisdom and guidance in her message moves you toward knowing her the way she needs to be known right now, and claiming her right now as your chosen one. When Robert stood unrecoiling in the face of Cathy's emotional storm, refused to collapse into attack or defense, but instead reached more deeply into her heart with the resolve to answer her genuine yearning for love with his unwavering masculine presence, he evoked her depth of love and hunger to be known and claimed by him.

Known and claimed.

There are countless aspects of knowing and claiming. Offering loving direction to your feminine partner for her sake, and then resolutely accepting her response by detaching from needing her to follow your direction is one example. Looking into her eyes and proclaiming your love is another. A huge amount of conflict can be addressed from the masculine pole by feeling into what is valid in the feminine partner's distress, acknowledging that validity to her, and immediately committing to improve that area. This form of knowing and claiming is a great way to transform conflict into loving connection. It also tends to be soothing to the feminine and to evoke her trust.

Offer her direction.

One central way the masculine partner helps the feminine partner to bloom is by offering direction. Direction is his current sense of what is in her best interest. You offer what you believe is best for her, and then resolutely accept her response whether she follows your direction or not—you love her regardless. A first stage man offers direction primarily to get his needs met, a second stage man offers direction in service of fairness and takes offense if direction is not followed. A third stage man offers direction as to what he believes will open her the most to pleasure, light, and love, and accepts and loves her whatever her response.

Add depth to the sexual occasion.

If sex feels too shallow, the masculine partner needs to add depth; if sex is too boring, the feminine partner needs to add life, humor, play, and energy. Depth comes from feeling into what most opens both of you, and holding that as an organizing principle of lovemaking. If a guy gets too serious in this activity, it's time for the feminine partner to inject a little fun, play, or irreverence.

Penetrate/open each moment.

Deida calls this "fucking the moment open."

A word here about words. Some clients prefer "lovemaking" to "intercourse", or "pussy" to "vagina." One woman I worked with said she felt a sense of liberation calling her vaginal area her "pussy," and especially loved Mama Gena's admonitions to consult with her pussy on important decisions. I personally want to use the language that most supports growth in my clients, but I avoid certain words that close me down personally. The words, "cock, prick, cunt, twat, bang, and fuck" generally don't meet my subjective beauty standards, but there are sometimes exceptions, depending on the worldview/language style of whomever I'm working with. I encourage you to consciously examine your and your clients' semantic charge on various language forms, and use the insight you gain to enhance your work.

When Deida refers to fucking the moment open, he means the masculine principle of penetrating and opening the world through masculine agency. Masculine agency experiences bliss in finding meaningful problems and solving them—turning somethings into nothings. This is the masculine imperative that moves a man forward through life, simultaneously seeking meaningful activities (problems to solve), and solving them into blissful nothingness. Deida sometimes calls this "fucking the moment open." He says a first stage man fucks for his own pleasure, a second stage man opens his heart and head but holds back his shadow and can become soft literally and figuratively, and a third stage man fucks the world open from all levels, ravishing the world open to God. First stage passion, self-centeredness, and desire progress to second stage egalitarian boundaries and respect, which progress to third stage transcendence and ravishment. They include and transcend as the masculine practice of being consciousness and opening each moment matures and deepens.[11]

A focal point of Deida's work is teaching people how to discern and direct opening and closing the moment. In his workshops, he uses a variety of individual and couples' practices to teach this. One of his couples' practices is the following: Sit across from someone else and look into his or her eyes. Feel into your heart, and, when you've identified the sensation, feel into your partner's heart:

- On a scale of 1–10 (1 being completely closed down, and 10 being wide open) rate how open you are as you do this.

- On the same 1–10 scale, rate how open your partner is. When this exercise is done in groups, there is amazing group concordance, indicating that people often reliably share perceptions of openness and closure.

- Open yourself farther than you were before. You might try deepening breath, resolute acceptance, and commitment to open your partner. Feel the difference in you and your partner as you do this, and keep monitoring 1–10 levels of openness.

- Engage in some activity (emotional, spiritual, transactional, or physical) that opens your partner farther, and then feel (and score) the differences. Share your experiences with each other.

This ongoing sensitivity to whether you are opening or closing your partner can be a foundation skill in supporting erotic polarity.

A measure of masculine practice is how effectively you use your presence, breath, integrity, voice, and body to open the moment. If you discover that people are closing down in response to you, you probably have some block or resistance that you need to resolve through introspection, dialog, therapy, yogic or spiritual practice, physical discipline, rest, diet, medication, or some other attention. Often you'll feel some corresponding block in your body (head, face, throat, heart, solar plexus, abdomen, genitals, legs, hands, or arms), and it's useful to breathe through that physical block until you feel the spot opening.

These same principles apply to lovemaking. Feel into yourself, feel into your feminine partner, and open her to pleasure as far as you can with your presence, breath, integrity, voice, hands, and body. If you feel a block in you or her, breathe through it until you feel a sense of opening.

Cultivate humor.

Freud called humor the most mature defense.[12] Remember, in circular breathing, you cultivate the faintest smile on your lips and continue the practice until you can feel the smile in your heart even when it is not visible on your face. I tell my clients, "If you've lost your sense of humor, you've probably regressed a least one or two developmental levels."

Humor evokes humor. One principle in the physics of relationship is that you evoke a complementary response from the person you're relating with. If you put out love, you tend to evoke love. If you put out violence, you tend to evoke violence. If you put out humor, you tend to evoke humor. A wonderful practice is to center in your heart, and try to reach into another's heart with love; it's easier when your partner is similarly engaged, much more difficult if they (or you) are radiating fear, anger, contempt, pain, or coercion. If you and/or your partner are in pain, the practice is to resolutely accept that pain arises, and then to love your partner with gentle humor through the pain.

Congruence with your body/energy.

The main communication a feminine person feels is the energy and congruence of your body/voice/expression. This communication generally registers more strongly with her than the content of your words. "I'm angry and I'm struggling to do right and not harm you," is usually felt as more trustable than, "I'm fine; no problem." "I don't have good attention right now. I need to work (exercise, meditate, rest, etc.) and then I'll be able to be more present with you," is usually felt as more trustable than, "Sure, I'm listening." The more you speak directly from your heart with the intent to serve, congruent with your tone, demeanor, and body, the more trustable a feminine person will find you.

The masculine grows best in the presence of loving challenge.

If you observe two good male friends, their style of connection is very different from two good female friends. Masculine intimacy tends to involve more challenging humor, while feminine intimacy more loving praise. Masculine contact revolves more around deep purpose such as work, projects, ambitions, existing at the edge of death (as in sports, gambling, and other extreme experiences), and frank acknowledgment of feminine radiance ("Look at her!"). How consistent or adept a masculine client is with masculine practice is an ongoing subtext in most psychotherapy with masculine clients. Opportunities to relate, teach, inspire, confront, interpret, and direct in these areas occur throughout each session. The following exchange with Ben illustrates this:

Ben: "I'm only in town for a week, and I don't want to see my mother."

Keith: "Why don't you want to see her?"

Ben: "She worries and complains, and it's just uncomfortable."

Keith: "What's the highest good for everybody?"

Ben: "I don't know what you mean."

Keith: I knew my question would be confusing, but I asked to stimulate his interest in the area, and to model how it serves the moment to ask yourself, "What's the highest good for everybody?" "Depth of consciousness is the masculine gift. Feeling into a situation and discerning what best serves love for everybody, *including you,* is an important aspect of depth of consciousness."

Ben: "She'll just be pissed off if I don't visit her. So, what do I do, visit her to placate her?"

Keith: "If you visit her out of fear of her critical judgment, that's a codependent collapse. If you visit her because it is in the highest good for everybody, that's depth of consciousness and good masculine practice."

Ben: "How do you tell the difference?"

Keith: Teaching him how to cultivate depth of consciousness while knowing that masculine people want solutions. They want to turn something, a problem, into nothing, a solution. "You ask yourself, given what you know about yourself and her, what's in the highest good for everybody, and then go with the solution that seems best."

Ben: He's suddenly getting it, waking up. His expression becomes more resolved, and I sense a stronger presence. "I should visit her in the morning through lunch on Saturday and then go. She'll complain of course, but she always complains."

Keith: "Do you feel the difference in your body and voice as you say this? This is presence and depth of consciousness." He nods thoughtfully.

If Ben had a lover present in the session, I'd teach her corresponding feminine practices, both to support her health and development, and to enhance their sexual polarity.

1. Deida (2004)

2. Maslow (1962)

3. Masterson (1981)

4. Dweck (2006)

5. *Ibid*

6. Deida (2004)

7. Musashi (1974)

8. Erikson (1998)

9. Deida (2004)

10. Deida (2005)

11. Deida (2006)

12. Freud (1949)

11

Feminine Practice: Being Love Through the Body

Becky asked me, "What are you going to say when they ask you, "How can a man teach a woman feminine practice?"

I told her, "The best I can."

Becky engaged in her own spiritual odyssey looking for women to teach her feminine practice. Sophia Diaz (an extraordinary woman who taught with Deida's group for many years) led a woman's weekend and the group expanded through dance, teaching, dialog, and other practices. Becky read lots of books and Regena Thomashauer's *Mama Gena's School of the Womanly Arts,* and *Mama Gena's Owner's and Operator's Guide to Men*[1] were two of her favorites. Becky read *Womanly Arts* to our son, Ethan (then seventeen), and me on the way to his freshman orientation at University of California at San Diego. Ethan and I kept laughing and telling each other that this was the secret knowledge about women that all men needed to know. To read Mama Gena's books is to love her and I'll keep referring to her as one of my main guiding lights for feminine practice.

Pleasure.

Pleasure is of huge importance to both the masculine and feminine. If someone makes any gift or offering to us in the form of compliments, physical caress, appreciative expressions, or devotional love, our pleasure is the indicator that we have received the offering. Absence of pleasure reflects a refusal to receive, sometimes for healthy reasons as when an offering comes from manipulative or false intent, or for unhealthy reasons as when we are conflicted about feeling pleasure or receiving gifts.

Feeling pleasure in the body is a central part of feminine practice. Pleasure nourishes the feminine as water nourishes a garden. The abilities to run healthy pleasure daily through her body in a variety of ways (sensual, sexual, aesthetic, spiritual, and relational pleasures are all important examples) are foundation attributes of many feminine practices.

Give your best gift of love.

It often feels natural for a feminine person to anchor herself in how she most deeply wants to give and receive love. Such practices often begin with feeling the love that flows from your deepest heart and opening up to manifest that love as pleasure. In relationship, a feminine person offers her love through pleasure in the body in devotion to her partner's deepest consciousness. Feminine erotic radiance pulls a masculine person out of the void, out of his head, and into his body. Devotional, erotically radiant love is the one form of love a mother, friend, dog, or acquaintance can't fully offer a masculine partner. Erotic radiance is the feminine anchor of erotic polarity. It tends to evoke masculine presence, and can open him to profound spirituality.

Circular breathing.

Practice circular breathing and feel yourself an open channel of emotion. Feel the "yes" to life with each inhalation down your front and through your genitals. Feel the release and flow up your spine with each exhalation. As you breath, do you feel any blocks in your body? If so, breathe through them until the area (head, face, throat, chest, solar plexus, abdomen, genitals, back, or legs) opens up wide as your most open area.

A central aspect of cultivating self as a clear channel of primary emotion is the capacity to feel blocks or closure and breathe them open. Are you more open inhaling or exhaling? Practice until you feel equally open doing both. The Sanskrit word for breath, prana, also means life and energy, reflecting the eastern spiritual traditions' understanding of the interconnectedness of breath, life, spirit, and energy. Breathe your body open until you are an interconnected network of freely flowing rivers of energy, a living embodiment of life's force.

Primary emotion.

Primary emotion is the pure expression of your open heart, be it angry or loving, light or dark. If there is a block in your body, breathe through it until it relaxes open. Express emotion with spontaneity, exaggeration, gestures, and sounds. If your emotion is blocked, even for seconds, it might become a residue that is expressed in ways (defensive states) that close down your partner or the world in general. Pointless arguments, holding anger, or recoiling anxiously from truth are all examples of emotional residue (Deida calls it "toxic residue"[2]) being expressed in destructive ways.

Cathy, in our earlier example, would criticize and rebuke Robert and, when he protested even mildly, would say, "I have a right to my feelings." First of all, her distorted critical beliefs were not feelings, they were distorted beliefs. Feelings are anchored in sensations, which drive thoughts or beliefs, but are not themselves thoughts or beliefs. Secondly, the pain and anger driving those beliefs was mostly old residue from a lifetime of injury, stimulated by a current cue (often provided by Robert) and attributed solely to that cue. You can see primitive emotional fusion here, locked down by neurotic conflicts. Cathy had to deepen her consciousness to discern the difference between free flow of emotion and toxic residue. When she learned to be in the moment, angry at Robert's current collapse, but still available to shift to pleasure when he regained his presence, Cathy was able to experience real emotional flow that became a resource for both of them.

Toxic residue (generally expressed from defensive states) can be released and resolved through psychotherapy, open talk with a loving friend, trauma work such as Peter Levine teaches in *Waking the Tiger*[3], or by letting it go into the void with a "No, thank you." Amplifying it or engaging in passive aggressive-attacks on yourself, or sadistic attacks on another, just hardens the block and deepens the wounds. Primary emotion, emotion that is present and immediate, might sometimes appear terrible, but it is also almost always beautiful like a waterfall is beautiful, a free flow of energy. The following exchange is from an individual session I had with Cathy:

Cathy: "Robert is so weak."

Keith: "How so?"

Cathy: "He never follows through. He's never interested in me."

Keith: "He's frightened of you."

Cathy: "He has no reason to be frightened of anything. I do nothing but give."

Keith: "He's frightened of your critical judgments, and of your capacity to withdraw your warmth from him."

Cathy: "He doesn't care about my warmth unless he wants to have sex."

Keith: Knowing that the feminine grows best in the presence of loving praise. "Your warmth is probably one of the most pleasurable things in his life. If you wanted to maximize his growth as a man, it'd be best to show him your pain though your body at his being less than his best, and show him your pleasure through your body whenever he's being his best self."

Cathy: "He's never his best self."

Keith: Confronting her distorted belief. "That's your residue from a lifetime of pain. You don't perceive it when he's his best self, and so you deny yourself and him the pleasure of your body's 'yum'."

Cathy: "You're right. When I'm mad it's hard to be nice."

Keith: "It's not about being nice, it's about being a full spectrum woman. You let yourself perceive and be angry at his collapses, but you are blind to his beauty, strengths, and presence. An important part of feminine practice is perceiving when he is present and in integrity, feeling the pleasure, and expressing that pleasure through your body; despite the anger you unconsciously cling to."

Give the gift of your pleasure to the world.

Much of the feminine aspect is about love, relationship, and opening your heart to love and pleasure. Once you open your heart to your pleasure, you can give the gift of pleasure to your lover, and then through your lover to all beings. Regena Thomashauer says that pleasure makes a woman friendly, free, and generous.[4] Her whole approach to the womanly arts is drenched in pleasure. She brings the *Massive Sexual Orgasm*[5] couple, Steve and Vera Bodansky, to New York twice a year to teach their technique. An unapologetic and enthusiastic practitioner of their system, she suggests women include their man in their commitment to pleasure. Like Deida and other teachers, she suggests women help each other by playing together, seeking pleasure together, and praising themselves and each other frequently.

Sacred dance.

Deida, Sophia Diaz, and Regena Thomashauer all suggest that women practice sacred dance alone and together with other women, spending time daily with music, delicious fabric, pleasing scents, massage, and deep sensual movement designed to open up every part of your body to pleasure, especially those physical and emotional parts you most hide from yourself and others, your physical and emotional shadow. The practice is to use the dance to blossom like a flower so that you are able to inhabit the full spectrum of feminine radiance, from light to dark. Much of Sophia Diaz' workshop that Becky took was dance and non-verbal expression designed to open up all aspects of current feeling through movement. You can practice daily or weekly, for a few minutes or hours, alone or with women friends.

Create a beautiful feminine environment with material, texture, light, scent, food, drink, and color. Wear outfits that emphasize your erotic radiance, or those aspects of your body and personality you hide. A woman comfortable dancing in sexy lingerie might be embarrassed and blocked if she were dressed like her mother. You can start with sensual music, standing and vibrating in place. Beginning with your root chakra and working up the seven chakras (perineum, abdomen, solar plexus, heart, throat, between your eyes, crown), breath through each area, move in increasingly large movements to open first your hips, and then the rest of your body. If you are dancing with women friends, help each other by suggesting garments and movements that open you further. If a friend resists opening her hips, or dancing her shadow, or breathing fully, help her to dance those areas open.

Sophia Diaz suggests you feel what's tight and fix it, and love your hips into openness in a regular practice. As you become more at home in your body you'll discover habits of closure like nervous fidgets, high or tight breath, muscle tension, a tight pelvis, rigid postures, or distressed expressions that you can relax open and let love and light flow through.[6]

Identify your desires and communicate them.

Regena Thomashauer reaches into the souls of women and pulls them into the world of total self love first, and then the ability to surrender to loving their partners. She believes that if a woman loves herself daily, it is easier to identify her desires and communicate them to the world, and especially her lover. She and Sophia Diaz both recommend daily and weekly pleasure rituals such as massages, or sensual baths with scented oils and delicious self-pleasuring. These rituals open you to pleasure, desire, and insight, all of which you can share with your lover, family, and friends.

Give the gift of your shadow to the world.

A feminine person in a third stage moment opens to whatever serves love. She can be soft or hard, angry or gentle. Shadow is her darkest power used in the service of love. Shadow is all those parts of us we have difficulty perceiving, acknowledging and/or showing. It might be your angry self, your wanton self, your brilliant self, your dense self; or whatever other selves you hide from your own awareness and the world. In many ways, women are stronger than men emotionally and sexually, capable of reducing them to "nubs."[7] Regena Thomashauer says, "Make friends with your inner bitch."[8]

If you have a trustable man and he collapses, you open him with erotic heat, humor, gentleness, rage, or whatever it takes. When he opens to his deepest masculine presence, you show him your pleasure through your body in devotion to his deepest consciousness. The ability to show your distress or pleasure as your lover shifts into collapse or presence is one of the most difficult practices to sustain. Our defenses resist showing our shadow in service of love. Feeling when your lover collapses and showing him your suffering (not by complaining or whining but by allowing your suffering to radiate from your body) is as important as feeling when he is trustable and expressing your pleasure through the body. This use of shadow is a central skill in creating sexual polarity.

The following exchange between Cathy and Robert illustrates how to help a feminine client discern between toxic residue and shadow in the service of love:

Robert: "I just offend Cathy when I initiate sex."

Cathy: "'How about a roll in the hay?' is not sexy when I'm doing the dishes."

Keith: Noticing Robert's hurt, resentful expression. "What is your most favorite kind of sexual overture from Robert?"

Cathy: "When he's gentle, and kind of nuzzles my neck without interfering with what I'm doing."

Robert: "You always have to have things your way."

Cathy: Now in the more familiar, and less vulnerable, territory of conflict. "Why should I tell you what I want? You don't care."

Keith: "She just gave you a gift and you ignored it. She told you how to approach her to make it easier for her to welcome you erotically, and you collapsed and complained. Try another response."

Cathy: "It's too late now."

Keith: "That's your toxic residue talking. It's rarely too late. Look at him and feel into him. If he's coming from his love and integrity, it needs to feel pleasurable in your body, and you need to show him that pleasure. A simple, heartfelt, 'yum' will do it."

Robert: Sensing an opportunity and looking at her with genuine affection and humor. "He's right. It was a gift. I will try gently nuzzling you."

Cathy: A tiny smile appearing at the corners of her mouth. "Yum."

Keith: "That's it. You become beautiful when you offer that smile to his presence. Robert, that's the way to always approach her. With love, presence, and humor."

Bring the Goddess into your life and honor the divine feminine daily.

Sophia Diaz suggests creating a feminine place in your home, offering a flower to something you love, and sitting in divine devotion each day. She and Thomashauer both suggest keeping a journal with emphases on the themes of pleasure, radiance, growth, opening, shadow, and love. Journaling is especially useful with feminine clients because women tend to think relationally.[9] When journaling, there is often an imagined dialog with various aspects of self, God, or other people. Journaling is thus often experienced unconsciously as a relational activity, even though it is primarily done privately.

Cultivate humor.

As we explored in the previous section, humor tends to evoke humor. Third stage humor opens people in the moment and evokes pleasure and laughter in yourself and your partner. First stage humor is primarily for the enjoyment of the speaker whether or not it hurts the listener. There is not a lot of humor in second stage negotiation and strict egalitarianism.

Cultivate your erotic radiance, and use it to open your partner.

Masculine people often respond to argument with enthusiastic debate. One form of masculine bliss is combat where he seeks meaning at the edge of death, and debate is a form of combat. I encourage my feminine clients to cultivate their warmth and erotic radiance and turn it like a searchlight on their partner to support his presence and to evoke positive transformation when he is hostile, selfish, or disconnected. The fewer words and the more erotic radiance the better. This often evokes his deepest presence and depth of consciousness. Sophia Diaz suggests you feel your thighs caressed by God, feel your vagina open, and then feel infinity coming in until you are receiving the universe, feeling ravished open by God.[10]

Relax open to your deepest heart of love and light and let it shine and serve love.

The feminine is life and light. The masculine often feels most at home in pure emptiness of deepest consciousness, while the feminine often feels most at home in the world immersed in the richness of life's tapestry. The feminine is light, so her practice is giving the gift of her warmth and erotic radiance to her lover, her children, her friends, and to the world. Sophia Diaz suggests you feel spirit infusing your vagina and body, and then feel light shining out of your heart, your breasts, and your body to your lover and the world.[11]

Feel into your lover.

If he is trustable, relax and let him open you farther than you can open yourself. If he feels not trustable, show him your suffering (don't tell him with complaint or attack, show him through your body), and, when you feel him shift back into presence and integrity, show him your pleasure until you see it reflected back in his pleasure. The difference between showing suffering through your body and attacking destructively is reflected in your immediate intent and responses.

If your intent is to get relief by attacking, you'll speak to the worst part of your partner with the intent to hurt him as he has hurt you. You might explain or argue how he is repulsive or bad in some fashion. If he tries to become more present, you are unlikely to perceive it and/or be able to respond with pleasure.

If your immediate intent is to reach through to love, then your cry of anger, sadness, or distress is directed at the best part of your lover, designed to evoke his presence. If he struggles to love you and/or return to presence, you immediately feel pleasure and express it with feelings, movements, and sounds.

When the masculine is angry, it is often useful to get close to him, stroke his energy down his body with your hands, and open him with your radiance.

Communicate through the body.

Show him sounds of pleasure and pain, give him a clear "yum" and a clear "yuck." The best feedback for trustable men from feminine partners is often sound, gesture, humor, and expression through the body. Words invite the masculine into argument, debate, and battle. Words are necessary for couples to move from first stage lack of safety to the respectful boundaries of the second stage. As you move more into the third stage, words become less relevant as conscious intent increasingly is to act consistently from love and good will. Rational analysis of ideas and behaviors can progress into deepening consciousness to be able to experience mind, body, cultural influences, internal habits, blocks, and predispositions as different facets directed by a deeper self. Deepening consciousness can lead to the capacities to be able to experience the interface between a deeper self and the infinite field that is constantly arising. Third stage relationship is guided by such depth and beyond, where words become less necessary to resolve conflict, since both partners take on the responsibility of doing whatever it takes to open and reach through to love with self and others.

Open.

Open heart, open body, open breath, open hips, open channel of emotion, open wellspring of love. A great artistic expression of the power of opening to love is the movie, *Love Actually*, where, again and again, feminine radiance from an open heart irresistibly attracted masculine partners. The women who closed down were the ones leaving and left. In over three decades of working with couples I've seen these patterns happen endlessly.

Yearn.

If you don't have a partner and want one, yearn for a trustable man. If you have a partner and he collapses, yearn for his presence. I suggest to my single feminine clients who want partners to spend five minutes a day yearning for a trustable man who can open them farther than they can open themselves. I encourage them to feel and allow their yearning and send it out over the world. The women I work with love this exercise, enjoy practicing it, and have discovered it seems to result in attracting trustable men.

Serve love.

In any situation, but especially in difficult situations, a wonderful question to ask yourself is, "How can I serve love right now?" The feminine is love and light, and if you experience yourself serving love you are most likely to be relaxed wide open into your deepest feminine essence. The "Does this serve love?" standard is amazingly effective at evoking our best self in most situations, and distinguishing between clean contact and subtle attack.

Feel your body, breasts, and genitals.

After Becky was doing this practice for a while, she was walking alone across a street one day when a man in a sports car slowed down and called out, "Beautiful." Regena Thomashauer says you are beautiful if you feel beautiful. She says all she has to do to get a guy to ask her out is to, "look into his eyes, smile, and think about my pussy."[12] Deida suggests to go about your day feeling God stroking your inner thighs and infusing your vagina, or feeling that your breasts are headlights illuminating everything before you.[13] Energy flowing from nature into your body through your breath, skin, and genitals, and flowing out of your body through your light, love, and pleasure is your magnetic feminine gift of light to the world.

The feminine grows best in the presence of loving praise.

Studies show that stressed women tend to seek affiliation, while stressed men more often seek solitude. The feminine blossoms in the presence of loving praise. John Gottman has observed that satisfied couples have an over five to one ratio of praise to criticism. It is often difficult to teach this to masculine people. "She knows I love her. She knows I think she's beautiful," are frequent responses from men when I suggest that they praise or compliment feminine partners regularly.

In general, when doing therapy of any sort, I try to remember what part of my client I'm addressing. If I'm dealing with a more feminine aspect I'll often intervene with loving praise, and if I'm dealing with a more masculine aspect I'll tend to use loving challenge. Good therapy finds the strength, beauty, integrity, and radiance of clients, and honors and encourages it. When a client is in a more masculine moment, the ratio of praise to challenge often needs to shift towards loving challenge, while, when a client is in a more feminine moment, the ratio often needs to shift towards loving praise.

Objective and subjective cues for therapists.

In therapy we observe the various constellations of our clients' masculine/feminine aspects, essences and polarities, and how informed they are of the practices and responsibilities inherent in them. Externally observable indicators of essence and polarity are how clients dress, move, speak, look at you and/or each other, smile, breathe, and behave both in and out of sessions. A spouse who doesn't look at a partner while complaining or criticizing is usually not feeling into the other's heart. A masculine partner who defends or attacks when confronted with his feminine partner's suffering is not a trustable presence. A feminine partner who refuses to feel or show pleasure at a masculine partner's authentic offering is probably caught up in toxic residue. Another important indicator is whether people are breathing higher in their chests or lower in their bellies, with lower breathing more often associated with healthy responses to the present moment, and higher breathing more often associated with defensive states.

Subjective cues to presence, radiance, and relative polarity in clients involve how clients feel to the therapist in the session. If you feel a subjective sense that your client is attractive or repulsive, in integrity (living their principles) or out of integrity (not living their principles), your body/mind/spirit system (your therapeutic healing instrument) is informing you that they are opening or closing the moment, as well as giving you information about whether they are in a more masculine or more feminine moment.

Most couples come into therapy with issues and, after initial intake sessions, I'll often encourage them to go more deeply into issues until their individual and relational defensive states and structures are revealed. I'll then relate, teach, inspire, confront, interpret, and direct until they are cultivating new, healthier perspectives, and contemplating or engaging in new, healthier actions. Effective psychotherapy in general, and conjoint therapy in particular, often involves frank discussion of masculine and feminine types, practices, and responsibilities, and candid appraisals of the nature and state of sexual polarities in clients' lives. Once intimate partners start understanding their strengths and weaknesses as masculine/feminine poles of their sexual polarity, and begin to accept responsibilities associated with their deepest essences, exciting awakenings can occur and new possibilities for love can emerge.

One hazard of teaching this material is that partners, delighted with the new information, will make swift progress for several weeks, and then collapse into old defensive states and despair. I've found it useful to predict this to clients, and, when it happens, to offer a developmental perspective. Just like all developmental lines, we can have peak experiences on our psychosexual, masculine/feminine lines of development, but we don't skip levels. It often takes years of practice before we stabilize at new, higher levels of functioning. The beauty of love as a shared spiritual practice between intimates is that we can co-create regular peak experiences that support upward movement on lots of developmental lines while simultaneously optimizing love and health in the present moment.

1. Thomashauer (2002, 2003)

2. Deida (2004)

3. Levine (1997)

4. Thomashauer (2002)

5. Bodansky (2002)

6. Witt (2003)

7. Deida (2006)

8. Thomashauer (2002)

9. Gilligan (1993)

10. Witt (2003)

11. *Ibid*

12. Thomashauer (2002)

13. Deida (2006)

Section Four

Cultivating compassion and depth of consciousness

12

Cultivating Compassion

In 1991 I was having a session with Jean, a woman in her early thirties who had been in therapy with me periodically for a year. I had just given her what I felt was an incisive interpretation involving one of her central relationship issues, hoping, as always, that it would help wake her up to new, healthier, perspectives. Jean looked at me in mild irritation and said, "I'm much more complicated than you think."

I was literally dumbfounded by how completely true her statement was. At that moment she woke me up to a new perspective, and many times since then I've remembered that moment and smiled.

Every client is too complicated to ever be completely understood. The central conundrum of psychotherapy is trying to help people who are complicated beyond belief grow one simple step at time.

As I suggested in Chapter One, since no single perspective can address all issues, good therapists cycle through multiple perspectives, alert to discerning the ones that best serve each moment.

There are multiple psychotherapeutic systems and techniques. An Integrally informed approach provides the epistemology of quadrants, lines, levels, states, and types.[1] David Deida's work provides further granularity in discerning masculine and feminine types and practices.[2] In combination, these perspectives can help us scan ourselves and our clients systematically to amplify understanding and impact, and to help guide us from the hopelessly complex, to the blatantly simple, to the hopelessly complex, to the blatantly simple, and so on throughout the session.

In this Section we'll begin with some simple constructs defining psychotherapy, and then expand them as practical operating principles in the therapy session. In general, every form of psychotherapy that I've studied and practiced, and every therapy session I've conducted or supervised, has involved establishing and maintaining a foundation of a healing culture between therapist and clients in the session, while the therapist intervenes to maintain a healthy relationship and advocate for health. Therapists' interventions usually emphasize either relating, teaching, inspiring, confronting, interpreting, or directing, though every intervention is, to some extent, an amalgam of more than one of these activities:

Two definitions of the psychotherapeutic encounter describe the therapist as:

- **Cultivating compassion and depth of consciousness to support healthy perspectives and actions.**

- **Co-creating a culture in which the client and the client's universe is cherished, each moment is experienced as a gift and an opportunity, and healthy perspectives and actions are considered beautiful, good, and true.**

The purposes of therapy across disciplines can be characterized as:

- **Remediating symptoms, enhancing health, and supporting development.**

The process of therapy across disciplines can be characterized as involving:

- **Relating, teaching, inspiring, confronting, interpreting, and directing.**

Compassion is beautiful.

At first impression, compassion seems purely a subjective phenomenon. I experience compassion as pleasurable warmth in my chest and stomach area, combined with a felt sense of oneness with, and care for, whoever or whatever I'm considering. This experience can be compassion for other people, for other people's actions or perspectives, for other living things, for objects, or for my own or others' vulnerabilities, strengths, spirit, or energies. Compassion seems very similar to the "felt oneness with" that Deida defines as love[3], or the unconditional positive regard that Rogers included with congruence, transparency, self-disclosure, and empathy as core characteristics of a helping relationship.[4] Compassion, however, is not only a subjective experience. Compassion, like every human experience, can be processed through lines, levels, states, types, and multiple subjective and objective perspectives.

Compassion is good.

Compassion is almost always considered right and good. Most of us find compassion moral as well as beautiful. "Love thy neighbor as thyself,' "Do unto others as you would have them do unto you," are precepts that are supported by most moral codes. Thus it feels good, or moral, to have compassionate understanding be a standard for psychotherapy.

Compassion is true.

Compassionate understanding is overwhelmingly more objectively accurate than other forms of understanding, especially in relationship to other people. Therapists observe multiple perspectives and decisions made in various emotional states. Most therapists will agree that compassion is the most reliable indicator of clear discernment and right action. Compassion can observe shadow, evaluate fault, and confront mistakes without the emotional violence of critical judgment. John Gottman's couples' research has demonstrated compassion for spouse as being a major predictor of happiness and marital longevity.[5] An example of cultivating compassion is the following exchange with Deana, a client in her early forties who is processing her husband's infidelity and her codependence:

Deana: "He was coming home and I thought I should put on something pretty, but then I didn't want to."

Keith: "You thought you should, but you didn't want to."

Deana: "Now that he says he's not seeing his lover I should feel like being sexy."

Keith: "You're not saying you felt sexy, or even wanted to feel sexy. What could Tim do to actually evoke sexiness in you?"

Deana: This evokes a blank stare, and then some heat. "He's been such a jerk. He's lied to me. I don't even really know if he's stopped seeing her."

Keith: Knowing that what makes a man attractive is presence, humor, and access to shadow while being trustable, and also knowing that Tim is largely blocked in discerning and dealing with his shadow. "What if he said, 'I realize I have some deep wound I've never acknowledged or addressed that causes me to compulsively womanize. I'm entering therapy to deal with it so I can love you the way you deserve to be loved.'"

Deana: Tears brim up in her eyes. "He'd never say that."

Keith: "Exactly, and that's why you don't feel sexy with him. He has presence and humor, but he denies his shadow, and attacks you if you threaten him. He's not a trustable man until he takes responsibility for dealing with his shadow, and that means acknowledging that he needs help, and then getting help. Until then, your own masculine side is a more trustable source of masculine discernment and direction than Tim is."

Deana: Her voice level rises. "He says no therapist can know him better than he knows himself, and that he knows what to do."

Keith: "Does he?"

Deana: "I don't think so. He talks to me but if I don't agree he gets mean."

Keith: "So you are in what seems to be an impossible situation. Confront him and be attacked and perhaps deserted, accommodate him and pretend to be attracted when you're repelled, or leave him when what you really yearn for is love in your family. This all largely because he won't deal with his shadow; so your choices are be codependent, or animate your own masculine because you can't trust his."

Deana: "I'd rather not do all this. I feel so dense."

Keith: "You're a feminine person. You'll always struggle and suffer when you can't trust your masculine partner and have to be your own man. You'll always resent your masculine partner if you have to mobilize your own masculine side because he won't step up and occupy the trustable masculine pole in your relationship."

Deana: "I wish he would."

Keith: "To me, one of the saddest things about this whole mess is that he probably wishes he would too."

Compassionate understanding doesn't deny moral discernment or scientific data. Instead, compassion looks with clear, loving regard on everything, focusing on the beautiful, the good, and the true without critical judgment of self or others.

Form of compassion can vary with level of development on different developmental lines.

Developmentally, the experience and understanding of compassion shifts depending on what lines and levels are involved. On the self-line, compassionate understanding co-varies with the capacity to empathetically take the role of other. Thus, four-year-olds—and RED, power-God viewpoints at any age—can have caring moments and peak experiences of compassionate understanding for others, but their worldviews are primarily egocentric. In psychotherapy, compassionate understanding of four year olds, or adults with RED worldviews, appreciates the reality that individuals inhabiting these worldviews often need external, environmental boundaries to contain egocentric impulses, and often respond better to more egocentric motivational systems.

Knowing that levels can't be skipped helps therapists support a client's movement from a current level (center of gravity) he or she has on a given line toward fully inhabiting that level in a healthy way to support their natural transition to their next developmental stage. As someone expands to fill up a current worldview (or a current developmental level on a given line), new perspectives are increasingly required for experiences that aren't adequately explained by that worldview's perspectives, thus leading the individual to differentiate from their current worldview, and then integrate into the deeper understanding (often involving a wider range of caring) of the next developmental step. Knowing levels can't be skipped further helps a therapist avoid condescension and/or critical judgments about the levels the client currently inhabits or is unable to inhabit, and possible frustration at a client's apparent inability to grasp some perspectives.

In an emotionally abusive, first stage relationship, each partner of a couple needs to cultivate second stage clear communication, safe boundaries, and 50/50 fairness before they can move to third stage openness to whatever serves love in the present moment. An egocentric, selfish man needs to learn to value and respect rights in his immediate, personal affiliations before he can truly embrace universal rights for all, just as an egocentric, selfish woman needs to learn to care for those she has personal contact with before she can truly embrace universal care for all.

Compassion indicates healthy states.

In all states of consciousness, the presence of compassion indicates more likelihood of a healthy response to the present moment rather than a defensive state. Further, there is consensus among many spiritual traditions that ascending (or deepening on) a spiritual line of development involves increasing feelings of compassion for larger groups of beings in wider ranges of situations.

This is not just true for clients, but also for therapists both in and out of sessions. A therapist committed to horizontal and vertical health in their own life is better equipped to support such practices in clients' lives. When a therapist is feeling compassion for his client in the session, his perspectives and interventions are more reliably valid and useful than when he is not feeling compassion.

Compassion supports understanding and valuing different types.

Understanding and valuing different types of individuals requires compassionate understanding. This is particularly hard for more masculine therapists who tend to naturally be drawn to responsibility for self, being unrecoiling in the face of karma, and to solving problems (agency). Feminine healing is more compassionate embrace without agenda. The unconditional positive regard that Rogers identified as being essential to the therapeutic relationship is harder to maintain in the face of agenda, or attachment to the masculine needs for agency, progress, or creation. In the following exchange with Kurt, a single man in his mid forties, struggling with the conflicts his narcissism brings him, cultivating compassion became my primary psychotherapeutic focus:

Kurt: "I'm with this wonderful woman who's crazy about me."

Keith: "Sounds great."

Kurt: "The problem is, she has a three year old son that I don't want to be responsible for, and she doesn't like me seeing other women."

Keith: I feel repulsed. "You want relationships with other lovers?"

Kurt: "I don't want relationships. I just want to fuck them."

Keith: This is probably a test. I suspect that he's showing me this egocentric side because he doesn't know how to adequately care for it himself. Recognizing my anger at the suffering this pattern is almost certainly causing, I reach for compassion. It helps to know that one major therapeutic path in dealing with narcissism is to mirror pain. His feminine aspect, powerful and distorted in narcissistic characterological defensive structures, needs to feel both safe and beautiful for me to have access to his deeper masculine essence. "This must be difficult to process with your lover."

Kurt: "She says it's OK if I date other women, but I can tell she hates it."

Keith: "I'm sure you're right."

Kurt: He looks up suspiciously. "What do you mean?"

Keith: I feel more connected and less repulsed. I'm getting how he wants love and compulsively sabotages it, and suspect he's unconsciously doing this right now with me. Feeling more compassionate, I'm more confident to press deeper. "You describe her as a 'wonderful woman.' You generally choose wonderful women. Wonderful women almost always eventually want to be claimed exclusively by their man, and they suffer in the absence of that claim."

Kurt: Relaxing as he feels understood without being critically judged. "She should understand."

Keith: "I know you want to be true to yourself and not hurt her, and that seems impossible in this situation."

Kurt: "Exactly."

If I just passively tolerate my irritation and repulsion without internally reaching for compassion, I'll lose the delicate therapeutic connection that I have with him (and also likely fall into a defensive state similar to those he evokes in his lovers). If I can find compassion for his suffering, and gently suggest that he has a problem that currently can't be solved, I'm supporting his wounded feminine aspect, while subtly challenging his masculine essence to create a solution. Even though his current solution is to find a "wonderful woman" who'll be sanguine about him "fucking other women" (a solution that will almost certainly result in more suffering for everyone involved), the fact that we're discussing this issue in a non-charged context is significant progress.

Compassion tends to evoke compassion.

Communication is almost always reciprocal and complementary. Cocreating a culture in which the client and the client's universe is cherished generally requires the therapist to be relentlessly feeling and expressing compassionate understanding to help evoke similar feelings and understanding in the client. When Kurt asked, "What do you mean?" in a hostile tone, he typically would have pulled a complementary defensive response of fear and/or hostility in another, which would likely have devolved into some kind of relational defensive pattern that resisted real exploration and change (in this case, since Kurt has characterological narcissistic defensive structures, the eventual result would most probably involve him demeaning me and withdrawing from our relationship). By responding with compassion, I disarmed his hostility and pulled him deeper into our therapeutic culture where he and his universe are cherished.

1. Wilber (2000)

2. Deida (2006)

3. Deida (2004)

4. Rogers (1961)

5. Gottman (2001)

13

Cultivating Depth of Consciousness

Much development is characterized by increasing depth of consciousness.

Carol Gilligan[1], Abraham Maslow[2], Lawrence Kohlberg[3], and many other developmental researchers have documented how development on a variety of lines involves progressive decentering from more egocentric worldviews, and identifying with progressively wider classes of other.[4] The infant, undifferentiated, discovers a separate physical self, and then a separate emotional self. In each case, there is a disidentification with the previous worldview, and a reintegration into a new worldview that includes wider possibilities. The young child hungers for affiliation and acceptance, and so disidentifies with exclusive egocentric worldviews and learns to discern and abide by the rules/roles that allow him or her to identify with social groups of family and tribe. The adolescent can disidentify with the rigid boundaries of rules/roles, hold and examine conflicting viewpoints, inhabit "what if" situations where it is more possible to take the role of other, and identify with larger groups of nation, humanity, or all living things. The adult engaging in self-exploration, can disidentify with just body, emotions, or thoughts, and identify with a deeper self that can observe body, emotions, and thoughts. This progress of disidentification and reintegration into new, broader worldviews is literally deepening consciousness.[5]

The developmental breakthrough into a second tier center of gravity necessarily involves deepening consciousness. Felt appreciation for all worldviews and dramatically reduced fear turbocharges understanding and learning. In psychotherapy, a felt appreciation for a client's perspectives, especially their regressed, defensive perspectives, combined with compassionate awareness of what their distortions are in their defensive states—and what their next developmental steps are on relevant lines—reflects depth of understanding of where the client is. Such understanding often indicates possible adjustments they need to make to reduce symptoms, enhance health, and support development.

Depth of consciousness in therapy moves toward post (and post-post) formal operational thought, post conventional moral perspectives (to draw from Lawrence Kohlberg's pre-conventional, conventional, and post-conventional[6] equivalents of Gilligan's selfish, to care, to universal care in women[7]), and Deida's concept of third stage functioning where the organizing principle is serving love in the moment[8].

Depth of consciousness is beautiful.

The subjective experience of depth of consciousness for me is similar to the pleasurable warmth in my stomach and chest I associate with compassion plus an added sense of fullness and clarity in my throat area, confidence in my healing connection with my client, confident understanding of at least some aspects of my client's current blocks to love, and a felt sense of clarity to paths that will probably facilitate exploration and resolution of those blocks.

Your subjective experience of depth of consciousness will, of course, be different from mine. I suggest that the next time you feel a deep, loving understanding of yourself and/or another, you monitor your sensations, emotions, thoughts, and impulses. There will probably be a constellation of experiences that, with practice, you will consistently identify as your signature sense of depth of consciousness.

Depth of consciousness is good.

The subjective indicators of depth of consciousness are often a shared sense by therapist and client that useful work is being done, deeper and more profound perspectives are being generated, and that this process is inherently moral. Even if your client disagrees with—or even seems offended by—your understanding, if you're cultivating depth of consciousness you will tend to reach for language forms and perspectives that will probably eventually resonate with your client's validity standards.

Depth of consciousness is a psychotherapeutic edge.

One great advantage that a therapist has in the session is that most clients' functioning tends to be regressed in conflicted areas that manifest as defensive states. Since defenses resist insight and change, they constitute relative blind spots in clients' consciousness, invisible to them; much clearer to others, and especially clearer to a trained, experienced, and compassionate "other" such as a good thera-pist. A therapist usually doesn't share the same constellation of defensive struc-tures and states as their client, and this allows the therapist to perceive the client's defensive patterns deeper and clearer than their client because the therapist has more depth of consciousness in those areas. The deeper consciousness the thera-pist inhabits in dealing with defensive areas gives the therapist the same edge an experienced wilderness guide has in leading someone through unfamiliar geo-graphic territory. When dealing with my client's defensive states, I often have the advantage of perceiving what my client cannot perceive, and thus being able to compassionately point out hidden spots to encourage insight and awakening.

Masculine practice is being consciousness, feminine practice is expressing love through the body.

Just as compassion is central to communion, a descending more feminine spiri-tual principle, depth of consciousness is central to agency, an ascending more masculine spiritual principle. Together they bring a non-duel focus to the art of psychotherapy. In the previous example with Kurt, he was unaware of how his narcissistic wounds were dominating his relationships with women. My job, while always maintaining a compassionate attitude towards him and his universe, was to discern and support progressive steps towards healing those wounds, rely-ing on my greater depth of consciousness in those conflicted areas to help guide both of us.

Depth of consciousness is what enables us to feel and understand how each moment is a gift and an opportunity, and what healthy perspectives and actions are beautiful, good, and true, and might help our client remediate symptoms, enhance health, and support development.

How can we develop depth of consciousness?

The following list is by no means complete, but it is a starting point to develop-ing and enhancing depth of consciousness:

- Study, training, and spiritual practice all support depth of consciousness.
- Feeling into another person's heart and discerning how they open and close in response to our offerings supports depth of consciousness.
- Identifying the principles and practices we teach and courageously living those principles and practices supports depth of consciousness.

- Embracing new perspectives as gifts rather than threats supports depth of consciousness.

- Seeking out and receiving feedback from teachers, friends, family members, and other intimates about our strengths, weaknesses, and blind spots supports depth of consciousness.

- Knowing that, no matter how many times we awaken, there are always new awakenings stretching out before us supports depth of consciousness.

1. Gilligan (1993)

2. Maslow (1962)

3. Kolhberg (1985)

4. Wilber (2000)

5. Wilber (2000)

6. Kohlberg (1985)

7. Gilligan (1993)

8. Deida (2006)

14

Remediate Symptoms

In the 60's there was a movement organized by the American Psychiatric Association and the American Psychological Association to arrange to be able to bill insurance companies for psychotherapy, the same way medical doctors billed for medical treatments. To do this, psychotherapy had to be conceptualized as treating psychological symptoms in the same way traditional allopathic American medicine treated physical symptoms.

In some ways this medicalization of psychotherapy was a perfect fit. A patient comes to a therapist with arachnophobia (irrational fear of spiders). The therapist does progressive desensitization (a technique of learning how to relax and gradually deal constructively with fears), and, hey presto, no more arachnophobia. The symptom has been remediated. A patient comes in with depressive symptoms, is referred to an MD as part of a standard evaluation, and is discovered to have either low thyroid hormone, premenstrual dysphoric disorder, sleep apnea, low seratonin, or some other biochemical or physiological problem, and is prescribed appropriate medication or other medical treatment with positive results. Once again, the symptom has been remediated.

On the other hand, in some ways the medicalization of psychotherapy was forcing a square peg into a round hole. A client comes in unhappy with her life, unfulfilled erotically with her husband, and sensing there is a better, deeper way to live. Her biochemistry is all in the normal range, and she has no discernable physiological disorders. Psychotherapy progresses and in the unfolding sessions she begins to feel happier with her life, more fulfilled erotically, and experiences herself as having a better, deeper existence. Clearly this is important, healing work, but it's healing work more in the tradition of Eastern medicine where a main function of the healer is to support general health and balance in the individual's many interconnected body, mind, energetic, environmental, professional, and social systems. How do you bill insurance companies for this?

Diagnostic and Statistical Manual (DSM).

Enter the Diagnostic and Statistical Manual (DSM) in 1952. This first attempt has been elaborated on and revised throughout the years and the DSMV is due soon[1]. This document attempts to describe, in observable, externally verifiable terms, many of the various emotional, behavioral, developmental, and relational problems that humans are prone to. Each of these problems is presented as a constellation of observable symptoms and statistical representations that can have observable remediation. Depression, for example, is having a severely depressed mood not caused by other identifiable physical problems, that causes major interference with personal and/or professional life, and that persists for two weeks or longer.

Since all issues that bring people into therapy have some externally observable characteristics, the original DSM was a bridge and a language that could legitimatize the subjective, internally observable concerns that brought many people into therapy. It was a language that could discus those concerns in concrete terms that were mostly acceptable to the scientific establishment that was dominant in the medical culture at the time. The unhappy, erotically unfulfilled, existentially yearning woman in our previous example could be diagnosed as dysthymic, with relationship problems, and sexual anorexia.

Each revision of the DSM has improved and deepened the document (further refined and expanded it as an objective language) until, with only a little bit of whittling, we can now fit most square pegs into round holes, and anyone who wants therapy can get a diagnosis that is reasonably honest and justifies some sessions on most insurance plans. Typically for traditional western science, subjective phenomena are under-represented, but the language the DSM has created can be wonderful when communicating with other therapists, when evaluating whether to make medical/medication referrals, when doing research on psychopathology, psychopharmacology, and psychotherapy, when describing disorders that are sometimes embarrassing or repulsive to clients in non-judgmental, behavioral terms, and when billing insurance companies.

Remediating DSM disorders is generally acceptable to most worldviews.

If there is a behavior that interferes with someone's life (like compulsive hand washing), or a mood that interferes with someone's life (like depression or anxiety), or thoughts that interfere with someone's life (like constant obsessions about fatal disease), there is consensus that it's useful and moral to offer support and help until the symptoms are remediated and suffering is reduced. The language of remediating symptoms is particularly soothing to RED egocentric clients because they don't have to acknowledge psychological problems as representative of personal weaknesses or flaws, soothing to BLUE traditionalist clients because they can feel like a normal person with an illness, and soothing to ORANGE rational, achievement oriented clients because they can deal with emotional/spiritual/relational problems in a scientific way that doesn't demand airy-fairy worldviews, or diminish their drive for achievement. The following exchange is with Dennis from the couple we met in Section One. He was first referred to me by the partners in his firm. He presented as an ambitious ORANGE businessman in his late forties who regressed to RED power-God defensive states when feeling threatened:

Dennis: "I don't see what the problem is. I just got a little angry at work."

Keith: "Your partners were alarmed enough at your outbursts that they insisted you get therapy or they wanted you out of the partnership."

Dennis: "They're over-reacting."

Keith: "How so?"

Dennis: "Anyone would have gotten mad at that technician. He made a mistake."

Keith: "He reported feeling frightened for his physical safety, and the other office workers reported feeling intimidated and alarmed."

Dennis: "They should know me well enough to understand that I just want things done right."

Keith: "Dennis, you suffer from Intermittent Explosive Disorder,[2] and you need help to address it."

Dennis: "What's that?"

Keith: "It's when someone periodically feels driven to explode emotionally, or physically, by extreme rage. It always involves distorted negative perceptions, amplified negative emotions, little if any impulse control, and diminished empathy for what damage is inflicted on the people around them."

Dennis: he relaxes a bit. He has a disorder, but he's not crazy. "But it hardly ever happens."

Keith: "A wife beater might only strike his wife once every few months, but every day she's frightened of abuse."

Dennis: This makes sense to his logical, scientific worldview. "That's a good point."

Keith: "I'd like you to talk to a psychiatrist about what might be happening and about some medicines that might help you feel less anxious and driven, and make it easier to control your temper. Also, there are a variety of adjustments you can make in how you think and behave that could potentially make a big difference in how satisfied you are with life, and how effective you are when you feel provoked."

Dennis: "I'm interested."

Symptoms from subjective perspectives.

Of course, as all therapists know, lots of symptoms are experienced subjectively. "I feel despairing, I think I'm an ugly person," or "I feel ashamed, I don't think I'm a good person," reflect suffering that can benefit from psychotherapeutic attention. "I feel lost and anxious because I have no sense of meaning in my life," is devastating to a more masculine client who suffers from lack of deep soul's purpose. "I feel frightened of people not liking me, I have no women friends I can be fully myself with, I think I'm invisible to people, and I don't believe that there will ever be a man who will truly love me," is equally devastating to a more feminine person who needs to shine as erotic radiance, and believe that love is being served in her life.

Most psychological symptoms, whether or not they are created or amplified by biochemical conditions, are associated with defensive states of consciousness characterized by distorted perceptions and beliefs, amplified or numbed emotions, destructive impulses, and diminished capacities for self-reflection and empathy. The popularity of cognitive behavioral treatment in modern psychotherapy is driven, at least partly, by the fact that cognitive behavioral constructs are comprehensible, practical bridges between subjective defensive states and objective definitions of disorders.

The current "third wave" of cognitive behavioral therapy (Dialectical Behavior Therapy is a good example that has been experimentally validated working with difficult borderline patients[3]) is beginning to interweave existential and spiritual components (especially mindfulness orientations and practices) into more traditional cognitive behavioral approaches[4]. These systems benefit from an explicit embrace of the importance and utility of spiritual and existential concerns in psychotherapy. Let's continue with Dennis, using a cognitive behavioral paradigm to address his periodic regressions into destructive defensive states:

Keith: "What were you thinking when you got real mad at that technician?"

Dennis: "That he deserved it because he screwed up."

Keith: Guiding him deeper into his distorted schema, or belief systems. "He deserved you raging at him because he made a mistake?"

Dennis: A little uncertainly. "Well, when you put it that way, it doesn't really make sense."

Keith: "And yet, when you're in a certain kind of angry, aroused state, it seems like the right thing to do."

Dennis: "I don't really think about it, I just do it."

Keith: Introducing the idea that he currently can't consistently control surrendering to his distorted beliefs, amplified emotions, and destructive impulses. "Maybe you can't control how you think or behave when you're angry past a certain point."

Dennis: "There's only so much anybody can take."

Keith: "Before it's a good idea to rage at someone who's made a mistake?"

Dennis: "No, it's never a good idea."

Keith: "Then perhaps, at those times, you're out of control."

Dennis: Uncomfortable. We are now up against one of his main rationalization systems, or pathological schemas, that his outbursts are reasonable responses to provocation rather than destructive, out of control events. "Well, maybe sometimes I am."

Keith: "There are ways of thinking and behaving you can cultivate that can help you be more in control."

Dennis: Intrigued. "Like what?"

Keith: "Like cultivating a mindfullness practice and embracing the principle of zero tolerance for emotional violence. Like noticing when you're getting tense and doing sixty seconds of relaxation training. Like telling yourself you are in danger of emotionally hurting others and yourself when you feel anger."

Dennis: "I can do those things."

Keith: "Let's practice them now. The real test comes when you're angry, feeling provoked and justified, and suffering your distorted thoughts, amped-up anger, destructive impulses, and reduced capacities for self-reflection and empathy. If you can do the practices when you're mad, you will have made great progress in letting go of a bad habit that's hurt you and the people you care about for decades."

You'll notice I'm appealing to his moral and aesthetic self as well as his rational self. Whether consciously or unconsciously, most people routinely evaluate their experiences by aesthetic, moral, and externally observable validity standards. It's useful in therapy to routinely appeal to different validity standards, adjusting emphasis to the type, state, and developmental levels of your client to maximally motivate risk-taking and change.

The nature of symptoms and remediation can vary wildly with type of client and levels of development.

What constitutes remediation can vary wildly with the type of client and level of development. Remediation of social problems with a shy person probably involves encouraging more expression, self-revelation, and assertion. Remediation of social problems with an extroverted, aggressive person probably involves more moderation, quiet listening skills, and less talk about self. Progress for a dominating RED husband in conflict with his wife might involve him practicing zero tolerance for striking her and raging at her, while progress for a egalitarian GREEN husband might involve direct expression of his anger and increased sensitivity to her subtle closing in the face of his implied criticisms in quid pro quo negotiation.

Masculine and feminine types often need to remediate in opposite directions for what appear to be similar problems. An anxious feminine person often needs to cultivate daily pleasure in the body and other opening practices to help her be a more immediate, expressive, open channel of emotion, and be better able to express devotional love through her body towards her masculine partner when he is being his best self. An anxious masculine person often needs to cultivate resolute acceptance of death, standing unrecoiling in the face of stress, and feeling into his feminine partner and opening her with his presence, humor, and shadow to deeper pleasures.

Remediation of symptoms: important, but not the whole story.

Psychotherapy focuses on remediating symptoms by monitoring and utilizing multiple perspectives applied through whatever theoretical models the therapist chooses to learn and practice. As this process unfolds the therapist pursues and is informed by two other primary agendas of psychotherapy, enhancing health and supporting development.

1. Diagnostic and Statistical Manual: Fourth Edition. (1994).

2. *Ibid*

3. Linehan (2001)

4. Siegel (2007)

15

Enhance Health

What is health?

Dan Siegel, the originator of interpersonal neurobiology suggests that a healthy person is one whose brain is integrated, whose relationships are empathetically sound, and whose mind (defined as a process that regulates the flow of energy and information) is harmonious. Integration is the linkage of differentiated parts in a hierarchical, energized system that doesn't get lost in chaos or rigidity. Practically, he maintains that a healthy mind/body system is flexible, adaptive, coherent, energized an stable.[1]

As an operational definition, mental health as an integrated (or integrating) mind/body system has a lot to recommend it. Most therapists will agree that identifying different parts of self, world, and worldview and linking them with acceptance and compassion results in enhanced emotional, mental, and relational health.

On the other hand, an open secret of all psychotherapy is that the general health of the individual is the foundational concern of the work, and that general health includes physical, professional, relational, developmental, spiritual, and pschosexual components that are all interwoven into the life of the client. This calls for a somewhat broader view of health, though the linkage of differentiated parts to support integration is a process that can apply to all areas.

Balancing the quadrants.

Ken Wilber suggests that health can be looked at by how fully one has expanded into a current worldview (horizontal health), and by how effectively one is allowing and supporting upward movements on central developmental lines (vertical health).[2]

Since each moment is happening simultaneously in all four quadrants from a variety of perspectives, horizontal health can be monitored and guided by balanced consideration from all quadrants, or, balancing the quadrants. Balancing the quadrants utilizes multiple subjective and objective as well as individual and group perspectives and validity standards to evaluate current functioning, provide directions for thought and action, and deal with the myriad issues, decisions, and questions that are constantly arising in life. Doing this involves linking different perspectives with awareness, acceptance, and compassion.

Health from externally observable, objective perspectives.

Objectively, good health can show up as optimal blood work, healthy diet, good grooming, adequate sleep, relationships characterized mostly by positive expressions and interactions, successful performance at work/school/other performance based settings important to the individual, abstinence from, or controlled use of, euphorics, and, in general, practices and behaviors that have been shown by research to be associated with healthy metabolism, satisfying relationships and successful functioning in the individual.

Systems theory yields ongoing streams of data about what group research has taught us about health. More blueberries are associated with decreased risk of some cancers[3], couples that positively idealize each other report greater satisfaction and live longer lives,[4] workers with good people skills tend to advance faster and farther, smokers shave decades off their expected life spans, and mentally active individuals are more resistant to Alzheimer's disease.

Health from individual subjective perspectives.

Health in the broad sense that we're using it involves a subjective sense of well-being, positive feelings about self and others, feelings of attraction to objectively healthy activities, and repulsion towards the corresponding indicators of imbalance and disease.[5] When we enter a defensive state, one form of healthy response involves discerning the state shift into characteristic amplified or numbed emotions, distorted perspectives, and destructive impulses and then using conscious intent and resolve to self-regulate to non-distorted perception and thought (compassionate understanding), to self-soothe to appropriate and proportionate emotion, and to self-direct to constructive impulses and actions.

Healthy ascending spirituality (especially nourishing to the masculine) involves increasing compassion, deepening consciousness, more decentering, and identification with a progressively deeper and wider sense of self that witnesses body, sensation, emotion, thought, and impulse, but is not primarily identified with any of them. This deeper self tends to feel one with progressively larger groups and entities, moving toward feeling consistently one with the ultimate vibrant emptiness from which everything is always (and always has been) arising.[6]

Healthy descending spirituality (especially nourishing to the feminine) involves feeling progressively more at one with (loving towards) all the delicious objects, beings, and processes in nature and the manifest world, surrendering to constant change, and moving toward oneness with the vibrant spirit that shines up through all.[7]

Health from shared inter-subjective perspectives.

From an inter-subjective perspective, health involves feeling the satisfying, "good," sense of living life according to our personal moral code, which usually includes the principles, guidelines, and rules we mostly share (usually in reality, occasionally in fantasy) with the cultures we are embedded in.

A more masculine aspect of a client will likely feel it is especially "good" to live each moment of life in a way that is consistent with deepest purpose. A more feminine aspect of a client will likely feel it is especially "good" to lead each moment of life in a way that serves love in relationships, and expresses caring for those individuals who are members of the cultures he or she feels a member of.

Health is relative to life conditions and developmental levels.

Being sensitive to where our client is on their various developmental lines is useful in enhancing health, because the moral standards and beauty standards our clients most need to be true to are their own, not ours. In the following exchange with Josh, an intelligent, somewhat depressed eighteen year old, the focus of the work is on him identifying and being true to his own moral sensibilities. In this segment I'm exploring data from multiple perspectives while encouraging him to discern, refine, and be true to his own values:

Josh: "I've been drinking and using drugs for a couple of years now."

Keith: Starting with the aspect of drug/alcohol use that is most often neglected by health practitioners: the subjective pleasure. "What do you enjoy about it?"

Josh: "I like the pot high, though I get anxious sometimes. Beer is fun, but I don't like to drink too much."

Keith: "Why not?"

Josh: "There's lots of alcoholism in my family and I don't want to be an alcoholic."

Keith: "So when and how much pot and alcohol is it healthy for you to use?"

Josh: "Pot maybe three days a week, and beer maybe two or three days a week."

Keith: "Specifically, how much is the right amount by your standards."

Josh: "No more than three or four beers at a time. It's not good to be stoned all day or to drink during the day, unless it's a holiday. I like to get stoned once, and sometimes have another hit later. I don't think you should get drunk hardly ever."

Keith: "Are you consistent with these standards, or do you violate them ever?"

Josh: "I'm pretty good, but I do get drunk once in awhile at parties, or get stoned in the morning once in awhile."

Keith: Giving him objective data on health. "Research shows that progressive (more over time) or out-of-control (can't say 'no' to the next dose) use of euphorics are signs of addiction. Your pattern and standards of use are on the high end of moderate for regular users in your age cohort of seventeen to twenty-three. If you were older there would be a strong possibility of addiction because of the frequency of your use and the episodes where you break your own rules by getting stoned in the morning or getting drunk at a party. A lot depends on whether you continue to use more or break your own rules more, or whether you use less and are more true to your own health standards."

Josh: "I know I don't want to use more."

Keith: "I guess we'll find out over the months and years ahead if you can keep to that resolve, or if you'll drink more, smoke more, or still use in out-of-control ways. One alcohol expert named Dutch Shultz once told me that it often takes one to five years of progressive use to develop alcoholism. The guy had been a practicing alcoholic, been in recovery from alcoholism, or had worked with alcoholics all his life, so, as far as I was concerned, he had street credibility[8]. With pot, I've found in my work that people who progress to daily use are usually addicted."

Josh: "I know I don't want to be an alcoholic or a pot addict."

Keith: "You have healthy standards for your cultural context. We'll see if you can be true to them."

As I explained to Josh, his patterns of use were on the high end of moderate by the standards of his peers, but they could strongly indicate abuse or dependence in other age cohorts, and so could be indicators of major problems for him. The first step towards evaluating these areas was helping him identify his own health standards and joining with him in interested observation on whether he could be true to those standards.

Enhancing health: a lifelong practice.

One of the things I love about physical, emotional, spiritual, relational, and professional training, is that you can dedicate yourself to systematic growth in those areas, make progress almost every day of your life, and die having had the subjective experience of more or less constant growth and improvement throughout a lifetime. Each moment provides us with opportunities to balance the quadrants and enhance health. Sometimes we make good decisions, sometimes bad, but an integrally informed approach cultivates awareness of the decision making process from a variety of perspectives. This approach reminds me of the Buddhist principle that most physical and mental disease is caused by ignorance. Compassionate understanding is a reciprocal inhibitor of ignorance.

On the other hand, healthy thought and action at one moment of our lives might be inappropriate at another point. To have a fuller picture it's useful to understand and support balancing the quadrants from a developmental perspective. This is a central aspect of vertical health.

1. Seigel (2005)

2. Wilber (2003)

3. Hitti (2007)

4. Gottman (1999)

5. Cloniger (2004)

6. *Ibid*

7. *Ibid*

8. Schultz (1977)

16

Support Development

Balance the quadrants and think developmentally.

Focusing on health in the present moment from multiple perspectives sets the stage and provides the impetus for developmental growth. We progress from our current development level to our next level on any given line to the extent that we "fill up" our current level; inhabit it so thoroughly that we begin to be constrained by its limitations.[1] Cognitively, as a ten-year-old's brain matures, he becomes so adept at concrete operational thought that he is frustrated by its limitations and instinctively moves to the "what if," multiple perspectives that formal operational thinking provide. Athletically, a woman may improve in tennis to the point she is beating all her usual opponents and, hungering for more challenge, finds more difficult matches that stretch her. Relationally, a couple in their early thirties can inhabit second stage functioning until their intimate relationship is pervasively fair, honest, and equal, and any topic can be safely discussed and negotiated, but then one or both might yearn for the surrender to inner voices, deeper penetration and more soulful, passionate ravishment that often characterize the third stage. In all these examples, behaving optimally within current worldviews naturally leads to developmental shifts to new worldviews.

In psychotherapy, simple thinking developmentally supports development. Remembering and teaching the following axioms has been invaluable to me in supporting development. Some of these principles have been explored in previous chapters, and some require further elaboration:

- **We are constantly progressing and regressing on numerous developmental lines, reflecting the glop and slop of development.[2]**

- **As meaning-making beings, we will create meaning at each level of development, inhabiting what Robert Kegan calls "evolutionary truces" between our worldviews and the stimuli our environments provide.[3]**

- **We include and transcend as we rise through developmental levels.**[4]
- **We do not skip levels.**[5]

We can have peak experiences on much higher levels (for instance, flashes of post-formal operational insight), and regressive experiences to lower levels (both healthy responses to the present moment like engaging in silly play with a four-year-old, or regressed defensive states where we use our adult capacities in service of primitive resistance to change; for instance blaming someone else for our own mistakes). These peak and regressive experiences are normal and often useful if they are healthy responses to the present moment and/or if we use them as opportunities to cultivate compassion and depth of consciousness. If we deepen in discernment, we naturally view perspectives and actions on higher levels as positive and move towards them. There are spurts, stops, starts, peaks, and regressions, in the glop and slop of development, but each consecutive level must be fully inhabited for us to progress to stably inhabiting the next level on that line.

- **It is generally desirable and healthy to rise in levels.**

More mature functioning on any given line is generally preferable to regressed or arrested development on that line unless it involves self or other destructive actions. An example of climbing levels at the cost of health is using steroids to enhance athletic performance. Aside from the legalities, such behavior isn't moral to most of us, though it can result in genuine improvement on a particular athletic line (football, cycling, and baseball are current, high profile examples).

- **The higher the level, the more felt sense of spirituality.**

Spirituality can be defined variously as a separate line of development, a state of nature mysticism (oneness with nature), deity mysticism (oneness with a transpersonal being or force), or formless mysticism (oneness with emptiness, or the void) that we can occupy at any level, and a quality that characterizes higher levels of development.[6]

In my studies of martial arts, I've noticed lots of disagreement among moderately skilled practitioners, while the advanced teachers in most systems speak in very similar terms, appreciating other adepts, and referring to more universal, often spiritually charged, qualities like practice, focus, chi, love, and discipline. The higher we climb, or the deeper we evolve, on most developmental lines, the more we are likely to feel a sense of the sacred associated with our functioning in that area.

- **Different life conditions evoke different developmental levels of response.**

To me, part of the genius of Spiral Dynamics is the core insight that characteristic life conditions evoke characteristic worldviews. Cultural MEMEs pull the individual up to the cultural center of gravity and then inhibit the individual from going beyond. Adolescents generally leave a family (the first, most influential, culture we are embedded in) at the same developmental levels on self and other lines that their parents inhabit. A PURPLE, tribally oriented, individual brought into an ORANGE rational culture will constantly be deluged with input that supports his development towards rational, achievement-oriented, hierarchical, ORANGE consciousness. First he will be forced by RED power-God tactics to comply with local rules. Then he's likely to learn and follow the new rules until he inhabits a complementary BLUE consciousness that finds the "Book" of rules sacred. As (or if) he outgrows, or looks for deeper truths beyond, the "Book," he might pursue more individual, ORANGE, hierarchical, achievement oriented goals.

Beck and Cohen tell a story in *Spiral Dynamics* of how, when Bushmen adolescents were taught soccer in Australia, they initially played until there was a tie and then quit. The concept of competition was an alien one to their PURPLE tribal worldviews, but I assume that, at least for some of those boys, they eventually changed in response to the dominant cultural demands of their English boarding school cultures. The contemptuous incredulity of their Anglo teachers was doubtless a force that would condition some Bushman boys away from intra-tribal cooperative consciousness towards RED power-God forced obedience to the rules of the school ("Play to win or you will be punished"). Over time this forced obedience could develop in some youths into the BLUE conformity of accepting the rules as inherently sacred ("It is moral to follow the rules of the game, and to do your best to win"). As the young men became more distant from their tribal culture and more invested in the new culture they were originally forced to be embedded in, they might be drawn to the individualistic, ORANGE, achievement oriented hierarchical aspects of their BLUE/ORANGE environment ("I just scored two goals, I'm a star"). If these Bushmen adolescents embraced competitive, achievement oriented, merit-based ORANGE cultural standards, fully inhabited those standards, and deepened to GREEN non-hierarchical, multi-cultural egalitarianism, the dominant BLUE/ORANGE colonial culture would then inhibit and interfere with their development; finding their emerging, egalitarian, non-hierarchical GREEN worldviews irritating and offensive ("How dare you imply that your primitive Bushman culture is as valid as our traditional English way of life?"). In this case the center of gravity in the culture first pulled the young men up to the cultural norm, and then inhibited them as they began to ascend beyond the cultural center of gravity.

In the following exchange with Lance, a man in his early fifties, we are processing his recent experiences with changing his center of gravity on his self-line and the resultant reorganization of his worldview:

Lance: "I can't stand being around my brother and father anymore."

Keith: "What's difficult?"

Lance: "They're crude. They make lots of rude comments about women. They put me and other people down all the time. I just don't like it."

Keith: "How did it used to be?"

Lance: "Frankly, I was more like them. I was used to it. I'd kid them back and make the same comments. But I just can't do that anymore."

Keith: "It feels ugly and wrong to you now."

Lance: "Exactly."

Keith: "This is what happens when you grow developmentally. Your values are refined into new understandings. In a very real sense, you're a different Lance; one who has included the old Lance, but has transcended into a new Lance who has somewhat different standards and sensibilities."

Lance: "My wife loves it. She never could stand being around my brother and father."

Keith: "I think one of the reasons you chose her was that she enjoys the same values and worldview that you've been growing towards."

Lance: "You're right. I've always admired how she is practical, successful, and treats people with respect."

Thinking developmentally is especially important when working with parents. As we'll see in the next Section when we explore developmentally informed parenting, it doesn't merely guide parents in supporting their children's development, it guides them into addressing their own emergent developmental needs that are evoked and accelerated by having children and creating a family. I encourage parents to conceptualize family as a culture where everyone is developing, and everyone has their current work and challenges.

In Section Five we will more deeply explore developmental lines and levels including developmentally informed parenting, clinical applications of evolutionary psychology, critical developmental differences between masculine and feminine types, and clinical implications of different developmental levels on central developmental lines.

Summary.

We began Section Four with examining how psychotherapy cultivates compassion and depth of consciousness to cultivate healthy perspectives and actions. We continued with examining the purpose of therapy being to remediate symptoms, enhance health, and support development. The next seven chapters will explore the process of therapy from the perspectives of relating, teaching, inspiring, confronting, interpreting, and directing.

1. Wilber (2004)

2. Wilber (2000)

3. Kegan (1982)

4. Wilber (2000)

5. Wilber (2003)

1. *Ibid*

17

Relate

Cultivating compassion and depth of consciousness to support healthy perspectives and actions reflects the inner orientation of most psychotherapists. Remediating symptoms, enhancing health, and supporting development define the goals of most therapeutic sessions.

Co-creating a culture in which the client and the client's universe are cherished, each moment is considered a gift and an opportunity, and healthy perspectives and actions are considered beautiful, good, and true, reflects the intersubjective nature of the psychotherapy process. The therapist engages the client in ways that are intended to support the co-creation of a healing culture in their intersubjective relationship. The activities the therapist engages in to do this are mostly relating, teaching, inspiring, confronting, interpreting, and directing.

Therapist regularly are informed by and responding to the streams of data flowing constantly from self and client. Every therapist is also informed by knowledge of what the responsibilities, limits, and goals of self and client are in the session, all of which vary from client to client and, to some extent, from therapist to therapist (depending on licensure, training, experience, depth of consciousness, and type of person the therapist is). Anchored in formal and post-formal cognitive abilities, and reaching for post-post-formal processes, most therapists find themselves variously emphasizing relating, teaching, inspiring, confronting, interpreting, or directing in any given moment of the session.

Just as there is rarely just one source of input, or one single perspective that the therapist attends to at any instant, there is rarely just one kind of healing activity the therapist is engaging in. What does shift is the emphasis the therapist chooses to have in what area to best maximize healing and growth:

- **Relating** involves the therapist attuning to self and client in the intersubjective fields that infuse the therapeutic relationship in each session[1] and providing contingent communication (the client's messages are heard, understood, and responded to their satisfaction[2]), while focusing on remediating symptoms, enhancing health, and supporting development. Relating is the context, fabric, and atmosphere of each session and the sine qua non requirement of psychotherapy as a healing art.

- **Teaching** happens, to some extent, each time the therapist speaks or acts.

- **Inspiring** clients to reach for healthier perspectives and actions is an important measure of how effective therapy is, and involves the therapist and client cocreating moments where healthy activity seems more discernable and available to clients.

- **Confronting** is reflecting compassionate understanding and truth to clients.

- **Interpreting** supports the human drive to create meaning as a healing (rather than a wounding) activity, by providing contexts that help the client shape their autobiographical narrative into one that is coherent, optimistic, and positively directed towards the future.

- **Directing** involves suggesting (or even insisting on) the presence or absence of certain behaviors, insights, or processes. It is often the therapist's responsibility to offer guidance, or set boundaries determined by what's required for maximizing benefit (and by the laws of the States we practice in).

During a therapy session, therapists are often consciously and/or intuitively drawn to different constellations of the above activities as the session unfolds. In the following Chapters we'll look at relating, teaching, inspiring, confronting, interpreting, and directing in more detail.

Relating: The Sine Qua Non of Therapy.

Relating is the foundation requirement, the sine qua non, of therapy. It is the medium (the atmosphere) in which the therapeutic encounter occurs.

Whenever we are in the presence of another, we are generating intersubjective fields of relating. These fields are perspectives we share, complementary roles we play, and actual energies we radiate, receive, and co-create. Intersubjective fields are determined by each individual's state of consciousness, and how those states naturally constellate together in intimacy.

There is persuasive evidence that humans radiate gross, etheric, astral, thought, and causal energies from our atomic/molecular selves, living selves, sexual being selves, thinking selves, and causal selves, respectively. Empirical science has observed and documented these energies, as well as the ongoing shifts in all of them when in relation to others.[3] In a form of dual Heisenberg principle, we influence, and are influenced by, everyone around us. Often, we are either predominantly in a state of healthy response to the present moment or a defensive state and, since states tend to evoke complementary states in others, we'll tend to evoke or reflexively inhabit healthy or defensive states with intimates.[4]

In the psychotherapy session, effective therapists tend to consistently maintain personal states of healthy response to the present moment, while seeking out and engaging the client's defensive states. In the ensuing tension, as the client's defensive states are brought into the light of conscious awareness, therapists learn to discern their own impulses to inhabit complementary defensive states and continually adjust to states of healthy response, thus subtly influencing the client to enter complementary states of healthy response. As the client shifts to states of healthy responses to the present moment, healthier perspectives and actions become accessible and desirable.

There is a wealth of data supporting relating as a healing activity. Carl Rogers maintained that relating, characterized by congruence, empathy, transparency, self-disclosure, and positive regard, helps people heal psychologically and spiritually.[5] These qualities form the core "listening skills" that are taught, in one form or another, in almost every psychotherapy training program.

Each therapist has his or her own body of subjective experience and knowledge that relationships of trust, mutual acceptance, and caring intent promote healing, and maximize their client's courage to consider new perspectives and actions in service of love and health.

There are a number of subjective indicators of successful relating that a therapist can experience. I'll briefly list four of them:

- A fascination with, an absorbing interest in, the client's universe, worldview, and current experience from multiple perspectives.

- An intense caring for both your client's welfare, and the welfare of everyone with whom they are affiliated.

- An excitement at the possibilities of remediating symptoms, enhancing health, and supporting development for your client, their significant others, and everyone in their life.

- A hunger for your client to feel understood, accepted, supported, and cherished in each moment of the session.

This last characteristic of relating is particularly important in prioritizing interventions. If your client doesn't feel understood, accepted, or supported, the focus of the session shifts from whatever insight, technique, positive change, or potential transformative experience that you are unavoidably invested in to some extent, back to attuning to your client so that they feel understood, accepted, and supported. Attunement usually is a function of attending to what you are feeling, thinking, and wanting, and extending your focus to what your client might be feeling, thinking, and wanting, all with caring intent.[6]

Intersubjective indicators of successful relating are the subjective ongoing senses in therapist and client that the activity of therapy is worthwhile by individual and societal standards.

The following exchange between Sally and Martin (the couple in their late thirties we met in Section Two) illustrates relating as an organizing principle. Their initial presenting problems were chronic fights, isolation and deception in Martin, and sexual aversion in Sally:

Martin: "We had another horrible fight on Friday night."

Sally: "Martin came home and insulted me."

Martin: He turns to me with a "This is so unreasonable" expression on his face. "All I said was I like you better in the green dress."

Sally: "Meaning I look ugly in the blue dress."

Keith: Wanting to encourage understanding that the content of such fights is inconsequential compared to the process. "How did it resolve?"

Martin: "It didn't. Sally's still pissed off."

Sally: "I'm pissed at you for a lot more than that."

Keith: "So it hasn't resolved. You are still angry at each other for this and other stuff."

Sally: "You guys don't understand what it's like to have someone attack how you look."

Keith: This triangulating of "therapist and partner against me" is a common characteristic of certain defensive states in conjoint therapy, and can be especially disruptive with clients who suffer from borderline traits or borderline personality disorder. It's often first apparent to me when one partner includes me in a distorted belief that is primarily associated with their partner. It's my cue to leave the current agenda and focus on relating, specifically on attuning Sally's and my relationship. "I do know how devastating it can be to a feminine person, who is light and radiance, to feel perceived as repulsive."

Sally: She's still in a defensive state, defending her position, but is relaxing as she feels safer at my refusal to engage in conflict, and my insistence on relating to her in a supportive manner. "You're a guy, how could you understand?"

Keith: I'm feeling more attuned, liking her, and aware of compassion for her suffering and admiration of her courage to deal with these scary topics. "Explain it to me. Tell me what it's like for you."

Spiral Dynamics as a shorthand attunement system.

For the therapeutic relationship to thrive, clients need to feel that their worldviews are compatible with their therapist's worldviews. Spiral Dynamic is a magnificent shorthand system for adjusting perspective and language to complement a client's worldview. If the therapist does not share the client's worldview (or is not operating out of a YELLOW, integral, felt appreciation for all points of view), adjustments to a client's worldview and language can be calculated manipulations with possible accompanying subjective indicators of a sense of falseness to both the client and therapist. The absence of compassionate understanding is often felt as significantly as its presence. If the therapist is feeling compassionate understanding, adjustments to a client's shifting worldviews are felt as soothing and authentic. For example, let's examine some motivational systems that might be more soothing for different worldviews:

- **PURPLE** tribal worldviews need motivational systems consistent with their magical orientation, ethnocentric consciousness, and reverence for Shamanic power. A member of a gang, an indigenous tribe, or occasionally even a dominating extended family with some magical orientations, needs motivational systems that honor their sense of magical connection to the divine, and don't threaten their beliefs of their tribe being unique and special. Motivational systems need to be consistent with their insular and mystical tribal standards. A PURPLE teen member of a gothic high school subculture needs language that supports (or at least doesn't threaten) her people-dressed-in-black look, her anti-establishment views, and her rights to find the dark and forbidden beautiful.

- A **RED** teacher, who dominates his class with power-God authoritarian techniques, will actually tend to relax to hear that, if he doesn't conform to specifically defined boundaries, his principle (or superintendent if the principle is not a powerful enough power-God) will crush him. RED tends to respond well to power dominance (either dominating or being dominated) in authoritarian hierarchies.

- A **BLUE** police officer needs to believe that a change in perspective and behavior is consistent with his code of what is right by the rules and laws he lives by (his sacred "Book"). BLUE conformity finds comfort in dogma, and needs to subjectively experience a therapist as being a member (or at least an honorary member) of the "people of the Book," for the therapist to have credibility in advocating new perspectives and behaviors.

- An **ORANGE** student needs her drives to self-sacrifice for achievement honored, and her need for externally verifiable data respected, to feel trusting of her therapist. ORANGE is especially comfortable with a therapist as a "coach" who helps establish position on merit based hierarchies.

- A **GREEN** social worker needs to feel her egalitarian, anti-hierarchical, multicultural sensitivities honored, and her own moral certainty of her "good" perspectives respected before she can relax and consider other perspectives. Though consciously believing herself open-minded, she's likely to react with distrust and moral condemnation if the therapist expresses views contrary to her own egalitarian, multicultural, and non-hierarchical standards.

Adapting Spiral Dynamics to psychotherapy is not just all about worldviews. One reason the Integral Institute shifted away from Spiral Dynamics to their own system of color indicating altitude on specific developmental lines (with magenta replacing purple, amber replacing blue, and teal replacing yellow) is that we have varying centers of gravity on different developmental lines, and we shift altitude on any line depending on whether we are in a relaxed, defensive, or transcendent state.

Types figure prominently in how a worldview manifests in individuals. Risk adverse RED clients will need their genuine desire to avoid conflict honored, while risk seeking RED clients will need their hunger for thrills on the subjective edge of death respected. A client in a more masculine moment will tend to grow best in the presence of loving challenge, while a client in a more feminine moment will tend to grow best in the presence of loving praise. Masculine types are often more inspired by meaning at the edge of death; feminine types often more inspired by serving love, and so on through the masculine and feminine domains.

Since defensive states almost always involve regression, it's important for therapists to be alert to what worldview, language, and sexual aspect is being exhibited on the self-line in the present moment, and to be able to adjust to soothe and connect with shifting worldviews, altered states, and the current predominant sexual aspect. How well we, as therapists, relate depends on how well we feel and coordinate with our clients on a variety of continua in the ongoing dance of the session. A therapist rides these shifting forces the way a surfer rides a wave, with clear purpose and direction while constantly adjusting to a variety of ever-changing environmental influences.

As the previous session with Sally and Martin continues, observe how many worldviews are represented, and how my language shifts to stay in tune with them:

Sally: "Martin just wants to have sex. He thinks that will solve everything. It's so wrong."

Keith: Responding to her conformist, BLUE moral judgment. "You believe it's wrong for him to want sex with you?"

Sally: "No, of course not. It's wrong to think that it will solve everything."

Martin: "It's not fair to be married and not have sex. We should have equal power and we don't."

Keith: "You should have equal power because …?"

Martin: "Because it's not right for one person to have more power than the other."

Sally: "You make all the money."

Martin: "That's our money."

Keith: "I can see how it feels unfair to you, Martin, that you have no power to create sex, and Sally does. But it's also not fair that you find sex attractive and exciting while Sally finds it scary and repulsive. Relationships are balanced and complementary, but they are asymmetrical. Often one person has more of one kind of resource and less of another."

Sally: Finding this frightening, she regresses to a primitive RED worldview where she needs to dominate Martin. "This is such bullshit. All I have to do is spread my legs and you think everything's fine."

Martin: He smoothly enters a complementary RED defensive state. "You are so selfish and so wrong. As if you care at all what I need."

Sally: "You, you, you."

Keith: I need to become a compassionate power-God and provide RED boundaries that direct them out of their RED regressions. I invite egocentric Sally to receive love by challenging Martin to offer something she can enjoy. "Stop. Now you're both trying to get relief by hurting the other, and that just creates more suffering. Martin, tell Sally what's valid about her point."

Martin: He looks confused. "What?"

Keith: I want to inspire them by encouraging a peak experience where they can briefly inhabit higher levels on their self-lines. "Each of your positions has validity, but you, Martin, are the more masculine partner. It's your responsibility to feel into the moment, understand what's needed to serve love, and then offer masculine direction. Rather than go with your reflexive, stingy attack, I suggest you lead with a generous offering of what's valid in Sally's position. This makes you a more trustable man, so she can feel safer, relax, and be a more loving, radiant woman."

Martin: He looks at her rather than away from her for one of the first times in the session. "It's valid that it's much harder for you to be sexual. It's valid that you need to be loved in a lot of ways. It's valid that, when we have sex, I feel that everything is OK for awhile."

Keith: I appeal to ORANGE rationality, BLUE justice, and feminine essence. "Sally, what's valid about Martin's position. I know you agree with him that you need to be loved in many ways."

Sally: Laughing. "It's valid he wants a sex life. It's unfair he can't have it."

Keith: They are both caring, egalitarian GREEN at this moment. "So how does it feel to organize your thinking and behavior to better serve love?"

Martin: "I love you Sally. This is what I want."

Sally: "It feels so easy when we just love each other."

Keith: As is often the case when clients enter states of healthy response, my emphasis shifts towards teaching and inspiring. "This needs to be your stan-dard, your fall-back position when you're angry and want to be stingy and hurt each other. Ask yourself, 'What do I have to do right now to best serve love?'"

Self as instrument in relating.

Each therapist has his or her own constellation of perceptions and experiences that reflect the presence or absence of relational attunement. Two of the most profound revelations of Carl Rogers were the simple (in retrospect) observations that a client needed to feel accepted and understood in the session, and that the best way for the therapist to accomplish these goals was to focus on feeling understanding and accepting.[7] Your body/mind system can tell you with relaxation, compassion, love, joy, or concern if you are relationally attuned, or with irritation, confusion, condescension, or fear if you are out of relational attunement. As we accumulate experience, training, and practice in our careers as therapists, the attunement process tends to become more reflexive. Within this process there are regular surprises that can broaden understanding of when our relational foundation is solid and when it needs conscious attention.

1. Witt (2007)

2. Siegel (1999)

3. Wilber (2004)

4. Witt (2007)

5. Rogers (1961)

6. Witt (2007)

7. Rogers (1961)

18

Teach: A Central Function of Therapy

Misunderstandings that have given teaching a bad reputation in therapy.

The importance of teaching was down played—even disparaged—in much of my early training in psychotherapy. The behaviorists and cognitive therapists seemed least conflicted about teaching clients how to identify maladaptive behaviors, distorted thoughts, and amplified or numbed emotions, and then training them in healthier alternatives. The humanistic and psychoanalytic schools were more suspicious of therapists having teaching agendas. I believe these suspicions were due to a variety of factors. There are three that I believe are especially significant:

- Misunderstanding of what Rogers meant by "unconditional positive regard."

- The myth that therapists should be values-free in dealing with clients.

- The Freudian ideal of therapist as a blank slate upon which the transference is projected.

Lets briefly explore these three areas of misunderstanding.

Unconditional positive regard is arranging to feel love, not pretending to love

Unconditional positive regard involves constant respect for, and acceptance of, your client's worth as a human being, respect for and acceptance of your client's right to make their own decisions, and a refusal to indulge impulses to make critical judgments about your client's basic nature. Unconditional positive regard is not pretending that all decisions are equally valid, healthy, or consistent with our client's, or our own, goals, principles, and moral precepts. To pretend in this fashion can reflect a GREEN egalitarian bias in which levels and hierarchy are often regarded as morally suspect.

One important function of the therapist is to help elicit the values and goals of the client and to teach him/her how to be true to those values and accomplish those goals in ways that are consistent with the therapist's (hopefully second tier) values. This is a central aspect of congruence, which is necessary to sustain trust in the therapeutic relationship.

The myth that therapists are values-free.

The idea that psychotherapy is values-free is accurate only in the narrow sense that there are different constellations of values for different worldviews, and good therapy respects and finds validity in most of them. It is not accurate in the wider sense that the therapist brings no personal values into the session. Therapists bring a plethora of values into the session. The following list is just the tip of the iceberg of the body of values that most therapists would automatically acknowledge:

- **Growth is better than neurotic reenactment.**
- **Recovery is better than addiction.**
- **Truth to self and others is better than lies.**
- **Self-awareness is better than blind spots such as denial, rationalization, projective identification, projection, somatizaton, reaction formation, repression, suppression, and emotional and/or physical violence.**
- **Hurting others is a poor response to internal pain.**
- **Development/growth on whatever developmental paradigm you ascribe to is good.**
- **It is better to create comfort and the subjective experience of love than to create suffering.**
- **Using love and compassion as organizing principles of decision-making is better than using fear or anger as organizing principles (revenge, preemptive attack, and so on).**
- **Good boundaries are necessary for healthy relationships.**
- **It is better to know objective facts and perspectives than to be ignorant of those facts and perspectives (as in teaching evolution, sex education, and family planning).**

Therapists have their own moral standards that are as important (sometimes more important) to them as their aesthetic or empirical standards. Personal values inform and influence the therapist constantly throughout the session.

The misunderstanding of transference.

Transference has no need for a therapist to be a blank slate. Transference happens independent of any position a therapist takes for or against anything. Fritz Perls used to act like his client's parents to try to speed up the transference, and then abandoned the technique as unnecessary.[1] Transference is a function of intimacy in general, and the therapeutic relationship in particular. When intimacy approximates family-of-origin levels, we naturally activate family-of-origin idealizations, projections, and defensive structures.[2] For example, the therapist, as an arbiter of what's moral and true, will always attract parental projections.

As therapists relate, teach, inspire, confront, interpret, and direct, transference is happening in ways that are consistent with their clients' defensive structures and states, their developmental levels on different lines, and their type of person (especially more masculine or more feminine type).

As therapists help clients remediate symptoms, enhance health, and support development, transference happens, and becomes a perspective/dimension that can be (and sometimes needs to be) used to support the work. When therapists perceive the positive or negative distortions characteristic of transference (or counter-transference), they can adjust to use these distortions as guides to support the work, sometimes directly, sometimes indirectly. We'll explore this in more depth in our discussions of states in Section Six.

Teaching is a natural and necessary part of psychotherapy

Often, teaching is what's happening in a session when our clients are not in defensive states. We teach material that meets our own standards of what is in our client's best interests. Cognitive Behavioral Therapy and it's many offshoots including Dialectical Behavior Therapy[3] and Acceptance and Commitment Therapy[4] all involve extensive teaching of skills, schemas, perspectives, and practices. When people are open, relaxed, and in the moment, they learn phenomenally well.

Therapists have knowledge and experience regarding remediating symptoms, enhancing health, and supporting development, and clients expect therapists to share such knowledge and experience. As therapists get to know their clients progressively better, they develop opinions of what perspectives and actions are in their client's best interests. Clients generally want to hear, and generally benefit from hearing, those opinions. In the previous example with Martin and Sally, part of the work was teaching them masculine and feminine practices. Martin suffered from not knowing his purpose in the moment, his responsibility to stand unrecoiling in the face of Sally's rage in order to create safety for them both, and the necessity of feeling into Sally and opening instead of closing her. Sally suffered from feeling restricted in the lower part of her body, not feeling erotically radiant, and not being able to discriminate between free flow of emotion and toxic residue. A central aspect of therapy is uncovering such deficits, discerning when our clients are open to new input, and teaching remediating information.

Teaching happiness.

Positive psychology, pioneered by theorists and researchers such as Seligman[5], Diener[6], and Kahneman[7], has generated persuasive data supporting happiness and fulfillment as healthy and necessary components of a good life, as well as a variety of attitudes, practices, and techniques that support happiness. For example, gratitude, optimism, and positive anticipation have been correlated with decreased cardiovascular risk, enhanced immune function, lower cortisol levels, and increased subjective happiness.[8] Since increased happiness is always an implicit and/or explicit agenda of therapy, I believe it is useful to know and teach this material.

Interestingly, pleasure in the body, loving affiliation with family and friends, service to others, personally meaningful work and play, and being fully present in the moment are central characteristics associated with happiness in the emergent literature. These characteristics line up, point for point, with central constructs of masculine and feminine practice.[9]

Depressed and/or anxious perspectives can resist the validity of happiness-enhancing or health-enhancing perspectives and actions, or the possibility that these perspectives and actions can be personally cultivated. Knowing and teaching the truths of this material from multiple perspectives can be a central aspect of how a therapist co-creates a culture where the client and their universe is cherished, each moment is considered a gift and an opportunity, and healthy perspectives and actions are considered beautiful, good, and true.

Teaching can establish psychoactive transformative internal systems.

New perspectives can be internalized into <u>psychoactive internal systems</u> that naturally support ongoing psychological, relational, spiritual, and behavioral transformation. Knowing if you are in a more masculine or feminine moment helps you feel and understand progressively more of the intersubjective polarities that we all experience daily, and provides guidance to opening rather than closing moments. Being informed by the four quadrants and bringing to bear the three validity standards supports compassionate understanding and healthy action in the present moment while minimizing the risk of discounting, avoiding, or privileging any given perspective. Understanding developmental lines and levels is invaluable in recognizing general worldviews and current perspectives. Teaching clients to distinguish a relaxed state of healthy response (which usually opens the moment) from a constricted, defensive state (which almost always closes the moment) supports self-soothing and self-regulation in service of love and health.

1. Anderson (1983)

2. Witt (2007)

3. Linehan (2001)

4. Hayes (1999)

5. Seligman (2002)

6. Diener (1984)

7. Kahneman (1999)

8. Childre (2005)

9. Deida (2006)

19

Inspire: Encouraging Transcendent States in Healing

Of all the healing arts, psychotherapy relies most on the client to make adjustments to remediate symptoms, enhance health, and support development. Even in the face of the vast contributions of psychopharmacology and biophysiological interventions, the measure of psychotherapy is how effectively it guides and inspires people to make healthy changes in their perspectives and actions. Empirical research has consistently shown that happiness is overwhelmingly more a function of psychological orientation than of environmental circumstances.[1] The ongoing challenge of psychotherapy is to inspire clients to risk new perspectives that support their power to love and to inhabit joyful lives.

We've already discussed how different language and motivational emphases are more welcome to different worldviews. Robert Kegan in *The Languages of Change*[2], and Beck and Cowan in *Spiral Dynamics*[3] brilliantly illuminate the potential for maximizing the effectiveness of communication by using understanding of development, meaning making, and type. As we've expanded on the three validity standards, we've seen how drawing from the beautiful, the good, and the true provides a wide and satisfying evaluative system for most decision making. All this material and more is central to one of the basic functions of psychotherapy, inspiring clients to risk change and growth.

Inspiring through visions of superior functioning.

In general, therapists inspire by co-creating visions of superior functioning. Two ways they accomplish this are living the principles they teach, and helping clients inhabit peak experiences both in and out of sessions. These peak experiences are often characterized by joy, love, compassion, deepening consciousness, erotic radiance, and deep soul's purpose that is experienced by the client and shared empathetically by the therapist.

The basis of a therapist's capacity to inspire is their absolute conviction that it is possible, beautiful, and good for anyone, at any time, to chose love over violence, truth over lies, health over disease, and deepening spirituality over existential despair. The great Roman Catholic concept of redemption is, at its heart, the confidence that, at any point in life, a person may genuinely acknowledge their mistakes, shadow influences, and imperfections, and choose to surrender to their best understanding of God's will. This echoes Krishna, in the Bhagavad-Gita, telling the warrior Arjuna that Karma yoga is doing your best to make each action an expression of God.[4]

Understanding levels and lines helps therapists inspire clients by providing clear visions of superior functioning on each level of every line, and by demonstrating how an increasing sense of the sacred accompanies progress on—and peak experiences on—most lines.

Transcendent, potentially transformative, states can happen to any individual, at any level of development, at any time. Wilber describes how one can have a nature mysticism experience (one with nature, or objects in waking, gross reality), a deity mysticism experience (one with a perceived transcendent entity), or a formless mysticism experience (one with the formless void) at any level of self development.[5] Each experience will be interpreted through whatever worldview the individual is occupying at that time. A BLUE fundamentalist might interpret a transcendent state as a direct experience with the God of their "book." An ORANGE scientist might interpret a transcendent state as a biochemical event in their brain. A RED egocentric might conclude from such a state that they have been chosen by God to lead or dominate other people.

Inspiring transcendent states often happens in therapy when clients shift from defensive states to healthy responses to the present moment characterized by compassionate understanding, joy, love, free flow of current emotion, or generous impulses. These shifts are especially dramatic in conjoint therapy where both partners can redirect themselves—often quite suddenly—from savaging each other to loving each other.

Therapists can use confidence in clients' ability to transcend, knowledge of higher levels of functioning, and abilities to work with a variety of states of consciousness to inspire clients to experience and embrace healthy perspectives and actions. In the following exchange with Josh (the eighteen-year-old from one of our earlier examples), I use his response to a previous interpretation (which he hated) to inspire him to embrace his power to control and direct his life. This is our first session after a two-month hiatus:

Josh: "I think you might have been right; what you said about my wrestling."

Keith: Sometimes I don't remember what my client is referring to, and then I'll usually frankly acknowledge it. This time I do remember what I said, but realize that what I remember might not be what Josh remembers, so I explore. "What did I say?"

Josh: "After I told you I'd lost four straight matches, but I'm a good wrestler, you said maybe I was losing because I was afraid to really try to win."

Keith: Laughing. "I seem to remember you telling me I was full of shit."

Josh: Laughing. "Well, I've won six of my last seven matches."

Keith: I feel happy for him, and proud of him. "That's so cool. What do you conclude?"

Josh: "Maybe I have the power to, you know, do things, or accomplish things by focusing my mind."

Keith: I want him to explore more deeply. "What do you mean?"

Josh: "You know, maybe I can do lots of things if I really commit to them and don't block myself."

Keith: Feeling a warm wave of love wash through me. "Josh, I believe, if you fully commit yourself, you have the gifts to accomplish practically anything."

Almost every session provides moments of opportunity to inspire clients. Masculine/feminine teaching is particularly useful in this regard because acknowledging and being in harmony with our deepest sexual essence resonates so strongly that the process often yields peak, inspirational moments. The following exchange with Tom and Anne is one example. Tom is forty-two and Anne is thirty-three. They've been married seven years, have one child, and have both suffered from narcissistic/borderline traits throughout their lives:

Anne: Her brows are furrowed and her voice is cold. "I was trying to fix the leak yesterday and you just laughed at me."

Tom: He speaks with a whiny, defensive tone, indicating a collapse into a defensive state. "I wasn't laughing at you. You are way too sensitive to any kind of criticism."

Anne: She slumps down, looks away, and talks exclusively to me and not Tom. Hypersensitive to criticism, Tom's attacks often result in her closing down almost completely. "He's so critical and selfish. It's all about him."

Tom: Now his tone is hostile. "This always happens. You just close down. You ..."

Keith: Because I know that Tom's optimal response to her abandonment depression, or major closure, is becoming more compassionate and present, not engaging in hostile analysis, I interrupt. I suspect that a productive way to help Anne through her closure is to confront Tom, since at this moment he feels more accessible. "Tom, look at Anne. She's completely closed down. When she enters this state, your job is to love her and be a safe, embracing presence."

Anne: She relaxes a bit, but is still curled up in her chair, angry with Tom, and looking at me. "He can't do that. He has to be right."

Keith: Tom bristles but, sensing an opening in Anne's defensive state, I confront and direct her. "Anne, when you close off so completely you can't discern if Tom's being his loving self or defensive self. Look at him."

Anne: She reluctantly turns her head. Tom is experienced enough from previous sessions to do his best to stand unrecoiling and reach for his most compassionate self. "He looks better."

Keith: Feeling movement, I continue directing. "Tell him, not me."

Anne: "I hate it when you attack me."

Tom: He's now realizing his responsibility to create safety. "I'm sorry. I know I did it, and I love you. I don't want you to hurt."

Anne: She relaxes, smiling at Tom. "That's better."

Tom: "Thanks for giving me a second chance." He walks over and kisses her. She relaxes back into love and returns his kiss.

Keith: I want to support them being inspired by this moment. "What you just did can happen any time either one of you loses it. You can get back to love. Anne, all you need to do is look at him, notice when he's trying to do right, and feel the pleasure of his offering and love him. Tom, all you need to do is to keep reaching to be your best self when you feel defensive."

Of course they need to do much more than that, but this little peak experience is emblematic of what they are both capable of with work and dedication. My job is to frame the experience in a way that inspires them to keep choosing the loving option that is consistent with their deepest sexual essence, even when they are gripped by defensive states.

Development is not linear; it is glop and slop, three steps forward, two steps back, and one step to the side. Each moment a client feels inspired is a beacon they can orient to, a validation that they can change and transcend, and a confrontation of their power to heal and grow.

1. Kahneman (1999)

2. Kegan (1982)

3. Beck (1996)

4. Prabhavananda (1944)

5. Wilber (2004)

20

Confront: Telling Healing Truths

As we relate, teach, and inspire in therapy, we naturally deepen our intimacy with clients and flow to those conflicted places that are hard for them to discern, and natural for them to defend. These conflicted places are the inevitable defensive structures and states that accompany development. The nature of human consciousness is such that nobody makes it out of childhood without hard-wired defensive capacities in their nervous systems[1]. As we develop we bring our defensive states (resistance to change, habits of closure, and entrenched distorted beliefs) along for the ride until we mature enough to integrate them into states of healthy response. Externally observable indicators of defensive states are unhealthy habits, expressed distorted beliefs, unsuccessful relationships, repetitive failures, and destructive behaviors.

In clients, subjective indicators of defensive states can include confusion (the great signpost to internalized conflict), distorted perceptions and beliefs, amplified or blunted emotions, destructive impulses, diminished capacities for empathy and self-reflection, self-righteousness, moral revulsion, or critical judgments about self and/or others.

In therapists, subjective indicators of the client's defensive states can include anxiety, irritation, moral condemnation, identifying the client as a helpless victim, or some urgent internal pressure to accomplish an agenda right now to prevent some perceived disaster.

When I encounter defensive states in my clients, the focus of the session often shifts to engaging and resolving the defense, usually through emphasizing relating, confronting, interpreting, and/or directing. As a defensive state shifts to healthy response to the present moment, the focus of the session often shifts more towards teaching, and/or inspiring.

The difference between a client open to change and a client caught in defensive resistance can be perceptible in the therapist's body. I often feel a slight tightness in my chest and a mild irritation or anxiety when a client enters a defensive state. I usually feel a pleasurable relaxation and relief in my chest and easier, deeper breathing when a client shifts into a healthy response to the present moment.

Create optimal tension between support and advocating healthy risk-taking.

The organizing principle of resolving defenses is to engage them deeply enough to support change, but not to push so hard as to compromise the therapeutic relationship. Part of the art of therapy is finding the optimal tension between providing a safe environment and encouraging and challenging clients to take the risks of considering and embracing threatening changes in perspectives and actions. Too little tension might subtly support unhealthy homeostasis, while too much tension might drive clients away from treatment.

Discerning and adjusting sexual polarities is central to this process. Since I have a more masculine sexual essence, I need to help my more feminine clients grow with enough loving praise and energetic opening to help them bloom without allowing erotic polarity that might be thus created to interfere with the work. I need to help my more masculine clients grow by providing enough loving challenge to inspire them to step into masculine responsibilities, without evoking unnecessary competition or masculine dominance display. Since we all have both masculine and feminine essences, both these energetic tensions, ongoing shifting event horizons, are often present and need attention to some degree with both men and women.

Confronting is telling observable truths.

Confrontation is telling your client truth that is directly observable to them and/or you. "Your eyes narrowed when you mentioned your sister." "I suddenly felt tense when you brought up your wife's illness," "You sigh each time you discuss sex with you husband," "Everybody just relaxed when you laughed," "Each time you criticize your boss, it works out badly for you," are all examples of confrontation.

Confrontations can come from objective and subjective perspectives.

Confrontation can come from many perspectives. "You'll lose your license if you get one more DUI," or "You're not looking at you wife as you talk about her," are examples of externally observable perspectives.

"I find it beautiful that you want to care for your elderly neighbor," or, "I always feel a wave of sadness when you mention your dead father," are examples of confrontation coming predominantly subjective experience, where information is internally observable to the therapist.

"It feels wrong to me for you to publicly shame your son when you're coaching his soccer team," or, "It doesn't feel right that you lie to your husband about your lover," are examples of confrontation coming predominantly from inter-subjective perspectives, where information can be based on (mostly) shared inter-subjective senses of morality.

"Research shows that seventy percent of people who drink as you do die between the ages of 45 and 55," or "My experience suggest that, if you and your husband can't learn to love each other more effectively, you'll probably divorce within the next five years," are examples of objective confrontations where the information is based on systems theory, externally verifiable group behavior, or statistical representations.

While interpretation involves suggesting causes, frameworks, motivational systems, and organizing principles, confrontation presents clients with the truth of the current moment or of specific situations. These truths tend to arise from the ground of the therapist's perceptions, knowledge, experience, choice of perspective, compassion, and depth of consciousness.

Confrontation either opens or closes.

Confrontation tends to elicit a response of either more opening or more closing in a client. Therapists can feel this opening/closing and use it to further uncover a client's beliefs, processes, perspectives, and impulses, and hold them in the light of both therapist's and client's perception and evaluation.

Relating is usually the first optimal response to resistance (or closing). If the therapist is relationally attuned, the client cannot easily resist opening in response to relating by discounting the therapist as unsafe, unworthy, uncaring, or incompetent.

Confrontation often becomes the second optimal response to resistance since the client—still being influenced by a defensive state but relationally attuned with the therapist—can observe and validate the substance of the material by direct experience, and usually trusts the therapist is doing his best to tell the truth.

I've spent long periods of many sessions engaged mainly in staying relationally attuned and confronting clients. These sessions often develop their own rhythm: get connected, confront with truth, deal with the reaction, attune, confront with truth, deal with the reaction, attune, and so on. This is especially the case with borderline clients, who tend to twist interpretation into masochistic, self-flagellating constructs of themselves and their lives, or into projective identification where they split and become consumed by an angry, dark self who is driven to cling to and sadistically torture others (frequently their therapist).

Confrontation often becomes the intervention of choice with borderline clients because confrontation is generally internally and externally more verifiable than interpretation, and is thus less vulnerable to distortion. The following is an exchange with Billy, a twenty-five-year-old practicing alcoholic with borderline personality disorder who has recently passed from the contemplation stage of change to actual, conscious admission of her alcoholism, and real behavior change. In this session she has just entered an outpatient treatment program for addiction, has encountered the huge blocks she has against sobriety and health, and is decompensating in response:

Billy: "Everyone thinks it's all about alcohol."

Keith: Confronting from my subjective experience. "That's not what I believe."

Billy: Defensively. "Yes you do."

Keith: Confronting. "I believe that you have profound personal and relational issues. If you continue to use all your gifts to support recovery, you have significantly more likelihood of having more beauty and love in your life. If you go back to surrendering to the disease of alcoholism you have much less chance of progress, and much greater chances of premature death. I believe the best course for you is to continue to devote yourself to your recovery."

Billy: "It's just too hard."

Keith: "You look and sound so sad as you talk."

Billy: She begins to cry. "The only people who are interested in me are people like you I pay, or people at the bars I buy drinks for."

Keith: I shift to relational attunement, looking her in the eyes and feeling an echo of her despair. "You believe, or fear, that I care for you just because you pay me?"

Billy: Defiantly. "Yes."

Keith: I feel love and compassion for her and I know, if I open to her, I'll show it through my face, voice, breath, and body. "It's true you hire me to help you. It's also true that I care for you and want you to be healthier, happier, and more fulfilled."

Billy: Connected with me again, she begins crying harder. "Life doesn't seem worth living."

Keith: I shift back to confronting. "Life not seeming worth living is a classic symptom of depression. There was once a study done on everybody who jumped off the Golden Gate Bridge and survived. Without exception, they all thought on the way down, 'This is a big mistake'[2]."

Billy: Laughing. "I'm not going to try to kill myself, but I liked life better before I tried to change. Also, I'm afraid of going to jail. I've been driving drunk."

Keith: Confronting from statistical reality. "Driving drunk will almost certainly result in you dead or in jail."

Billy: "I don't want to go to jail. I didn't drive drunk before. I liked life better before I tried to stop drinking."

Keith: Relating, confronting, and inspiring. "Of course you did. You had reliable pleasures in drinking, and reliable companions in the bars. I believe you can have a more joyful life than you can currently imagine. There is more beauty and love in you than you give yourself credit for."

Discerning how, when, and what to confront.

How to best confront in any given moment is informed by what center of gravity your client has on what line of development, whether they are in a defensive state or healthy response to the present moment, and what type of person they are.

I confront from all levels with most clients, but their worldview of the moment needs to be honored to give validity to other perspectives. For instance, if someone is in an egocentric, RED moment, they need to hear how some power-God (the police, parents, bosses, institutions, and other authorities) will dominate them if they indulge destructive impulses. Billy was in a RED moment in our previous exchange and needed to hear that the police would put her in jail if she kept drinking and driving. If a client is in a conformist, BLUE moment, they need to hear how destructive thought and/or action violates their sacred "Book," and constructive thought and/or action is consistent with the "Book's" teaching (common examples of "Books" are the Bible, the Koran, the Talmud, and the Constitution). If Billy had been a devout Catholic, I would have confronted her with the fact that her sacred beliefs dictated that self-destruction, especially suicide, was against her beliefs about God's will, and that alcoholism is a form of slow suicide.

When a client is in a defensive state, relating becomes particularly important. As Billy accused me of caring for her solely because of money, the agenda of the session shifted from confrontation to relating/attunement. When she felt again that she and her universe were cherished by me, we returned to confrontation.

Partly because feminine people tend to grow best in the presence of loving praise, I focused on Billy's capacity for beautiful transformation. If she had been a more masculine person, or in a more masculine moment, I might have been more challenging, perhaps by confronting her with how repulsive she was to her lover when she was drunk and abusive, and how she had responsibilities to her intimates to care better for herself.

Reality testing is a form of confrontation.

Much of the reality testing that therapists provide comes from confrontations of what we observe and believe to be the most compassionate and deepest truth of each moment. The instrument of our body reacts to distortion and falseness in a variety of ways that are unique to each therapist. I often will feel tension, irritation, anxiety, concern, interest, and/or impulses to correct distorted perspectives when my clients enter defensive states. Every time we feel or observe falsity, distortion, or observable data that we know or feel to be useful to our client, a confrontation will suggest itself. The focus and language of each confrontation can be guided by our conscious and intuitive understanding of what type of person our client is, what states of consciousness they're inhabiting, and what developmental levels they are currently manifesting.

1. Witt (2007)

2. Friend (2003)

21

Interpret: Supporting Healthy Contexts

Healthy perspectives are characterized by more compassion and deeper consciousness as opposed to less compassion and less consciousness. As we help clients open through relating, teaching, inspiring, and confronting, we can further help them deepen compassionate understanding and better organize their experience of themselves and their world by co-creating interpretations of their experience (new autobiographical perspectives) that support more compassion and deeper consciousness, and that help remediate symptoms, support health, and enhance development.

Robert Kegan, in *The Evolving Self,* maintains that we are meaning-making beings.[1] As such we have an ongoing hunger for—and tendency to pursue—deeper understanding of ourselves and our world. This hunger is supported and fed by interpretation.

An interpretation is simply orienting current experience and/or memory into a conceptual framework. Since humans are capable of infinite perspectives, therapists have a daunting task in choosing which frameworks to use in interpretation. We can study, practice, and stay open to new ideas, but there is always the possibility that there is a better framework than the one we're currently using. For this reason it's useful to hold all frameworks loosely, remaining cognizant of the possibility that a new, better, perspective can appear at any time. Ultimately, choice of perspective is a function the client's worldviews, capacities, and needs, combined with the therapist's training, intuition, and biases.

The organizing principle of healthy frameworks are that they support positive, coherent autobiographical narratives in each client where the client's present and past life makes sense to them, and they have some sense of being a positive author of their future.[2]

Interpretations support less critical judgments and more compassion.

In general, interpretations provide frameworks that have less critical judgments of—and more compassion for—self and others. The presence of a critical judgment, usually indicated by superiority (one up), inferiority (one down), contempt, hopelessness, powerlessness, distorted thought, or destructive impulse and/or action, can be framed as the self/soul of the client crying out and yearning for new perspectives that better support compassion, love, depth of consciousness, agency, and communion.

The Myriad Sources of Interpretations

Externally observable interpretations.

Externally observable interpretations can be drawn from the biophysiological and behavioral realms:

"You recoil when you find yourself in a situation that calls for you to voice an opinion. I imagine that in your family-of-origin you were hurt, criticized, or somehow negatively reinforced for having a point of view different from your parents'," is an example of an interpretation based on learning theory.

"You seem to have an innate capacity for anxious arousal, yet you describe your upbringing as supportive and non-traumatic. Some people are born with more capacity for anxiety and/or depression than others[3]. I suspect you have always carried the burden of being more emotionally reactive than many of your peers, and you tend to interpret the world as more dangerous and dark than it actually is." This is an example of an interpretation based on systems biophysiological research combined with externally observable data on the individual.

Systems and statistical interpretations.

Systems data is quite useful in interpretation for normalizing symptoms and opening up possibilities for possible paradigm shifts in perspective. The following is an example an interpretation based on statistical data combined with other, more subjective, material:

"You are inhibited about thinking and talking explicitly about sex with your husband. You were raised in a strict Christian, fundamentalist family. Christian fundamentalists overwhelmingly assert that sex education should take place in the family, but over seventy percent of fundamentalist parents (including your parents) have effectively no conversations about sex with their children.[4] It is no wonder you have very little information about sex and lots of inhibitions talking about it. Things that parents do not talk about are often interpreted as "bad" or forbidden by developing children. You know that talking about sex with your husband is a healthy thing, but to you it often feels wrong, ugly, or forbidden to actually begin doing it."

Discrepancies between beliefs, values, or perceptions can guide interpretation.

The woman in the previous example was experiencing a discrepancy between her belief that talking about sex with her husband was a good thing, and her emotional resistance to engaging in such talk. Such discrepancies set the stage for productive and enlightening interpretations and dialogue that, in the safe holding environment of the session, can lead to healthier perspectives and actions. Notice how the interpretation I offered her leaves room for compassionate understanding that her parents would probably have wanted her to have healthy knowledge of sexuality and the capacity for healthy dialogues with her husband about sex, but might have been constrained by their own taboos and inhibitions from teaching this to their children. This focus on most people's core desires to be good and do good, even though they might collapse into distortions or regressions, provides an organizing principle for many interpretations. We absorb most of our maladaptive, destructive perspectives and defensive capacities while relating to intimates who were not operating from their most mature, most knowledgeable, or most compassionate selves when our learning took place.

Subjective interpretations.

Subjective interpretations can vary wildly depending on therapist's type, training, levels of development, and orientation. Some theoretical orientations have been largely unsupported by empirical science. For example, resolving anger and reducing aggression simply by promoting catharsis has simply not been supported by research. To the contrary, studies show that catharsis techniques applied to anger tend to result in increased aggression and extended amplified feelings of anger.[5] On the other hand, the infinite complexity of people is reflected in an endless array of unique individuals with unique needs. To an introverted, passive-aggressive, repressed masculine type, a cathartic explosion that harms no one can be liberating, exhilarating, and can help him feel and understand the power that resides in his shadow. To a repressed feminine type, a cathartic explosion might be a positive step in the direction of opening herself to being a clear channel of current emotion.

Traditionally, a popular interpretive framework for psychotherapists has been Freudian theory. The following exchange is from an individual session with Tom (from our previous couple, Tom and Anne):

Tom: "My mother lives nearby and I hate it."

Keith: "What do you hate about it?"

Tom: "She wants special attention. She only talks about herself, and she never understands or really supports me or my family."

Keith: "What's important to you about her understanding and supporting you and your family?"

Tom: "She should care about who we are and how we're doing. She doesn't. It's always about her."

Keith: This is a familiar theme; I'd like Tom to press deeper and use the emotional charge he has from cumulative injuries from his mother to support his sexuality and relationships rather than stunt them. "How often have you somehow protested to her about her selfishness?"

Tom: Laughing. "All my life."

Keith: I focus my confrontation on the discrepancies between his knowledge and behaviors. "And not only do you keep hoping she'll change, you keep trying to elicit understanding and care regularly, and are always angry and disappointed when she can't deliver. The child-like hurt and anger you show when you talk about it is very much like the hurt and anger you show when talking about Anne's anger and sexual rebuffs. I suspect there's a connection."

Tom: Sarcastically. "Must be my Oedipal complex."

Keith: Offering a Freudian interpretation. "Absolutely it's your Oedipal complex. You had to provide sexual boundaries for your mother's infantile sexual attachment to you when you were a kid. You always hungered for real love and care, and still indirectly express and nurture your outrage by going again and again to her poisoned well; passive-aggressively setting her up to fail, while hopelessly yearning for her to provide mature love. You keep trying to elicit love and passion from your sexually conflicted wife (who needs a mature, present man) by presenting her with a hurt, needy, child whom she usually finds repulsive. You could embrace this knowledge, and use it to support maturation by setting consistent boundaries for your mother, and cultivating a mature loving presence with Anne."

Interpretations are usually better received when they harmonize with worldview.

Interpretations tend to work best when they complement the worldviews, biases, and personality theories that are favored by clients. To a client who believes in past lives, astrology, Jungian theory, Freudian theory, or the tarot, interpretations generally need to harmonize with, rather than create dissonance with, such beliefs. Similarly, if a client has a spiritual path oriented to an organized religion and/or an individualized spiritual practice, interpretations will tend to feel better if they support deeper, more joyful spirituality and opportunities for inspiring new insights into idiosyncratic feelings, beliefs, and behaviors. In the following exchange with Cheryl, a woman in her early thirties who is beginning a relationship and who has extensive experience and training in Eastern mysticism and East Indian spirituality, the interpretation needs to harmonize with her sense of being a figure in her own emergent myth:

> Cheryl: "I dreamed about my ex-husband on Monday night, so of course I ran into him on Tuesday."
>
> Keith: I respect her genuine psychic power. Her ex-husband lives hundreds of miles away and it is a staggering coincidence that, on the one day he was in her city, she should see him. "How did you run into him?"
>
> Cheryl: "He was in town on business. I walked into a record store and there he was. I was shocked and sad afterwards."
>
> Keith: "Sad because?"
>
> Cheryl: "I know he's not the right man for me, but I still miss his power and magic."
>
> Keith: "What was the dream?"
>
> Cheryl: "We were in the mountains in India, by the lake where he asked me to marry him, the lake I dreamed about before I ever saw it. He took my hand and walked with me into the water. I had a moment of panic, and then relaxed as we sank below the surface. It was beautiful under the water. Then we saw a beautiful radiant fish swimming past us in the water. He let go of

me and went off after it. I felt a sense of panic and resentment. Then I woke up."

Keith: Operating from within her framework of dreams providing access to our personal myths. "What is the dream message?"

Cheryl: "I miss the magic we had in India. I don't trust him. What do you think the dream's saying?"

Keith: Offering an interpretation consistent with her spiritual orientation. "I think the dream was telling you to value the gifts and deepening you received in your marriage, but also to further accept that he cannot practice love with you at the level that you need to practice love to serve the highest good with your masculine partner."

Cheryl: Tears well up. "It was so magical with him, but you're right, I can't stay with a man who cheats on me."

Once Cheryl feels attuned with me according to her central worldview, I might gradually try a variety of interpretations from different theoretical orientations to see if she responds favorably to any others. This is especially the case in initial therapy sessions when I'm discovering a language that is comfortable for a particular client. The following are a few examples.

Family systems theory.

Family systems' theory is organized around understanding and healing family members in the context of the intersubjective webs in which each family member lives. An axiom of family treatment is that each family member lives and grows in a subjectively different family, with different relationships physically and energetically with other members. All these relationships fit together in a Rubric's Cube of the family system in which altering any relationship alters all.[6] A family system's oriented interpretation of Cheryl's dream might be: "Your family of origin was organized around the premise that people loved each other, but also betrayed each other. You tend to feel at home with a man who both loves and betrays you, and so are still drawn to your Ex, even while you're repulsed by how he treated you."

Object relations theory

Object relations theory maintains that how each of us negotiate early relationships with parents (mostly mothers), and especially how we resolve the separation/individuation challenges we encounter before age three, largely determines our personality structure for the rest of our lives.[7] An object relations interpretation of Cheryl's dream might be: "It was never safe for you to be wholly yourself because you always had to adapt to your mother's need for you to make her look good, and to your father's coercive, abusive anger when he felt threatened by you. This makes it feel natural for you to want to stay with someone who loves you, abuses you, and expects you to normalize his or her behavior."

Developmental theory

We've explored various aspects of development in previous chapters and will explore many more in the next Section. Robert Kegan's position that as the subject—I—of one stage becomes the object—he or she—of subsequent stages is particularly soothing to clients if presented in a comprehensible manner.[8] A developmental interpretation of Cheryl's dream might be: "The self you used to be was comfortable taking direction from an untrustable man. You notice that you relaxed when you got beneath the surface of the lake. The self you are now knows depth and is comfortable there, but no longer feels comfortable taking direction from a man when he is untrustable."

Understanding different worldviews naturally creates interpretations from a developmental perspective.

Lines and levels naturally emerge in the mix as we are cognizant of different worldviews in offering interpretations. What worldviews a client is most comfortable with will largely determine what interpretations they will comprehend and tolerate, and will reflect developmental levels on various lines the client is currently inhabiting. Interestingly, more spiritually based interpretations ("It sounds like God's will that you seek depth and love in healthy ways" for example) are often more attractive to power-God/RED, conformist/BLUE, and integral/YELLOW worldviews, and somewhat less attractive to rational/ORANGE, or egalitarian/non-hierarchical/multicultural/GREEN.

Interpretations and the masculine and feminine.

The masculine and feminine often inhabit different domains that provide dramatically different templates in development, sexuality, relationship, spirituality, morality, deep soul's purpose, erotic radiance, pleasure in the body, and deepest consciousness through the body.[9]

Interpretations for someone with a more masculine essence assume he probably has some basic needs for deep soul's purpose, confidence to stand unrecoiling in the face of death, abilities to evoke feminine erotic radiance, and the knowledge and freedom to engage in masculine practices.

Interpretations for someone with a more feminine essence assume she probably has some basic needs for pleasure in the body, communion with other women, being an open channel of emotion, trustable masculine presence, surrender to a trustable present masculine partner who can open her into deeper feminine erotic radiance, and experiencing herself as a wellspring of love.

In the interpretation for Tom, you might have noticed how I was challenging him to take on the responsibilities of mature masculine presence, and in the interpretation for Cheryl I was supporting her feminine yearning for a trustable man to open her into deeper love. Even though each of us has both masculine and feminine aspects, more deeply masculine people will generally respond better to interpretations consistent with the Way of the Warrior, or the Man of Wisdom, and feminine people will generally respond better to interpretations consistent with their need to serve love and be seen as light.

Interpretation in conjoint sessions.

Couples present special challenges in interpretations, with partners originally developing in different family cultures and then forming a unique culture of their own. Usually there is a more masculine and a more feminine partner with individual needs and combined needs to create polarity and practice love. Interpretations with couples often begin with confronting them with observable patterns of how they are either creating love through healthy responses to the present moment, or creating suffering through indulging relational defensive patterns. These observable patterns are natural bridges to pointing out similar patterns in other relationships and/or historically in families-of-origin.

Such observations lead to interpretations of how each partner's strengths, sexual essence, and wounds attract and/or repel the other in the moment, and support or inhibit self and/or other's growth. David Deida suggests that satisfying relationships require both polarity and the willingness to practice love at the same level.[10] Since intimacy evokes progressively deeper capacities for transcendent love and defensive regression, there is incredibly rich ground in conjoint sessions from which to offer useful perspectives on the development and expression of sexual essence, the connections between historical support or interference with sexual/relational development and current functioning, and how to deepen compassionate understanding of self and other starting with awareness of the enactment of relational defensive systems. The following exchange is with Martin and Sally in an early session in which we were beginning to understand the interplay of their historic sexual wounds in their current problems:

Sally: "I couldn't keep my hands off him in the beginning. Now I can't stand the thought of being sexual with him."

Martin: "That's no way to have a marriage."

Keith: "What do you mean, Martin?"

Martin: "I love her. I want to spend the rest of my life with you, Sally. We're married. We need to have a sex life."

Sally: "I love you too, Martin."

Keith: "You seem drawn to Martin right now, Sally."

Sally: Smiling. "I like when he says he wants to spend his life with me."

Keith: "What happens as you get more affectionate, sensual, or sexual?"

Sally: "As soon as sex is mentioned, I freeze up."

Keith: "Freeze up like …?"

Sally: "You know my history."

Keith: Knowing her history of abuse, I interpret gently to support resolution of historic wounds. "When you feel threatened, I don't think your unconscious discerns between Martin and the historic abusers."

Sally: "What do you mean?"

Keith: "When your sexual abuse occurred, the abusers wanted your pleasure. Sometimes child molesters want the child's terror and pain, and sometimes they want the child's pleasure. As a child you felt revolted and terrorized and did what children often instinctually do, you dissociated from your body and refused them your pleasure. Now you're a grown woman who yearns to be opened sexually by a trustable man, but when he wants your pleasure and you feel threatened, that same reflex, the old body memory, kicks in. You have trouble caring for the traumatized part of you that has been restimulated, and you have difficulty discerning between your husband, whom you love and trust, and the people who abused you. Your revulsion is a memory that blocks you from being in the present moment."

Sally: "As if Martin's trustable."

Keith: I offer an interpretation indirectly to Martin while confronting Sally. "Often Martin's trustable, and often he collapses into anger or whining. He was not taught how to honor his sexuality and take on the responsibility to make a woman feel safe, but he's learning. He is never abusive like those wounded historic figures that molested you. When you dissociate and are repulsed, you lose your capacity to feel into his heart and discern when he's a trustable man, or when he's collapsing into anger or whining. The abuse taught you that sex is exploitative and abusive. You were never taught how it is necessary and beautiful in loving relationships. Even when Martin's trustable, you feel no responsibility to yourself or him to surrender into pleasure in your body, the pleasure you both need."

Sally: "But why was I so turned on at the beginning with Martin?"

Keith: Interpreting to help her make sense of apparently conflicting responses. This can help her form a coherent narrative that can guide her when old, implicit memories of trauma are restimulated. "When you first met, you projected a perfect, trustable man onto Martin; the trustable man you've secretly fantasized about all your life. When you discovered he's not perfect, and when your depth of intimacy with him approximated the depth of intimacy with members of your family-of-origin, your reflexive historic defenses against unwanted sexual intrusion began to kick in, and, rather than face the fact that you have historic wounds, you've been trying to pretend that Martin's as bad as those childhood abusers. He's not. He's a good man."

Martin: Getting in sync with healthy perspectives, he becomes excited by insight. "Just like me whining and complaining and feeling hopeless and unattractive instead of being trustable and loving."

Keith: "Yes. If you consciously decide to, you can now often discern between healthy appropriate responses and unhealthy repulsive responses. You now know what it is to stand unrecoiling, be present, and show depth of consciousness through your body."

Martin: "I keep forgetting."

Sally: "It's easy to forget this stuff."

Easy to forget.

It *is* easy to forget. Defensive states resist positive, empowering memory, and amplify negative, immobilizing memory. This is one reason I usually offer my clients the option of recording the session for them to take home. Over time, interpretations help clients develop worldviews that empower them to be aware of, self-regulate, and remember defensive states. The disadvantage of relational defensive patterns is that couples evoke and sustain each other's defensive states. The beauty of intimacy is that, when one person breaks through to healthy responses to the present moment and fully inhabits their appropriate position in the sexual polarity, complementary healthy responses are often evoked in their partner.

Interpretation supports love.

Some psychotherapy, especially behavioral therapy, has tended to de-emphasize the importance of understanding the interfaces between current thought/emotion/behavior/relationship and historical conflicts through interpretation as a healing force. My clinical experience is that people hunger for perspectives that empower them to put their past, present, and future strengths and weaknesses, light and shadow, into positive, non-judgmental frameworks that support deep understanding (depth of consciousness), compassion for all, healthy choices, and love. This is consistent with adult attachment research that shows how coherent autobiographical narrative is associated with secure autonomous adult attachment.[11]

Effective interpretation thus supports an integrative process that results in an increasing sense of our body/mind organism as a healthy network of developing systems presided over by a deeper, wiser identity that chooses what aspects of the system to mobilize in any given moment. These perspectives (presented through interpretation) naturally support a deeper self that is aware of the whole, multifaceted system, and disidentifies with, rather than dissociates from, any one aspect, especially pathological aspects. This deeper self can take on the responsibility of organizing the whole system to give our best gifts of love and deep purpose to ourselves and the world.

Go back to the well.

Once a client has embraced and used a healthy perspective, a therapist can continue to go back to that well in subsequent sessions to build and expand frameworks of understanding that support compassion and depth of consciousness. As therapy continues, each client increasingly participates in creating and deepening new, healthier, perspectives and worldviews, until occupying, maintaining, and expanding a coherent autobiographical narrative becomes a stable trait in the client's personality.

1. Kegan (1982)

2. Siegel (1999)

3. Cloniger (2004)

4. Levine (2002)

5. Bushman (1999)

6. Nichols (2007)

7. Bowlby (1988)

8. Kegan (1982)

9. Deida (2006)

10. Deida (2004)

11. Siegel (1999)

22

Direct: Necessary Masculine Agency in Therapy

A significant requirement for safety in the holding environment of the session—the immediate psychotherapeutic culture—is clarity about the therapist's beliefs and agendas, and clean, clear inclusive and exclusive boundaries.[1]

Inclusive boundaries involve the therapist insisting on certain things happening. Insisting on payment for sessions, sobriety during sessions, and respect for others during sessions are examples of inclusive boundaries.

Exclusive boundaries involve the therapist refusing to allow, and/or taking action to address, such things as physical violence, dual relationships, child/elder abuse/neglect, or client requests to misrepresent them to insurance companies, other individuals, or other institutions.

Boundaries are a form of direction that the therapist has the responsibility of articulating and maintaining, often independent of how comfortable or uncomfortable she is setting them. Many of these boundaries are mandated by the legal and ethical requirements of the profession.

Directing is agency in service of love through depth of consciousness.

Each therapist, man or woman, serves his or her clients from both their masculine and feminine aspects. Just as relating largely reflects the feminine healing principle of communion without agenda (empathy and unconditional positive regard), directing reflects the masculine principle of agency in service of love through depth of consciousness. This involves telling a client exactly what you believe is in their best interests, and resolutely accepting their response. An example of clear direction to a repetitively battered wife might be, "I think it's best you find another place to live before he beats you again." Whether she finds another place or not, the therapist—never value free—has offered direction in service of her client's best interest. Another example to an unresolved masculine partner with a dissatisfied feminine lover might be, "I believe you need to dedicate yourself to opening your lover to feeling safer with you as a man, and to help her feel a deeper emotional and erotic claim than she's ever felt before."

Clients crave and resist direction.

Every experienced therapist knows that clients both crave and resist direction. I find that my clients only intermittently follow the directions I provide, but are always intensely interested in what I believe is in their best interests. I cheerfully offer any direction that might help remediate symptoms, enhance health, or support development, and then examine the results with interest, often in the session with my clients. Directions they choose to follow or not follow provide revealing access points to deeper understanding of them and their universes. For example, in the following exchange with Tom and Anne, we first process the directions they avoided, and then I offer new directions based on our conversation:

Tom: "We didn't follow any of your suggestions."

Anne: "We were bad."

Keith: I'm curious about what they remembered the directions to be, what they resisted, and what their experience might reveal to help me help them. "Well, well, well. This is interesting. What didn't you do?"

Tom: "We didn't lie down and breathe together. We didn't go out and have fun. I didn't compliment Anne more."

Anne: "I didn't focus on pleasure each day and I didn't hug Tom when I was glad to see him."

Keith: Laughing. "A perfect zero. What do you make of this?"

Tom: "I don't know what to make of it. We should have followed through."

Keith: "Why's that?"

Tom: "All the things you suggested are good things."

Anne: "I thought so too."

Keith: "What makes you believe they are good things to do?"

Anne: "They just feel right, and they make sense."

Keith: "So they seem like good things to do, and yet you didn't do them. Do you often avoid doing different things, especially with each other, that seem like valid activities?"

Tom: "I guess so. We should do them."

Keith: "What stops you, personally, Tom?"

Tom: "We were getting along much better, and I got busy with other stuff."

Anne: "This is the second week of school, and our son had lots of appointments."

Keith: "It sounds like it's much harder to be deliberately different around each other than either of you imagined."

Anne: "I think you're right. Nothing was going badly, so why mess with it?"

Tom: "Exactly."

Keith: I'm sensing an opportunity to surprise them, perhaps wake them up for a moment, to confront them with their power to be the authors of their futures. "If you had to pick one thing the other person could do differently that would make you feel the most loved, what would it be? It can be anything that we have discussed or something we haven't discussed."

Anne: "That Tom took responsibility for us holding each other and breathing together each night."

Tom: "That Anne smiled and hugged me when she was with me."

Keith: I Wait a few seconds to let this sink in. They are looking at each other with a little surprise. "What do you want to do with this information?"

Anne: "I want to smile and hug him. I want him to feel more loved. But I wanted to last week and didn't."

Tom: "Yeah, me too."

Keith: "You can do something about it."

Tom: He looks confused. "What do you mean?"

Keith: "Part of the reason Anne's often distrustful of you is that you can collapse and let her down like this. You have an opportunity here to give her something that will help her feel loved and help you feel strong and competent."

Tom: "I'll do the holding every day."

Keith: "I think you're offering too much. What if you forget one or two days? Then Anne will experience it as another collapse. I suggest you create the holding and breathing a minimum of three times before the next session. You could do more if you want."

Anne "I want to smile and hug him more."

Keith: I know Anne probably needs to practice showing pleasure in the body when she feels it before she can cultivate it in defensive states. "Especially when you feel good about him. An important component of feminine love through the body is showing him your love when you feel it."

Anne: "I think I'll remember this week."

Keith: I want them to feel accepted by me whether they follow my direction or not. "I'm looking forward to talking about whatever happens."

An infinity of directions.

There are endless directions that are potentially useful to clients. Healthy diet, healthy exercise, healthy rest, masculine and feminine practices, self support, gratitude exercises, social risks, professional risks, affirmations, self-confrontations, sexual practices, parenting practices, spiritual practices, service to others, journaling, dream exercises, and assertion exercises are common examples. Masters and Johnson had huge success with structured touching exercises leading to progressively more intimate and satisfying sexuality.[2] Behavior therapy is practically all direction.[3]

Some therapists refuse to give direction, preferring individuals and couples to simmer, boil, and explode into creating their own new perspectives and actions.[4] This is particularly useful in situations that don't lend themselves to compromise such as "You want another child and I don't," or "You want sex once a day and I want sex once a month," but can miss the real benefits of exploring clients' willingness/resistance to change and direction, and an emergent therapeutic relationship where everybody is transparent about what they believe best serves love and is in the highest good for all.

Since I am a more masculine, extroverted, revealing type of person, I tend to easily be actively transparent about what I believe is in my clients' best interests, and then process what arises. It sometimes requires effort for me to let my clients simmer without interruption when I discern that backing off best serves the moment. More feminine, introverted, or concealing types of therapists will naturally offer less direction, and need more effort to interrupt and direct. We adjust our responses to our client's state and type as we adjust our responses to be congruent with our own state and type. Each licensed therapist commits to offering a minimum of direction through the legal and ethical requirements of their license. Beyond that we develop our own natural discernment about what direction to offer that is congruent with who we are and what we believe best serves our clients in each moment of the session.

1. Witt (2007)

2. Masters (1970)

3. Lazarus (1976)

4. Schnarch (1997)

23

Tools

Therapists draw from a number of tools that empower and focus the work of relating, teaching, inspiring, confronting, interpreting, and directing. These tools provide organizing principles that can focus and guide us through the often messy and stormy ebbs and flows of the psychotherapy session. The following tools seem particularly important to me.

Love.

You love your client from your deepest heart and deepest consciousness. You love them through defensive states, habits of closure, and biases. You love them as deeply as the boundaries of health, professional responsibility, and personal capacity allow.

Humor.

We are all going to die. A hundred years from now, nothing we do, say, or experience is going to matter much, if at all, to anyone. Life is absurd and bizarre beyond belief, and we usually do best when we're enjoying it, and especially when we're entertained by the present moment. Your laughter with clients models humor, clear channels of emotion, and resolute acceptance of everything.

Integrity.

Living your principles, being true to your deepest sexual essences, and fulfilling your concept of your responsibilities as a therapist, spouse, friend, parent, family member, and human being is the best platform for supporting your clients to do the same.

Intent.

"Think always of the healing" is an adaptation of Myamoto Musashi's famous dictum for the Warrior, "Think always of the cutting." Ideally, each word, glance, tone, gesture, reference, and intervention in each session is informed by your intent to help your client in every way you can within your personal and professional parameters as a therapist.

Courage.

Courage is doing what you believe is best, even though you are afraid. Therapy sessions can involve moments which feel threatening to therapists. When feeling threatened, it often takes courage to say what must be said and do what must be done. We need to accompany our clients into the scary places they fear to go alone, and model for them how to inhabit those places artfully with grace and humor. Telling a wife she might lose her husband if she doesn't cultivate feminine radiance, telling an addict he will die if he doesn't break out of denial and embrace recovery, or going with a client into her most horrific trauma and inhabiting that place with compassion and depth of consciousness, all require us to practice courage as best we can. The beauty of courage as a practice is that it is a learned skill. As we direct ourselves to do what we believe serves the highest good—independent of how frightened we are—we tend to become progressively more courageous.

Knowledge.

Dedicating ourselves to the calling of psychotherapy means dedicating ourselves to a lifetime of self-discovery, emotional, spiritual, and relational growth, and endless study. Each therapist has his or her own limitations, but we also each have our own expanding breadth of knowledge and experience that we bring to bear in each session. It's important to be aware of our limitations, but it's more important to be aware of the gifts we offer from our dedication and study to help our clients remediate symptoms, enhance health, and support development.

Conclusion.

In this section we took core concepts of psychotherapy and expanded them. We explored the therapist's mission of cultivating compassion and depth of consciousness to support healthy perspectives and actions, and examined a variety of practical examples of co-creating healing cultures with clients. We examined therapy's goals of remediating symptoms, enhancing health, and supporting development, and therapy's process of relating, teaching, inspiring, confronting, interpreting, and directing.

In the next Section we'll more deeply explore developmental lines and levels, and how the knowledge we discover there can be used to help us and our clients heal and thrive.

Section Five

Lines and Levels

24

Thinking Developmentally

A typical workday for me begins at 9:00 AM and ends at 7:30 PM. During that time I might see a forty-five year old housewife, a sixteen year old cheerleader, a couple in their early twenties with a newborn and two other kids under five, a mother of eleven-year-old twins, a married seventy-year-old college professor, a single homosexual man in his thirties, a couple in their forties with adult kids in college, and a single fifty-three year old realtor. This group will be primarily Anglo-American, but can include Afro-Americans, South Africans, Latinos, Canadians, Asians, or Europeans.

All of these people, their children, their families, and their friends occupy different levels on different developmental lines; levels that shift regularly depending on center of gravity, defensive states, and peak experiences.

It's a good idea for me to be able to think and speak developmentally.

Evolutionary Psychology

Phylogenetically, evolutionary psychology helps us understand, normalize, and address a variety of vital issues with our clients. Humans developed from hunter-gatherer groups that functioned as biological colony organisms in the wild. To this day, forager indigenous cultures reveal to us the peculiar strengths, weaknesses, and predispositions of such groups. Jean Liedoff in *The Continuum Concept[1]*, and Thom Hartmann in *The Edison Gene[2]* describe tribal societies who engage in group childrearing where there is minimum stress on individual mothers and phenomenal adaptability of children of all ages to the tribe's social and physical environments. Societal and gender roles are naturally presented and inhabited on all levels, supported by daily ceremonies and spiritual practices that balance interpersonal energies and maintain and strengthen connections to nature. Individuals in these cultures occasionally have peak post-post-formal operational cognitive experiences (genuine psychic abilities) that are accepted and normalized by the tribe.

Clearly, a tribal context is potentially strong in supporting parenting, nature mysticism, and secure development into gender and other roles.

On the other hand, it's important to not romanticize indigenous hunter-gatherer cultures (or any culture). Individuals from such tribes tend to be enormously less able to adapt to different cultures than individuals raised in the current western nuclear family model. The hunter-gatherer center of gravity is usually PURPLE/tribal. Most such tribes tend to function like single entities, much less able to adapt to changed circumstances than individual human beings. History has demonstrated repetitively that power-God RED, fundamentalist BLUE, and capitalist ORANGE cultures encroach, exploit, and supplant hunter-gatherers. Further, indigenous peoples tested least altruistic in altruism studies and are usually deeply ethnocentric, with different words for "human being" (a member of our tribe) and "person other than human being" (someone outside our tribe).

The genetic level of sexuality.

According to some anthropological geneticists, human evolution accelerated to one hundred times its historic rate with the advent of agriculture forty thousand years ago.[3] Not only are humans still *genetically* evolving, but we are evolving at a tremendously accelerated rate compared to other mammals. This does not even take into account the cultural evolutionary processes that have also been accelerating throughout human history to the point where, in our current cultures, we are seeing social/technological shifts in a few years that previously took centuries.[4]

Evolutionary anthropologists ascribe accelerated genetic evolution to the effects of disease and diet on large, stable populations. I believe consciousness itself has been a huge influence on human evolution, since various cultures and individual humans have consciously directed human reproductive patterns over generations, potentially causing significant effects on gene pools.

In human relationships, the above raises questions of how attraction, sexual functioning, fidelity, and infidelity might have developed from genetic imperatives in hunter-gatherer groups to their myriad expressions in modern societies. David Deida calls this the genetic level of sexuality.[5]

From an evolutionary standpoint, the central question is, "What characteristics optimize chances of successfully passing genes on to the next generation?" The slightest advantage amplifies over generations into genetic imperatives. Let's examine some possible characteristics that might impart advantage in passing genes onward:

- Men who could better choose healthy young women, claim them, and protect/support them through childrearing would have an advantage.

- Women who better attracted alpha males to both impregnate them and claim them would have an advantage.

- Women who more easily affiliated with, and mutually supported, other women would have an advantage.

- Men who better practiced obligate jealousy, the refusal to allow their women to have sex with other men, would have an advantage.

- A woman who practiced discriminative jealousy, preventing another woman from romantically/emotionally bonding with her mate, would have an advantage.

- Men who could have indiscriminant sex without risking their lives (rape or secret liaisons are two possible examples) would have an advantage.

- Women who had secret liaisons with high status males (but not low status males) would have an advantage.

- Quick orgasm would give a reproductive edge to a man, but not necessarily to a woman.

- A woman being able to sustain prolonged sexual ecstasy (which is highly arousing to a man, valuable to a man, and would potentially keep him around and evoke more and quicker orgasms) would have an advantage.

- A group that had felt responsibility for shared childrearing, and thus constantly supported young mothers and their children, would have an advantage.[6]

How can principles like the ones postulated above help in psychotherapy? One example is in understanding how modern western childrearing exhausts women because it does not recapitulate the genetic template of tribal existence. Marilyn, an otherwise healthy woman in her early thirties, walks into my office looking like Count Dracula has been draining her blood each night for the last week:

Keith: "Do you have children under five?"

Marilyn: Surprised. "Why yes, I have a one-year-old and a four-year-old. Why do you ask?"

Keith: "Because you look tired and drained. This culture does not optimally support mothers raising small children. Small children are genetically programmed to hunger for a tribal context, and, since you love your children so much, you unconsciously are probably trying to provide that mostly by yourself, and are being exhausted by the effort."

Marilyn: "Thank God! I thought I was exhausted because I'm just not a very natural mother."

Later in the session, evolutionary psychology again provides an opportunity to help:

Marilyn: "My husband uses pornography, looks at other women, and really likes the babes on T.V. I hate it."

Keith: "Studies have shown that men tend to be more visual erotically, and are drawn to the feminine shape. Women tend to be more relational and are drawn more to a successful, well-connected masculine presence.[7] In the hunter-gatherer societies we evolved from, men who went after the feminine shape when they saw it had a reproductive advantage over men who didn't. Women who attracted, and were attracted to, the alpha males had a reproductive advantage. Most men now share these hard-wired tendencies. The ones who had less of these tendencies just couldn't compete in the long run."

Marilyn: "I still hate it."

Keith: "Of course you do. Women who blocked their men from sexually bonding with other women had a reproductive advantage. If your husband is not suffering from some form of sexual compulsive disorder, I'm sure there are ways you and he can connect, or behaviors you can accept, that can ease your suffering. It's just that he'll still have a biological tendency to be attracted to the feminine shape."

The evolutionary perspective helps normalize behaviors while supporting possibilities for health, development, and reduced suffering. Knowing genetically driven, biological foundations of feelings, thoughts, and impulses gives therapists non-judgmental language and interventions that can guide us to what might be possible and realistic (Marilyn's husband not staring rudely at other women), and what might not (her husband actually having no interest in looking at other women).

The last two decades have produced wonderful research on attraction and affiliation. How do you imagine the following data could be explained by evolutionary psychology?

- When presented with the smells of infants' receiving blankets, men's testosterone levels go down and oxytocin and estrogen levels go up. Testosterone has been associated with aggression and competition. Oxytocin and estrogen have been associated with affiliation and bonding.

- Men who experience themselves as alpha males (high status, or winners) tend to have higher testosterone levels than men who don't.

- A nursing mother's testosterone/estrogen ratio is less than a non-nursing mother, resulting in less libido for the nursing mother, and thus more attention for—and attachment to—her vulnerable infant.

- Couples caught up in romantic infatuation have more highly activated dopamine/norepinephrine brain systems associated with pleasure and thrill seeking. Couples in long-term commitments who have passed through romantic infatuation have more highly activated oxytocin/vasopressin systems associated with bonding.[8]

Biology is not destiny.

Of course, biology is not destiny, but knowing and teaching our biological predispositions, their possible evolutionary roots, and how they need to be included (not denied or repressed) in supporting love, passion, and health, add valuable perspectives to therapy. Issues such as jealousy, sexual attraction, different relating styles of men and women, fidelity, and most taboos can be addressed with more value free language, and less moral condemnation.

Individual Development

Ontogenetically, we all start at the bottom of each developmental line, and grow upward through the same levels, never skipping levels, with each level including and transcending previous levels. In what Robert Kegan calls the dialectic of development, each level presents both enhanced function and the advantages of wider perspectives, but also new risks of developmental arrest and pathology[9] (which set the stage for new symptoms, new defensive states, and new forms of regression under perceived stress).

Certainly, we are born with advantages and disadvantages. Research has demonstrated that we have genetic and congenital effects on our temperaments. At birth we have more or less tendencies towards harm avoidance, novelty seeking, dependence, cooperativeness, persistence, self-transcendence, self-directedness, and emotional reactivity.[10] Some of us are more shy, and some of us are more extroverted. Some of us are more anxious, and some of us are more sanguine. Some of us are more gifted in math, and some of us are more gifted in languages. Some of us are more prone to depression, and some of us are more prone to light-heartedness.

Human development is very much a call and response process. Our various temperaments call out differently for different environmental elements as we grow through developmental levels on a variety of lines. Research overwhelmingly supports the superiority of stable, contingent, caring, enriched social and physical environments for maximizing development, and creating secure attachment in important relationships.[11] These environments provide the widest range of supportive responses to the varying yearnings and needs of each human for affirmation, affiliation, social position, boundaries, and meaning making.

Psychotherapy resolves blocks to development.

Psychotherapy is often about helping clients resolve blocks to growth, health, and love. Defensive patterns, both individual and relational, almost always involve some form of developmental arrest; regression under perceived threat to primitive patterns of self-protection, usually egocentric, and usually with roots in the alchemy of our biophysiological nature shaped by our ongoing experience.

In the following exchange with Tom and Anne, you can track the subjective level of maturity of their responses. Both are highly educated, psychologically sophisticated, mature adults, and yet there is an immature, childlike feel to their defensive states. This is defensive regression in action:

Anne: "You came home and used a pissy tone when I said I couldn't drive Linda to school tomorrow."

Tom: "All I did was ask . When you said 'no,' I said 'OK'."

Anne: "Then you were pissy all night."

Tom: "So were you."

Keith: "How did this resolve?"

Anne: "On Sunday he asked me how I was. I told him he was using a mean tone, and he changed it."

Keith: "Is that accurate to you, Tom?"

Tom: "Yes, then we felt better."

Keith: "So, Anne, when you told him you didn't like his tone, and when you, Tom, instead of defending, softened you tone, Anne relaxed and felt loved. When Anne showed you her affection, you relaxed and felt better."

Both: "Yes."

Keith: "Anne, it seems that you want more warm tones and affection from Tom."

Anne: She bursts into tears and speaks with childlike protest. "He only does it to placate me. He doesn't mean it like he used to."

Tom: His voice is plaintive. "What about when you walked into work last week and I was glad to see you? It's too much with the kid, your job, and my job. We don't have enough time for anything anymore."

Anne: Looking at me, not looking at Tom, she speaks in a despairing tone. "See, all he does is get mad." Tom, visibly frustrated, looks out the window.

Regressed Tom doesn't understand that his habit of defending and rationalizing shuts Anne down. Regressed Anne doesn't understand that under stress her distorted beliefs about not being loved by Tom cause her to over-interpret his temporary collapses and habits of closure into not really loving her. Neither of them consciously noticed in the exchange how they temporarily matured, and then swooped down into regressed, immature defensive states. As I notice these things, I can first emphasize relating, confronting, interpreting, and directing to help them through their defenses to states of healing response, and then emphasize relating, teaching, and inspiring them to love. As I engage in this, I'm modeling for both of them how to reach for more compassionate perspectives and more loving actions:

Keith: "You both were in loving connection, and then you regressed. Tom, you get insulted by her anger and then defend and counterattack. Never diminish her pain. Challenge her by loving her. Try saying in a loving way, 'I'm sorry I used a hostile tone.' Anne, when you're distressed, you resist accepting that Tom loves you and is working at loving you better. He's loving you right now. Look at him; do you see?"

Anne: "I see him trying."

Keith: "And does it please you to see his effort?"

Anne: "Yes."

Tom: Touched by her warmth. "That's all I want sweetheart; for you to know how much I love you."

Keith: Confronting Anne through Tom. "It's important for you, Tom, to realize what courage it takes for her to show you her pleasure when she has recently felt wounded."

Anne: "It is hard."

Keith: "Is it worth it?"

Anne: "Of course it is."

Decreasing insight and empathy co-vary with magnitude of developmental arrest.

What level of developmental arrest a defensive structure entails is reflected by the amount of insight your client can have about their defensive states, and, in relation to intimate partners, the extent to which they can maintain an empathetic sense of their partner when distressed. In this session, Tom has some capacity for insight and empathy when defended, reflecting neurotic defensive structures. Anne has practically no capacity for insight and empathy when defended, reflecting more characterological defenses. We'll deal with neurotic and characterological defenses more extensively in Section Six.

Couples have complementary defenses.

Since we tend to choose our reciprocal[12] and unconsciously harmonize our relationships around each other's strengths and weaknesses, there will almost always be a complementary response in one partner to regression in the other. One of the advantages of working with a couple is that one partner can be indirectly affected while witnessing the therapist working with the other partner. In the above example, stressed Tom has resistance to using a loving tone and more tendencies to using hostile tones than he consciously realizes. Encouraging Anne to request and expect a loving tone will create situations where he can discover his resistance to using it when he's mad. It also confronts Anne with how difficult it is for her to be different and ask for a different tone instead of surrendering to her destructive impulses to attack or withdraw when she's caught in a defensive state.

Speaking developmentally is likely to encourage self-soothing and disidentification with defenses.

Thinking and talking developmentally is often soothing to clients, and tends to evoke mature, caring, healthy responses to the present moment. In conjoint sessions, partners who regress easily when discussing their relationship will often act more mature when discussing their personal development, and parents tend to become more mature and cooperative when talking developmentally about their children.

I tell parents that I conceptualize a family as a culture where everyone is developing and everyone has issues they're working on to be healthier and to love better. This has the dual value of helping clients be more flexible parents and further normalizing and supporting the idea that healthy people are not issue free, but rather are aware individuals who can be curious about and responsible for their current issues, and who can be committed to a lifetime of growth and self-discovery.

The Self-line

The chart on the following pages is one that I use in most of the classes I teach. In *Integral Psychology*, Ken Wilber has many charts like this one from all kinds of developmental perspectives[13]. The self-line, cognition line, sexual/interpersonal lines, and moral line, are particularly relevant to individual and conjoint psychotherapy. The F-0 to F-9 represents Wilber's fulcrums of development of the self-line.

The "self" is the "I" that looks out my eyes. The self-line is composed of two aspects. Subjectively to me, my self feels like the same person I was at three, five, twelve, forty-two, and fifty-four. I suspect that this subjective self involves unconscious identification with the unchanging, unrecoiling, ever-present witness, which can be considered the pure masculine principle. Objectively, this self includes worldviews, cognitive capacities, and interpersonal, sexual, and moral perspectives that have changed dramatically as I've matured. This constant change in the richness of the world can be considered the pure feminine principle. Together they constitute the self-line of development.

SELF			COGNITION
F-9	Coral		**LINES &**
Transpersonal			Include and
	Turqouise		Post-Post-Formal Operational
F-8			
Integral	Yellow		
F-7			Post-Formal Operational
F-6			
Pluralistic	Green		
F-5			
Rational	Orange		Formal Operational
12 years and up			
F-4			
Conformist	Blue		Concrete Operational
7–12 years			
F-3	Red		
Egocentric	Purple		Pre-Operational
6 months – 7 years			
F-2			
Archaic	Beige		Sensorimotor
F-1 0–6 months			
F-0			

SELF   **COGNITION**

Ken Wilbur   Jean Piaget
Clare Graves
Don Beck

LEVELS

Transcend

	Integrated Care and Rights

Third Stage

- Give best gifts to the world
- Be true to deepest masculine or feminine essence
- Open each moment
- Give gift of radiant love
- We are here to serve

Universal Care   Universal Rights

Second Stage

- Communication is the religion of the second stage
- Egalitarian
- Denies shadow
- Boundaries / Safety

Care   Rights

First Stage

- Egocentric
- It's all about me

Selfish

Feminine ↑ Masculine   Feminine ↑ Masculine

Relational Focus   Hierarchical Focus

SEXUAL INTERPERSONAL   MORAL

David Deida   Carol Gilligan

1. Liedloff (1975)

2. Hartmann (2003)

3. Kaplan (2007)

4. Toffler (1970)

5. Deida (2004)

6. *Ibid*

7. Fisher (2007)

8. Fisher (2004)

9. Kegan (1982)

10. Cloniger (2004)

11. Siegel (1999)

12. Deida (2004)

13. Wilber (2000)

25

Meaning Making

Robert Kegan in *The Evolving Self* suggests that the instinct to create meaning drives human development.[1] We create meaning with a progressive series of compromises in the tensions that inevitably arise between our current worldview and ongoing experience. His research demonstrates how we fuse with our perceptions of the current culture in which we are embedded, how we differentiate as we "fill up" and press against—and ultimately through—the edges of our current worldview, and how we re-integrate into a new worldview where we often regard our past selves as objects of our current self's attention. Especially through early development, the cultures we are embedded in revolve mainly around our family.

Fusion with our perceptions of the environment and the evolutionary truce.

Our perceptions of the environment are constructed of a fusion between our current worldview and sense of self, and the actual stimuli entering our senses. The parameters of this fusion are defined by our physical, cognitive, psycho-emotional, spiritual, and social capacities, and the physical/social environments (or cultures) we are embedded in.

Many believe that infants in the womb experience oneness with the entire universe in the sense that there is no differentiation between self and environment. By around six or seven months, children demonstrate awareness that there is a difference between self and the physical world. Children can observe that their body is separate from other features in the environment. Now there is a subject (body/self), and object (everything else).

Kegan calls this interface between subject and object an "evolutionary truce." The world presses in and our instincts to create meaning press out, resulting in our current worldview, our current evolutionary truce or equilibrium. It is a "truce" because, as we expand into this worldview, it eventually proves inadequate to process our deepening capacities and understandings, and we are drawn

233

to separate, differentiate from it, and reintegrate (fuse) into a new, more satisfying evolutionary truce. Kegan postulates six primary stages of development:

- **Incorporative Stage:** Beginning with infant becoming toddler and absorbing the world through all senses.

- **Impulsive Stage:** Progressing to more mature attachment, rivalry, and fantasy in the growth from toddler to small child.

- **Imperial Stage:** Hungering to inhabit roles, explore interests, and feel membership with family and school in the growth from younger child to older child.

- **Interpersonal Stage:** Finding one-to-one intimate relationships progressively more compelling in the growth from older child to adolescent.

- **Institutional Stage:** Becoming an independent adult with corresponding hungers for adult identity, career identity, and long term relationships.

- **Inter-Individual Stage:** Interior integration of self-systems accompanies the capacities for greater self-understanding and deep, interdependent, intimate relationships.[2]

Kegan believes that the innate human drive to create meaning is a fundamental force propelling us through developmental levels. In what he calls, "The dialectic of progress," he asserts that with each ascending level we have new capacities for understanding, and also new possibilities for pathology, distortion, and developmental arrest.

I agree that the drive to create meaning is a fundamental evolutionary force, but I also believe that our human needs to relate, be true to our deepest sexual essences, and to establish position on social hierarchies are also fundamental evolutionary driving forces. Several reflections of this are:

- Autism, a widely researched pervasive developmental disorder, involves a dramatically reduced interest in relating, which cripples relational, cognitive, moral, and values development.

- In Section Three we explored the omnipresent nature and importance of sexual essence.

- Almost every human in every society tends to seek and maintain positions on a variety of social hierarchies.

As we'll explore in this chapter, the instinct to create meaning, the hunger for deeper relatedness with others, the drive to be true to our deepest sexual essences, and striving to inhabit positions on social hierarchies propel us through developmental levels on many lines—especially on the self-line.

The subject becomes the object of the new subject.

Two major aspects of self are the unchanging "I" who subjectively stays the same from birth to death, and the constantly changing "I" whose values, beliefs, perceptions, and identifications are always in flux. A eight-year-old boy, whose center of gravity is the imperial stage (conformist/BLUE), identifies with his roles of family member, school member, team member, and temple/church member. He accepts the rules and roles of these memberships and unconsciously experiences his "self" ("I" the "subject" of his life) as someone who is embedded in—fused with, at one with—these cultures. The meaning he creates is consistent with the rules/roles of these cultures.

At eighteen, this boy has likely entered Kegan's institutional stage. He can now experience formal operational cognitive processes and more mature relating. He can reevaluate his worldviews and deepen into a "self" that has wider identifications with other groups, institutions, and value systems. He might reevaluate associations and identifications with family, school, team, or temple/church, and experience himself as a different person, with different understandings, than the eight-year-old he once was. That eight-year-old that used to be the subject ("I") is now the object ("he") of the new, eighteen-year-old "I" (the new subject).

When discussing his eight-year-old values, identifications, and understandings, this eighteen-year-old might speak in the third person ("he") as if that eight-year-old was another person. The subject becomes the object of the new subject.

Daryl encounters the second tier.

How can such information be useful in therapy? Consider the following exchange with Daryl, a 57-year-old man. Daryl's profession of consultant to a number of very wealthy and powerful people had historically involved being unable to say "no" to most of them:

> Daryl: "I did some things that I haven't done before. I was offered a job with this guy who screwed me twice twenty years ago, and I said 'no.' I decided that, when I talked to him, it wasn't going to degenerate into 'fuck you.' I supported his request, reminded him of the best work we had done together, said I couldn't sign on, and wished him good luck."
>
> Keith: "This feels healthy and right to me. You said there were other 'things.'"

Daryl: "I asked our local carpenter for a bid, and told him my maximum amount of money I was willing to spend on the project. He was a little hurt, but I told him I needed to be clear. Another thing I did two days ago was sit on the deathbed of my friend Dave. I talked to him and kept him company all afternoon. I couldn't do that when my mother died, my sister died, or my best friend Bob died."

Keith: "Sounds like you are a somewhat different person now."

Daryl: "What's really strange is that my wife, Sally, was in Puerto Rico. I've always thought it was Sally who gave me what little strength I had to do stuff like this."

Keith: Interpreting. "You're reminding me of something Robert Kegan describes in *The Evolving Self.* He says that emotional wounds we experience as small children can lead to needing others' approval to feel we exist. Your mother gave you great warmth unless you challenged or disagreed with her. Then she cut it off, so to speak." We both laugh.

"This kind of relationship can lead kids to need the subjective sense of acceptance and approval from whomever they're with to feel they exist. Nobody wants to risk their sense of existence to make assertions. But, if you grow and anchor your sense of self as legitimate and worthwhile, you can stand up for principle in the face of disapproval. Now you look back and say, 'I used to have to agree—to not offend—to try to avoid emotional pain. Now I can disagree, feel pain, or say 'no,' if my principles direct me to, even without the presence of Sally.' You are a new 'I' looking back at the old Daryl who is now 'he'. This is development. The previous subject—the old 'I,'—of one developmental level, becomes the object—the 'he'—of our new developmental level, the new 'I.' How does it feel?"

Daryl: "If feels wonderful. It makes sense. I really used to feel that some huge catastrophe would descend if anybody got mad at me or was disappointed. I'm not nearly as scared as I used to be."

The diminishment of fear, and the felt appreciation for multiple worldviews that Daryl is exhibiting in this exchange are emblematic of the shift to what Clare Graves calls the second tier, YELLOW in the Spiral Dynamics system, a TEAL altitude on the self-line in Wilber's Integral Operating System. As we keep growing, these shifts are eventually not just peak experiences we have in extraordinary circumstances. They become our most typical way of behaving and responding to the world. States of enhanced functioning in one worldview become traits of a new worldview. The subject (the "I") of the previous worldview becomes the object (the "he") of the current worldview.

1. Kegan (1982)

2. *Ibid*

26

Developmental Fulcrums

There are dozens of developmental systems, generated and supported by the research of hundreds of scientists. Some theorists, like Piaget, emphasize cognitive development. Others, like Kolhberg and Gilligan, emphasize moral development, and some, like Erickson and Kegan, focus on psychosocial development. Wilber, Fowler, Almaas and others are interested in spiritual development. All have their own stages, principles, and characteristics. All reflect the include and transcend rhythm of development.[1] How can we consider these systems collectively, and how can we use them to support psychotherapy?

Ken Wilber has integrated Kegan's concepts of progressive developmental truces in response to the instinctive human drive to create meaning, with a number of developmental systems and lines in his Fulcrum 0 to Fulcrum 9 formulation.

The concept of fulcrums is particularly elegant in the glop and slop of development, because people don't make developmental shifts instantaneously or discretely. Instead, we hold our most natural, current worldview roughly fifty percent of the time, more primitive regressive worldviews around twenty-five percent of the time, and progressive worldviews around twenty-five percent of the time. As our life conditions, defensive structures, and consciousness dictate, we move forward and back from one to the other, but, as we grow and expand to fill up our current worldview, we change the amount of time we inhabit each, until the fulcrum tips, and we are naturally spending significantly more time in a new balance; a balance where a former progressive worldview is now our most current, dominant worldview, and our peak experiences include higher levels than before. Where we spent twenty-five percent of our time, we now spend fifty percent of our time. What was once superior functioning is now our more normal way of being. This shift creates a subtly new sense of self. A new evolutionary truce has been established between the self—or selves—that assign meaning, and our subjective universe.[2]

Fuse, differentiate, reintegrate.

We fuse with the current worldview, differentiate as it proves increasingly inadequate to contain and support our expanding consciousness/experience, and re-integrate new perspectives into an expanded worldview we can explore as we become fused with it, flowing naturally into repeating the process again and again—ascending spirals of development. We include and transcend into new worldviews.[3]

As we grow, we can have peak experiences of vastly enhanced functioning or regressive lapses into old ways of being and understanding. We can change worldviews momentarily and also change our center of gravity of the worldview that feels most natural to us when we're most relaxed and open. We never lose our capacity for any previous way of being, or our potential for transcendent peak experiences.

Culture pulls us up, and then holds us down.

Spiral Dynamics has observed that the center of gravity of the culture in which we are embedded (the sum total of beliefs, understandings, and shared perspectives) will first pull us up towards that center, but then slow us down as we are moved to grow further. For example, on the moral line, an infant girl embedded in the culture of a devout religious family will probably, by late childhood, have a moral center of gravity that mirrors her family's beliefs. If, as she matures, she differentiates from those beliefs and begins to reintegrate into a more relativistic, flexible moral structure, her family and religious community might protest and resist in a variety of obvious and subtle ways. Her emerging differences might alarm and threaten them, and thus cue critical judgments and coercive maneuvers designed to "bring her back into the fold."

American academic culture tends to pull students up into disciplined, formal operational cognitive capacities. "What if" thinking, being able to assume the role of other, and Aristotelian logic applied to concepts as well as concrete objects tends to be the norm, and there is academic and social pressure to inhabit this norm. Post-formal and post-post-formal cognitive processes, where intuition and true trans-rational abilities are integrated into an individual's cognitive style, can be met, systemically, by incomprehension, suspicion, or outright hostility. This discourages cognitive growth in that direction.

"How did you do this?"

In 1970, a colleague of mine named Carrie Ramey worked as a graduate assistant for a Physics professor. One day he left a problem he was working on written in chalk on his office blackboard. Carrie walked into the room, glanced at the problem, and impulsively scribbled an equation under it. The professor incredulously examined the equation, meticulously checked it against the problem, and realized it was the solution he had been seeking. He spent the next hour browbeating Carrie until she was helplessly weeping, trying to extract from her how she had arrived at the solution. "It just felt right," was not a satisfactory answer for him. It enraged him that he couldn't understand the processes she had accessed to solve the problem, and essentially punished her for engaging in what was clearly postformal operational functioning.

Carl Jung observed that, if an individual becomes "inflated" (very different from) the collective, the collective will tend to pull that person down.[4] Since the principle of "greater depth, less span" is true for every developmental line, the higher someone ascends on any line, the fewer people there will be at that level. Thus, the higher we ascend on any developmental line, the less support and understanding, and the more resistance, we are likely to experience from the collective.

Allen and Evalyn

The lines and levels chart at the end of Chapter 24 shows a variety of roughly corresponding levels on different lines of development. An extraordinary aspect about such lines is that they exist as similar potentials in all human beings, relatively independent of culture, and all humans progress through the same levels as they ascend these lines.

On the other hand, different cultures have different percentages of citizens who are higher or lower on different lines, demonstrating how different life conditions evoke different depth (or altitude) on different lines as each person matures in each culture. The miracle of human consciousness is such that differences in levels within cultures are usually far greater than differences in levels between cultures.[5]

Let's follow fraternal twins, Allen and Evalyn, from in utero onward through their lives. As I delineate Allen and Evalyn's development, it's useful to remember that both have masculine and feminine developmental lines, though the masculine line will be more central and important to Allen, and the feminine line more central and important to Evalyn. Both are capable of all the reactions, desires, feelings, thoughts, and impulses of the human experience. My descriptions mostly reflect statistical data about how most boys and girls develop. Some boys enjoy wearing dresses, but most do not. Some girls are more drawn to violence and meaning at the edge of death than to caring and relationships, but most are not.

In therapy it's useful to honor the fact that statistical tendencies exist to guide our understanding. It's also useful to remember that any person can occupy any spot on most lines, including inhabiting any position on the masculine/feminine continuum, at any time. Such awareness helps us acknowledge and honor each client's idiosyncratic nature, deepest sexual essence, and yearning to be true to their unique constellation of drives, principles, needs, and current worldviews.

Developmentally informed parenting.

Development by necessity involves conflict. Children often discover the world by pushing into it until boundaries (often from environmental limitations including parents) push back. Children and parents largely inhabit different worldviews through much of a child's development, and different worldviews invariably lead to conflict in the first tier (tribal/PURPLE, to power-God/RED, to conformist/BLUE, to rational/ORANGE, to pluralistic/GREEN). Conflict is usually stressful. If conflicts are handled by parents who regress under stress into defensive states, there is more risk of creating disease and/or varying levels of developmental arrest in children. For example, one study showed that seventy percent of American mothers spanked their toddlers.[6] The statistic is strikingly at odds (pun intended) with the current, widely held belief that corporal punishment is generally bad for children. When I've asked parents how they've felt when they're spanking their kids, they often give some version of the following exchange:

Mother: "I couldn't take it anymore, so I lost it and spanked him. Not real hard, but he knew I was mad."

Keith: "What couldn't you take?"

Mother: "He just seemed to be asking for it. I told him to not hit his brother, and then he did it right in front of me! I just got so mad I grabbed him and spanked him and shouted, 'No, bad boy! That's a nasty, rotten thing to do!'"

Keith: "How did he react?"

Mother: "He started screaming, so I put him in his room and he finally calmed down."

Toddlers occupy what Kegan calls the incorporative stage of development—roughly corresponding to BEIGE and PURPLE in Spiral Dynamics. They are egocentric, impulsive, and demanding, and often require physical limits (such as restraint, time outs, and otherwise losing control of their body or immediate physical environment). They can push boundaries with verbal and physical demands until they are externally controlled. Conformist, rational, or pluralistic parents, usually fatigued from raising small children in the exhausting, non-tribal, child-centered manner that's currently typical of much American child-rearing, are stressed and often offended by their toddler's egocentric verbal and physical demands. They are hurt by the obvious lack of empathy and apparent selfishness they see in their children. Under these stresses, parents can have impulses to regress to power-God and conformist worldviews. They can become dictatorial power-Gods, or self-righteous moralists who establish dominance the way power-Gods and self-righteous moralists have always established dominance, through the threat and presence of physical intimidation and by moral condemnation.

A developmentally informed mother observes this dynamic constellating between herself and her toddler, and has access to less alarmed and defensive interventions. The child in the above example still receives physical limits for striking his brother (he might be restrained, or given a time-out, or even spanked), but without the regressive rage or global moral condemnation that accompanied the previous spanking. She might say, "It's wrong, and against the rules, to hit your brother. That's why you're getting a time out." She still feels the *impulse* to regress, and still needs to set a physical boundary and deliver a moral lesson, but she normalizes the exchange and is less offended and outraged. She has access to a more mature and compassionate response that answers her child's need for a power-God and moral arbiter, but is a wiser, more compassionate power-God, and a less condemning, self-righteous moral arbiter.

All mammals share a social development system that involves toddlers' nervous systems going into parasympathetic collapse in response to caregivers' non-verbal signals of disapproval (with the accompanying subjective experiences of shame emotions). Human toddlers can be externally regulated back to happy sympathetic arousal by the loving touch and gaze of a caregiver, having had their nervous systems conditioned by *social learning*. Approval generates happy sympathetic arousal and positively reinforces what is approved of. Disapproval generates painful parasympathetic collapse and punishes what is disapproved of. Thus parents need to judiciously utilize approval and disapproval to insure healthy development and, *by modeling compassionate and reasonable approval/disapproval*, set the stage for the child to learn effective self-regulation as her nervous system becomes progressively more capable.

This social learning system is turbocharged with the advent of conscious self-awareness in the past/present/future, which starts coming on line around two. Now the child can approve/disapprove of herself in the past/present future. *She can condition her own nervous system.* Thus our interior, lower left quadrant, "good," moral/cultural sense is established and developed throughout life, in conjunction with our interior sense of approval/disapproval, and our social experiences of approval/disapproval.[7]

Since children can't self regulate the shame emotions associated with parasympathetic collapse, they instinctively maneuver to avoid them using emergent capacities to manipulate attention and concepts to create defensive habits of suppression, repression, projection, denial, and the plethora of defensive strategies observed by Freud and others. While children are relatively immature cognitively (sensory motor through much of concrete operational), they need primarily external regulation for defensive patterns and states in the form of boundaries from caregivers and rules and roles they learn to follow to feel "good." As they become formal operational they can become significantly more adept at self-regulation using insight, empathy, and self-awareness capacities that usually accompany such cognitive development.[8]

FULCRUM 0

Allen and Evalyn are conceived and born: Fulcrum 0.

In Fulcrum 0, the children are in utero, fused with their mother's body, differentiating into the outer world at birth, and integrating the universe outside the womb with their sense of self.

Cognitively, we know that there is brain activity in fetuses.[9] How this is subjectively experienced we can only speculate. Much of Allen's and Evalyn's temperament is already set before birth genetically and congenitally by the interplay of their genes and the relative health and well being of their mother's body (which is functionally their body until birth). They will be born more with more or less novelty seeking, harm avoidance, persistence, cooperativeness, self-directedness, self-transcendence, and emotional reactivity.[10]

There are a number of aspects of the birth experience itself, which can have far ranging effects on physiology and temperament. Oxygen deprivation, brain trauma, and viral infection have all been associated with developmental problems. Some psychoanalytic theorists and pre and perinatal researchers have found that the nature of the birth experience itself as well as parental thoughts and attitudes during pregnancy can affect personality development.[11]

Allen, born to crave freedom.

Sexually, XY Allen is already programmed to grow to be aggressive, hungry for deep soul's purpose, and sexually attracted to the feminine shape and feminine radiance. He's likely to grow morally with more emphasis on rights than on care, and think more hierarchically than relationally. Erotically he will seek to penetrate and crave emptiness. He will probably suffer without deep soul's purpose and feminine radiance, and feel blissful if he has purpose, can effectively claim feminine radiance, and can experience himself as high on personally important hierarchies. Allen will tend to be more naturally drawn to spirituality that is ascending, many into one, involving austerity and solitary spiritual practices, and will probably seek some form of meaning at the edge of death in competition, sports, or direct or vicarious violent striving.

Evalyn, born to yearn for love.

Sexually, XX Evalyn is already programmed to be less aggressive, hungrier for fulfilling love relationships, and more sexually attracted to trustable, high status, socially connected masculine partners. Evalyn will probably grow morally with more emphasis on care than on rights, and will think more relationally than hierarchically. Erotically, she will probably yearn to be known and claimed by a trustable masculine partner, and to be penetrated energetically and physically to a sense of fullness. Evalyn will probably suffer without the experience of love being served in her life, or by the absence of a trustable masculine partner to claim her emotionally, spiritually, and erotically. She will feel more blissful if she experiences herself as radiant (seen as light and beauty that shines and dazzles in socially appropriate ways) and as a wellspring of love that attracts the masculine. It will likely feel beautiful and good to her to be able to offer devotional love to a trustable masculine presence, and spread care and love into the world. Evalyn will probably be more naturally drawn to spirituality that is descending, one into many, involving pleasure, music, dance, community, and children. She will likely be nourished by pleasure in the body, and suffer emotionally and physically if denied it.

Genetic and pre-natal roots of pathology.

At birth, Allen and Evalyn are already predisposed to certain strengths and weaknesses, successes and pathologies. Schizophrenia, depression, bipolar disorder, anxiety disorders, autism, ADHD, addiction, as well as susceptibility to a number of other illnesses including heart disease and many forms of cancer all often have genetic components. Many of these problems can be prevented, ameliorated, or remediated, by the life conditions Allen and Evalyn encounter after birth, and increasingly as they develop, by the decisions they make using their human gifts of self-aware consciousness, attention, and intention.

Parenting at Fulcrum 0.

Parenting at Fulcrum 0 revolves first around the physical and emotional well being of the mother. Good nutrition, a loving and secure emotional holding environment, and good pre-natal and post-natal medical care for mother will support the infants' development. Poor nutrition, drug or alcohol abuse, chronic maternal stress, or poor pre-natal and post-natal medical care will create risks of compromising the children's development. After birth, parenting revolves around the physical and emotional nourishment and care (the holding environment) of the infants. Relatively constant (some believe continuous[12]) physical contact with loving caregivers combined with breast milk and nursing tends to optimize development in the first six months after birth. One theory is that, due to the size of human brains, human children need to be born earlier than other mammals, and that the first six months of development constitute an extension of time in the womb. This would explain why infants, unlike other mammals, are non-ambulatory and completely dependent for this extended period after birth.

1. Wilber (2000)

2. Wilber (2003)

3. *Ibid*

4. Jung (1965)

5. Wilber (1995)

6. Tescher (2005)

7. Witt (2007)

8. *Ibid*

9. McCarty (2004)

10. Cloniger (2004)

11. *Ibid*

12. Liedloff (1975)

27

Fulcrums 1 and 2

Fulcrum 1: The Birth of the Physical Self

Fulcrum 1 begins at around six or seven months. The children, fused with the external environment, differentiate through gradually discerning the difference between physical self and external world (they experience their physical body as separate from everything else), and integrate into the internal world of images. This is the birth of the physical self. Still fused emotionally with mother, the children experience themselves as discrete physically. They can hold images of objects and people in their consciousness, and discern differences between individuals. As early as four months they might become alarmed if a strange caregiver appears.

Cognitively, they are sensorimotor, literally thinking and relating instinctively through their bodies' whole range of sensory interface with the environment. This is consistent with BEIGE life conditions, since the children are driven by instinctual forces that mandate survival behavior.

Externally, there is little to distinguish Allen and Evalyn from each other sexually and interpersonally at Fulcrum 1. Both take pleasure in their body and bodily functions (in Freudian terms, their sexual cathexis is their whole body rather than discrete erogenous zones). Both need physical strokes, eye-to-eye gaze, and physical embrace by caregivers.[1] Internally, the powerful forces of masculine and feminine development are driving Allen and Evalyn in separate, though parallel, directions.

Both children are extremely egocentric. Having no real conception of an emotional other, there is little possibility of conscious empathy, though resonance circuits in their nervous systems automatically mirror other's states of consciousness including intentionality when they attune with physical proximity, touch, and eye contact[2].

Pathologies of Fulcrum 1.

Pathologies of Fulcrum 1 (such as the pervasive developmental disorders, childhood schizophrenia, and mental retardation) are often created by genetic problems, gestational problems, birth problems, trauma, or by the absence of, or interruption of, essential needs for contact and sustenance. Dietary deficiencies, or the absence of physical touch or emotional resonance, can interfere with body and brain development. The significance of our need to relate is reflected in the fact that the absence of physical holding and touch can cause wasting away and even death.[3]

Parenting at Fulcrum 1.

Parenting now involves attending to the children's physical/social needs, and their increasing ability to hold images in their consciousness. The children increasingly demand familiar caregivers. Images increasingly intrude into their consciousness, and they develop the abilities to roll, creep, crawl, and walk. They are more easily interested and alarmed by changes in the environment, and Mother and Father need to interpret behavioral and energetic communications and respond physically and energetically by holding, attuning, or adjusting the environment. Around one-year-old, as the children learn to walk, they increasing cue parental approval and disapproval which socializes and instructs their nervous systems through a variety of pleasurable states (feeling securely loved) and painful states (feeling shame emotions at parental disapproval). Children need parents to be verbal during this stage to support language development. They also need parents to set clear physical boundaries to protect and instruct them (like physically constraining a temper tantrum), as well as psychological boundaries of approval/disapproval to activate and support social learning.

The principle here is that parents are beginning to provide the external physical/psychological regulation that the children progressively internalize as self-regulation. Thus firm and kind physical boundaries as well as clear approval and disapproval can optimize later compassionate self-soothing and behavioral self-regulation.

I have what I call "the one year rule" in my practice. Up to one-year-old a parent can bring an infant into a session with relatively small impact on the psychotherapy. The mother might need to nurse, or change the baby, but most baby distress is relatively easily dealt with as we engage in the session. Starting about the end of year one, it becomes increasingly impossible to do therapy with the child in the room. Toddlers are more demanding, more mobile, more interested in knocking things over and ripping things apart. As they pass from what Kegan calls the Incorporative stage into the Impulsive stage, more adult attention is necessary to tend and balance the child, and the child is progressively less tolerant of attention (usually Mother's) being on anything, or anyone, other than herself.

Fulcrum 2: The Birth of the Emotional Self

Fulcrum 2 begins at around fifteen months. Fused emotionally with mother, Allen and Evalyn differentiate through gradually discovering, through their instinctual drives to relate and to create meaning, that self and mother are separate emotional beings. As this differentiation occurs, they are integrating from the world of images into the more expanded internal world of images, symbols, and beginning concepts. Interestingly, around sixteen months is when children can put on a "social face" that can mask their inner experience.[4] This period can be viewed as the birth of a separate emotional self.

Cognitively, this expanded world of images, symbols, and beginning concepts is pre-operational in Piaget's cognitive developmental hierarchy. It is magic in the sense that the two children often subjectively experience direct control of the physical universe. They say "banana", and a banana appears. They say "no" and an aversive stimulus stops. They cry for Mother, and she appears. This magic orientation is similar to the nature mysticism of PURPLE tribal cultures, where there is often a sense of directly controlling or influencing the external world. A Shaman friend of mine believes he can move clouds and call the eagle through the force of his will and spirit.

Sexually, Fulcrum 2 marks the advent of what David Deida calls the physiological level of sex, where the goal is pleasure. A child rubbing or stimulating his or her genital area might feel different pleasurable sensations than from rubbing other areas.

Children need embracing love and loving boundaries.

Interpersonally, Allen and Evalyn now must deal with the genuine discomforts of expanded separateness and expanding self-awareness. A separate emotional self means that more losses and separations are possible than before. Expanding self-awareness means that the child is beginning to experience an infinity of interior and interpersonal perspectives. If the terrors associated with a separate emotional self and the hugeness and intimidating possibilities of infinite perspectives are met with the appropriate emotional and physical holding (generally associated with feelings of love and security), and appropriate boundary setting (generally associated with the feelings of frustration) by some version of Winnicotts's "good enough" mother[5], the children will tend to have a secure attachment with their mother. Children with secure attachment styles with primary caregivers tend to have sense of security that their needs for contact and withdrawal will be met, and tend to grow into adults with secure autonomous attachment styles.[6] Intrusive, inconsistent parenting, dismissive parenting, or terrifying parenting can cue defensive systems available to the Fulcrum 2 consciousness. Two general categories of such systems are fusion and dissociation.

In extreme cases caused by either extraordinary neglect or abuse, and/or temperamental vulnerability (tendencies towards depression, high anxiety, or extreme emotional reactivity), the defensive capacities to fuse and/or dissociate can eventually result in adult personality disorders, such as narcissistic personality disorder or borderline personality disorder, where there is a periodic lack of a coherent sense of self.

Under stress, an adult suffering from these disorders cannot experience themselves or another as being simultaneously good and bad, light and dark, and cannot consistently feel empathy for others. These disorders of self can result in the characteristic "cling and torture" defense of the borderline personality disorder, and the "demean and withdraw" defense of the narcissistic personality disorder.[7]

In adults, psychotherapies for these disorders are designed to help construct and maintain a consistent, reality testing, observing ego, especially during subjective stress which tends to cue the most urgent impulses to enter regressed defensive states. Most therapists have had the experience of a borderline or narcissistic client decompensating during a session and becoming relatively unavailable to any external reality testing. This is very much like the tantrum states a toddler can enter, where verbal boundaries have no impact. These states are the dissociated or fused defensive places where differentiation and integration of emotional self has not taken place. Psychotherapy for adults in these cases is often lengthy and dangerous due to the primitive demonic projections the client instinctively engages in under threat, and dramatically diminished capacities for insight and empathy.[8]

A typical session with an adult client suffering from narcissistic personality disorder will cycle from mirroring the pain they usually deny, to interpreting their psychology in attempts to help them move toward self-reflection on the wounds they have organized their lives to avoid.[9] An example is the following exchange with Ellen, a professional woman in her forties. In this exchange, she is outraged at not receiving preferential treatment in her graduate program:

    Ellen: "I submitted my paper and the professor criticized it."

Keith: Mirroring her pain. "That must have felt bad. What did she say?"

Ellen: "She said I didn't write on the subject she assigned. What I wrote about was much more relevant and interesting than what she assigned."

Keith: "I can understand how that could hurt. You believed you were giving her a different, even superior, perspective, and she criticized you."

Ellen: "Yes, and it's not the first time."

Keith: "How do you mean?"

Ellen: "It's happened with lots of teachers."

Keith: "It sounds like you instinctively want to offer a different, more special, perspective, and then, instead of being praised, you're attacked."

Ellen: "Yes."

Keith: "Do you think there might be some part of you that is attempting to get these teachers to see that you are special?"

Ellen: With no irony."Yes, and they never do."

Keith: "Then why do you keep doing it? If you can predict that it will happen, it seems that there is a part of you that is inviting the attack for some reason."

Ellen: "Maybe, though I don't know why I'd do that."

Keith: "It's interesting to me that you have enough depth of consciousness to consistently come up with unique perspectives, and yet not enough to notice that this pattern keeps causing you suffering."

Ellen: "That is interesting."

Eventually, such careful exploration can take us to original Fulcrum 2 wounds, insight into destructive defensive states, and increased abilities to have empathy for others' suffering (her teachers' for example), leading to opportunities for Ellen to learn how to self-regulate angry impulses instead of lashing out at—and then rejecting—others.

Fulcrum 2; morally selfish.

Morally, Fulcrum 2 is selfish in the extreme, influenced by primitive boundaries of reward, punishment, and physical containment. This is a wider embrace than

Fulcrum 1 where there was much less sense of emotional other, but the absence of empathy and low frustration tolerance of Fulcrum 2 lead Allen and Evalyn to have little real altruism or consistent care for others. Still, as they are driven by the instincts to make meaning, to relate, to be true to their deepest essences, and to have position on social hierarchies, they are gradually coming to the understanding that separate emotional others exist and are important.

This decentering will continue throughout development. The undifferentiated stage leads to the egocentric stage, which usually leads to identifying with and caring for family, which often leads to identifying with and caring for larger social groups, which can lead to identifying with and caring for all people, which occasionally leads to identifying with and caring for all beings, which, in rare circumstances, can lead to identifying with, and caring for, everything that is arising. "Greater depth less span" reflects how few individuals develop to the point that their center of gravity is consistently identifying with and caring for everything that is, has been, and will be, but these progressive levels of decentering from self, and increasing care for others, exist as either realities or potentials for us all.

Vertical movement on the moral line (as well as the spiritual line, masculine/feminine lines, Clare Graves' values line, and Maslow's needs line) involves decentering away from merely identifying with self, to identifying with larger and larger groups.[10] Spiritually, this can take the subjective form of identifying less with our body, emotional self, cognitive self, relational self, or professional self, and more with the deeper, ever present essence (or consciousness, or soul, or Self) that most spiritual traditions agree we always have been and always will be, and that is one with the vast sea of consciousness (what Myamoto Mushashi called "the Void"[11]) from which everything is arising.[12]

For Allen and Evalyn in Fulcrum 2, all the above factors exist as potentials in the context of their current, egocentric existence.

Parenting at Fulcrum 2.

Parenting of fulcrum 2 children is often extremely difficult. Parents feel a responsibility for their children's safety and well being, while children are often consumed with plunging recklessly through a physically dangerous world, and by inhabiting the often bewildering and terrifying experience of emotional separation (with the concomitant capacity for an infinity of threatening internal images, symbols, and beginning concepts). The language that Fulcrum 2 children speak most fluently is PURPLE/RED, physical, and magical interface with the world, while the language their parents are most likely to speak is more conformist BLUE, rational ORANGE, and/or egalitarian GREEN.

Parents' higher centers of gravity pull upward developmental movement in children, but there is often an unconscious assumption by parents that children understand more than they really do. This can lead parents to have the subjective experience of being ignored, defied, and even abused. Developmentally informed parents focus on consciously discerning what capacities their child has for understanding and self-regulation, and adjusting accordingly. Providing an enriched physical environment is often much easier than discerning when a verbal "no" is sufficient, or a non-verbal intervention of physical restraint or other environmental adjustment is required.

1. Siegal (1999)

2. Siegel (2005)

3. Taylor (2002)

4. Schore (2003)

5. Rodman (2003)

6. Siegel (1999)

7. Masterson (1981)

8. Kernberg (1975)

9. *Ibid*

10. Wilber (2003)

11. Musashi (1974)

12. Almaas (2004)

28

Fulcrum 3: The Flowering of the Representational Mind and the Capacity for Repression

Fulcrum 3 begins around four. Allen and Evalyn have integrated physically and emotionally into separate physical and emotional selves. Fused with the world of images, symbols, and beginning concepts, and extremely egocentric, they are driven genetically, socially, and intrapersonally to grow. What drives them is physical development and the instinctual imperatives to create meaning out of an ever-widening world, to relate to family members in deeper, more participatory roles that support a felt membership in the group, to invoke approval and avoid disapproval, and to be increasingly true to their deepest masculine and feminine essences. Central to this process is the blossoming of language and the representational mind. Increasingly, Allen and Evalyn can hold and manipulate concepts internally, and communicate those concepts to others. This enormous power to inhabit a potential infinity of internal and interpersonal perspectives, to understand more of the world, and to manipulate concepts, combined with the inadequacy of their previous worldview to hold their experience, drives them to differentiate from their magic, Fulcrum 2 worldviews, and integrate into the more mythic linguistic world where there is an identification with a mental, or conceptual self. This is the birth of the conceptual self; the representational mind.[1] Neurologically, both children have matured to the point where they can string together life episodes into autobiographical memory, and are beginning to have a sense of self in this process creating the beginnings of autobiographical narrative.[2]

Repression.

The Fulcrum 3 world is often a threatening place for Allen and Evalyn. There are real and imagined things to fear, and interior and/or external disapproval can cue painful shame emotions.[3] Using maturing abilities to manipulate concepts, they can increasingly respond to perceived threat by unconsciously rearranging concepts using repression, suppression, projection, rationalization, or denial of what is alarming. These capacities are unconsciously utilized by each child's nervous system to create templates for neurotic defensive structures that they can carry for the rest of their lives. Under stress, these reflexive, primitive distortions will tend to manifest as defensive states characterized by distorted beliefs and perceptions, amplified or numbed emotions, destructive impulses, and decreased capacities for empathy and self-reflection.

Adult problems with their roots in such defensive structures often respond well to the uncovering aspects of various, often insight-driven, therapies such as Relationship therapy, Gestalt therapy, the cognitive therapies, and the analytic therapies. Held in the safe environment of the therapeutic relationship, the holding culture of the session, the hidden distortions can be explored, uncovered, and held in the light of conscious attention and evaluation of therapist and client.

The shame and guilt that characterize neurotic symptoms often revolve around internal senses of unacceptability and reflexive devaluing of the self or another. Therapeutic interventions can uncover and heal through self-exploration, self-acceptance, and integration of various conflicted aspects of self. The following exchange reflects a Jungian style of uncovering and healing with Ben, a twenty-five-year old graduate student:

Ben: "I saw the movie, "Stealing Beauty," and I cried at the love scene."

Keith: "What was it that moved you?"

Ben: "She was so sweet, and he was so pure and good."

Keith: "It reminds me of the dream you had where you were trying to save the young woman from the police."

Ben: Embarrassed. "But I didn't save her, and they arrested me too in the dream."

Keith: "What embarrasses you?"

Ben: "I'm not that strong or pure. I feel weak or weird a lot when I'm around women. I say stupid things."

Keith: "How do you feel about the part of you that feels weak and says less than the perfect things?"

Ben: Looking thoughtful. "Ashamed, I guess. I know we've talked about accepting that he is like a scared kid part of me, and having compassion for him, but sometimes that's hard."

Keith: "Is there any part of you like the guy in "Stealing Beauty?"

Ben: "Sure. I try to do right with women. I don't try to use them or screw them over like some guys."

Keith: "Is that part of you beautiful or ugly? Is he good or bad?"

Ben: "Obviously beautiful and good, but I can't feel like that guy all the time."

Keith: Interpreting. "Maybe your dream and your reaction to the movie indicate that he symbolizes a direction you've decided to grow in. That's certainly what your body, your dreams, and your feelings seem to indicate. I think the archetype of the pure young warrior knowing and claiming the radiant young woman resonates with you. I believe that's who you're becoming."

Ben: "That feels true, but what about the other side of me, the weak and inept side?"

Keith: Teaching and inspiring. "The warrior with integrity still feels weak and afraid sometimes. He still has destructive or embarrassing impulses, and he still collapses in some situations. He just does his best to resolutely and compassionately accept those feelings, impulses, and collapses, while struggling to do right and live according to his principles. That's how you develop and practice courage, by doing your best to do right when you feel weak or afraid."

Ben: "That is my goal, to accept who I am and grow to be a better man."

A Gestalt style of uncovering and healing in the above situation might focus on making it more immediate and experiential, following the Gestalt therapy guidelines of making the implicit explicit, pointing out the obvious, and staying in the present moment.[4] For example:

Keith: "I'd like you to imagine the hero from "Stealing Beauty" sitting across from you. Tell him how you feel about him."

Ben: To the imagined hero. "I envy you. You're pure and not afraid to make love to her."

Keith: "Sit in his chair, be him, and respond to Ben."

Ben: As the hero. "I'm just being myself, Ben. You could do the same."

Keith: "Be Ben and respond."

Ben: "I get too scared and weak."

Keith: Having helped him evoke a sense of being the hero, I initiate a dialogue between the part of him that feels strong and the part of him that feels weak. My goal is to have them relate until there is insight and integration. You'll notice I'm referring to his strong side simply as "Ben." This is intended to help him experience his strong side as more dominant in his personality. "Put the scared, weak Ben in the chair, and tell him how you feel about him."

Ben: To his scared, weak self. "You disgust me."

Keith: "Be the scared, weak Ben and respond."

Ben: "I'm scared. What do you want me to do? I don't know what to say. Why are you so much on my case?"

Keith: "Be Ben and respond."

Ben: With anger and power in his voice. "I'm tired of not feeling confident and strong. I'm sick of you."

Keith: "Be the scared, weak Ben and respond."

Ben: "Why don't you help instead of giving me so much shit?"

Keith: "Be Ben and respond."

Ben: Looking a little surprised. Sounding more compassionate. "You've got a good point. I shouldn't attack you. It doesn't help. I'll try to show you how to do stuff right."

In both the Jungian and Gestalt scenarios, we are uncovering hidden material that is marked by distressed feelings and distorted beliefs, we're identifying conflicted aspects of his self, and we're supporting Ben's resolve to integrate and grow. This dynamic appears regularly in working with Fulcrum 3 neurotic defensive structures. These can be his primary defenses, or they can be a layer on top of deeper, Fulcrum 2 characterological defensive structures that require more extensive work in helping him develop a resilient observing ego. As I relate and attune to Ben, I become increasingly oriented to his unique constellations of strengths, weaknesses, easily perceived selves, and shadow selves (the Jungian complexes[5], the Gestalt introjects[6], or the psychosynthesis subpersonalities[7]), and can adjust my therapeutic style accordingly.

Magic to mythic in Fulcrum 3.

In Fulcrum 3 the magic orientation of the younger child is supplanted with a more mythic orientation. Allen and Evalyn have discovered that they personally rarely, if ever, directly control the universe, but there are powerful arbiters—adults—who seem to be able to. Parents evoke the archetypes for mythical heroes and Gods.[8] RED cultures are dominated by power-Gods, humans with a cult of personality (perhaps a mantle of Deity as in the divine rights of Kings), which is tacitly accepted, feared, and respected by the populace. Healthy families of Fulcrum 3 children are led by parents whose authority and power the children generally accept, respect, and, to some extent, fear. If this is not the case, if the child through extravagant demands or displays of emotion dominates the family, then the child becomes the power-God whose authority is tacitly accepted and feared by the parents.

Salvador Minuchin's Structural Family Therapy is centered on establishing healthy hierarchies in families with the parents firmly on top of the pyramid.[9] Jay Haley makes a similar point when describing working with oppositional adolescents in *Leaving Home*. His clinical work has shown him how teens, seizing power by out-of-control behavior, need power-God boundaries from parents and other adults before they can benefit from emotional processing.[10] All this underscores the importance of understanding how we cannot skip developmental levels. If a child or adult's center of gravity on the self-line is RED power-God, then they usually require RED power-God interventions to support them growing to BLUE conformist commitment to the "book" (specific rules, based in tradition, that support the collective).

Fulcrum 3: cognitively preoperational.

Allen and Evalyn are expanding their abilities to think conceptually from two to five, but frequently operate non-logically, with images and symbols often taking precedence over concepts, fantasy being mistaken for reality, and appearances often trumping physical reality testing. Piaget's famous "the tall glass has more liquid than the short glass" example reflects the preoperational cognitive capacities that Fulcrum 3 children typically inhabit.[11] They can have peak experiences of concrete operational (and occasionally formal operational) functioning, but easily fall into magical thinking and non-rational decision making.

Sexual experimentation and taboo in Fulcrum 3.

Sexually, Allen and Evalyn are discovering increasing differences between their subjective experience of their genital areas and other parts of their bodies. They might discover the capacity for true, genital sexual pleasure, which is qualitatively different from other sensual experiences. Simultaneously they are presented with a bewildering array of rules and taboos they must abide by or risk punishment and censure. Innocent, age-appropriate, sexual examination and play with other children might take place, but eventually taboos and rules begin to dominate their sexual selves. Much sexual feeling, thought, or behavior is repressed and interwoven into defensive structures. Allen is discovering impulses to dominate and penetrate (not necessarily sexually, but perhaps with pretend weapons play, and roughhousing), while Evalyn is discovering impulses to wear pretty clothes and shine as radiant feminine light.

Allen and Evalyn are increasingly hearing contradictory messages about sexuality; messages that will echo and accelerate in the years to come. American middle-class parents have a public position of openness ("We talk about things in our family; you can ask me anything you want"), and a private position of taboo ("Shut that door! Knock before you come into our bedroom!"). The result of this, as chronicled by Judith Levine in *Harmful to Minors*, is that more than seventy percent of American children have no conversation of consequence about sex with their parents.[12] Parents who are more open about discussing sexuality run the risk of censure from even the most liberal of community cultures. The following is a typical exchange between an alarmed mother and me:

Mother: "This terrible thing happened at the pre-school."

Keith: "What happened?"

Mother: "The teacher walked in on my son and another little boy playing with each others' penises in the cloak room."

Keith: "Did you ask your son about it?"

Mother "Yes. He said it was their favorite game, and that lots of the children played it with them."

Keith: Sometimes children being interested in genital sexuality is a sign they've been molested and sexualized by an adult or older child. It's important to rule this out by evaluating whether there was other activity with older individuals, whether there were age discrepancies in the participants, whether there was coercion, and whether drugs or alcohol were involved. This mother had an unusually open dialogue with her son, and it was clear to me that, almost certainly, none of these factors were involved in his case.

Keith: "How's the school handling it?"

Mother: "The teachers seem kind of freaked out, and the mothers seem to be blaming my son. I don't know what to do."

Keith: "What did you tell your son?"

Mother: "I told him he couldn't do it anymore."

Keith: "What was his reaction?"

Mother: "He seemed let down."

Keith: "I imagine so; he said it was his favorite game."

Mother: "What should I do?"

Keith: "First, be aware of how everybody gets alarmed in this culture when kids explore their sexuality with each other. It sounds to me like your son was engaged in age appropriate sexual play, but that can get him in trouble. I suggest you take on the responsibility of cooling everybody down."

Mother: "How do I do that?"

Keith: "I recommend you send your son to this great Marriage Family Therapist I know to be extra certain no adults or significantly older children have been sexual with him in some way. Next, you can tell the other mothers that I suggested they could do the same with their children. Even though your son almost certainly hasn't been the object of inappropriate sexual attention, one of the other children might have, and so that child might need help. Last, you might tell your son some version of, 'In this country, kids can't play with each others' genitals until they are teenagers and have a girlfriend or boyfriend they really like.'"

I want to help this mother think developmentally, and respect the values of everyone's culture while encouraging her son to not pathologize himself for disagreeing with, or even violating, those aspects of culture that he doesn't find serve love and health. We don't all have the same standards. In later sessions, I might encourage this mother and her husband to more deeply explore their son's sexual essence as a (probably) more masculine individual, and help guide him into whatever directions he needs to travel to support that essence.

Masculine and feminine play.

In Fulcrum 3, Allen and Evalyn's play is becoming less egocentric and more focused on their emerging masculine and feminine identities. Allen is increasingly more fascinated with power and agency. Trucks, guns, trains, and action/sports figures are pulling his attention. Evalyn is increasingly more fascinated with radiance and relationships. Dresses, jewelry, make up, and dance are more fascinating for her. When they play (Allen mostly with other boys, and Evalyn mostly with other girls), their activities are increasingly different. Allen's play is more competitive and hierarchical. When he and his friends disagree on a game, they tend to argue the rules and rights of the situation before recommencing. Evalyn is playing more relational, non-competitive games and, if someone disagrees or has a bad time, the girls will often stop playing rather than argue.[13]

Morally preconventional, on the threshold of conventional.

Morally both children are still egocentric and selfish, but increasingly social life conditions and reward/punishment contingencies are supporting more care for, and interest in, the rules and roles of their cultures. Allen and Evalyn are beginning to recognize that there are rules that must be obeyed, and fairness now has some significance in decision-making. These characteristics put them at the end of Kohlberg's pre-conventional moral stage and at the dawn of the conventional moral stage, where the rules/roles of their cultures are firmly internalized and dominate much decision making.[14]

Parenting Fulcrum 3 children.

Parenting Fulcrum 3 children now increasingly becomes a function of parents' center of gravity and cultural biases. Middle class American children are provided with much cognitive, emotional, and physical enrichment. They are read to, played with, given dance, swimming, music, martial arts, sports, and/or art lessons. Their diets are rich in calories and nutrients. Interpersonally they are increasingly being urged to be aware of, and comply with, rules, roles, and "appropriate" behavior. Sharing is rewarded while keeping resources for yourself is not.

Allen and Evalyn might be required to participate in whatever spiritual orientation their family has. Prayer, attendance at temple or church, participation in marriage, funeral, and other ceremonies are expected, and these experiences stretch the children's worldviews. Their emotions are observed and translated to them by adults as in "you're angry," or "you're happy." Values are communicated by what receives praise (sharing for example), what receives censure ("It's bad to lie"), and by what is acceptable or forbidden to discuss or examine. A developmentally informed parent is aware of his or her own taboos and biases and cultivates the standard of consciously choosing what to teach and model for children. If talking explicitly about sex, pleasure, penises, vaginas, death, violence, excretory functions, or insanity doesn't meet a mother's instinctive moral standard, she can still choose to endure the discomfort of such discussion when she believes it is in the best interests of her child. A developmentally informed mother with a rebellious or permissive nature might determine that it's "good" for her child to have a parent be an enforcer of rules, and discipline herself to parent accordingly, while an developmentally informed father with a more rigid, controlling nature might determine it's "good" to lighten up and "let kids be kids" more than he finds naturally comfortable.

1. Wilber (2000)

2. Siegel (1999)

3. Witt (2007)

4. Perls (1968)

5. Jung (1968)

6. Perls (1968)

7. Assagioli (1965)

8. Wilber (2001)

9. Nichols (2007)

10. Haley (1980)

11. Wilber (2000)

12. Levine (2002)

13. Gilligan (1993)

14. Kohlberg (1983)

29

Fulcrum 4: The Rule/Role Self: The Conformist

Starting around six, fused in egocentricism and preoperational cognitive capacities, differentiating through increasingly concrete operational cognitive capacities, internalizing rules as good in themselves, and hungering to inhabit roles in the family, school, team and other important groups, Allen and Evalyn integrate into more other-oriented rule/role selves where they have more ability and desire to take on the role of other and be a functional member of important cultures. This process constitutes a decentering from the more egocentric previous Fulcrums to identifying with a group. "My family, my tribe, my religion, my nation" are important identifying constructs. Others outside these groups might be viewed as different in significant ways, with less credibility, fewer rights, and less worth as human beings, but still this is a huge decentering developmental shift into the children's beginning to be able to take the role of other and to want to comply with group standards.[1] This is the conformist stage of development, a central aspect of the BLUE MEME.[2]

Fulcrum 4: from preoperational to concrete operational.

Cognitively, from six to eleven, Allen and Evalyn are expanding into concrete operational thought where they experience the world as full of stable, invariant facts and relationships. The children are developing an intuitive grasp of Aristotelian reasoning. If Allen is taller than Evalyn and Evalyn is taller than Mary, then Allen is taller than Mary. They might find pleasure in listing objects in concrete categories (there are four members of my family, and twenty kids in my class), and they will understand others in terms of concrete, observable parameters ("This is Sally. She has two brothers, a rabbit, and a hamster. She lives two houses down from me").[3]

266

Fulcrum 4: the blossoming of the cultural level of sexuality.

The cultural level of sexuality is where acceptance becomes the goal of sexuality.[4] Allen and Evalyn have long since discovered that explicit examination of—or talk about—genitals, genital pleasure, sexual activity, or sexual roles other than those condoned by their culture is usually met with alarm and censure. As a result, any subjectively forbidden aspects of their emerging sexuality are likely to be expressed secretly, indirectly, or transgressively, or be completely repressed. Freud called this period "latency" because he believed there was little, if any, sexual awareness or sexual activity.[5] Subsequent research has proved him largely wrong. Just as it was discovered that Samoan children told wildly exaggerated tales of sexual exploits to Margaret Mead, I imagine Victorian adults and children distorted in the opposite direction (though I've never encountered any data indicating that Freud actually talked to a sampling of Victorian children).

Fulcrum 4 children can have fascination with genitalia, sometimes enjoy any of a variety of individual and group sexual exploration or masturbatory play, and can have a charged sense of interest in, and/or revulsion to, the forbidden aspects of body and sexuality. These activities are variously supported or punished depending on family culture and especially taboos. Family taboos are often reinforced by BLUE religious principles based in moral biases that children should be "protected" from sexual content and experience.

Jesus wants us to have hot sex.

This BLUE conformity can develop into major moral blocks to adult couples trying to have more joyful and fulfilling sexual relationships. Adults will often resist explicit sexual talk, change the subject, become ashamed, or become embarrassed discussing sexual anatomy or physiology. They might have preconscious beliefs that explicit sexual talk and behavior is somehow immoral. With Christian clients, I sometimes meet such biases head on. I believe that if Jesus were alive today he would wholeheartedly support sexuality as a bridge to deeper intimacy and spirituality, especially with married couples. The following is an outline example of this approach:

Keith: "Jesus wants us to love each other; right?"

Couple: "Yes."

Keith: "And Jesus wants love in our families; right?"

Couple: "Yes."

Keith: "And for love to bloom in a family, Mom and Dad need to have love blooming in their relationship with each other. Doesn't that feel true?"

Couple: "Yes, it does."

Keith: "And love blooms much better between you two when you're able to have regular hot sex; right?"

Couple: "Yes, it certainly does."

Keith: "So, Jesus wants you to have hot sex."

Couple: "Yeah, Jesus wants us to have hot sex."

If religious clients have doubts about this (which they rarely do in session because the culture of the session acknowledges and admires healthy perspectives and actions), I encourage them to talk to their minister, priest, or Rabbi, confident that these guides will support the couples' hunger for romantic/erotic union.

The subjective sense of cultural censure or acceptance is of huge importance in sexuality. Most adults I've worked with have experienced some aspect of their sexual functioning, sexual programming, or sexual practice as wrong or forbidden. Much of the healing value of Kinsey, Masters and Johnson[6], and Hite[7] was in normalizing varieties of sexual charge and experience. An example of this normalization applied in a therapy session is this exchange between me and Cheryl, the woman in her early thirties whom we met in Section Four:

Cheryl: "I don't think I'm normal sexually."

Keith: "So, what sexual fantasies turn you on the most?"

Cheryl: Flustered. "What do you mean?"

Keith: "When you masturbate, do you think of any images, people, or scenes, for instance? Are there sexual stories or themes that turn you on more than others?"

Cheryl: "Sometimes it's a turn-on to think about being held down while a man makes passionate love to me."

Keith: "You mean, like being tied down, or restrained, or do you mean more like being raped?"

Cheryl: Ashamed. "More like being raped."

Keith: "Is he angry, violent, or demeaning? Or is he just hungry for you and won't take 'no' for an answer?"

Cheryl: "More like that, where he won't take 'no' for an answer."

Keith: "In the fantasy, are you having a good time or a bad time?"

Cheryl: "I'm really turned on."

Keith: "That sounds more like ravishment than rape. Some experts suggests that being forced, with love, can be ravishment, and that one characteristic of a great masculine lover is having the sensitivity to discern when his partner craves that attention, and the power and presence to deliver it.[8] It's one of the most common fantasies that women describe to me."

Cheryl: "That's such a relief, I thought I was so weird."

Keith: "Have you ever discussed this with your lover?"

Cheryl: "I'm too embarrassed."

Keith: "He seems to me like the kind of guy it would be safe to talk about these things with. I've found it promotes intimacy and sexual polarity to share these kinds of things with each other."

Cheryl: Intrigued. "I suppose I could try."

Sometimes a therapist is the first person to hear about a sexual practice, fantasy, or experience that a client has believed to be forbidden, but has practiced or imagined for decades. Just normalizing that most of us have some eroticism that wanders one or two standard deviations (a great statistical term for this subject) from the top of the human sexual bell curve is tremendously reassuring for many people. The importance of this is reflected in one early seventies sex therapy acronym, PLISSIT, that was designed as a guide in prioritizing interventions. PLISSIT stands for Permission, Limited Information, Specific Suggestions, and Intensive Therapy.

The hunger for relational acceptance dominates fulcrum 4.

Fulcrum 4 marks significant shifts in interpersonal relationships. Six to eleven year old children yearn to be accepted by family, friends, and other important social entities. Hunger to be accepted, liked, and admired results in strong impulses to meet social norms and not violate taboos.[9] Fairness takes on increasing importance, giving an early glimpse of the 50/50, egalitarian nature of second stage relationships that Allan and Evalyn will likely begin yearning for in adolescence. This can be seen in various forms of play the children engage in.

Six to eleven year old Allen and his masculine friends will likely find bliss in weapons, fantasy wars, and meaning at the edge of death. They'll like action movies, and hunger to feel physically potent and able to dominate in sports or other power displays. The real and fantasy experiences reflected in this play almost all involve the subjective sense of being admired and approved of by important social groups, and include sometimes intricate rules and protocols that must be observed for the activities to feel fair.

Six to eleven year old Evalyn and her feminine friends will likely find bliss in relationship play, jewelry, dolls, dresses and clothes, and relationship movies. While Adam will probably more enjoy movies and books where the hero grows to discover personal power and use it for good and social justice (to the acclaim of important social networks), Evalyn will probably more enjoy movies and books where the girl is discovered to be special, perhaps a princess, who becomes a well-spring of radiant love, and attracts alpha males, perhaps a prince. Part of the play is that she is admired and seen as light by important social networks, while being an advocate for caring attitudes toward others. The Tolkien trilogy is a great example of the masculine myth, while "The Little Mermaid" and "The Princess Diaries" are examples of the feminine myth.

Fulcrum 4: The feminine moral shift from selfish to care, and the masculine moral shift from selfish to rights.

Morally, Evalyn is shifting from selfish to care. She thinks others should be cared for as well as required to follow rules. Allen is shifting from selfish to rights. Rules are important in that they define rights and responsibilities and take precedence over individual distress.[10] Both children are somewhat Old Testament in their moral orientation, as in "an eye for an eye." Punishment, or equal suffering, balance out transgression. Still, while Allen will argue with friends over the rules with little regard for personal distress, Evalyn might seek exceptions to rules if someone is suffering.[11] The children are decentering, identifying with larger groups, and becoming more moved to participate and contribute to collectives.

We tend to relate to ourselves the way we relate to others.

An interesting psychodynamic is illustrated in the moral predispositions of Fulcrum 4. Becoming visible in Fulcrums 2 and 3, expanding in Fulcrum 4, and continuing throughout life, humans tend to relate to themselves in the ways they relate to others, and tend to relate to others in the ways they relate to themselves. This capacity is strongly influenced by how children are related to by parents, since children's nervous systems are literally guided in how to grow through attunement with parents' nervous systems.[12] This attunement tends to be healthy when parents are in states of healthy response, and unhealthy when parents are in defensive states.[13]

The capacity for moral condemnation of others is often reflected in moral condemnations of ourselves in the forms of guilt for specific transgressions, and shame over real or imagined flaws in our being. To the extent Allen and Evalyn are shamed or critically evaluated by caregivers, up to and including physical violence, they will tend to have impulses to shame and critically evaluate themselves and/or others in similar ways throughout their lives. A child, contemptuous of weakness in his friend, will experience self-loathing at perceived weakness in himself. The pain associated with such self-condemnation will be acted on in different ways. Allen, a more masculine individual, might, under stress, be more likely to seek solitude, distraction, or displacement (attack someone or something else). His self-loathing might be turned into solitary activity, stimulus hunger, or injuring others to relieve internal pain. Evalyn, under stress, might be more likely seek affiliation and/or someone else to care for or tend. I suspect this is why I've found that in alcoholic family systems the boys are more likely to act out and the girls are more likely to become codependent caregivers.

As we explored earlier, disapproval and shame emotions are necessary parts of socialization and moral development. How parents express disapproval and how they manage shame emotions can become templates for eventual self-regulation in children. When parents are in states of healthy response, disapproval eliciting parasympathetic collapse and shame in children can enhance development—is actually necessary for healthy development. Prompt parental disapproval of self-destructive and/or other-destructive behavior followed by loving contact as soon as the child's nervous system has registered the forbidden behavior and experienced the shame emotion will tend to result in the child dealing with himself in similar ways as he develops.

There are rules that support justice and care. We violate them, feel a shame emotion, adjust our behavior and/or refine the rule, and move on feeling a subjective sense of satisfaction and inner forgiveness. This is optimally harnessing of our social conditioning capacities. When parenting, an emphasis on process, effort, and progress in these areas, rather than absolute standards—such as "good children go to heaven and bad children go to hell,"—encourages children to develop growth mindsets which find challenge interesting, other's excellence stimulating, and assume that life-long learning is preferable, possible, and moral.[14]

Knowing these principles and tendencies is of benefit in therapy, especially in teaching assertion. For instance, men often need more direction and support to seek out affiliation when stressed, while women often need more direction and support to set effective boundaries for others when stressed. Such principles can help guide therapists to choose perspectives in therapy sessions. In the following segment with Tom and Anne, you can observe how approval/disapproval of self and other figure hugely in their current issues:

Tom: "Just get out of my face and leave me alone when I'm mad."

Anne: "You never talk to me when we're fighting. How are we supposed to work things out if we can't talk? Right Keith?"

Keith: Anne is confident that I, as a psychologist, will completely support her need for processing when in conflict with Tom. "Well, Anne, it depends. There's productive talk, and non-productive talk."

Tom: He loves this. His distaste for processing is being normalized and supported. "Yeah, we go around in circles and nothing gets accomplished."

Keith: "Tom, you seem to have the impression that the reason you're talking is to solve a problem, to figure something out."

Tom: "Isn't that what processing is for?"

Anne: "He never talks about anything, no wonder we never solve anything."

Keith: "Productive talk moves you towards love, non-productive talk moves you away from love. Both of you forget this when you're mad."

Anne: Stunned by this. "I don't forget it, I always want to talk when we have problems."

Keith: "When you're angry, Anne, the form of your talk is often criticizing Tom, and accusing him of being anywhere from insensitive to abusive."

Anne: "If the shoe fits …"

Tom: "Fuck you, Anne."

Keith: Confronting. "Classic non-productive talk. Do either of you feel more loving now?"

Both reluctantly acknowledge they don't.

Tom: The masculine partner wanting a solution. "How do we solve it?"

Keith: "When you're angry, your nervous systems are conditioned to automatically enter defensive states where you're stingy with yourselves and each other. Neither of you is feeling particularly attractive or loving, and neither of you is interested in being generous in the service of love. A generous response is figuring out the genuine need of your partner, or the injury that your partner is experiencing, and attending to that need or injury with care, *even when you don't especially want to do it*. When you do this you feel like a better person."

Anne: "I tell him he needs more friends all the time. I tell him he needs to exercise, work less, drink less, and be nicer. He just ignores me."

Keith: "Does all that feel like a generous offering to you, Tom?"

Tom: "She's just bitching at me. What can I do? Just take it, or bitch back?"

Keith: "Then you're both a couple of bitches."

Both laugh. The humor breaks the tension, implicitly forgives both for being unkind, and models shifting perspectives.

Keith: To Tom, who cares about content. "Tell her what's valid about her position, and what you're willing to do about it. For instance, 'I get it you're mad I missed the conference. You're right I screwed up and I won't let it happen again.'"

Anne: Sarcastically. "That'll be the day."

Tom: "I can do that."

Keith: To Anne, who cares about energy. "Your defensive states show him your most repulsive side when you're mad. This causes you to secretly feel unattractive and hate him for not being attracted to you. What if you recognized his genuine desire to be there for you and your son, and said, 'I know you wish you'd remembered the parent conference. It just hurts me that you weren't there.'"

Tom: "That'll be the day."

They both laugh.

Keith: "These are practices you can get better at. Tom, you can tell her what's valid and what you're doing about it right now. Anne, you can feel into and love his heart and, if he feels like he's genuinely working on being better, show him your pleasure at his effort. That will encourage him to talk.

Your pleasure at his offerings attracts him toward you. The most important thing to remember about this *is to engage in these generous acts even when you don't feel like doing them.*"

In this exchange, I'm showing Tom how affiliation in the form of productive talk can sometimes "solve the problem" of her hostility. I'm showing Anne how setting inclusive boundaries by relating to Tom's mature, loving side, and showing him pleasure at his efforts encourages the affiliation she yearns for.

His critical attitude toward her probably reflects a similar critical attitude toward himself, and his shifts to being generous can help him feel like a better man. Her attacks and demands for perfection in him probably reflect her own demanding, perfectionistic standards for herself, and her shifts to being more loving can help her feel more radiant and attractive. I keep emphasizing the need to engage in generous behavior when in the grip of defensive states because I know that defensive states involve secret disapprovals of self, and that reaching for generous behavior can resolve such disapprovals into approval of self and other. Such resolves make defensive states more accessible for self-reflection and self-regulation, and create more interior compassion for conflicted aspects of self, which in turn can lead to more compassion for others. This is one specific dynamic of the central psychotherapeutic processes of cultivating compassion and depth of consciousness.

Therapy for Fulcrum 4 children.

Much of adult therapy is insight driven, relying on formal operational capacities to understand how seemingly unrelated events and processes can influence each other in our current life. Because children are generally preoperational to concrete operational, insight-driven therapy, which benefits enormously from formal operational cognitive capacities, has somewhat limited value with them. Cognitive behavioral therapy with children usually needs to be anchored much more in utilizing their concrete operational, or even preoperational, cognitive capacities. For example, a child who is chronically anxious can learn to notice anxiety, take three deep breaths, and imagine Mother, Father, or therapist with him saying, "Everything is fine." I've had the most success helping children by teaching them such practices while helping parents support the practices and then further learning how to adjust the family culture to support healthy self-esteem and healthy development in all family members.

I've found other approaches useful in treating children. For example, behavioral interventions (structured mostly by adults) can help children suffering from a variety of mood and behavioral problems. When working with kids directly I use concrete language and/or magical intervention (such as hypnosis, sand tray, or paradoxical intent), or function as a teacher or an alternate power-God or moral arbiter who advocates powerfully for the family to be fair, caring, and have clean, appropriate boundaries. I suspect the effectiveness of Minuchin's structural family therapy is based largely on parents identifying their responsibilities to love and set boundaries appropriately and, with the help of the therapist, explicitly committing to and living those responsibilities to help guide and liberate their children's innate drives to develop and be part of a healthy family hierarchy.

1. Wilber (2001)

2. Beck (1996)

3. Wilber (2001)

4. Deida (2004)

5. Freud (1949)

6. Masters (1970)

7. Hite (1976)

8. Deida (2006)

9. Wilber (2001)

10. Gilligan (1993)

11. *Ibid*

12. Siegel (2005)

13. Witt (2007)

14. Dweck (2006)

30

Fulcrum 5: Formal Operational and Reaching for Deeper Understanding and Relating

Fulcrum 5 begins to tip at around eleven. Fused in identification with social rules and roles, anchored in concrete operational thinking, the children begin to have peak experiences where they can hold opposing concepts in their minds at the same time, and are increasingly able to consider "what if" scenarios.[1] At the same time, the kids are finding situations where they disagree with the legitimacy of the rules. "Why do I have to go to bed at 9:00? I'm old enough to stay up later." "It doesn't seem right that Jacob will burn in Hell forever just because he's Jewish and not Christian."

As they differentiate from their rule/roles selves, they begin to integrate into the formal operational world of being able to critically examine concepts, rules, and ethnocentric roles, and make shifts in perspectives based on rational analysis. Socially, academically, and athletically, Allen and Evalyn are encountering merit-based hierarchies that they are motivated to join and compete on. This corresponds to the ORANGE MEME which is rational, hierarchical, and interested in individual advancement, especially in institutions that feel subjectively important.[2] Allen may join Youth Football, and Evalyn might start seriously studying ballet. Grades become more personally important to the children, either as sources of self-esteem if the grades are high, or as sources of self-criticism and/or possible signs of defensive resistance or learning disabilities if the grades are poor.

Fulcrum 5: the psychoemotional level of sexuality where the goal is fulfillment.

Sexually, at eleven to thirteen, the children are entering the psychoemotional level of sexuality where the goal is fulfillment.[3] Many people remain at this level for the rest of their lives, with occasional peak experiences of erotic transcendence.

Allen starts being more interested in girls, begins to find the idea of a girlfriend more appealing, and begins masturbating to orgasm with erotic fantasies that will probably remain more or less the same throughout his life. He wants to appear strong and successful to other kids, both boys and girls, and he wants his body to look strong and be strong. He might start working out, seriously pursue sports, or study martial arts. On the other hand, he might react to his hunger to be strong and attractive in oppositional fashion by ignoring his body, embracing drugs and/or alcohol, or by rebelliously hanging out with low status males and/or females that the dominant culture he's embedded in has contempt for. Energetically, he notices feminine erotic radiance and wants to penetrate it with his attention and his body. He either desires to seek out and claim a desirable girl, or actually seeks out and claims one, hungering for sexual experiences that go deeper and farther into fulfillment.

Evalyn has emotional charge associated with her developing body. If it's positive charge, she enjoys her breasts, menstruation, maturing genitals, and increasing yearning for masculine attention and romance. She'll want her clothes to look "cute" to enhance her erotic radiance. She might want attention from boys and affiliation/acceptance from high status girls. She will probably be drawn to care for and nurture her friends, both masculine and feminine. She might develop crushes on high status boys, or movie/rock stars, and fantasize being known and claimed by them.

If Evalyn has a negative emotional charge on her body, she might feel reflexive self-loathing that could be reflected in ignoring her body, hiding her body, starving herself, or stuffing herself with comfort food when she's anxious. A local middle school counselor told me that in a random survey of nine middle school girls about their biggest concerns, all nine listed body image as number one.

Sexually/interpersonally, Allen and Evalyn are beginning to face the culmination of American culture's institutionalized conflicting messages about sex and relationship. Their bodies are sending them increasingly more urgent signals physiologically. The social cultures they're embedded in are promoting attraction and romance (Evalyn's family wants her to look good, but not too sexy, and Allen's family wants him to be popular and attractive, but not too sexually active). Evalyn has high status if boys want her, but lower status if she surrenders herself too much sexually, while Allen gets strokes from his friends for being sexual active, but contempt from girls if he's a "player." These increasing internal and external pressures are met by the now internalized BLUE standards of having it feel "not good" (immoral) to want sexual contact, or talk explicitly (especially with parents) about hungers for, and fears about, erotic feelings, behaviors, or physiology. Since Allen and Evalyn have these sensations and engage in some of these behaviors, but feel transgressive when they do, much sexual thought, feeling, and behavior goes further underground and becomes suppressed and/or repressed. Such material might be shared somewhat with lovers or friends, but more rarely is it risked with parents.

The emotional charges of these tensions are regularly exploited by ORANGE and BLUE institutions, largely driven by achievement or conformist goals. "Sex sells" whether you are selling cigarettes, SUV's, your local university, or a spiritual fellowship that promises relief from conflict through conformity to specific moral codes.

Adding to the confusion is the general cultural ambiguity about what exactly are the responsibilities of masculine and feminine partners in intimate relationships. ORANGE, merit-based hierarchies are idealized as gender neutral, and are often mandated so by law. Sex educators have been constrained since the late eighties by Federal law to teach abstinence as the preferable response to sexual urges, and to not discus abortion as a possible viable alternative to unwanted pregnancy[4]. Meanwhile, sixty percent of American teens have intercourse by sixteen[5], and most of them make important decisions about themselves, their bodies, age appropriate sexual activity, and masculine/feminine responsibilities in intimate relationships in the absence of the ability to talk openly and explicitly with either their parents or the most sexually/relationally expert individuals in their social networks: responsible, educated, experienced adults.

The miracle of love.

The miracle of love is that, in the face of all the aforementioned impediments, Allen and Evalyn both hunger for intimate, erotic affiliation, have innate urges to occupy and develop their deepest sexual essences, and courageously begin to look for and experiment with sexual relationships and behaviors. Since "communication skills" are now socially accepted and widely taught, Allen and Evalyn begin expanding into the realm of second stage relationships as they take on the more caring and fair standards that are consistent with their developing morality. It feels moral to them to have a relationship be 50/50. It feels right to "talk it out" if there are problems in relationship, and search for solutions that allow each partner to get their needs met.

This is a beautiful developmental shift that mirrors Allen and Evalyn's moral centers changing from caring or justice for tribal members, to caring or justice for much more extensive groups. They feel moral obligations to be fair in their dealings with most others (perhaps all others), and it might not seem good to be cruel to anyone. They still unconsciously assign more rights and consideration to "their" institutions and cultures, and to individuals associated with those institutions and cultures, but they are decentering and developing empathy for larger groups.[6] Allan and Evalyn's attitudes toward hierarchies are moving from the caste system of BLUE (where social position and family status determine rights and opportunities) to the more merit-based, ORANGE, systems of SAT's, academic achievement, athletic achievement, financial achievement, and corporate productivity.[7]

At this point the principle of "greater depth, less span" becomes more pronounced in the developmental process. Increasingly, there are going to be significant figures like parents, family members, friends, teachers, coaches, pastors, and lovers who will have fundamental differences with significant aspects of Allen and Evalyn's beliefs, habits, character structure, or principles. This stresses their needs to be powerful (RED), be accepted (BLUE), and be successful (ORANGE). Add to this the possibilities of internal conflicts, developmental arrests, and constitutional vulnerabilities, and we see emotional, cognitive, constitutional, environmental, and/or relational weather patterns that can translate into the storms of adult defensive structures/states and psychopathology.

Developmentally, most humans are solidifying on the self-line, and other lines, at adolescence, and by twenty-six plateau, especially on the self-line. Charles Alexander, researching Transcendental Meditation, found little movement on significant developmental lines (such as the self, cognitive, spiritual, and moral lines) between twenty-five and early fifties unless an individual cultivated a daily meditation practice. Four years of daily meditation was associated with an upward shift of two levels on these lines. This research found psychotherapy and other forms of self-improvement to result in, at most, a one half level upward shift on the same lines.

This is one of many reasons I encourage my clients to choose ascending and descending spiritual practices that appeal to them, and engage in them daily; even if only for a few minutes.

More stable worldviews by late adolescence.

By late adolescence, most people will have stabilized at BLUE, ORANGE, or GREEN worldviews, and will stay in these MEMEs, often for the rest of their lives. Under stress, most of us—no matter what our center of gravity—remain vulnerable to defensive impulses to regress to more primitive worldviews.

First tier MEMEs often feel instinctive distrust for other first tier MEMEs.[8] In this context, we can see the importance of the psychotherapist being comfortable and familiar inhabiting each first tier MEME while being exclusively aligned with none of them. Common threads that can help organize the therapist's worldview are felt appreciation for all perspectives, and unrelenting advocacy for the vertical and horizontal health of clients. This is not independent of social, cultural, or relational context, but rather is the field out of which these contexts arise.

For example, in this next exchange with Tom and Anne, we see how, in psychotherapy, the individual's right to choose her own path trumps the social contract of the couple to stay married. It also demonstrates one way of working with the common dynamic of relational ambivalence as a defense against risk-taking in the interest of love:

Anne: "I don't want to be married."

Tom: "Great. Now you pull out the old threat. Just because I wouldn't go to your mother's, you …"

Anne: Interrupting. More urgent. "No, I don't want to be married to you."

Keith: "Wait a second; we need to stop and examine this. Anne, what do you …?"

Tom: Interrupting me. He does not want to stop and examine this. "She's just threatening me. She'll …"

Keith: Tom's interrupted me because it's less threatening to attack Anne than to listen to the real possibility that she wants out of their marriage. It's my job to deal with the superseding issue that Anne just raised, and not accommodate his defense. I need to direct, confront, and teach. "Tom, stop. When someone says they want out, I need to evaluate what's going on. If Anne really wants out, that completely changes the agenda of what we're doing right now."

Tom: "She's so full of shit. All she wants is …"

Anne: Unconsciously complementing and cooperating with Tom's defense. She scared to examine what she just said. "Fuck you, Tom. You always …"

Keith: "Excuse me for interrupting, but, stop! Anne, I need to ask you some questions, and, Tom, we can process after I'm done. Anne, what do you mean when you say you want out?"

Anne: "I don't want to be married. I'm tired of working on it. I've thought about it, and I want to separate."

Keith: "Are you looking for a place?"

Anne: "Yes. I can stay with a girlfriend."

Keith: "Does it feel wrong for you to keep working on improving your marriage?"

Anne: "We never get anywhere. Tom always attacks me. We never ..."

Keith: Interrupting her unconscious attempt to avoid the issue. "I asked, 'Does it feel wrong to keep working on improving your marriage?'"

Anne: Relaxing somewhat as she faces the issue. "Yes, I think it does. I've thought about it, and I don't want to keep struggling with him."

Tom: "I don't have to listen to this crap."

Keith: Addressing Tom, but speaking to both, and especially confronting Anne on what is happening right now. "Look, Tom. If Anne is serious, then we shift from trying to resolve issues to creating a separation (and probable divorce) if you do separate. The new agenda would be to help you through the separation process with a minimum of suffering to you two and your kids. You can't work on a marriage if one partner doesn't, in their heart, believe working on improving the marriage is the right thing to do."

Anne: More uncertain, and somewhat less resolved. "I don't want you, me, or the kids, to be hurt, Tom, but I don't think we can work out our problems and ever really be happy together."

Whether Anne remains firm in her resolve or not, I've staked out the psychotherapeutic territory of relating to each one of them as having the right to choose to go or to stay. I've also set the boundary that, unless they *both* believe working on improving their marriage is the "right" thing to do, I'm not going to be an agent of some other entity (spouse, family, church, or society) to try to coerce either of them to go against their deepest inner voices. If I think Anne's making a mistake and that leaving Tom is not what's best for her, I'll tell her. But, when she decides on a course of action, my job is to respect her decision and help her follow that path in the healthiest way possible. If doing that violates my own principles (such as wanting me to collaborate in keeping an affair secret) I might need to terminate therapy and make appropriate referrals.

I assume this psychotherapeutic position is part of what has occasionally caused some to reject (or suspect) psychotherapy in particular and secular humanism in general. Most therapists I've known, when faced with a conflict between the teachings of "the Book" and what he or she perceives are the best interests, health, or prerogatives of clients, will overwhelmingly choose the latter.

I believe a good therapist does their best to reconcile and see the value in different perspectives, but, if all points of view get to be valid, some are going to be more valid than others in different situations.

These issues become increasingly important in therapy as clients develop. "Greater depth, less span" means an increasing reliance on personal validity standards and flexibility of response to changing environmental cues, and less reliance on habit, custom, or blind obedience to anything.

Fulcrums 4 and 5 teenagers: ready for insight driven therapy, but not yet adults.

Allen and Evalyn are now teenagers with formal operational cognitive capacities, sexually mature enough to have children, sexually/interpersonally able to fall into romantic infatuation, and morally moving deeper into valuing care and rights with increasing peak experiences in valuing universal care and universal rights, and regularly regressing to selfish and egocentric perspectives. They are able to value and inhabit second stage, 50/50, egalitarian relationships where they can often set good boundaries and engage in clear communication. They might be disinterested in, or deny, shadow material (hostile, vulnerable, or destructive aspects of themselves that they can't easily perceive), and be relatively unaware of defensive states in themselves, but they can observe such states in others and find them repulsive.

All the above means that they are now able to more consistently benefit from insight-based psychotherapy, and have enhanced possibilities of genuinely feeling in charge of their lives and development. Up to this point, most effective therapy for them will have involved largely systemic, concrete operational, and/or behavioral interventions, mostly in the context of the dynamic systems of their families or social networks. These interventions will have been driven much more by their parents' capacities for self-reflection, insight, and conscious behavior change than by the children's capacities for healing insight. On the other hand, therapy has had the potential to help the children be able to learn and apply principles and rules, and (through teaching, behavioral rehearsal, and support) learn new behaviors, perspectives, and/or energy release and balancing through indirect or symbolic means (dialogue, expressive art and play, paradoxical intent, story-telling, or hypnosis). Now Allen and Evalyn have the formal operational abilities to engage in more mature self-reflection and have deeper transformative insights of their own.

1. Wilber (2001)

2. Beck (1996)

3. Deida (2004)

4. Levine (2002)

5. CDCP survey (2005)

6. Kohlberg (1983)

7. Beck (1996)

8. Wilber (2003)

31

Teenagers Are Not Adults

Teens might be physically mature, cognitively formal operational, at the psychoemotional level of sexuality, and morally caring, but teenagers are not adults. Therapy often looks and feels quite different with them individually, in family sessions, and in conjoint sessions with their lovers. Our brains reach full development at twenty-six, and then continue to change in response to aging, learning, and life experience. Teens have been demonstrated to have less emotional recognition capacities, more impulsivity, and less capacity for empathy, than adults. Teens (and college students) routinely test two standard deviations higher than adults on the paranoia and psychopathic deviancy scales on the MMPI (the Minnesota Multiphasic Personality Inventory, one of the most famous and widely used psychological tests of the last sixty years). Teens want autonomy, but also crave parental boundaries, and can communicate boundary needs behaviorally (like younger children) in symptoms such as acting out, drug/alcohol abuse, school failure, or angry/depressed withdrawal.

Confidentiality with teens is a much more slippery concept than with adults. Parents need to be informed of some behaviors and activities (depending on legal obligations of the therapist, and levels of maturity and acceptance of the parents), while other behaviors and activities are best kept private to maintain the therapeutic relationship and encourage responsibility and self-regulation in the teen client.

Teens are quite able to fall into romantic infatuation as deeply and passionately as adults, but often lack the abilities to self-soothe and self-regulate when relationships end, or the abilities to deal with interpersonal, sexual, and moral issues when they inevitably arrive.

In my experience, teens are less able than adults to remember and follow through on therapy assignments. They will listen with interest but will more often than adults report completely forgetting about the suggestions made or insights discovered in sessions.

Teenagers can inhabit spiritually charged nature mysticism, deity mysticism and causal (formless) mysticism states and practices, but seem to rarely maintain spiritual practices outside sessions unless supported by group participation involving peers, church, or temple.

BLUE belongingness is hugely important to teens, but they are also driven by ORANGE achievement needs to excel in school, sports, jobs, or college aspirations. This, of course, adds conflict to their social relationships since, as teens get older and deeper, friendships and lover relationships face inevitable separation and loss as the teens and their peers enter college, join the military, or enter job cultures. A wonderful book that delightfully explores the challenges of parenting teens is Anthony Wolff's *Get Out of my Life, but First Could You Drive Me and Cheryl to the Mall.* A psychologist and father of two daughters, Wolf details and normalizes many of the idiosyncrasies and paradoxes of teen and parent existence.[1]

Psychotherapy with teens can be very similar to working with adults if the teens are available and if their life conditions support the work, or very similar to working with younger children or doing social work if they are not available and/or their life conditions don't support the work. Three factors figure hugely in determining what kind of interventions are possible and appropriate with teens:

- Whether they are willing or unwilling clients.

- Whether their parents are healthy enough to support treatment rather than interfere with treatment.

- What peer cultures teens are embedded in.

Let's examine these three factors.

Willing and Unwilling Teen Clients

Teens that are motivated clients are delightful. When treated with respect, they can respond respectfully and with huge interest in their developing adult identities. There is a purity they bring to sessions that is heartbreakingly beautiful in ways often commented on by helpers who have worked with enthusiastic teen clients. BLUE/ORANGE, Fulcrums 4 and 5, they are hungry for truth and insight, often can embrace GREEN and YELLOW peak experiences, and are frequently embedded in family and social cultures that value self-awareness, health, and growth.

The following is a typical exchange with such a client, an intelligent, emotionally stable, fifteen-and-a-half-year-old (the "half" is often still important to teens) named Kevin:

Kevin: "I want my parents to give me more freedom."

Keith: Teaching. "Besides being a healthy teenager who wants more freedom, your deepest sexual essence is masculine. The masculine almost always hungers for freedom. What kind of freedoms do you believe they should give you?"

Kevin: "I think they should let me stay out till midnight with my friends. I know I screwed up before and got in trouble with the police, but I won't let that happen again."

Keith: "What makes you sure you won't let it happen again?"

Kevin: "I'm not going to drive with kids that are drinking or smoking pot. I've already refused to do that a couple of times."

Keith: When working with teens, it's especially important to elicit their moral standards, and encourage them to be true to their own emergent values. "So, it feels wrong to you to drive with people who are loaded?"

Kevin: "Duh. It's also stupid. It's so easy to get busted, or do something stupid."

Keith: "So, it seems wrong, dumb, and ugly to let yourself do it, and you're able to withstand the social pressure to go along with it."

Kevin: "I've already said 'no,' and my friends are cool with it."

Keith: "That's great. Let's invite your parents to the next session and we can discuss it."

Kevin: "OK, but it's hard to talk to my Dad."

Keith: "What's hard?"

Kevin: Tears forming in his eyes. "I hate to disappoint him."

Keith: "There seems to be a lot of emotion around pleasing and disappointing your Dad."

Kevin: "Yeah, I don't know why it makes me cry."

Unwilling teen clients: more danger, not as much fun.

An unwilling teen client rarely has exchanges like the above. They will complain about being forced into therapy, lie or refuse to discuss transgressive activities, and often be contemptuous of the therapist's offerings. I rarely work with unwilling clients. I've found forced therapy to usually have limited impact, but sometimes the only possibility of reducing suffering and supporting health is to agree to see an unwilling client. I tell parents I'll see their son or daughter two or three times but, if the teen remains unwilling, I'll refer them elsewhere.

The combination of destructive behavior plus unwillingness to participate in therapy moves treatment back to the external, environmental and behavioral interventions of childhood. Jay Haley in *Leaving Home* details how, in these cases, the therapist best works exclusively with behavioral contingencies, and refuses to discuss feelings or inter/intrapsychic analysis with resistant, acting-out teens. Rather than allowing them to use emotional talk to avoid change, attack parents, and refuse personal responsibility, teens are constrained to self-regulate, act respectfully, and take responsibility to earn privileges. Ultimately, talking about feelings becomes a privilege that must be earned by constructive, appropriate behavior.[2]

The following is a typical exchange between me and an unwilling teen client: a sixteen-year-old, oppositional girl named Tina:

Tina: "I don't want to be here."

Keith: "Why not?"

Tina: "It's useless. The problem is my parents. They are just trying to control me."

Keith: "Your mother said you're failing school, using drugs or alcohol almost every day, and having unprotected sex with your boyfriend."

Tina: "She is so clueless."

Keith: "Is she right?"

Tina: "It's none of her business."

Keith: "To the contrary. If you keep acting self-destructively, she and your Dad will feel obligated to control you much more. I suspect they'll put you in a special school of some sort where there will be strict rules and major consequences for acting out."

Tina: "They wouldn't dare!"

Keith: "You might be right, but I think they'll do whatever they can to stop you from failing and hurting yourself."

Tina: "Do you think they will? Are you telling them it's a good idea?"

Keith: "Tina, parents will do what it takes to stop their children from hurting themselves. If it came to it, I'd do it for my kids, and I think, if nothing else works, your parents will do it for you."

Tina: "I don't want that to happen."

Keith: "You're in control of whether it does or not."

Tina: "What do you mean? They don't listen to me. I have no control."

Keith: "If you begin making better decisions and taking better care of yourself, you'll have rapidly increasing power to direct your own life. If you continue to act self-destructively, the adults around you, and especially your parents, will intrude and try to protect you and force you to develop."

The most impactful part of our dialogue started with a boundary. I'm letting her know that, if she doesn't decide to self-regulate, her parents will probably mobilize to regulate her. This is the difference between working with a teen and a much younger child. I know that Tina has a capacity for formal operational thought and self-reflection. I want to confront her in each step of this unfolding drama that, if she takes on the responsibilities of self-reflection and self-regulation, she will be dealt with progressively more as an autonomous adult and less as an out-of-control child. Conversely, if she insists on acting out destructively, she will be dealt with progressively more as an out-of-control child who needs external boundaries. This theme continued with Tina though parental boundaries, placement to a special school, and two years of milieu treatment at that school. In initial family sessions I discouraged emotional talk and encouraged concrete boundary setting by her parents. It took some time before inter and intrapsychic issues could productively be the main agendas in individual and family sessions.

A common error of BLUE/ORANGE/GREEN parents like Tina's is their unconscious resistance to recognizing that their teen is out of control, and that the whole family is using emotional wrangling to avoid the real issue. Tina needed a healthy RED system where she was dominated and forced into BLUE morality (we don't skip levels); otherwise she became the RED power-God who dominated her family system. Her parents were challenged with the question,

"Will we allow Tina to self-destruct, or take on the job of controlling her life in ways that she refuses to for herself?"

Healthy and unhealthy parents

There is a brutal physics of health and development that can help us understand some harsh realities. A self-destructive teen plus abusive or non-functional parents is a positive feedback system the same way a steam boiler without a thermostat is a positive feedback system. It will cycle until there is an explosion.

If a teen son of emotionally abusive or non-functional parents is a willing client, there are possibilities of teaching him how to handle his parents until he can escape the toxic family system and become self-sufficient. This work is similar to teaching an employee with an emotionally abusive boss how to "manage up."

If this teen boy is unwilling, the referral is often coming from the courts or social services, and his therapist's work will probably revolve around understanding the boy's scene, empathically addressing his dilemma of sick parents, trying to hook him up with a firm, caring RED milieu that does not allow acting out, and confronting him with healthy alternatives. Prognosis in these cases is poor because the odds for successful treatment co-vary with the extent the teen is a willing client and lives in a supportive milieu.

Sick parents who drag their unwilling teen in to be "fixed" by a therapist are quick to terminate their child's therapy, and to refuse therapy themselves when confronted with their own pathology. Parents who respond to such confrontation by deciding to work on their own issues immediately become much more functional just by their willingness to awaken to their problems.

Peer cultures

Teenagers may be BLUE, ORANGE, or GREEN in many capacities, but their social milieu will reflect their social center of gravity.

Conformity based BLUE, merit based, competitive ORANGE, and egalitarian, multi-cultural GREEN teen cultures often have achievement standards and self-regulation standards that support health, resulting in willing clients interested in growth.

Self-destructive teens are often embedded in unhealthy tribal PURPLE, power-God RED, or conformist BLUE with self-destructive conformity standards (like violence, crime, or drug use). Healthy PURPLE, RED, or BLUE cultures support teen development. In our hunter/gatherer genetic roots, it was in the crucible of PURPLE tribes that adolescents came of age and were initiated as adults. One reason I sent my two children to the Santa Barbara Middle School is that its founder, Kent Ferguson, knew the tribal needs of developing teens, and organized his school to be a healthy tribal society, anchored in magic and mythic ceremony and tradition, with institutionalized ordeals (multi-day community bike trips), and structured on every level to support horizontal and vertical health for the individuals and the group. Kids were dealt with compassionately, but every aspect of the culture, including most of the peer cultures (teens always develop cliques), assumed healthy values and personal responsibility.

Unfortunately, there are tribal groups that kids form and join that are self-destructive and oppositional. These are often associated with regular drug and/or alcohol abuse. Independent of whether a teen is using, abusing, or dependent on drugs and alcohol, being embedded in a culture that normalizes regular use is almost always associated with some level of self-destructive symptoms.

I met a couple of delightful young Austrian brothers at a men's retreat on the Green River near Sedona. The two young men had moved from Austria to Washington State as teens. They described to me how appalled they were at the cultures of binge drinking and drugging that they encountered in American high schools. Not only do such cultures predispose the participants to reckless behavior (seventy percent of sexual assaults are on women nineteen and under), but once a teen is embedded in such a culture it is often almost impossible to motivate and empower him or her to leave it and seek tribal cultures that find healthy, successful behavior preferable. An axiom of treatment for teens addicted to coke or crack is that their best chance of lasting recovery is to leave town for treatment, and often to permanently relocate away from their self-destructive social milieus.

Fulcrum 5: development is now more of a conscious choice.

Fulcrum 5 begins in early adolescence and marks the point where Allen and Evalyn accelerate their differentiation from their family into more autonomous and increasingly self-directed lives. They can stay power-God RED, conformist BLUE, or competitive, achievement oriented ORANGE for the rest of their lives, or continue to decenter and hunger for new perspectives.

Driven by their needs to relate, to be true to their deepest sexual essences, and to claim and be claimed erotically, either Evalyn or Allen can, at any time, fall in love, bond, marry, and begin to have children of their own. Having a committed lover relationship creates new opportunities and pressures. Such relationships provide opportunities to grow emotionally, interpersonally, sexually, and spiritually. There are internal and external pressures to love well and create a good life in a committed relationship. These pressures amplify as children are born and Allen and Evalyn discover the huge responsibilities of parenthood, and the fierce desires to give their children a good life filled with love, joy, and opportunity. On the other hand, as intimacy with lovers and children approximates family-of-origin levels, the defensive structures and states developed in early life are increasingly cued. Allen and Evalyn's most primitive defenses then manifest in their lover relationships, cuing similar regressions in their lovers. They can use these regressions as opportunities to grow, or they can indulge defensive impulses and endlessly reenact historic pathology (in my opinion, the dynamic origin of the concept of "the wheel of karma").

Let's assume they continue to decenter and grow.

As Allen and Evalyn achieve mastery and success in their ORANGE, merit-based, achievement oriented hierarchies, stabilize in second stage relational standards of fair, egalitarian relationships with "good communication," and normalize moral standards of care and rights within institutional rules and personal relationships, they find that they still yearn.

Allen hungers for deep soul's purpose and a profession where he can give his best gifts to the world. He's beginning to find the concept of universal rights for all attractive. Evalyn yearns for personal and relational fulfillment for herself, her intimates, and everybody else. Both Allen and Evalyn feel increasing respect for other cultures and increasing distress over the obvious inequities both within and between cultures. They idealistically want universal care and universal rights for everyone and sense that there are deeper, post-formal operational ways of thinking and knowing that are possible.

All the above begins to tip them towards the GREEN MEME where egalitarianism and multiculturalism exist in an anti-hierarchical, idealistic context.[3] This is the beginning of Fulcrum 6.[4] GREEN has its limitations. Shadow tends to be repressed or denied, multiculturalism and egalitarianism often are translated into moral judgments at others who acknowledge and value the legitimacy of hierarchy, and there is the first tier distaste for, and felt superiority to, other MEMEs. On the other hand in GREEN, the last first tier MEME, we encounter the staging area for the leap into the second tier, where the Fulcrum 7 integral perspective will become the new center of gravity and Allen and Evalyn can have stable felt appreciation for all points of view and dramatically reduced fear.

1. Wolf (1991)

2. Haley (1980)

3. Beck (1996)

4. Wilber (2001)

32

Fulcrum 6: The Emergence of the Centaur

Fulcrum 6 begins as Allen and Evalyn are fused in formal operational functioning, ORANGE achievement hierarchies, sexual yearning for fulfillment, second stage relationship styles, and moral commitment to care and rights. Through yearning, relating, seeking, and struggling to grow, Allen and Evalyn differentiate away from their current worldviews, and integrate into the ability to identify mind and body as objects experienced by a deeper self. Wilber calls this the "centaur" in reference to the mythological figure that clearly divided higher functions (the human head, hands, and torso), and powerful, instinctual, biological drives (the horse's body) in one being. I have a body, but I am not my body. I have thoughts, but I am not my thoughts. I have feelings, but I am not my feelings. I have impulses and judgments, but I am not my impulses and judgments. I am something deeper and more profound than all these things. These are the existential discoveries of Fulcrum 6 that can be experienced with existential despair (as in, "The old mythological systems of childhood and adolescence seem false. We are all going to die, and all that we do is ultimately pointless"), or with spiritual hope ("As I decenter away from identifying with body, mind, emotions, impulses, and judgments, I have an intuitive feel that there are deeper, larger, more profound truths and awakenings awaiting me").

Wilber defines spirituality variously as a developmental line, as a charged, sacred experience of nature mysticism, deity mysticism or formless mysticism at any level, as a felt sense we can experience at any time, and as a common characteristic of the higher levels on most lines.[1] A felt sense of the sacred can involve the spiritual charge associated with disidentifying with "smaller" aspects of self in service of "larger," deeper, more fundamental, and abiding senses of self (as in feeling one with an unrecoiling, ever-present witness), and can include a decentering away from self and increasing identification with larger groups; moving

toward including all people, all sentient beings, all life, and everything that is arising in the present moment. In Fulcrum 6, this process can move to where Allen
and Evalyn are experiencing peak moments of post-formal operational cognitive
abilities (what Wilber calls, "vision logic") that are no longer limited to Aristotelian either/or frameworks, but instead hold and integrate seemingly opposing
viewpoints in subjectively truthful, internally consistent systems that integrate the
intuitive and the purely rational into the transrational.

Fulcrum 6: the blossoming of the psychoemotional search for fulfillment, and the beginning of the yogic level of sexuality, where the goal is healing.

Sexually, Allen and Evalyn are capable of having moments where sex has a transcendent feel that seems to deliciously energize their bodies. These moments are
glimpses of the yogic level of sexuality where the focus is healing and opening
energetically.[2]

Primarily, though, they are more fully living the psychoemotional level of sexuality pursuing fulfillment. They might experiment with their lovers, or have different lovers, looking for new thrills. If they are untrained in masculine and
feminine practice (as are most people), they might begin to feel vague yearnings
and dissatisfactions with themselves and their lovers. Allen might not like himself
when he is unresolved around his lover and, under this or other stressors, have
tendencies to regress and feel a diminished sense of self, impulses to be self-
destructive, and/or impulses to blame her for real and imagined flaws that he
believes account for his suffering. Evalyn might feel distress when she doesn't
experience herself as a wellspring of love, or her lover as a trustable presence. Her
distress might create impulses to regress, try to fill herself with food, euphorics, or
shopping, obsess about her appearance, complain about (or to) her lover, or conclude that she must direct her life independently since she can't find a trustable
man.

In the midst of this real and potential suffering, Allen and Evalyn are learning
how to maximize the benefits of second stage 50/50 relationships. Allen is
becoming more able to acknowledge and celebrate his feminine side in art, dance,
or nature. Evalyn is feeling more independent and capable in professional skills
and independent living. Both value and practice "good communication" in their
relationships, which are now more likely to progress into more stable bonding,
and creating family.

Fulcrum 6: the moral shift to universal care and universal rights.

Morally, as Allen expands into Fulcrum 6, he progresses to normalizing the GREEN ideals of universal rights and respect for other cultures. Evalyn progresses to normalizing the GREEN ideals of universal care and respect for other cultures. Both have peak moments where they inhabit the integrated space, what Kohlberg called post-conventional, where they value both universal care and universal rights, and are principle driven (rather than rule driven) in their decision making. Both are now philosophically multicultural, non-ethnocentric, and anti-hierarchical. Hierarchy is now appearing less moral and attractive, and (without perceiving the irony) Allen and Evalyn find themselves feeling irritated by, and morally superior to, others who don't share their views.

Therapy with clients in these (mostly) GREEN Fulcrum 6 worldviews benefits from validating their egalitarian values while subtly encouraging peak experiences of Integral (YELLOW and above) functioning. Enhancing horizontal health in therapy deals with resolving the pain, symptoms, and regressive defensive states that accompany and drive symptoms in clients' interpersonal and intrapersonal lives. Supporting development (vertical health) includes identifying and normalizing peak experiences of expanded spirituality, care and rights for all beings, post-formal and post-post-formal operational thought, hunger for growth from fullness rather than lack, and helping clients use such experiences to enhance their development. An example of such a therapeutic exchange is the following segment with Henry and Nancy, an egalitarian, multi-cultural, anti-hierarchical GREEN, Fulcrum 6 couple in their early forties, who occasionally have extended periods of integral YELLOW functioning on some lines:

Nancy: "We tried to follow your suggestions about our love life."

Keith: "How was sex last week?"

Henry: "It's never good enough for her. She always has something negative to say, or some correction to make."

Nancy: "I try to be specific and positive."

Henry: "It always sounds like criticism to me."

Keith: "Henry, how do you react when she corrects you?"

Nancy: "He pouts."

Keith: Raising my eyebrows at Henry.

Henry: Defensively. "I'm sick of it. I'm never good enough for her."

Keith: "It sounds like you feel there are always hurdles you have to jump, and you never successfully jump them all."

Henry: "Yes, and I'm sick of trying to jump hurdles."

Nancy: "I'm just communicating clearly what I want. Isn't that what I'm supposed to do?"

Keith: "Absolutely. How do you show him you like what's happening?"

Henry: "She's great at that. She moves, makes sounds, and smiles. It's fun when she's having a good time."

Keith "Henry, What does Nancy mean when she says, 'pouts?".

Henry: "I just get frustrated and I'm not in the mood anymore."

Nancy: "Forget about sex then."

Keith: "Is that accurate? When you're frustrated you withdraw and sex stops?"

Henry: "I'm sick of the hurdles."

Keith: "Henry, a feminine person will never be satisfied with anything for very long. And besides, when she recoils or requests, isn't she indicating how you can be a more effective lover?"

Henry: Defensively. "I get frustrated."

Keith: "It sounds like when you're frustrated you're surrendering to defensive impulses to collapse and losing your ability to adjust back to presence and serve her open with pleasure; both hers and yours. Isn't that your job as a masculine partner, to adjust to her signals and serve her open to deeper pleasure? Hurdles are your friends."

Henry: Laughing. "Hurdles are my friends. I love that."

Keith: "What's the best way for Nancy to give you feedback during lovemaking?"

Henry: "Just show me, or tell me and not go on and on."

Nancy: Defensively. "I want to communicate clearly."

Keith: "The feminine partner supports sexual polarity by primarily reacting rather than directing. The shorter, more graceful, and less verbal the better."

Nancy: "I can do that if he doesn't pout. I hate pouting."

Keith: "Can you show him juicy pleasure if he adjusts back to presence and humor?"

Nancy: Warmly. "I like that. Anything, if he doesn't pout."

Henry: Laughing. "Hurdles are my friends."

You can see the combination of regressive states and enhanced functioning in Henry and Nancy's exchange. All therapy oscillates in this fashion to some extent. Henry and Nancy are mostly GREEN, with flashes of regression and peak periods of YELLOW Integral functioning. They can accept and value hierarchy and, as Henry demonstrated with hurdles, shift to new perspectives with direction and encouragement. There is also the assumed presence of the sacred, the shared responsibility to serve love, and acknowledgement of the difference between masculine and feminine responsibilities in the sexual occasion. They are comfortable with my position that they have different constellations of responsibilities as a more masculine partner and a more feminine partner, and are willing to explore them. Since development is include and transcend, I know that either Nancy or Henry can regress to any previous Fulcrum under the right combination of life conditions. Also, either may have specific conflicted areas of regular regressed functioning where they easily flow into destructive defensive states. As each session unfolds, clients will reveal temporary or habitual defenses, which help guide interventions. The higher their center of gravity, the more resources they can bring to bear on remediating symptoms, enhancing health, and supporting development.

1. Wilber (2007)

2. Deida (2004)

33

Fulcrum 7: Welcome to the Second Tier

Fulcrum 7: in the year 2003, three percent of the population.[1]

Fulcrum 6, generally GREEN, marks the last of the first tier MEMEs. The next developmental step is into YELLOW, Integral. As of the year 2003, in Wilber's estimation, three percent of the American population had a Fulcrum 7, YELLOW, Integral center of gravity.[2] Statistically, Allen and Evalyn will have small chance of growing through Fulcrum 7, but let's assume they have the right combination of individual gifts, yearning to grow, and stable and enriched enough life conditions to develop beyond Fulcrum 6.

Allen and Evalyn are fused in the observing self's ability to experience mind and body as objects of a deeper consciousness, and are comfortable with the existence of, and regular practice of, post-formal operational thought. They are confident in their ability to have clear communication and clean boundaries in relationships, have experienced good sex (on occasion, transcendent sex), and are solid in their conviction of the legitimacy of universal care and universal rights in non-hierarchical frameworks. As they yearn and sense that there is more to life and love, they differentiate from GREEN, Fulcrum 6 worldviews toward deeper understanding and deeper purpose.

Deficiency needs and being needs.

As Abraham Maslow observed, the needs we struggle with in the first stages of our development come from a sense of lack; deficiency needs. I want food, water, security, sex, and recognition because there doesn't seem to be enough of these things for me. He observed that, as people develop, their needs begin to come from a sense of fullness; being needs.[3] Allen and Evalyn are successful, secure, and happily related, but with this fullness comes a yearning to give more deeply, to experience the world and spirit more profoundly. This yearning from fullness helps move them to differentiate from GREEN, Fulcrum 6, and integrate into an increasing awareness that there are realms of consciousness and service beyond the boundaries of self. In these realms they sense there are mysteries and wisdom inherent in every perspective, and that there is a unity of everything which can be experienced but never completely described.

Hierarchy returns in YELLOW.

In Fulcrum 7, hierarchy no longer seems immoral, but instead is a natural outcome of the validity of all points of view.[4] Of course there are hierarchies of abilities and developmental levels, of course some people are higher on different developmental lines, or have more authority in different circumstances, of course we are one world and one people. From an Integral perspective there is a felt, world-centric, appreciation for all previous MEMEs, and a dramatic reduction in fear of death, fear of change, fear of people, and fear of the world.

A this level Allen and Evalyn accept the existence of, and have experienced moments of, post-post-formal operational thought beyond vision logic; true transpersonal experience of oneness beyond self. These experiences are often categorized as "psychic phenomena" by ORANGE and GREEN science.

A transpersonal experience under the stars.

In 1979 when I was studying Taoist healing I had such a transpersonal experience. I've since noticed that many people, after a year or more of intense spiritual practice, have psychic events occur, almost as if some part of them is bursting out and establishing the existence of connection to something deeper than an isolated self.

At twenty-eight I had been practicing martial arts and spiritual disciplines for thirteen years, finding one teacher or system after another and integrating the teaching into my life and work. I felt intuitively that there was a bridge between the psychological, spiritual, and Way of the Warrior, but hadn't found a system that provided that bridge until I encountered the martial artist/Taoist priest John Davidson, whom I briefly described in the Introduction. I surrendered myself to the dharma and practices and studied with him for about two years, using the emerging forms to guide me in writing my doctoral dissertation[5].

Toward the end of that period my studies led me to the University of California at Sant Cruz, where I was researching alternative healing. While there, I found myself alone one night under the stars in a hot tub next to a friend's house in the nearby mountains. I had discovered a wonderful text on Antoine Mesmer that afternoon, and was relaxing in the hot tub, synthesizing Mesmer's work with my Taoist practices. As I lay there feeling one with the forest and enjoying the night air, I began planning my next week's lecture in the psychotherapy course I was teaching at that time in Santa Barbara. In my mind I constructed the class, seeing my students and lecturing them on the healing techniques I had been training in. I asked for a volunteer and, in my vision, one of my students, Amelia, stepped forward. I directed her to lie down on a massage table in from of me, and I ran my right hand two inches over her imagined body, feeling her energy, and telling the class, "You feel the energy of your client's body with your hand as you move it slowly several inches above her torso from head to thighs. I feel a tingle coming from Amelia's lower abdomen; a block of some sort. I'm now extending my energy through my hand to release the block, with the intent to heal."

It was an extraordinarily vivid series of images I had that night, alone in the hot tub under the stars. The next week I approached Amelia just before class and had the following exchange:

Keith: "How were you last week?"

Amelia: "I wasn't doing well on Tuesday."

Keith: "What was going on?"

Amelia: "I had a pain over one of my ovaries. The Doctor said it was a cyst."

Keith: "What happened with it?"

Amelia: "About 7:30 Tuesday night I felt a sharp pain right on the spot, and then a 'pop' in the area of my ovary, and then the problem was gone."

Clearly Amelia and I were connected that previous Tuesday night at 7:30 in a way that was not explainable by empirical science at the time. Since then, quantum theory and research on healing has validated the process of feeling into someone at distance, imagining specific healing taking place, and stepping out of the way of some larger force working through the healer and helping the one being healed[6].

Interestingly, when I've told this story to people I would now identify as having primarily a first tier worldview, or who have no particular spiritual practice, they respond with something like "wow," and then, apparently, promptly forget what I just said. It doesn't seem to stick in their consciousness or affect their beliefs in any way. When I've told this story to people I would identify as having primarily a YELLOW, or higher worldview, or who engage in regular spiritual practice, they respond much differently. An expression of loving knowing comes over their face, and they'll tell me of a similar experience that they've had; one that validates their felt relationship with spirit, and their confidence that we are all connected in love.

Fulcrum 7: the yogic level of sexuality where the goal is healing.

Sexually, Fulcrum 7 allows Allen and Evalyn to inhabit what Deida calls the Yogic level of sex, where they can consciously direct energy, and practice sexual ecstasy and transcendence, with the goals of opening energy channels, cocreating sexual/emotional/spiritual bliss, healing themselves, healing each other, and giving love to the world.

Yogic sex involves practices of feeling and conducting energy through breath, awareness, and intention in your body, then in your partner's body through active penetration in the masculine and active reception in the feminine, and finally giving your gifts of love and transcendence through each other's bodies to all beings. As Allen and Evalyn choose YELLOW lovers and give their love to the world through the medium of sexuality as the melding of consciousness and light ("enlightened sex" as Deida refers to it[7]), Allen practices depth of consciousness and active penetration, and Evalyn practices love through the body and active reception. This moves them toward the sixth level of sexuality, the spiritual level, where the goal is to live each moment as an expression and offering of divine love.[8]

Living the third stage in Fulcrum 7.

Deida frequently asserts that teaching people how to live the third stage is the main focus of his work.[9] Sexually/interpersonally, Fulcrum 7 involves cultivating enhanced capacities to be able to live the third stage. The third stage involves opening to the point that you can fully express any spot on the masculine/feminine continuum if that expression best serves the moment. It involves giving your best gifts to the world, even when you're distracted by your defenses, resistances, and attachments.

Allen, whose deepest sexual essence is masculine, will either feel, or relentlessly pursue, deep purpose in giving his best gifts to the world, and will organize his life to give those gifts, as best he can, each waking and sleeping moment. With his lover, he will use his presence, his shadow, and his humor to serve her open as far as he can each moment he's with her, with the goal of opening her all the way to God.

Evalyn, whose deepest sexual essence is feminine, will do her best to feel her body wide open to pleasure, light, and love in each moment, and surrender to being a wellspring of love that serves the world. With her lover, she will express suffering when he is not being his best self, and radiate devotional love when he is trustable and present, letting his trustable presence guide her and open her farther than she can open herself, so that she is progressively more able to be a living offering of love and light.

Defensive structures and states, habits of closure, and painful or pleasurable distractions still exist and influence both Allen and Evalyn. What characterizes a third stage moment is Allen's and Evalyn's resolved efforts to give their best gifts and to love through all blocks and distractions.

Fulcrum 7: morally integrated universal care and universal rights.

Morally, in Fulcrum 7 Allen and Evalyn embrace both universal care and universal rights in an integrated fashion, and feel into each moment with the intent of maximally serving love, informed by, but not ruled by, customs, laws, preferences, cultural standards, and habits. Kohlberg called this stage the higher level of post-conventional moral functioning, where universal principles are applied to humanity with the goal of the highest good.[10]

Therapy with YELLOW, Integral clients: challenging and fun.

Therapy with second tier clients is challenging and intensely pleasurable. It is a dance where the client brings in dissatisfaction, pain, regression, or hunger for transformative growth and, with great sensitivity and attunement, the therapist harmonizes with each moment and offers his best energy and content. Since there is always regression associated with defensive states, an integrally informed therapist can often stay half a step ahead on the path, and thus provide support and guidance. An example of this is an individual session with Nancy from our previous conjoint example. Nancy's center of gravity is YELLOW on her spiritual line of development (or TEAL altitude in the Integral Institute's system):

Nancy: "I'm going to die in four years."

Keith: "What do you mean?"

Nancy: "I was sailing alone on the ocean two years ago, and I felt God infuse me and tell me I was going to die at forty-eight."

Keith: "How do you feel in your body as you tell me this?"

Nancy: "Frustrated, because you can't understand."

Keith: I feel love for her, and a strong impulse to offer direction by completely accepting her assumption. "I agree. I don't think I can possibly understand past a limited point what your experience with God was that day."

Nancy: With pain and yearning that feel completely authentic. "I don't want to die. I don't want to hurt Henry."

Keith: "It sounds like both of those things might happen, but it's hard for me to imagine God intending for those things to happen if they somehow didn't serve love."

Nancy: Comforted, connected, still aching. "I know, I fight against it, but the energy is too strong."

Keith: Drawn to "fight against it". There is a slightly tense feeling in my body associated with her statement that often happens when I'm presented with a defensive state, or internalized conflict. "How do you mean, 'fight against it'?"

Nancy: "I only let God infuse me to my third chakra. I resist allowing the energy to rise to my other chakras."

Keith: Responding purely from intuition, with the relaxed, peaceful feeling in my heart that I associate with vision-logic. "It feels wrong to me for you to block God infusing your body. It feels right to me for you to open up all your chakras to God."

Nancy: Comforted and interested. "I'll try. I don't know why I resist it so much."

Therapy is cocreative art. This is especially true when dealing with Fulcrums 6 and 7 issues. There are regressions and internalized conflicts here, but they feel surrounded and infused with a deeper spirituality. This is consistent with one of Wilber's definitions of spirituality, an increasingly characteristic quality on the higher developmental levels.[11] I follow my interest, my emotions, my intuition, my love, and my focused intent to stay in tune and to help.

The moment I need her validation, admiration, or acknowledgment, or the moment I need her to understand, grow, or change so that I'll feel better in some way, I lose my connection and much of my healing impact. If I can maintain my connection with her, my resolve to help, and my disattachment from outcome, I can use my training, understanding, and the instrument of my body to cocreate a healing culture with Nancy to help guide her toward deeper levels of health and growth.

1. Wilber (2003)

2. *Ibid*

3. Maslow (1962)

4. Wilber (2003)

5. Witt (1982)

6. McTaggart (2007)

7. Deida (2004)

8. *Ibid*

9. Deida (2006)

10. Kohlberg (1983)

11. Wilber (2007)

34

Fulcrums 8 and 9: Second and Third tier: Still evolving

I have what Zen calls "beginner's mind" when dealing with Fulcrums 8 and 9. I've had some moments that seem to fit the descriptions that Ken Wilber, Don Beck, David Deida, A. H. Almass, and others have given for these levels, but spend the bulk of my life inhabiting other levels on Fulcrums 1 through 7. I am sure that there have been great realizers throughout history whose self, moral, cognitive, sexual/interpersonal, and/or spiritual centers of gravity have been Fulcrum 8, and have had more than peak experiences at Fulcrum 9. Wilber and Deida both mention Ramana Maharshi, Aurobindo, and Buddha.[1] Wilber loves Plautinus who wrote in third century Rome about non-dual practice and appeared to live what he wrote.[2] Bahá'u'lláh of the Bahai faith expressed principles and practices that are consistent with what Wilber has described as Fulcrums 8 and 9 consciousness.[3]

Since the concepts and experiences of Fulcrums 8 and 9 don't seem to lend themselves perfectly to language which is always dualistic (every thesis has its antithesis), and since most great realizers taught to people who couldn't completely share their experience, I suspect that there is always mystery associated with Fulcrums 8 and 9 until, very occasionally (greater depth, less span; we are now dealing with a fraction of a percent of humanity) individuals are able to have direct experience of these Fulcrums, or even to stably live them. I agree that there are ascending levels (or waves) of decentering, expansion, and spiritual experience that we can aspire to, have peak experiences of, and potentially have centers of gravity in, and we can be certain that others have occupied these states and stages before us, and have special knowledge of them.

Wilber asserts that the spiritual practices that become increasingly attractive and even necessary at Fulcrum 7 take us to deeper levels of self until we feel a vast expansiveness of identifying with all Self, the Self that we and all others have

308

always been.[4] Entrance into the third tier (turquoise to indigo in the Integral Institutes color system) is characterized by a deepening sense of spirituality in self, a recognition of such perspectives in others, and a hunger to join with like-minded people to serve. In *A Brief History of Everything*, Wilber calls Fulcrum 8 the "subtle", and says:

"'Subtle' simply means processes that are subtler than gross, ordinary, waking consciousness. These include interior luminosities and sounds, archetypal forms and patterns, extremely subtle bliss currents and cognitions (shabd, nada), expansive affective states of love and compassion, as well as subtler pathological states of what can only be called kosmic evil, kosmic horror. As always, because of the dialectic of progress, this subtle development is most definitely not just a day at the beach."[5]

Don Beck, in *Spiral Dynamics*, offers a more social definition of Fulcrum 8, TURQUOISE. He suggests that, as someone expands into the Integral, YELLOW worldview, there is increasing emotional/spiritual need to expand personal practices to create and/or include communities, or sanghas, of like-minded individuals with the purpose of serving the world.[6]

Fulcrum 8 seems reflected in Deida's ideas about living the third stage. When living the third stage, you are feeling yourself and all beings, offering your love to all beings, and are constantly receiving feedback from the world as to whether you are opening or closing any moment. When you live the third stage, you open the moment generously, even recklessly. Giving your deepest gifts can involve risk or suffering, and also requires the deepest humility. Friends, strangers, or the world can (and will), at any time, confront us with our collapse, and a third stage practitioner needs to acknowledge collapse, and do his/her best to adjust back to presence or radiant love.[7]

Fulcrum 9: One with the Source

Fulcrum 9 is referred to as "causal" by Wilber. The following is part of his description from *A Brief History of Everything*:

"When, as a specific type of meditation, you pursue the observing Self, the Witness, to its very source in pure Emptiness, then no objects arise in consciousness at all. This is a discrete, identifiable state of awareness—namely, unmanifest absorption or cessation, variously known as nirvikalpa samadhi, jnana samadhi, ayin, verjezzen, nirohh, classical nirvana, the cloud of unknowing. This is the causal state, a discrete state, which is often likened to the state of deep dreamless sleep, except that this state is not a mere blank but rather an utter fullness, and it is experienced as such—As infinitely drenched in the fullness of Being, so full that no manifestation can even begin to contain it. Because it can never be seen as an object, this pure Self is pure Emptiness."[8]

Wilber suggests that beyond this causal state is the Non-dual where the Witness vanishes and becomes everything that is witnessed. "Form is Emptiness and Emptiness is Form."

A.H. Almaas writes extensively about experiencing the universe as essence morphing into consciousness morphing into soul existing as unity, and in his books provides hundreds of examples of different facets of the experience, and how they can be organized to guide our unfolding.[9]

The relevance of Fulcrums 8 and 9 in psychotherapy is subtle, but profound. First, an integrally informed spiritual practice honors all quadrants, lines, levels, states, types, all traditions, and includes knowledge of the levels that stretch ahead of all of us. This understanding supports health, helps identify pathology as it regularly arises, and guides us in inspiring our clients to grow. In the include and transcend dance of development we never lose our defensive capacities or reflexes, but they often become more subtle as we grow. The more we as therapists have felt appreciation for all points of view, the farther we can guide our clients and help them understand and integrate their own current existence, regressive states, and peak experiences. We can be guided in this process by what Robert Kegan calls the "dialectic of progress," which refers to the fact that there is health and pathology at any developmental level.[10] Knowing the dialectic of progress helps therapists perceive the unique constellations of strengths and vulnerabilities that each person brings into the session.

Waking up at different levels.

A first stage, Fulcrums 2 or 3, PURPLE or RED, selfish masculine partner might crave freedom, feel constrained, and beat up his wife in frustration. A second stage, Fulcrums 4 or 5, BLUE, ORANGE, or GREEN, fair, masculine partner might crave freedom, feel constrained, and blame his wife for some real or imagined fault. A third stage, Fulcrums 6 or 7, GREEN or YELLOW, universal care and rights, masculine partner might crave freedom, feel constrained, and not offer his wife direction that might genuinely serve her because he is distracted by his pain.

In each case, the same defensive impulse is being acted out through different levels of development and different states of consciousness. In each case, there is psychotherapeutic opportunity for a therapist to co-create a culture that cherishes the client and the client's universe, regards each moment as a gift and an opportunity, and that considers healthy perspectives and actions beautiful, good, and true. In each case there is room for the therapist to relate, teach, inspire, confront, interpret, and direct to reduce symptoms, enhance health, and support development.

Reflecting the developmental principles of greater depth, less span, and that the more mature we become the more spiritually charged our lives tend to be, the more self-regulating we become, and the easier it is to seek out and receive guidance, I've experienced relatively few clients who enter therapy from second tier fullness needs. I imagine such individuals, yearning from fullness, are more likely to seek out spiritual teachers than psychotherapists. Overwhelmingly, clients enter therapy from deficiency needs. Therapy sessions will almost always revolve around deficiency needs, and first tier, regressed defensive states.

On the other hand, a developmental perspective provides a framework to help clients understand most aspects of their interpsychic and intrapsychic functioning at every level, with the confidence that progressive developmental levels continue ahead for all of us on all our developmental lines, that people have occupied those levels before us, and that the experiences they've had and the wisdom they've accumulated can guide us. This same framework helps us, as therapists, to identify what perspectives and language to use in each second of a session to cultivate compassion and depth of consciousness to help remediate symptoms, enhance health, and support development.

1. Wilber (2003), Deida (2006)

2. Wilber (1995)

3. McLean (1994)

4. Wilber (2003)

5. Wilber (2000)

6. Beck (1996)

7. Deida (2006)

8. Wilber (2000)

9. Almaas (2003)

10. Kegan (1982)

Section Six

States in Psychotherapy

35

States: The Heart of Therapy

Our whole life from conception onward is an amalgam of shifting states of consciousness. States of consciousness dominate our worldviews, our relationships, our sense of self, and our work. The sensory screen of our nervous system filters thousands of inputs constantly from the environment. Our brain scans these inputs and matches them against internal representations of previous events, inscribed in our implicit memory system (which doesn't require focal attention like our explicit memory system, and doesn't have a sense of something being remembered when we recall things).[1] Some perceptual signals (often seven plus or minus two[2]) stand out because they are unusual, pose some threat, are associated with something of emotional significance, or resonate with current needs. These items cue our brain to create stories of the present moment that usually last from seven to ten seconds.[3] Within this period our state of consciousness can shift every three tenth of a second, or even faster.[4]

In the present moment we are manifesting states of consciousness cued by associations and anticipations rooted in implicit memories which are behavioral, emotional, perceptual memories, belief systems and behavioral cuing reflexively encoded and recalled with no sense of something being remembered. When cued, implicit memories create states of consciousness which have bodily memories, sensory memories, kinesic memories, auditory memories, belief systems that support meaning with subjective and objective perspectives, and behavioral priming that drives our impulses toward specific behaviors. These states of consciousness involving constellations of implicit memories will be interwoven with our explicit memories (memories that require focal attention and have the sense of something being remembered) and weighted by frequency, intensity, temperament, and emotional saliency towards characteristic biases and tendencies.[5]

Wow. Where is free will?

Free will is our consciousness. Conscious awareness gives us the abilities to focus attention, intention, self-reflection, and compassion where we want. We can either ignore or embrace compassionate self-awareness and surrender to impulses associated with each choice. We can observe our shifting states of consciousness and relax into the flow of superior perspectives and unity with our deepest purpose and essence. We can thus consciously harness and direct the past, present, and future from multiple perspectives including the "I," "you," and "we." The more we allow and practice these capacities, the better we guide the infinity of perspectives that continue to arise from our consciousness, and the more attuned we are to what eastern traditions call "the Way."[6]

If we're cued to constellate defensive states of consciousness (as we often are in intimate relationships), laid down as neural networks learned in the intersubjective relationships with caregivers in fulcrums one, two, and three, we can enter defensive states of amplified or numbed emotions, distorted perspectives, destructive impulses, and dramatically reduced capacities for empathy and self-reflection. If we can disidentify with these states (not dissociate because we usually must feel and accept them to some extent to optimally process them), we can choose compassion and depth of consciousness and reach for superior perspectives that maximize love and health.

Psychotherapy is all about states of consciousness. The therapist's goals of cultivating compassion and depth of consciousness to support healthy perspectives and actions, and cocreating a culture where the client and the client's universe is cherished, where each moment is considered a gift and an opportunity, and where healthy perspectives and actions are considered beautiful, good, and true, are all accomplished by the therapist inhabiting and guiding her own and her client's attention and intention in the intersubjective fields that constitute the therapeutic relationship.[7] Awareness of states of consciousness, and having the ability to utilize states of consciousness in the service of health are crucial psychotherapeutic skills.

What is my current state?

This Section begins with a summary of gross, subtle, and causal states, and proceeds in some depth into the nature and importance of defensive states, and how to work with defensive states in therapy to help liberate each client into maximizing states of healthy response to the present moment. I encourage you to attend to your own shifting states of consciousness as you read this material. Are you comfortable, or uncomfortable? Are you intrigued, or irritated? Does any part of the material feel right or wrong? Do you feel dense or clear with the different concepts and techniques? By the end of this Section you will probably have a much better sense of when you or your clients are in defensive states or in states involving healthy responses to the present moment. Hopefully, you will feel more confident in your ability to identify and work with a wide variety of states of consciousness.

GROSS, SUBTLE, AND CAUSAL
WAKING, DREAMING, AND DEEP SLEEP

Three great foundation states of consciousness are gross (waking), subtle (dreaming), and causal (deep dreamless sleep). Wilber suggests that being awake in the manifest world is at the gross end of a continuum, experiencing everything as pure emptiness is at the causal end, and the subtle is everything in between.[8] This concept of continuum is useful in understanding the myriad states we enter and exit constantly in waking life. Since gross, subtle, and causal coexist, states all have varying elements of image, feeling, impulse, and worldview, and varying levels of awareness of the deep, unrecoiling, unchanging, ever-present self-identity that, subjectively, is the same from birth to death.

The enormous variety of gross, waking, states.

During our waking (gross) existence, we are constantly shifting both consciously and unconsciously from one state to another. We are distracted, absorbed, irritable, euphoric, intoxicated, infatuated, meditative, defended, aggressive, open, closed, and so on. Each of these waking states has characteristic sensations, emotions, perceptions, thoughts, memories, and impulses.[9] Each of these waking states has observable behaviors, energetic and biochemical properties, subjective qualities and charge, and intersubjective properties and effects.[10]

The importance of states to psychotherapy is staggering.

Much of therapy begins with, and runs off of, awareness in the therapist of her own and her client's current states. Attending to compassionate understanding in the present moment of both self and client is a central activity the therapist engages in to cultivate awareness of current states of consciousness. Awareness of states of consciousness helps the therapist discern lines, levels and types, and how they are currently manifesting, thus guiding the therapist to understand the unique configurations of qualities and capacities that each client inhabits and expresses.

Therapists can determine where health and growth are blocked or stunted by discerning and exploring defensive states. This exploration reveals intrapsychic and interpsychic defensive structures that manifest as defensive states with characteristic distorted perceptions and beliefs, amplified or blunted emotions, destructive impulses, and reduced capacities for empathy and self-reflection. Discerning and working with these defensive structures and states in ourselves and our clients is a foundation skill in cocreating a culture where the client and the client's universe are cherished, and healthy perspectives and actions are valued. Defensive states are thus doorways in the process of therapy, and necessary instruments for the therapist to utilize in helping clients.

Intersubjective fields are amalgams of different states.

The intersubjective fields that saturate the therapeutic relationship can be experienced by the therapist and the client as obvious, and/or subtle, moment to moment shifts in their states of consciousness during the session. As a therapist, I want to cultivate in myself states that support compassionate integration of all perspectives. For example, observe the interplay of different states of consciousness in the following exchange from an individual session with Tom (of Tom and Anne from the previous Section):

Tom: Grimacing slightly. "I'm sleeping in the guest house."

Keith: I feel a sense of "wrongness," accompanied by a tiny surge of resentment in my body. "I felt a little surge of resentment when you said 'guest house.'"

Tom: "Yeah. I feel resentful. I also just don't want to be around her."

Keith: Interested. "You're describing yourself as literally repulsed by Anne."

Tom: His breath goes higher in his chest, his expression becomes a little alarmed, and his eyes look accusingly at me. "I'm not repulsed by my wife!"

Keith: Feeling pushed away energetically, combined with a sudden sense of danger between us. I have an impulse to focus on relating and to be soothing and delicate. "You sound angry. Am I misinterpreting why you don't want to be around her?"

Tom: Relaxing somewhat. Suddenly appearing childlike to me. "I don't want to hurt her. It seems when I'm with her, I hurt her."

Keith: Feeling compassion for his pain, and having an image of Tom and Anne both feeling lonely in their big house with their little son; simultaneously angry and yearning for love. "I imagine you both suffer from not being able to love each other better."

Tom: Plaintively. "I don't know if she wants to."

Keith: Feeling some sadness and loss at the sense of his and her defenses conspiring to avoid dangerous topics, and thus draining aliveness and juice from their intimacy. Feeling a desire to shift his perspective first by agreeing and then by going in an unexpected direction. "I'm sure both of you don't want to talk about hard subjects. I'm also sure that both you and Anne yearn to be wide open in love with each other."

Tom: Resonating with my last statement. "We are happiest when we're loving each other."

The different states I'm experiencing relating to Tom guide me in my goal of joining with him to cultivate compassion and depth of consciousness to support healthy perspectives and actions. I observe his physical reactions, hear the changing nuances of tone in his voice, attend to the content of his words, feel my own constantly shifting sensations, reactions, and impulses, and then, accepting everything, ride the energies like a surfer rides a wave; always with the intent of reducing symptoms, supporting health, and enhancing development.

As you attend to your inner experiences, you'll often notice how there is a fluid, complex sense of flow to such states. Each of us is a protean, shifting, evolving, multidimensional blob of physical, emotional, cognitive, spiritual, and relational processes that are generally dominated by both habits and evolving consciousness; interconnected with all consciousness.[11]

In the face of this complexity, it's extraordinarily valuable in therapy to discern what different perspectives are best emphasized at different times. Most experienced therapists consciously and unconsciously monitor a variety of internal and external perspectives the way a jet pilot monitors her vast array of instrument readouts combined with all other sensory and memory inputs. This ongoing flood of experience helps guide us in cocreating healing cultures in sessions.

1. Siegel (1999)

2. Siegel (2005)

3. Stern (2003)

4. Siegel (2007)

5. Siegel (2005)

6. Musashi (1974)

7. Siegel (2007)

8. Wilber (2003)

9. Siegel (2007)

10. Wilber (2003)

11. Almaas (2004)

36

Gross, Subtle, and Causal: the Foundation States

Each of us wake in the morning and enter the gross realm; the world of objects. We observe the external world, and generally identify with our physical body, and our social identities. I wake and discover myself to be Dr. Keith Witt, psychologist, husband, father, etc. I am lying on a bed, looking out a window at Santa Barbara and beyond to the Pacific Ocean and Channel Islands. My brainwaves reflect the characteristic combinations of gross, waking existence, largely amalgams of beta, alpha, and theta. If I have a nature mysticism experience gazing out at the world, the gross realm, it's likely to be feeling oneness with nature. This experience can range from oneness with a single blade of grass to oneness with all of nature that is arising in the moment, and will probably involve a predominance of theta brainwaves.[1] If I get up and begin to work on this manuscript and become absorbed in a flow state of harmony with the activity, I will feel a pleasurable sense of being lost in the experience and probably have a predominance of alpha brainwaves.[2]

Each night all of us lie down, relax, rest, and go to sleep. Soon we begin to dream, and so enter the subtle realm. We no longer observe objects as necessarily concrete, unchangeable things, or experience our physical body as necessarily the same as we do in the gross realm. We might be a disembodied observer, or a child, or an animal. We might be anywhere in time; past, present, or future. Our brainwaves usually have a predominance of theta in the subtle, dreaming state. If we have a deity mysticism experience in this subtle realm (either sleeping, or in a waking state with subtle elements), it's likely to be a subjectively intense encounter with a luminescent being, creature, object, or presence that feels archetypal or Godlike. This is God in the second person, or God as "you."[3]

During each ninety-minute sleep cycle we usually relax for a time into deep, dreamless sleep, physically and psychologically restorative. We consciously observe no objects, gross or subtle. Our brain waves even out at predominantly delta. Various spiritual traditions maintain that deep, dreamless sleep is an opening into the causal, formless realm, where there is a felt oneness with everything, and no objects arise. Some experienced meditators can maintain conscious awareness in deep, dreamless sleep. This is conscious awareness of pure emptiness and/ or pure fullness, what eastern traditions believe is an enlightened state, or formless mysticism.[4]

All humans, from infant to sage, at all levels of development, inhabit these three great states daily, and can have nature mysticism, deity mysticism, or formless mysticism experiences. Each night we dream and enter the subtle realm of shifting forms and sensations that feel real in the dream, drop further into the causal realm of deep, dreamless sleep, and wake to the gross realm of observable objects and identification with body, roles, and relationships.

Great realizers have reported that, at various points in their lives, they have had a subjective experience of *waking up* from the gross realm to new levels of understanding and experience that is similar to waking from sleep. These awakenings are associated with enlightenment, or nirvana. The literal translation of "Buddha" is, "the awakened one."[5]

We tend to interpret spiritual experience through our current worldview.

Even though we can all have nature mysticism, deity mysticism, or formless mysticism experiences at any time, we will tend to interpret them according to the worldviews we are currently occupying. In *Kosmic Consciousness* Wilber refers to the "Wilber-Combs grid" where he and his friend have mapped nature mysticism, deity mysticism, and formless mysticism throughout seven levels of development corresponding roughly to Spiral Dynamic's PURPLE though TURQUOISE.[6] For illustration's sake I'll simply explore how a transcendent experience might be processed at seven different levels of development:

- Tribal PURPLE might translate a transcendent experience as having magical control over nature.

- More mythic, power-God RED might translate such an experience as having access to, or influence over, the Gods that control nature or by being chosen by God to rule others.

- Conformist BLUE might feel a sense of transcendent infusion of the divine and feel personally visited by Jesus (a common description of the "born again" experience) and chosen to spread His message.

- Rational ORANGE might feel a sense of the transcendent and interpret it as a rush of endorphins associated with a cognitive/emotional peak experience.

- Egalitarian GREEN might feel a transcendent experience and be certain it is a divine state of grace that is equally available to all people at all times.

- Integral YELLOW might have a transcendent experience and conclude it could be any or all of the above, while knowing that certain practices support or disrupt the experience, and that people at different levels of development have different access to, and interpretations of, such transcendent states.

- World service oriented TURQUOISE might experience such a transcendent experience as unity with an intersubjective web of spirit, service, community with like-minded others, and oneness with all.

Spiritual practice enhances access to transcendent states.

Spiritual practices seem to enhance our ability to occupy nature mysticism, deity mysticism, and formless mysticism experiences. Meditative practices can enhance abilities to alter brain wave patterns, influence autonomic (considered by science "involuntary") functioning, and deepen developmental levels.[7] In general, the human brain reaches full development at twenty-six, and people do not deepen on their self, cognitive, values, needs, or moral lines until their mid fifties. As I mentioned in Section Five, some studies showed measurable development on these lines seemingly stalled at twenty-five and then accelerating again in our early fifties, with the notable exception of those who engaged in daily meditation practice. Four years of daily meditative practice was associated with a deepening of two levels on many meditators' self, cognitive, values, needs, and moral lines.[8] This suggests that the more we can consciously inhabit nature mysticism, deity mysticism, or causal mysticism states, the more likely we are to acquire stable traits of increased compassion and deepened consciousness. This is consistent with spirituality itself being a line of development with levels that include and transcend.

Since one of the main goals of therapy is to support development, it behooves us as therapists to support spiritual practice when and where we can. To do that, we need an understanding of what constitutes spiritual practice, and what practices might be best for what types of people at what levels of development. Not surprisingly, masculine and feminine types tend to hunger for, and seem to respond better to, different forms of spiritual practice. One way of understanding spiritual practices is by viewing them as ascending or descending.

Ascending spiritual practice: the masculine yearning for pure emptiness, the many into one.

As we've briefly explored previously, ascending spiritual practice involves progressively disidentifying with the body and temporal world, and identifying more deeply with God, pure spirit, pure emptiness, pure consciousness, or any other perspective on complete unity. It is the many into one. Most traditional religions such as Islam, Christianity, Judaism, and Buddhism developed out of agrarian BLUE societies where movement towards God was associated with movement away from the temporal world, away from pleasure, away from the body, away from sex, and generally towards "the next world": heaven, paradise, or liberation, where we are one with bliss, God, or pure emptiness.[9] As Myamoto Mushashi said in the last line of A Book of Five Rings, "Spirit is nothingness."[10] The Gods of ascending religions are mostly masculine, and many of these religions' spiritual practices tend to be solitary and ascetic.[11] The emphasis is on masculine agency. There is a hunger to know God's will, attain enlightenment, or transcend the material world into pure emptiness through study, philosophy, sacred texts, meditation, renunciation, action, or prayer. In many forms of Buddhism, masculine types seek causal, formless mysticism in rigorous meditation practices which are focused on feeling progressively deeper through their sense of a separate self (identified with body, thought, emotion, role, attachment, or social standing) to the changeless, eternal, unrecoiling, ever-present Self that has always existed, is one with everything, and is the changeless ground out of which everything else is always arising and has always arisen.[12]

Deepening consciousness involves disidentifying with body, mind, emotions, desire, thoughts, and impulses, and identifying with a progressively deeper Self that is not attached to any worldly thing, and that observes all with equanimity. This unrecoiling, ever-present Witness is the deep consciousness that Deida maintains is our masculine essence, and the defining aspect of masculine types. The deep soul's purpose and meaning at the edge of death that more masculine people crave is intimately connected with this attraction to ascending spirituality.[13]

Descending spirituality: the feminine yearning for fullness, the one into many.

Descending spiritual practice involves progressively identifying more with, and deeply inhabiting, sensation, body, sex, pleasure, nature, family, community, and the temporal world until we feel spirit radiating up through everything. Outlawed and persecuted by conformist BLUE traditions throughout most of agrarian human history, descending practices are making public comebacks in modern and postmodern societies. They are the one into many. The deities of the descending traditions are often feminine; the Earth Mother, Kali, Tara, or the Goddesses of hearth, home, family, sex, or feminine wisdom. Descending practices pursue fullness. Fulfillment is not in the next world or the next moment, but in this world at this moment.[14] The practices of descending traditions tend to emphasize communion over agency, pleasure over struggle, and yearning for fulfillment over the hunger for the ultimate emptiness of pure spirit. These practices often involve ceremony, pleasure, community, family, food, dance, sex, sensation, and yearning for all beings to be loved and loving.[15]

Descending spiritual practice tends to be more attractive and natural to the feminine. The feminine in us is drawn to nature and nature mysticism. Feminine types tend to gather flowers, collect shells, absorb beauty, and delight in the light. Feminine people are likely to experience deity mysticism as yearning for everyone to be filled with God's love. They are likely to be drawn to expressing such joyful yearning for God's love in community, dance, music, color, texture, food, and family.[16] Where BLUE masculine types more often want universal obedience to "God's laws," feminine types more often want universal receiving of—and expression of—God's love. Feminine types tend to experience formless mysticism as being living wellsprings of love and light that nourish all creation.[17]

Non-dual practice: the tantric tradition.

Ascending and descending practices, when taken to their extremes, end up in the same place, identification with, and love for, complete emptiness, and everything that's arising, which ultimately are the same. Since we all have both a masculine and feminine aspect, to some extent we all crave both ascending and descending spirituality, though our preferences will generally mirror our deepest masculine or feminine essence. A non-dual spiritual practice honors and utilizes both ascending and descending practices.[18]

I find pleasure and fulfillment in a variety of ascending and descending practices. I practice nature mysticism walking in the morning, deity mysticism in my morning prayers and imagery meditation, and formless mysticism in witness meditation. I've engaged in ascending practices of ordeal, study, martial arts, and vision quests, and descending practices of sacred sexuality, dance, music, and community. I've found all of them compelling, nourishing, and illuminating.

1. Wilber (2003)

2. Csikszentmihalyi (1990)

3. Wilber (2003)

4. *Ibid*

5. *Ibid*

6. *Ibid*

7. Alexander (1990)

8. *Ibid*

9. Wilber (1995)

10. Musashi (1974)

11. Starr (2002)

12. Wilber (2003)

13. Deida (2006)

14. Wilber (1995)

15. Deida (2006)

16. *Ibid*

17. Wilber (2003)

18. Wilber (1995)

37

Psychotherapy, Yoga, and Spiritual Practice

David Deida, in a lecture he gave at the Integral Institute in 2005, said that there are profound differences between therapy, yoga, and spiritual practice. He gave the metaphor of the self as a stained glass window. Therapy is repairing the panes, yoga is dusting and polishing the glass so the light can flow thorough more fully and radiantly, and spiritual practice is being the light.[1] They are different but related activities. Being a therapist, a yoga instructor, and a spiritual teacher are different but related callings.

I believe that good therapists, yoga instructors, and spiritual teachers have some familiarity and abilities in all three areas. I am not a yoga instructor or spiritual teacher, but sometimes the demands of the moment require me as therapist to support my client's expansion into yogas that "dust and polish the glass," and spiritual practices that support "being the light." I believe my psychotherapeutic work has benefited from my study, knowledge, and practice in these areas.

Both empirical and phenominological research suggests that a lifestyle that includes ascending and descending spiritual practices, and various yogas that address energy blocks and increase sensitivity to energy currents, supports health in general and development of psychotherapeutic expertise in particular.[2] One advantage of including such elements into your lifestyle is that you will probably naturally expand your own understanding of integrating spiritual practice and yoga into psychotherapy.

Integrating spiritual practice and yoga into psychotherapy.

Integrating spiritual practice and yoga into psychotherapy involves discerning and supporting where our clients are strong spiritually and energetically, and discerning and helping where they are suffering.

Descending practices in therapy.

One example of integrating descending practices into psychotherapy is this exchange with Bill, an anxious man in his late fifties. He is out of touch with his body, worries obsessively, and has little concept of healthy pleasures as healing nourishment, so I suggest a descending practice to help him self-soothe and feel pleasure in his body:

Bill: "I'm anxious all the time, and life seems like one struggle after another."

Keith: This is consistent with one essential masculine bad mood: a sense of constraint, and loss of freedom. My impulse is to direct him towards more feminine pleasures, a descending practice. I gesture toward the French doors in my office that look out onto a mature Morton Bay fig tree with the Santa Barbara Channel beyond. "Bill, look out these doors at the big fig tree and imagine you are this tree. Feel what it's like to be a massive, vigorous tree. Your roots are digging like strong legs into the earth, absorbing the water and nutrients that the earth provides. Your branches are reaching like huge arms to the sky to absorb light, warmth, and nourishment from the sun. Be one with the tree. Feel yourself as the tree.

Bill: "It feels good, Keith."

Keith: "You need this nourishment. You can do this with a blade of grass, a forest, or a boulder. Do it every day in nature, Bill. The pleasure is healthy. It can be a soothing, healing practice for you."

The following is another example of suggesting a descending practice with Enid. She and her husband, Paul, are in their mid thirties and have difficulty connecting sexually. Since her sexuality has been historically connected with self-destructive affiliation with egocentric, narcissistic jerks, Enid has difficulty relaxing into pleasure in her body with Paul, a good man who doesn't ring the old transgressive bells:

Enid: "I just don't feel sexy."

Paul: "I don't know what to do."

Enid: "In Dallas I used to go to the clubs. I'd drink and dance and go home and have sex with dark guys, selfish guys, who treated me badly."

Keith: Seeing and feeling the energetic charge as she says "dark guys". Noticing the erotic charge and the self-destructive anger in the drinking and dangerous relationships. "Sounds like you miss her."

Enid: "Who?"

Keith: "The Sex Goddess, the Dark Goddess, Kali, the destroyer."

Enid: "Yes, but she's sick, she's wounded."

Keith: "I agree. You need to heal her by loving her, embracing her, and teaching her how to have a great time with a good man. I suggest you do a daily practice to celebrate her and love her. Create a sensual environment. Put on sexy clothes and music that demands that you dance when you hear it. Then dance her through every part of your body, and especially your hips, pelvis, and breasts. Let her inhabit and fill your body, your voice, and your movement."

Paul: "Yeah!"

Enid: Alarmed. "I won't do that in front of you."

Keith: "Of course not. You should do it with women friends if you can. They can make this playful and you can help each other open up parts that are closed. The feminine grows best in the presence of loving praise, pleasure, and play. If you can't do it with friends, do it by yourself. It is a practice to love and heal that wounded, passionate young woman; to welcome her and cherish her existence by honoring the Sex Goddess she opens to so easily. That dark sexual energy is a resource you can cultivate and channel to create love for yourself, Paul, and everybody.[3]"

Enid: Intrigued. "I'll try it."

Ascending practices in therapy.

I'll often suggest ascending practices when a client is yearning for, and yet unconsciously blocking, greater depth of consciousness. The following is an example of encouraging deity mysticism with Blake, a dysthymic man in his early thirties. Often masculine people, who carry emotional pain like depression, sadness, rage, or anxiety, resist depth of consciousness because it involves having to feel the layers of emotional pain that they have been trying to avoid all their lives:

Blake: "I'm so pissed at myself. I came home drunk Monday and Sadie wants me out of the house. I'm moving out."

Keith: "I'm sorry. How are you going to spend time with your son?"

Blake: "For now, I'll see him Monday, Friday, and on the weekend."

Keith: Knowing Blake, a Christian, had a born again experience a year ago. "Have you been praying?"

Blake: "No, I've felt like a jerk."

Keith: "That's when it's especially important to reach out to God for love and guidance. I suggest you pray every morning, starting with gratitude for your son, your body, your faith, your work, and all your gifts. Then I suggest you ask for guidance about how you can be an instrument of God's will today."

Blake: "You're right. I always feel better when I start my day with prayer."

Keith: "I also think you should take your son to church on Sunday."

Blake: "I don't know. I'm kind of embarrassed."

Keith: "This is a time that you especially need support and guidance from God and caring people in a sacred environment. Go to church with your son."

Blake: "It feels right when you suggest it, and my son and I usually enjoy church together."

Sometimes more feminine clients need ascending practices to help them self-regulate defensive states. The following exchange is with Bertrand, a "bottom" (more feminine partner) in a three-year relationship with Howard, his more masculine lover. Bertrand is somewhat narcissistic and sadistic, with a borderline personality disorder and narcissistic traits. Howard's a relatively happy, rational, egalitarian ORANGE/GREEN top, deep in his ability to open a feminine partner to bliss, and somewhat dependent:

Bertrand: "I'm angry at Howard. I think I need to kick him out. I don't trust him."

Keith: "What makes you angry?"

Bertrand: "I wanted him to fuck me Thursday night and got everything ready, and he didn't even seem to notice."

Keith: Having an impulse to help him cultivate wisdom and compassion. "It's not a good idea for you to make impulsive decisions when you're feeling emotional pain."

Bertrand: "Well, what should I do then?"

Keith: "Well, first, make sure he knows it when you want sex."

Bertrand: "I always want sex."

Keith: Laughing. "True, but sometimes it's particularly important, like Thursday night, and he might not be as tuned into you as you think."

Bertrand: "That's what he said, but I didn't believe him."

Keith: "Do you believe him at this moment?"

Bertrand: "Yes, I do a lot more."

Keith: "So, in the hurt state you were in Thursday, you had an extra negative opinion of him. Which do you think is probably the most true, your opinion Thursday or now?"

Bertrand: "Now."

Keith: "I think you would benefit from five minutes of meditation each day."

Bertrand: Egocentric, with a "What's in it for me?" attitude. "Why should I?"

Keith "It helps you cultivate compassion and depth of consciousness which can help you see more clearly and make better decisions. Let's try it and see how you like it."

Bertrand: "OK."

Keith: "Sit comfortably. Close your eyes. Do circular breathing like we practiced last session. Feel your body. Feel your emotions, thoughts, and impulses. Observe how they enter and leave your consciousness. Notice how you feel your body, but you are not your body. You feel your emotions and thoughts, but you are not your emotions and thoughts. You feel your impulses and judgments, but you are not your impulses and judgments. You are a deeper, unrecoiling, ever-present witness. As this witness, you observe your bodily sensations, you observe your thoughts, feelings, judgments and impulses, but you are not any of them. You are an unrecoiling witness, relaxed into deepest consciousness. If you can observe that deep witness, then there is an even deeper witness observing, and so on until you are the deepest witness, the self that observes all objects, but is itself not an object. Rest in that deepest witness. Sink deeper into the sea of consciousness that we all share, and that we are always arising out of. As this sea of consciousness, observe Bertrand's body, thoughts, feelings, judgments, and impulses like waves on the surface. Your conscious awareness rises up from this sea, through your deepest witness and through your body, emotions, thoughts, judgments, and impulses into the manifest world. Let's just sit a few minutes and abide as the ocean of consciousness."

Keith: After a few minutes of meditation, I see Bertrand's eyes begin to open as he moves out of the state I've helped him to cultivate. "Well?"

Bertrand: "I feel more loving towards Howard. I feel really peaceful. How should I use this?"

Keith: I routinely tape sessions and send the tapes home with my clients. "I suggest you listen to this part of the tape each day, and do the meditation until you can comfortably do it without the tape."

Bertrand: "I'll try it."

Ascending practices away from the body, descending practices into the body.

Descending meditations involve going deeper into sensation, nature, pleasure, and communion. Ascending meditations involve disidentifying with a smaller self, often a self that is conflicted and suffering, and identifying with a larger self that is more compassionate, has more depth of consciousness, and can identify with, feel one with ("feeling one with" is one of my favorite definitions of love[4]), a wider more expansive, less material consciousness. These are almost always healing experiences in the session, and healthy practices at home. They also don't have to require conscious understanding or formal operational cognitive processes. For example, in the following exchange with Nathan, a nine-year-old boy, I encourage him to cultivate an ascending, deity-mysticism practice:

Keith: "Did you dream last week?"

Nathan: "I had a dream about a unicorn."

Keith: "Tell me the dream."

Nathan: "I was in a beautiful country, and a unicorn came and talked with me. It was big, and nice, and wise."

Keith: "Close your eyes and imagine yourself back in the dream."

Nathan: Closing his eyes. "I'm back in the dream. I see the unicorn."

Keith: "Tell the unicorn what you're feeling and thinking."

Nathan: "Unicorn, I think you're beautiful and wise. I like you."

Keith: "Now, be the unicorn looking at Nathan, and tell Nathan what you're feeling and thinking."

Nathan: "You're a good boy Nathan, and I'm going to take you for a ride."

Keith: "Be Nathan and answer."

Nathan: "Let's go."

Keith: "Let yourself ride for a little."

Keith: After a couple of minutes, Nathan opens his eyes with a smile. "We flew over this green country like the shire. It was fun."

Keith: "Nathan, each night, when you lie down to go to sleep, I'd like you to have a little talk like this with the unicorn. You can just check in, take a pretend ride, or ask him for advice. I think it would help you to sleep better, and be good for you. Could you try it for the next week?"

Nathan: "If I remember."

Keith: "I'll have your Mom remind you when she kisses you good-night."

Nathan: "Sure."

Nathan's mother may or may not remind him, and Nathan may or may not continue his practice. My experience is that clients of all ages rarely follow through systematically on meditation suggestions. I'll remind them to practice, occasionally keep including the practices in the session, and offer them new practices periodically. Sometimes they follow through at home. Sometimes they pursue similar experiences in the fabric of their lives or spiritual orientations, or sometimes they are just a little more willing and able to engage in similar activities when they appear later in life.

Whether there is follow through or not, these practices stretch clients' capacity for compassion and depth of consciousness, and provide little bridges between their smaller selves and their larger selves; bridges that help them find healthy perspectives and actions to be beautiful, good, and true.

1. Deida (2005)

2. Alexander (1990), Cloniger (2004), Childre (2005), Linehan (2001)

3. Deida (2006)

4. Deida (2004)

38

Dreamwork: Including the Subtle Realm in Psychotherapy

Each night we lie down and go to sleep. On average, it takes us between six and twenty minutes until we pass, instantly, from the waking state to sleep. Contrary to popular perception, there is no gradual transition from waking to sleeping. Rather, it is a sudden change of state. As we sleep, we deepen into the dreaming state, which is usually (but not always) accompanied by REM (rapid eye movements) and characterized by a predominance of theta brain waves.[1] During our dreaming state, a pulse of energy moves from our brain stem out through our cerebral cortex, resulting in a dream. This process is influenced and directed by seratonin systems in the Rafe area of the ventral medial hypothalamus, one of the emotional regulation centers of the brain, but it also involves the hippocampus (our memory center), our amygdala (the center for negative emotional arousal), and other brain areas. Some research suggests that for memories to become consolidated and independent of needing hippocampal support for retrieval, we need to dream about them.[2]

Dreams: multi-thematic, multi-dimensional, primitive, and transcendent: a unique language for each individual.

Having studied dreaming and dream work, and practiced dream work with my own, my family's, and my clients' dreams for over thirty years, I've concluded that dreams are multi-thematic, with multiple levels of meaning from the most basic (you're hungry and dream of food), to the most transcendent (an archetypal figure gives specific direction to guide you on a path with a heart). All these levels are somehow woven together by the miracle of our nervous system, and the genius of our unconscious, into an unending source of images, themes, memories, and messages. Past, present, and future combine. The most sacred and the

337

most profane symbols coexist. We encounter ourselves, our history, and our culture in personal mythic creations that continue to unfold throughout our lives.

Since much dream material flows up from unconscious sources, and relates to inner conflicts and forbidden impulses that go unrecognized and unexpressed in our waking state, there is an ongoing tension in our psycho-emotional being from simultaneous drives to express repressed or conflicted material so energy can be released and resolution of conflict pursued, and to conceal threatening material from conscious awareness (a legacy of our Fulcrums 2 and 3 capacities for repression or otherwise avoiding threatening material). This is consistent with some researchers' assertion that a major function of dreams is to rehearse potentially dangerous situations to make us more likely to survive in waking life.[3]

Dreams that are not written down or discussed immediately upon awakening usually quickly fade and are forgotten. Further, since dream themes and images draw from all levels of development (primitive primary process to post-post-operational, egocentric to altruistic), they form a unique, inclusive, personal language for each individual. Like all languages, the more the dream language is spoken and used in waking life, the more fluent we become in speaking and understanding it.

Dreams are healing/balancing systems.

Unquestionably, dreams function as healing and balancing systems for us physically, spiritually, relationally, and psychologically. People deprived of dreams, but not sleep, usually develop paranoid psychotic symptoms within a week of dream deprivation.[4] Conflicted intrapsychic and interpersonal material is often presented in real or symbolic form in dreams, usually with obvious or subtle indicators about solutions or remediations we can implement in the gross, waking realm. Every spiritual tradition has some provision for dreams being a bridge into the divine. In Vedanta, regular lucid dreaming (being consciously aware you are in a dream state while dreaming) is one marker of the transition from the third sheath to the fourth sheath in the five-sheath progression towards non-dual unity.[5] Dream analysis and interpretation are central aspects of the Freudian and Jungian psychoanalytic systems, and Shamans throughout human history have used dreams, and interpreted dreams, to guide and support their tribes.

Dreamwork is useful in a wide range of psychotherapies.

Dream work of different kinds can support the psychotherapeutic process on almost all levels. I'll explore and give examples of four different applications of dream work in psychotherapy:

- Supporting intimacy.

- Connecting and harmonizing conscious and unconscious processes.

- Free associations and interpretations from a variety of perspectives.

- Identifying, normalizing, and resolving internalized conflicts by using Gestalt dialogues to integrate various aspects of self that are dissociated to some degree.

These four examples illustrate the basic organizing principle of using dreams psychotherapeutically, that almost any form of conscious attention to our dreams tends to be beneficial. Let's explore these four in more depth.

Dreamwork that supports intimacy.

Often couples have no conscious secrets from one another, and yet lack juice and depth in their emotional/erotic connection. They may be bored, or mildly irritated, when in conversation, have minimal and/or tepid sex, or find other men or women more interesting than their spouse. Deida suggests that when the sexual occasion is boring the feminine partner needs to provide more life, energy, and juice, and that when sex is shallow the masculine partner needs to provide more depth of consciousness.[6] One method of supporting these activities is to suggest to couples that they tell each other their dreams in the morning. If couples follow through on this practice, it has immediate effects. Most adults can deny the significance of dream material only to the extent that they avoid dream material. Describing and discussing dreams quickly confronts spouses with the presence of charged images and themes with obvious relevance to waking life, and brings them face to face with the relative difficulty of discussing some images and themes with their partner. There is often a felt sense of intimacy in discussing dream material and a frequent irresistible urge to discover (or create through projection) meaning from dream material. Whether this is more or less difficult, if practiced by couples it usually supports juice and depth.

An example of this is the following exchange with Paul and Enid, the couple we met earlier who were lacking juice and depth in their sexual relationship:

Enid: "I had the same dream about a powerful, selfish, confident man making love to me."

Paul: A whiny, complaining voice. "It's never me."

Enid: Defensive. "I can't help what I dream."

Keith: "Did you discuss the dream with each other?"

Enid: "I told him, like you suggested, the morning I had it."

Keith: Modeling an interested attitude for Paul, and assuming the dream material is useful and relevant. "What did it teach you, Enid?"

Enid: "I want to be ravished by a powerful, masterful, selfish man."

Paul: Angry, humiliated, and collapsing. "Go find one then."

Enid: "This is why I can't talk to you, Paul."

Keith: Their relational defensive pattern is constellated. They are both in defensive states. Dangerous new perspectives and potentially challenging new actions are being avoided in a typically collaborative way. It's time to interrupt before one of them gets so emotionally charged that he or she becomes unavailable to risk a different perspective. Knowing the feminine often grows best in the presence of loving praise and that Paul needs help in learning how to be more present, I model presence while praising Enid. "You're both missing the point. It's wonderful that you have these sex dreams, Enid. You have a healthy libido, and you yearn to be ravished open."

Paul: The same defensive tone. "But not by me."

Keith: The masculine often grows best in the presence of loving challenge. "Paul, first you collapsed and took offense when she risked telling you her dream, and now you're still collapsing by trying to evoke her attraction by complaining. Complaining never evokes attraction in a feminine partner."

Paul: More present. Open to direction. "How do I respond, then?"

Keith: Teaching masculine practice from the dream, so Paul can more effectively occupy the masculine pole of their sexual polarity and actually evoke attraction from Enid. "Listen with interest when Enid tells you her dream.

This is a window into her primal sexual energy. These dark men are confident, hungry for her, and able to extend their shadow into her and open her to erotic passion."

Enid: More open from just hearing me suggest this to Paul. "That's what I want from you, Paul."

Keith: "Paul, your shadow material of anger and self-doubt comes out in condemning her for not feeling attraction. You need to care for these aspects and cultivate other aspects of your dark side, as well as your humor and presence, until you are the one confidently ravishing her open. You start by keeping your humor and presence when she tells you her dream, and looking for guidance in her dream in how to help her feel loved by you, and in how to open her erotically yourself."

Paul: Looking at Enid with a smile. "What exactly were you and that guy doing?"

Enid: Smiling back. "That's better."

Paul and Enid are learning how to use their dreams to enhance their sexual polarity and expand their comfort zone of charged subjects around which they can have enjoyable, intimate conversations. This adds juice and depth to their relationship.

Using dreams to connect and harmonize conscious and unconscious processes.

Most of the time, creating and supporting an active dialog between unconscious and conscious processes enhances health and supports development. The most basic way to use dreams in this fashion is to write them down when we wake. Over time, this simple practice puts us progressively in touch with themes, images, relationships, and symbols that our unconscious finds important enough to include in our dreams. Our natural curiosity, fascination, and drive to create meaning often then motivates us to pursue self reflective, healing insight.

Once the importance of dreams is established, and the natural mechanism of almost instantly forgetting dream material is addressed through writing dreams down, or talking about dreams with another upon waking, deeper work designed to connect and harmonize conscious and unconscious material is possible. The following is a brief list of examples of practices I've recommended and supported over the years:

- **Program your dreams.**

I might suggest to a client with a marital dilemma, "Tonight, when you lie down to go to sleep, I'd like you to say to yourself twenty times, "Tonight I will have healing dreams about my marriage." Write down your dreams when you wake, and bring them into the next session.

- **Create ordeals, or rites of passage with dreams.**

To a masculine person who is plagued with nightmares, I might suggest, "Before you go to sleep, tell yourself twenty times that, if a monster starts pursuing you, you will turn, walk toward it, and tell it "I'm not going to let you hurt me."

To a feminine person who is plagued with nightmares, I might suggest, "Before you go to sleep, tell yourself twenty times that, if a monster starts pursuing you, you are going to turn and love that monster with all the compassion, love, and light in your spirit. Illuminate it with love."

- **Reenter and integrate dream material.**

Another technique for dealing with nightmares as well as pursuing healing insight and integration is, "When you wake distressed or perplexed, lie still for a bit while doing circular breathing, and tell yourself to go back into the dream so that you can talk to the conflicted figures, and address and heal distressing or perplexing material."

- **Do morning dialogues with dream images.**

To support a dream channel of self-reflection, I might suggest, "When you wake, stay in bed a few extra minutes and go back into your dream. Become the different figures and talk to each other in various combinations while staying alert for conflicts, resolutions, and insights. You can write this dialogue or just do it internally."

The above are just a few examples of connecting and harmonizing conscious and unconscious material using dreams. As you do this work personally and with your clients you will naturally discover through study and experimentation what techniques fit best with your clinical style and your sense of what best fits with each client's unique worldview.

Free associations and interpretations of dreams from a variety of perspectives.

Freud[7] and Jung[8] were pioneers in bringing dream interpretation into the mainstream of modern, western conventional thought and clinical practice. Both had points of view that were similar is some ways and strikingly different in others. Together they set the stage for Perls (Gestalt Therapy[9]), Asagioli (Psychosynthesis[10]), Campbell (myth and symbols[11]) and other analysts and humanists who have followed in their conceptual and clinical footsteps.

Freud believed that wish fulfillment, personally forbidden feelings/thoughts/experiences/images/impulses, and Eros and Thanatos—the drives to create and destroy—dominated unconscious content and dream material.[12]

Jung believed that there was a rich tapestry of unconscious material that was largely universal in human existence. He mapped out the archetypes of Animus (the masculine principle), Anima (the feminine principle), Puer (divine masculine youth), Warrior, Synex (man of wisdom), Destructress (Kali for example), Queen, Crone, and countless others. Jung abstracted, expanded, and wrote about the universal themes of epic journey, sacred family, mandala, and many others that seem to have always appeared in human myths and dreams.[13]

Both Freud and Jung encouraged their clients to free associate on dream images and themes while they simultaneously associated from their different points of view on those same images and themes, and then offered interpretations.

I often ask my clients to first walk me through the dream in the first person, and then tell me what the dream images and themes suggest to them. This free association guides me to what perspective might best serve a particular client. For example, in the following exchange with Josh, the eighteen year old we met in Section Four who was struggling with anxiety issues, anger issues, dependency issues, and a fierce desire for independence and freedom, both Jungian and Freudian elements seemed to best harmonize with his associations and needs:

Josh: "I had this weird dream last night."

Keith: Smiling, wanting him to feel that he and his universe are cherished. "I love your weird dreams. Walk me through it as if it's happening right now."

Josh: "I'm eating a meal at a table with lots of people my age. This guy across the table and I are rivals somehow, and getting angry, and now we're fighting. We're rolling around the table, and, all of a sudden, he's turned into a woman and we're making love."

Keith: "What was the guy like?"

Josh: "About five feet ten inches, black hair, and blue eyes. He was in good shape."

Keith: "You could be describing yourself, Josh."

Josh: "O God! You're right. But what about him turning into a woman and us making love? That feels weird to me."

Keith: "What does it mean to you?"

Josh: "I was so mad. I was trying to beat this guy up and then he was this woman and I was, you know, loving her, and having intercourse with her. I don't get it."

Keith: "Who else do you get so mad at that you want to hurt them, and then feel loving and sometimes sexual?"

Josh: "Not my mother!"

Keith: "What do you mean, 'not my mother?'"

Josh: "I feel those things with her sometimes. It sounds so sick."

Keith: Josh and I have worked previously on the Oedipal theme, and also on his capacity for critically judging his sexual impulses, especially ones that are transgressive according to the rigid BLUE moral perspectives prevalent in his family, friend, and school cultures. This dream seems more positive to me than a reflection of pathology. There is a community of peers, struggle, and several significant transformations. I offer an interpretation designed to support acceptance, deeper explorations, and a transformative orientation. "I think this is a beautiful dream."

Josh: "Huh?"

Keith: "You're in a community of your peers, but they also are eating together like family. Just like in your real life family, you start fighting for position and recognition. You're heterosexual, but we both know you have homosexual masturbation fantasies where you become the feminine partner. You hunger constantly for a beautiful, luscious woman with whom you can be wild lovers. This dream normalizes your anger, normalizes your homosexual fantasies, normalizes your desire for a lover, and reflects your ongoing struggles to integrate your light and dark, masculine and feminine, in a harmonious inner community. The dream ends with you and her publicly resolving your anger into sexual communion and erotic passion. Hopefully, when you do find and bond with a feminine lover, you can learn to take your aggressive impulses, which are absolutely going to show up in every intimate relationship you ever have, and transform them into love and passion. This is a transformative dream on many levels."

Josh: Intensely interested. "What about the mother stuff?"

Keith: "Your mother's feminine, you're masculine, and so you feel polarity that has been mostly expressed through passionate conflict, though you have had sexual feelings and one sexual dream about her. She has poor sexual boundaries energetically, and so you as a masculine person have a natural polarity with her feminine erotic glow. She believes just not allowing sexual touch is enough sexual boundary, and so she doesn't adequately regulate her feminine energy around you. She's the woman you've been closest to in your life so far, and you both love each other."

Josh: "That's disgusting."

Keith: "Yes, disgusting and fascinating. You need a woman from a community of your peers; one you can bond with, go deeper with, and be fully yourself with, both masculine and feminine."

Josh: "Like the woman in the dream."

Keith: "Yes. I think she was both your feminine side that you're ambivalent about and need to integrate, and your idealized lover with whom you can be fully yourself."

Josh: "This all feels so true."

Keith: "It feels true to me too, and it also feels beautiful and good."

In this exchange I feel no need to be consistent with any analytic tradition. I use the ones I know to help guide me in co-creating Josh's unique constellation of needs, drives, themes, and inner figures, to help him create his own meaning, and to understand, accept, and cherish himself and his own unique universe.

Identifying, normalizing, and resolving internalized conflicts by using Gestalt dialogues to integrate various aspects of the self that are dissociated to some degree.

Fritz Perls maintained that each aspect of a dream represents an aspect of self. Thus conflicts in dreams represent internalized conflicts between different intra-psychic elements of our self.[14] "Internalized conflicts" is one of Freud's definitions of neurosis. Encouraging a client to inhabit different figures and characters, and act out relationships to other figures and characters, helps him or her identify with, and more fully integrate, these elements. Encouraging a client to act out and explore dream conflicts between self, objects, and characters supports movement toward resolving the internalized conflicts that dream figures express.

Gestalt therapy: making the implicit explicit and pointing out the obvious.

Fritz Perls' dialogic techniques revolutionized dream work. They added authenticity and enhanced emotional charge to the more formal (and often less threatening) techniques of association and interpretation, and provided a present moment, visceral immediacy to the more traditional "talking about" dreams.

An example of using the Gestalt dialogic technique is the following exchange with Cheryl, the woman in her early thirties we met in Section Four, who is somewhat depressed and still conflicted about her divorce three years previously. She yearns for love, both to receive a trustable man and to offer devotional love in return, and hopes it is her current lover Jake, but she is unsure. When threatened, she easily becomes angry and suspicious of him. This particular piece of work illustrates a variety of Gestalt principles and techniques:

- I first ask Cheryl to describe her dream in the first person present, as if it is happening right now.

- I then explore by question and observation where the strongest emotional charges seem to be, and especially what conflicts they might represent.

- As I direct Cheryl in the dialogic process, I keep attending to, and keep encouraging her to be aware of, her shifting sensations, emotions, thoughts, and impulses. Perls believed, with much support from psychotherapeutic practice and spiritual traditions, that awareness of immediate experience is itself a healing activity.

- Foundation principles for the practice of Gestalt therapy are making the implicit explicit, and pointing out the obvious. I continue to do this throughout the exchange.

- Finally, I encourage Cheryl to support resolution of conflict in the dialogue, and then apply the whole process to supporting healthy perspectives and actions in her waking life.

Cheryl enjoys dream work and is comfortable with the Gestalt system. Some clients can't stand the dialogic process and so with them I'll work with their dreams in different ways, some of which I've already described. The classical Gestalt method is to have your client change chairs when they change characters. Less awkward alternatives are having them simply change identity in the same chair, or to hold out their hands and speak left to right, and then right to left:

Cheryl: "I had this dream last Saturday after Jake told me his ex-girlfriend called him earlier in the week."

Keith: "Describe it as if it is happening right now."

Cheryl: "I'm in a field. Jake has been hurt, maybe in an accident, and he's lying on the ground. I'm upset and want to help him, and I'm bending down over him protectively. Suddenly, I'm in a shack on a beach and my ex-husband is coming to surf. I don't want him to come, but I'm looking forward to it also."

Keith: Noticing how her voice and energy surge when she says, "Jake has been hurt."

"Where is the dream most intense for you?"

Cheryl: "When I see Jake lying on the ground."

Keith: I could ask Cheryl to be any part of the dream. If she had no particular charge on any aspect, I could ask her to be the ground, be Jake, be the accident, be her ex-husband, or be the dream itself. Since there is more charge on the injured Jake, I'll suggest we start with addressing him. "Be there with him, and tell him how you feel and what you think."

Cheryl: "Jake, are you all right? I'm worried, you look hurt."

Keith: When I ask her to be Jake, I'll first have her describe what it's like to be him. I want her to re-own and absorb whatever part of herself that is separated and projected into the conflicted image. "Be Jake, injured on the ground. Describe your existence. Start with 'I'm Jake, lying injured in the field'."

Cheryl: Voice quavering a little. "I'm Jake, injured in the field. I've been hit by a car. I can't walk. I need help."

Keith: Wanting to pull the dream Cheryl into the dialogue, I'll ask "Jake" to talk to Cheryl. This tends to naturally evoke a response from her to the dream Jake. "As Jake, look at Cheryl. Tell her how you feel as she bends down over you."

Cheryl: As Jake. "Cheryl, it's so good to see you. I need some help. Call 911."

Keith: "Be Cheryl and respond."

Cheryl: "I'm sorry, Jake."

Keith: I feel a tingle of curiosity at her apology. "Tell him why you're sorry."

Cheryl: "Somehow I did this to you. This is my dream and you've been hit by a car."

Keith: If her unconscious hit him with a car, she's probably resentful about something. I encourage her to make the implicit explicit. "Tell him what you resent."

Cheryl: With some vehemence. "I hate it that your old girlfriend called."

Keith: "Be Jake and respond."

Cheryl: As Jake. "I couldn't help it she called. Besides, it's no reason to hit me with a car."

Keith: "You sound angry, Jake. Tell Cheryl why you're mad."

Cheryl: As Jake. "Sara calls me, and you get all pissed off. It's not fair."

Keith: "Be Cheryl and respond."

Cheryl: "She wouldn't call if you didn't encourage her."

Keith: "It sounds like you don't trust Jake to be faithful."

Cheryl: Defensive. "He'd never cheat on me."

Keith: "Tell him."

Cheryl: "I know you'd never cheat on me. I just hate her intruding on our lives."

Keith: "Be Jake and respond."

Cheryl: As Jake. "Then why crush me with a car? I don't deserve it."

Keith: The dialogue now has its own momentum. Cheryl is experiencing the difference between the real Jake, and the destructive part of herself that she is projecting onto him. In the process, all figures are coming together and are visibly integrating. "Be Cheryl."

Cheryl: "You're right. I'm sorry. I get suspicious and think you're someone you're not."

Keith: Pointing out the obvious. "You look and sound tender."

Cheryl: "He's a good man. I should trust him more when I'm upset."

Keith: Wanting her to feel the impact of her devotional love. "Be Jake and hear what Cheryl just said."

Cheryl: As Jake. "I know you work at being honest and loving. I know it's hard for you when Sara calls. I'm not perfect, but I love you."

This session continues with Cheryl being her ex-husband, the car that hit Jake, the shack she is waiting for him in, and the beach that is the surf destination. There is no particular charged dialogue until this last exchange with her ex-husband, Al, the embodiment of the untrustworthy man that she projects her own violent self onto:

Keith: "Be Al and tell Cheryl what you want."

Cheryl: As Al. "I just want to have some fun surfing. Why can't we be friends?"

Keith: "Be Cheryl and respond."

Cheryl: Angry. "Because you cheated on me, that's why. Jake would never do that."

Cheryl is now unconsciously discerning the very real differences between the two men, and also normalizing and owning angry, egocentric, aggressive aspects of her self that she projects onto others. As her therapist, I need to assertively inhabit a trustable masculine presence to offer her direction of what I believe is in her best interests. I also need to embody feminine care by cherishing her and her universe, independent of any content. These responsibilities are the same for male and female therapists, but there will be natural emphases in one direction or the other depending upon what type of person the therapist is.

This concludes our section on working with the subtle, dreaming state in therapy. We'll now move on to biochemically induced or influenced states, states that are healthy responses to the present moment, defensive states emanating from individual defensive structures, and relational defensive structures.

1. Dement (1999)

2. Siegel (2005)

3. Dixit (2007)

4. Dement (1999)

5. Wilber (2003)

6. Deida (2004)

7. Freud (1952)

8. Jung (1965)

9. Perls (1968)

10. Assagioli (1965)

11. Campbell (1949)

12. Freud (1952)

13. Jung (1965)

14. Perls (1968)

39

*Biochemically Induced
or Influenced States*

Scientific definitions of humans often involve references to each of us being complex, multidimensional systems of interdependent biochemical processes. These biochemical processes are central determinants of our states of consciousness. Each type of individual has their idiosyncratic biochemical capacities and vulnerabilities to a unique constellation of states.[1] How we experience and manage those states varies with what levels of development we have on different lines.[2] No one can be cognizant of, much less expert in, every possible type of state, but therapists take into account as many perspectives as possible in understanding and helping clients. In this Chapter we'll explore:

- Genetic predispositions to various states.

- The effects of chronic and non-chronic illness on states.

- Drug induced or influenced states.

Genetic predispositions: types influencing states.

Most developmental researchers (and I suspect all mothers) believe significant aspects of our temperament are determined genetically and congenitally at birth.[3] Certainly there is persuasive evidence of temperamental predisposition for thrill seeking, shyness, harm avoidance, persistence, self-directedness, self-transcendence, dependence, and cooperativeness.[4] Research has also yielded high incidences of genetic and/or organic involvement in all the mood disorders (anxiety, depressive, and bipolar disorders), most thought disorders (all the schizophrenias, schizoid, compulsive, and dependent personality disorders), attention deficit disorders, and most developmental disorders.[5]

Arguably, most DSMIV diagnoses reflect different types of constitutional predispositions to different symptom constellations. Most of these types are predisposed to different states of consciousness and unconsciously generate characteristic energies in their intersubjective fields with others. Anxious people tend to be faster paced, more vigilant, and have higher energy. Depressed people tend to be slower paced, more pessimistic and critical, and have lower energy. Masculine people tend to process distress from success/failure perspectives; while feminine people tend to process distress from "I am loved/I am not loved" perspectives.

In therapy, it's always useful to observe and explore the types, and accompanying states, of our clients, and use that information to help them understand and manage their varying states of consciousness. An example of this is from the following session with Lance, a fifty-five-year-old man who was referred to me for striking his lover, and abusing cocaine and other drugs. He is intelligent, anxious, intensely masculine, with narcissistic traits, and extreme emotional reactivity. This exchange is from our thirty-first session:

Lance: "I'm trying to not get so angry when people mess with me."

Keith: "I think anxiety is your more basic problem, not anger."

Lance: Curious. "What do you mean?"

Keith: "You grew up in a terrifying environment with a lot of natural capacity for anxiety. Let's face it. You endured physical and emotional threat and abuse at home, physical and emotional intimidation at school, and no support for being scared. To the contrary, in the cultures you grew up in males were considered cowards for feeling or acknowledging fear."

Lance: "That's all true, but I was mad a lot."

Keith: "It was acceptable to everybody that you were angry. Anger was an emotion that had power and evoked respect. You learned to turn your anxiety into anger. Most of the time when you talk about being really pissed about something, I'm hearing you say you're really worried and are having anxious, obsessive thoughts. One of your defensive habits, which you developed throughout childhood, is to look for someone or something to attack."

Lance: "It makes sense, but so what? I still get mad."

Keith: "How does it feel to consider that, when you get mad, there's a part of you that's anxious and worried about loss of something important?"

Lance: "That's weird. It's relaxing to think that I'm actually coming from anxiety when I get pissed off."

Keith: "Right. Remember when you get mad that part of you is anxious and needs to be reassured and soothed; first by you, and then by the people who care for you."

Lance: "How do I do that?"

Keith: Speaking to his masculine core, which is transitioning from the Warrior to the Man of Wisdom. "First, you begin by remembering none of it matters because we're all going to die. Your next step is to ask yourself, 'How does a Man of Wisdom handle a situation like this?'"

Lance: Laughing. "We are all going to die, and I do want to be a Man of Wisdom."

Chronic and non-chronic illnesses influence states.

I've always found it fascinating that the DSMIV suggests that one of the first things you're advised to rule out when doing differential diagnosis of major depression is a case of the flu. This is revealing in two ways. First, it's a measure of how much physical and emotional pain is involved in having the flu. In general, I've found that most people deny the sheer magnitude of physical and emotional pain associated with the most common illnesses. Second, it reveals how much physical and emotional misery accompanies major depression. Pain tends to make us regress, become more egocentric, and more prone to defensive states. Most illnesses, as well as many medications, have some effects on mood and state of consciousness. It's useful to remember that anxiety, depression, grief, and anger associated with physical illness are all incorporated into states of consciousness with characteristic perceptions, emotions, thoughts, memories, and impulses.

Recognizing and normalizing the interplay between illness, medications, and states of consciousness is soothing and reassuring to clients. It helps them more effectively self-regulate, perhaps the single most important skill we support in psychotherapy.

An example of using this information in therapy is the following session with Lance, who had a cold at the time:

Lance: "I should sell this damn business and move to New Zealand."

Keith: "Lance, you have a cold. You're sick and aching and the world sucks. I think your physical pain is influencing your current feelings and impulses about your business. Nobody wants to go to work when they're sick."

Lance: "I have been just wasted the last two days. I'm taking antihistamines and Advil, working all day, and collapsing each night."

Keith: "Antihistamines make you anxious as well as tired. You need to go home and go to bed. Think about changes in your business when you're healthy. If it's a good idea now to sell your business and move to New Zealand, it will still be a good idea when you're healthy."

Lance: His masculine relaxes in response to my loving challenge. "OK. I'm going home, going to bed, and resting until I get better."

Drug induced or influenced states: omnipresent throughout history, with attitudes toward euphorics varying with worldview.

Every human society has utilized euphorics for religious and/or recreational uses. Often the drugs themselves are assigned mythical or magical attributes. Some Southwest Native Americans communed with the spirit of Peyote. Iawasca is considered a deity as well as a ceremonial hallucinogenic substance in parts of Brazil. Wine is still used in Communion in many Christian churches. Each MEME seems to have its own emphasis in attitude towards euphorics.

- Tribal PURPLE has normalized euphorics for religious and social purposes, as in Shamanic ceremonies, and normalized daily chewing of Coca leaves by villagers in Peru.

- Power-God RED uses euphorics as sources of wealth, power, and self indulgence, as in the illicit drug trades.

- Conformist BLUE uses euphorics, like sex, as instruments of social control, as in prohibition, and the American War On Drugs.

- Capitalistic, achievement oriented ORANGE uses euphorics as sources of profit (U.S. drug companies) and relief from the pressures of ORANGE hierarchical struggles (the cocktail hour).

- Egalitarian GREEN uses euphorics as symbols of individual freedom (campus drinking and pot smoking), while holding powerful self-righteous biases based on non-rational, mostly unexamined critical judgments of alternative perspectives (pot should be legalized, while cocaine and heroin should not).

- YELLOW utilizes drugs depending on the needs of the moment and the social context.

Peeks (or peaks) with a price.

In general, euphorics seem to be "peeks" (immediately altered perspectives) or "peaks" (as in substance induced transcendent moments) with a price. Eating, drinking, smoking, snorting, or injecting a substance translates into instant mood shifts (often, but not always, to euphoria of some sort) and immediately altered perspectives, followed or accompanied by a variety of physical/emotional/behavioral side effects.

Euphorics tend to be feminizing in that they pull us into the sensations of our bodies.[6] They also tend to be chemically induced adventures where we change our perspectives, feel subjectively on an edge, and have license to avoid responsibilities. There are clear social dangers in using euphorics in America, since most of them are illegal and (with the minor exceptions of small doses of caffeine, amphetamine, cocaine, or other stimulants) euphorics universally result in diminished capacity, reduced or compromised reflexes, and challenges to immune function in particular, and health in general.

I've also found chronic abuse and/or dependence of euphorics to often be associated with arrested development on various lines such as the self-line in general, and particularly the cognitive line, the relationship line, the masculine and feminine lines, the needs line, and the morals line.

Serious problems are likely when euphoric use becomes progressive and/or out of control.

A health-based psychotherapeutic perspective on euphorics starts with cultivating awareness of personal and social biases, and is anchored in the goals of reducing symptoms, enhancing health, and supporting development. Research has demonstrated that use of euphorics causes serious health and behavioral problems when it becomes either progressive and/or out-of-control.

Progressive use means that over time more and more of a substance is consumed. For example, some addiction researchers suggest that it often takes from one to five years of use to develop alcoholism in someone who is genetically and/or psychologically vulnerable to addiction. During that time the amount consumed gradually increases until it reaches levels that are psychologically and physically toxic.

Out-of-control use means that there are regular situations where the individual can't say "no" to the next dose. I've observed that a sign of marijuana addiction is daily use, with the inability to go days without use if pot is available. Alcoholics will regularly say "yes" to the next drink, often until they pass out, with progressively less regard for what serves their health, their social milieu, their family, or the moment.

Since addiction is almost always characterized by states involving denial ("I don't have a problem. I can control it any time I choose"), rationalization ("I only drank so much because I was sad, or happy, or celebrating, or commiserating, etc."), and suppression ("Do we have to talk about my drinking? I'd rather not"), clients with substance abuse problems are often genuinely confused and thoroughly uncomfortable when talking explicitly about substance use/abuse. I've found it useful to normalize the discussion and talk frankly about progressive and out-of-control use, encouraging the client to enter a state of healthy response and take a stand about whether his use meets either of these two criteria. Further, it's important to evaluate potential abuse and dependence early in therapy since a practicing addiction to euphorics generally cripples progress in other areas.

An example of working with substance abuse is the following exchange with Gabe and Leslie. Both are in their late twenties, have been living together four years, and are college educated, successfully employed, with no children. Leslie says Gabe is not interested in sex, but she tries "to not take it personally." She is alarmed by his nightly pot use, heavy drinking (he says he stopped drinking two weeks ago), and recent cocaine use. He is angered by her going out drinking with her friends each Tuesday night, and "coming home drunk." Both report daily fights where they say "mean" things to each other. The following exchange happened at the end of our first (and only) session:

> Keith: "You two have a lot of issues and concerns." Both laugh nervously.

> Keith: "Let's focus on the drug and alcohol issues first. My experience is that, if either partner is a practicing addict or alcoholic, therapy results in little progress until that problem is being addressed. So, do either of you think you're addicted to alcohol, pot, or coke?"

> Gabe: "I stopped drinking two weeks ago, and I've stopped for a year at a time before."

> Keith: "Alcoholics can stop drinking. The fact that you stopped for a year previously—then started and stopped again two weeks ago—actually makes you statistically more likely to be an alcoholic. Non-alcoholics rarely feel an urgency to quit absolutely. What alcoholics can't do is drink in a controlled fashion. This is also true for pot and coke. For instance, it's a bad sign that you smoke pot every night. It's also a bad sign that when you buy a few

grams of coke you go through it for two or three days straight until it's gone."

Leslie: "I only get drunk when I go out with friends."

Gabe: Self-righteously. Couples tend to attack each other when their substance use is being examined. "That's not true. How about when Sharon came over last week?"

Leslie: "Oh come on. We only drank two bottles of wine."

Keith: "Leslie, I am concerned that you regularly drink to feeling 'drunk,' and that you drink one half to a whole bottle of wine each night. Do you think you're an alcoholic?" I deliberately use the words "alcoholic, addiction, addict, and alcoholism" frequently when discussing drug and alcohol use, abuse, and dependence. They are uncomfortable words for drug and alcohol users, but they serve to pop the little denial bubbles that naturally form around the subjects, and bring abuse and dependence issues out of the preconscious, and into the light of conscious appraisal.

Leslie: "I don't think so, but how can you know?"

Keith: Glad to hear her curiosity; it is a good sign. Disinterest—or avoidance of exploration—are bad signs. "Alcoholics and drug addicts can't use in a controlled fashion. Say you had a maximum of two wine glasses of wine a night, and a maximum of three when you went out. If you could do this, without exception, for six months, you probably are not currently an alcoholic. Similarly, Gabe, if you smoked pot a maximum of three nights a week for six months, continued to not drink, and could make one gram of coke last two weeks, and could keep to those levels, without exception, for six months, you probably are not currently addicted to pot or coke. Addicts can stop use, but they can't use consistently in a controlled way."

Leslie: "I could do that, easy." This is a bad sign. People who drink at her levels who *can* control their drinking are usually much more doubtful and concerned. They are rarely this confident.

Keith: "Do those sound like rules you would be willing to follow?"

Leslie: "I'll try it. How about you, Gabe?"

Gabe: Reluctant. "I don't know."

Keith: Not wanting this to be an issue between me and them, and wanting it to be a conscious topic in the culture of the relationship. "Don't decide now. Go home, listen to the therapy tape, and talk about this stuff a lot with each other and other people you trust. We can get more into it in our next session."

I suspected, accurately as it turned out, that they would not make it to the next session. This is often the case with addicts that are in the pre-contemplation, or contemplation stages of change, they will come to a session, receive feedback, information, and confrontation, and then not return. Knowing this, I want to impart as much ability to distinguish addiction from controlled use as I can during the time I have with them. Even when alcoholics commit to recovery, they slip an average of nine times before they become consistently substance free. The recidivism rates for alcoholics/addicts entering a twenty-eight day treatment center are seventy percent the first year after admission, and fifty percent the second year after admission, but, interestingly, only three percent per year thereafter. The good news about this last statistic is that if an addict can maintain abstinence for two years there is likely to be some shift in worldview/environment/consciousness/neural architecture that makes them much more likely to stay in recovery. The bad news is that, no matter how many years of abstinence an addict has, there is always that three percent danger of relapse.

The principles of dealing with drug/alcohol use/abuse/dependence issues are to keep the issues current and explicit in the therapy culture, and to encourage the client to add another dimension of support for each failure to control use. For example, if Leslie or Gabe had stayed in treatment, signed on to control their use, and failed in the attempt (very likely with the amount, types of substances, and patterns of their use), I might encourage them to try control again, but this time with the provision that, if they again failed, they would attend three AA meetings in the following week. Another failure might result in deciding on abstinence plus daily meetings for the following month. Another failure might result in a decision to enter an outpatient or inpatient treatment program, and so on.

When abuse/dependence is not an issue

If dependence and abuse are not issues with euphorics, it is often helpful to support a client integrating euphoric use into their life in ways that minimize physical and/or social risk, and maximize insight and gain. Many people have had insights, epiphanies, and transformative experiences while under the influence of euphorics. There are almost always physical and/or psychological costs to such breakthroughs (peeks with a price). Nevertheless, psychotherapists can help clients normalize and organize such experiences in ways that are compatible with their current worldviews and relationships in the same way that other altered states—or transformative experiences—are normalized and processed.

Any state of consciousness is a potential teacher, a guide to understanding new perspectives and supporting development. For instance, when helping a client process a psychedelic experience that they have previously had, many of the same principles and techniques for dreamwork are applicable. This is understandable considering the subtle, archetypal, dreamlike qualities that can accompany psychedelic intoxication.

1. Schore (2003), Siegal (1999)

2. Wilber (2007)

3. Cloniger (2004)

4. *Ibid*

5. DSMIV (1994)

6. Deida (2006)

40

States of Healthy Response to the Present Moment

Beck and Cowen detail in *Spiral Dynamics* how different life conditions evoke different worldviews, both on a large, cultural scale, and on an individual scale.[1] In the individual these worldviews are experienced as and expressed through shifting states of consciousness. One of my favorite studies from the seventies involved the filming of peoples' faces as they related, and then evaluating, frame by frame, of how frequently their emotional state shifted as measured by changes in facial expression. The results were startling. People seemed to shift emotional state about every three-tenths of a second.

There is a constant interplay between the rich, fluid, physical and energetic outer environment we exist in, and the rich, fluid, physical and energetic inner environment we bring to each moment. This interplay is experienced as—and expressed through—our immediate states of consciousness.

Each of these states is an amalgam of many forces that are unique in each moment and yet often consistent enough to make generalizations and predictions. For example, most people when they experience themselves as attacked feel hurt, then angry, and have defensive impulses that are usually more primitive than their general center of gravity. A competitive, hierarchical ORANGE driver, when cut off by an (apparent) reckless maneuver executed by another driver might feel alarm, anger, and impulses to honk his horn and scream obscenities. Honking his horn might reflect BLUE moral condemnation, while screaming obscenities might reflect RED attack. Whether the honking and screaming actually occur will depend on the amalgam of inner forces our ORANGE driver brings to bear in the moment. He might be egalitarian GREEN morally and have principles about equal respect, even to reckless drivers. He might be a more masculine type who feels challenged with a corresponding impulse to dominate this new opponent, but also be at a second stage relational level where he finds verbal or physical violence unattractive. He will have relatively more or less conscious awareness of all these tendencies and impulses, and more or less conscious abilities to discern and focus on healthy and unhealthy responses

When combinations of forces translate into a state that ultimately results in support for truth, health, love, and deep soul's purpose, and the conscious agenda is not self and/or other destructive, it is most likely a healthy, naturally occurring response to the present moment. Most of our moments are spent in this fashion, doing our best to do right according to our current standards. Healthy RED pursues power and gratification without requiring damage to self and/or other. Healthy BLUE values conformity without requiring damage to self and/or other, and so on. The self and/or the other might become injured, but such damage is peripheral to the basic agenda of serving the moment open. Healthy RED might injure others in the pursuit of power, but would probably prefer not to. A dominating boss reacts strongly to a subordinate advocating for decision-making power, but backs off immediately when the subordinate defers, rather than sadistically continuing to dominate. Healthy ORANGE might maneuver special advantage within the law over a competitor for enhanced profit, but would prefer the competitor to walk away feeling fairly treated rather than ripped off. If the deal goes badly for him, he accepts the pain, does his best to learn from the experience, and moves on.

Psychotherapy liberates and supports healthy responses to the present moment.

Arguably, primary goals of psychotherapy are to maximize the frequency of healthy responses to the present moment, and increase client's self-regulatory ability to discern and shift from defensive states to states of healthy response. If these become conscious growth principles that a client can remember and turn to in defensive states, that individual naturally organizes his or her life to reduce symptoms, enhance health, and support development. This is much of what therapy is about.

When combinations of forces translate into a state where the emphasis of the individual is on avoiding truth, health, love, and deep soul's purpose, so that injury to the self and/or others seems like an appropriate goal, that individual has almost certainly entered a defensive state. We all enter defensive states regularly. If we can discern defensive from healthy states and reach for states of healthy response, we naturally integrate toward progressively more moments of healthy response, and more stable centers of gravity where healthy response is our norm and defensive states can consistently be met with automatic self-regulation.

1. Beck (1996)

41

Defensive States: Doorways to Healing Work

Defensive states arise from intrapsychic defensive structures. Defensive structures are neural networks first constellated in infants' and toddlers' nervous systems in response to pain and threat, and then elaborated and/or resolved throughout development as they are cued by various internal and external stimuli to evoke defensive states. Defensive states have unique combinations of amplified or numbed emotions, distorted perceptions and thoughts, destructive impulses, and diminished capacities for empathy and self-reflection. The purpose of defensive states is to reflexively protect us from perceived threat. The perceived threat is usually some signal from the inner or outer environment that, if we were open in a healthy response to the present moment, would be a cue for potential healthy change and growth. In a defensive state, these cues are often misinterpreted as threats that evoke impulses for destructive internal and/or external thoughts, impulses, and behaviors.

A central feature of increasing health is an expanding ability to recognize and accept defensive states, and self-regulate them into states of healthy response to the present moment. Psychotherapy helps clients recognize, accept, and self-regulate defensive states with a therapist's help in sessions until clients can develop motivation and expertise to do the same by themselves and with others. Eventually this capacity to recognize and self-regulate defensive states can become both a personal/relational/spiritual strength, and a source of enormous insight and growth.

In the last examples from the Chapter Forty, a defensive RED boss might indulge impulses to sadistically humiliate a subordinate who challenges his power, or a defensive, competitive, hierarchical ORANGE driver might indulge impulses to drive recklessly himself to "teach the other driver a lesson," or "put him in his place." These destructive impulses would be driven by amplified or numbed emotions, and distorted thoughts and perceptions, and, when indulged, would probably be unchallenged, even rationalized, by these men.

Challenging destructive impulses usually involves disidentifying with defensive states and identifying with deeper agendas to serve the moment open. The RED boss who *does not* challenge his defensive state might feel a surge of fear and then rage as he perceives, and believes, his authority being attacked by his subordinate. The ORANGE driver, who *does not* challenge his defensive state, might feel sick, self-loathing, and then anger as he **perceives, and believes**, his weakness as a man is exposed by the other driver taking advantage of him. Both are then likely to indulge destructive impulses.

Perceived and believed.

"Perceived and believed" is an important distinction. Consider the consequences if, instead of surrendering to the pressure of amplified or numbed emotions, distorted perceptions and beliefs, and destructive impulses, an individual disidentifies with the defensive state, refuses to believe that his current perceptions, thoughts, and impulses are the deepest truth of the moment, and refuses to indulge them. This refusal to indulge destructive thoughts and impulses tends to evoke healthier states of consciousness where it becomes progressively more possible to reach for deeper truth (depth of consciousness), and compassionate understanding. Most of psychotherapy, in one way or another, encourages and supports clients to disidentify with defensive states, and to cultivate healthy responses to the present moment.

The following exchange with Tom and Anne is an example of teaching this directly in therapy:

Tom: "We had a rough episode, but we got through it."

Keith: "What happened?"

Tom: "We were mad. We started saying nasty things, and I wanted to just walk out, but I remembered what you said, and suggested we go shopping. Anne couldn't go, but it broke the ice."

Anne: "It was nice to be asked."

Keith: "You felt differently towards Tom after he asked?"

Anne: "Yes. He was trying and I liked it."

Keith: "You see how the critical variables here were your states of consciousness. When you were angry and defensive, you were repulsed by each other, and you were stingy and distrustful of each other's love and motives. Tom, when you made a loving offer to Anne, and you, Anne, received it with pleasure, you shifted your states of consciousness to feeling more drawn toward each other, and more generous and trustful. By offering and receiving love when your defensive states resisted it, you changed your states of consciousness towards healthy intimacy. This is the most important thing to do when you feel the amped-up emotions, distorted thoughts, and destructive impulses of defensive states."

Anne: "But you can't just flip a switch."

Keith: "I wish. You're so right. But, you can recognize your defensive state and make an offering of love through your resistance. That offering of love pulls you toward a more healthy and mature state of consciousness, and it will tend to evoke similar shifts in your partner."

Tom: "It's not fair that I always seem to be the one who has to compromise."

Keith: Confronting Tom while teaching Anne. "You're entering a defensive state right now. When you get caught up in 'It's not fair,' you're indulging destructive impulses to stay separate and angry, rather than take the risk of offering love. Notice your distorted belief that it's harder for you than for Anne, and that your relationship isn't fair. 'Fair' exists, but not in mirror image effort. You have no idea how difficult it is for Anne when she is absorbed in her defensive state of hurt/anger and distorted negative beliefs about you, to either receive your offering through her resistance, or offer you love through her resistance."

Anne: "It's the last thing I feel like doing, believe me."

Keith: "It is a beautiful act of love and faith to offer, or receive, a generous, loving gesture when you are caught up in a defensive state. The paradox is that the quickest way back to a state of healthy response to the present moment is to do the thing you most resist; to offer and/or receive love."

Tom: As both of them smile. "Well, I must say, it worked this time."

Defensive states can be perceived from multiple perspectives.

Defensive states are externally observable and objectively verifiable.

We can see defensive states when people become agitated or emotionally collapsed. We can hear defensive states in the critical, uncaring expressions that arise from them. If we had instrumentation, we could observe internal processes and changes caused by defensive states. For example, many people suffering from depression have increased arousal in the amygdala (a brain area that regulates negative emotion), decreased hippocampus volume (a brain area associated with encoding and retrieving memory that is literally poisoned by the increased levels of the stress hormone cortisol which is chronically elevated in depressed individuals), as well as less glial cells and less neuronal plasticity in their cerebral cortex.[1]

Defensive states often involve egocentric and hostile language (as with Tom's "It's not fair."), and increased critical judgments of self and others. People in defensive states can be more negative about themselves, others, and events than impartial others would observe as objectively accurate. The poster child for this is Eeyore in *Winnie the Pooh,* who could find possible negative outcomes in any situation.

Defensive states are internally observable and subjectively verifiable.

Phenominologically, defensive states are usually experienced as uncomfortable, and associated with painful emotions such as anxiety, despair, dread, anger, self-righteousness, irritation, or depression (with the occasional subjectively pleasurable exceptions of manic or hypomanic euphoria, narcissistic entitlement, self indulgent pleasure at engaging in destructive activity, or sadistic pleasure at hurting another). In the therapy session, defensive states include distorted perceptions, beliefs, or conclusions in the client that are at odds with the therapist's validity standards. For instance, in the following exchange with Anne, her distortions evoke a "not true" feeling in my body. To me, this feeling is often slight anxiety, tension in my chest, and a slightly sick feeling in my stomach:

Anne: "Tom is being a complete asshole."

Keith "How so?"

Anne: Shaking with anger. "He was deliberately late in taking our son to his friend's birthday party. He knows how angry Cathy's Mom gets when someone is late, and he deliberately hung out, finished the paper, and left late. I know he does this because he wants to hurt me."

Keith: Feeling the internal sense of anxiety/tension/sickness in me that usually indicates a defensive state in my client. Needing to stay connected. Wanting to work my way into her distortions gently, through relating, interpreting, and confronting. "I'm sure there is a part of Tom that is angry at you for being hurt and angry at him, and that angry side of him is unconsciously more likely to make decisions that hurt you. I also know that, when you feel hurt, you protect yourself by amplifying his negative characteristics and literally not seeing his positive efforts. When you feel this bad, these reactions are what you learned to cultivate as child to help you feel more safe."

Anne: Defending her distortions. Revealing her projective identification. "He doesn't care about anyone but himself."

Keith: Feeling connected enough to confront, and push a little against her distortions. "I disagree. I know that he is fiercely dedicated to you and your son."

Anne: Softening, beginning to enter a more healthy state. "I know. I'm just so mad at him."

At his point, Anne is beginning to disidentify with the defensive state, and reach for more healthy perspectives. She is less certain of Tom's complete darkness, and feeling slightly less rage, and slightly more care and willingness to change perspectives. I'm feeling a corresponding relaxation in my chest, and admiration for her courage in reaching through her pain in the service of love.

Moral components of defensive states.

Subjective senses of what is moral or immoral, right or wrong, influence defensive states of consciousness, and are almost always on display to some extent when a defensive state is evoked. This is partially the inevitable consequence of infants and toddlers learning defensive states in reflexively avoiding shame emotions associated with disapproval from caregivers, and partially a consequence of our nervous systems being entrained to expand this disapproval into internal disapproval of self in the past/present/future.[2]

Since internalized approval/disapproval is central to socialization, and the moral validity standard is a crucial interior compass that guides us constantly, "right" and "wrong" figure heavily in defensive states and structures. What's considered moral in the culture of a family, institution, or country figures heavily in the development of intrapsychic defensive structures, and informs and shapes most individual behaviors and social interactions.

The intersubjective fields involved in social activity give us constant signals, many of which reflect and cue defensive states. For instance, frustration often cues anger, which cues aggressive impulses. These emotions and impulses will be guided by collective subjective moral standards that differ from culture to culture.[3] In my childhood cultures, it was common for children of all ages to be struck by some adults (parents, teachers, relatives, older siblings, or police officers) if that adult was angry. The social milieu supported this behavior, even to the extent of condoning paddling children of all ages at public and private schools. When an adult entered a defensive state of amplified anger, distorted critical beliefs, and destructive impulses to strike children over whom he or she had some authority, it was generally considered "right" to strike the child in a variety of ways with hands or socially sanctioned implements.

Child culture involved commiserating, sympathizing, and bragging about various episodes of corporal punishment, but never morally condemning it. The children accepted the moral authority of adults to engage in corporal punishment. Often, sometime in the BLUE/ORANGE, formal operational, second stage, rights/care, teen years, some individual teen might take a moral stand against being the object of violence by physically threatening, or even assaulting, authorities (especially parents and older siblings) to back them off. Thi also was generally considered moral—even admirable—in many teen and family cultures. Contrast this with current American culture where corporal punishment is much more widely considered immoral at all ages, and has actually been banned in public schools in twenty-seven states and the District of Columbia in the last forty years.[4]

Current moral standards concerning skin display, sexual conversation, sexual activity, and sexual hunger influence many Americans to have impulses to critically judge, pathologize, or even attack self and/or another if these felt standards are violated. Many of these destructive impulses reveal defensive states generated by intrapsychic defensive structures designed to avoid dangerous encounters with sexual feelings and practices that might lead to engaging in, considering, or remembering embarrassing or shameful thought or action. Infants and toddlers don't have the cognitive development to self-regulate shame emotions, and so learn instinctively to avoid them by activating defensive states. These defensive structures/states function to block insight and growth in charged areas involving perceived shared community values of right and wrong, good and bad.[5] Thus moral standards, if unexamined, can both create and support intrapsychic defensive structures, which then under perceived stress generate defensive states of consciousness with corresponding destructive symptoms.

An exercise I've done with clinicians in my classes is to ask them to *imagine making* the following two statements to the parents of a sixteen-year-old female client, and observe their own inner experience as they *imagine* the dialogue:

- **First statement:** "Today your daughter and I discussed her cognitive development. We explored how she was becoming more formal operational, more able to critically evaluate ideas from different perspectives. We talked about how this was contributing to some of your disagreements about the rules of the house."

- **Second statement:** "Today your daughter and I talked about her sexual development. We discussed her attitudes about her developing body, and especially her breasts and genital area. We discussed masturbation techniques and age-appropriate sexual activity with her eighteen-year-old boyfriend."

First of all, I would *never* have the second conversation with a sixteen-year-old girl's parents. Most clinicians are comfortable with the first statement and literally squirming and groaning with distress at the second. It elicits a wide array of defensive states from self-loathing to anger at me for even suggesting such a conversation.

I always have a flash of alarm directing the exercise, and feel an anxious urgency to reassure my students (as I reassured you when I introduced the exercise with two "*imagines*") that I would never have the second conversation with a sixteen-year-old client's parents. Our intrapsychic defensive structures are mobilized by the explicit sexual references, and we automatically enter defensive states where we have amplified or numbed emotions, distorted thoughts and perceptions, and destructive impulses towards ourselves and/or others. In this case, some therapists are likely to feel amplified alarm, anger, and/or moral outrage at the imagined conversation, have distorted perceptions that I'm advocating inappropriate sexual talk with teenage girls, have distorted beliefs that explicit sexual talk is never appropriate, and have destructive impulses to attack me in some way for conducting the exercise. Therapists can never be values free, but we can cultivate awareness of our own and other's moral conditioning (depth of consciousness), care for all concerned (compassion), and then do our best to discern what best serves the highest good for all at any given moment.

Statistical representations: a cornucopia of data on defensive states.

The DSM1V (diagnostic and statistical manual) is an avalanche of statistical data about defensive structures and states.[6] One percent of the American population suffers from scitzophrenia, more women than men are diagnosed with depression, and so on for almost every diagnosis. Most psychotherapy research involves statistical representations of defensive states. Medication tends to work better than placebo at alleviating depressed states, and medication plus cognitive/behavioral therapy tends to work better than medication alone, are two examples. Psychotherapeutic research has also acknowledged and occasionally looked at therapists' defensive states in the form of counter-transference. Attachment research has looked at defensive states from the perspectives of intersubjective fields between mothers and children; noticing that insecure attachment styles in primary care givers seem to correspond to various forms of insecure attachment in children.

1. Siegel (2005)

2. Witt (2007)

3. Wilber (2000)

4. US. (2007)

5. Witt (2007)

6. DSMIV (1994)

42

Defensive States in the Flow of the Therapy Session

Successfully identifying and managing our own and our client's defensive states are two of the most important activities in psychotherapy. The intersubjective fields which the therapist perceives and directs in cocreating a healing culture involve regular surges of energy, frequent amplified or numbed emotions, repetitive distorted perceptions and thoughts, a variety of destructive impulses in both therapist and client, and perceptible fluctuations in empathy and self-reflection. One Jungian description of therapy is that the therapist takes on the wounds of the client and heals them in himself, and that this activity supports the client healing his or her own wounds.[1]

Self as instrument in working with defensive states.

Self as an instrument of healing is centrally important when dealing with defensive states. The session needs to feel safe to the client, but also needs to deal with threatening material, which often elicits defensive states that feel unsafe to the client. This issue is amplified in conjoint work, where the complexity of intersubjective fields in the room skyrockets. The therapist can orient to client cues of content, facial expressions, posture, body kinesthetic, voice and tone qualities, and interior cues of internal, subjectively observable sensations, emotions, perceptions, thoughts, and impulses.

When the therapist observes her own emotions becoming amplified or numbed, her own thoughts and perceptions becoming distorted, her own impulses becoming destructive, or her own capacities for empathy and self-reflection diminishing, it's usually the case that her client has entered a defensive state which is pulling complementary reactions in their shared intersubjective fields. Effective therapy involves cultivating awareness of such shifts (depth of consciousness), and managing them with the goal of the highest good for all (compassion). This often involves using the therapist's reactions as guides for interventions (self as instrument).

The reason that "relating" is the first activity in the "relating, teaching, inspiring, confronting, interpreting, and directing" sequence is that relating, attuning to our client, is the foundation activity of therapy. Relating cannot happen productively if defensive states in self and/or client are not being effectively addressed by the therapist. For healthy perspectives and actions to be cultivated, the client needs to feel safe enough to deal with threatening material. Clients often communicate lack of safety through entering a defensive state which the therapist can observe in client behavior and/or in their own subjective reactions. Signals of a client's lack of feeling safe are often cues for the therapist to shift to relating (focusing on relational attunement) until the client is feeling understood, accepted, cherished, and safe once again.

The following exchange with Sally is an example of my attending to self as instrument of healing. Sally enters a defensive state that indicates a lack of safety, thus shifting my therapeutic agenda to relating. Sally and Martin are a couple who have had lots of therapy over the years. Sally, a housewife, is forty-one, and Martin, an insurance agent, is thirty-nine. They entered therapy with the goal of being able to ameliorate their frequent vicious fights and to reestablish a sexual relationship that had languished over the years. Martin initially needed to work on being a trustable man to Sally and, as he accomplished this, she felt some guilt and responsibility for their sexual alienation (in addition to a deep, inarticulate fear of allowing herself to be loved, and simultaneous longing to be loved, by a trustable man). This led her into individual therapy to resolve her alienation, which involved a combination of early abuse issues, characterological and neurotic defensive structures, and genuine doubts about Martin's stability:

> Keith: "You've told me a fair amount about the emotional abuse in your family of origin, but you've made no references to any details or episodes of physical abuse." I feel compassion and a faint sense of anxiety as I say this. I know I am on the edge of a personal Sally taboo.

> Sally: Visibly recoiling. Appearing frightened, suspicious, and angry. Turning away from me toward the window. "Why do we have to talk about it? I try not to think about it."

> Keith: Recognizing that she's entered a defensive state, and is feeling diminished trust for me. Feeling compassion, a sense that relating needs to be emphasized, and an impulse to simultaneously validate her natural reluctance to reopen old wounds, while offering her potentially new perspectives

on her abuse. "We don't have to talk about it. It might not be necessary to revisit the old atrocities. It is necessary to have compassion and admiration for the child who had to endure them."

Sally: Angry, but interested. "I hate her."

Keith: Feeling compassion and curiosity. "What do you hate about her?"

Sally: Angrily. "She invited that abuse. She put up with it. She asked for it."

Keith: Interested. Feeling admiration for the little girl who managed to survive, transcend, and become the impressive woman in my office. I feel a solid connection and decide to confront some of her distortions. "I admire that child. I think it's magnificent the way she survived, and beautiful that she found a way through to love."

Sally: Contemptuously. "I can't love Martin. That's why I'm here."

Keith: Noticing her contempt for both her child self and current self as a felt connection between present and disassociated past. This is an opportunity to support integration towards a more loving perspective. I'll use the same adjectives for her current self that I used for her historical self. "To the contrary. Your very presence in this session is an expression of devotional love for him specifically. That devotional love is admirable and beautiful."

Sally: Looking confused, which is a good sign. Confusion generally indicates a deeper step into a defensive structure. She answers weakly. "You have no idea what it was like."

Keith: Directing. "Tell me. Help me understand."

Sally: Venomously. "Oh, so you can get off on the dirty details?"

Keith: I feel a surge of alarm, irritation, and an impulse to explain myself. This indicates to me that one of my defense states is being mobilized. Sally must be feeling enormously threatened at the thought of describing details to me. I feel impulses to shift to relating, to focus on understanding and cherishing, and to support her feeling more safe in the moment. "It sounds like it's terrifying for you to even consider talking about those times."

Sally: Relieved I didn't strike back or insist that she talk about her traumas. Feeling safer and beginning to cry. "They were so mean to me."

The brutal physics of the art of therapy.

This process of attending and reacting to Sally's goals, defensive structures, and immediate states of consciousness, while simultaneously attending to my own general knowledge, specific knowledge about Sally, and immediate states of consciousness reflects what most therapist do to some extent. The craft of therapy is cultivating all these perspectives with the goal of supporting healthy perspectives and actions. The art of therapy is maintaining a holding environment in which your client feels safe, while engaging your client's defenses on a level that pushes enough so that he or she maximizes progress, but not so much that he or she loses their sense of safety in the therapeutic relationship.

There is a sometimes brutal physics to this art. Often the more deeply wounded and resistant the client is to change, the slower they move in the process, and the sicker and more self-destructive they are willing to be to resist threatening new insights and actions. Similarly, the less deeply wounded and resistant the client is, the faster they are often willing to change and the less sick and self-destructive they are willing to get to resist threatening new insights and actions.

Whatever system you ascribe to, and whatever your level of therapeutic training and experience, each client has their own rate of growth at any given time and, once you have a therapeutic alliance and a certain rate of change has been established, it is often difficult, if not impossible, to accelerate that rate. Occasional exceptions to this are biophysiological interventions like medication, social interventions like entering recovery programs for addicts, and added psychotherapy in the form of individual therapy, conjoint therapy, family therapy, or group therapy. Some clients—mostly more healthy clients—become healthier relatively quickly, while others—mostly more deeply wounded and less healthy clients—can only progress at a glacial pace.

Another principle in this brutal physics is that, generally, less healthy clients enjoy therapy less and leave therapy sooner. Ultimately, clients usually decide how much therapy is tolerable for themselves and their families, with clients rarely staying in treatment long enough for the therapist to suggest that they've reached a self-sustaining growth process that no longer could benefit from regular psychotherapeutic intervention. The art of therapy is maximizing movement toward healthier perspectives and actions while maintaining a culture in which the client experiences her self and her universe as cherished.

DEFENSIVE STRUCTURES

Defensive structures are our intrapsychic predispositions to specific defensive states.

As we develop through the first three Fulcrums, we internalize a variety of predispositions to handle perceived threat. These were the best alternatives our nervous systems had at the time, but human development gives us the capacities for vastly more sophisticated responses to threat as we mature. Perceived threat handled in an optimal fashion that serves love and health usually reflects healthy responses to the present moment. Perceived threat handled with amplified or numbed emotion, distorted perceptions and thoughts, destructive impulses, and diminished capacities for insight and self-reflection usually reflects defensive states.

Defensive structures are our natural tendencies to constellate specific defensive reactions in response to perceived threat. They are neural networks hardwired into our brains and bodies to serve us under perceived threat. They can't be extinguished entirely, but they can be incorporated into wider networks reflecting more mature understanding and more flexible responding. Identifying and then disidentifying from a defensive state and reaching for a state of healthy response is a superb human capacity for including and transcending defensive states into states of healthy response.

Defensive states arise naturally from the interplay between intrapsychic defensive structures—hard-wired tendencies to activate specific neural firing patterns—and environmental cues. In general, the more deeply entrenched and pathological the defensive structure, the less important the environmental cue is in eliciting a defensive state. A deeply depressed person will have amplified negative emotions and distorted perceptions and thoughts in the most benign and supportive environments. A highly anxious person will find things to fear in the safest environment, and so on. Most defenses that therapists encounter in their clients arise from one or more of three levels of intrapsychic defensive structures, characterological, neurotic, and relational.

Characterological, neurotic, and relational structures are evoked by perceived threat, and are expressed as defensive states in our moment-to-moment existence. In this and the next three Chapters we'll explore defensive structures in general, and then delve more deeply into these three levels of intrapsychic and interpsychic defensive structures, their ontology, and how they are expressed as defensive states on different levels of development on the self, the cognitive, the sexual, the interpersonal, and the moral lines in more masculine or more feminine individuals.

People have always observed defensive structures and states.

Defensive states and structures have been observed and described throughout human history. The archetype of demonic possession is present in most cultures, and reflects the fact that there are times when human beings appear to be driven by destructive forces, even entities, that don't seem to be congruent with who that individual is generally considered to be (or considers himself to be). Freud postulated that much psychopathology involved competing drives to create (Eros) and destroy (Thanatos) that were repressed, internalized, and later expressed as neurotic symptoms which were often distortions of, and destructive to, reality in some fashion.[2] Jung believed these internalized conflicts had actual character, a form of independent existence, and called them "complexes."[3] Roberto Assaglioli preferred the construct of "subpersonalities," literally cohesive personalities that are usually subordinate to the larger, central personality of "self," which is a reflection of the deeper, brighter, larger, "Self," which is transpersonal and, ultimately, one with the infinite.[4] Perls popularized the Freudian concept of "introjects," where important early figures like loving father, rejecting father, or loving mother, rejecting mother are absorbed and then later inhabited as either resources (loving father, loving mother) or destructive entities (rejecting father, rejecting mother).[5] Object relations theorists postulate that, in the intersubjective dance between mother and infant/toddler/child, the child can either differentiate successfully and integrate into a whole emotional self, or fuse with a mother who cannot (or will not) effectively support differentiation, with the result that the child is never fully born into a separate emotional self. Under the influence of abuse and/or neglect, primitive sadistic and/or masochistic aspects of this primitive self are split off into subpersonalities that are unconsciously activated and projected in later life.[6]

The signature borderline and narcissistic defense of projective identification is a common example of split-off sadistic aspects being activated and projected under stress. Projective identification involves projecting one's demonic self onto another, and then compulsively clinging to and torturing that other (a more borderline defense), or demeaning and withdrawing from that other (a more narcissistic defense).[7]

Defensive tendencies develop, at least partially, from a developing individual instinctually responding to external influences from their idiosyncratic amalgam of:

- Physiological responses to social conditioning.
- Constitutional pain.
- Attraction to death.
- Yearning for transcendence.
- Impulse control.

My belief is that defensive structures arise from an alchemy of development that includes evolutionary socialization imperatives, temperament, family culture, larger culture (community, tribe, nation, etc.), and environmental circumstances of early development. Each of us is born with relative constitutional amounts of temperamental pain (anxious arousability, depressive tendencies, or angry tendencies for example), relative tendencies to move towards death (thrill seeking, oppositional tendencies, or addiction tendencies), tendencies to move towards transcendence (desires to love, be loved, be good, be self-reflective, or to pursue a sense of the sacred), and impulse control. We can have strong or weak tendencies in all five realms of physiological responses to social conditioning, constitutional pain, attraction to death, yearning for transcendence, and impulse control. These developmental imperatives and temperamental dispositions manifest in an infant, who is born into a family where he or she will be more or less welcome, and more or less expertly responded to. The environmental circumstances of our early development can be stable, secure, and nurturing, or unstable, insecure, or abusive. Out of the alchemical cauldron of all these influences defensive structures arise, designed to generate defensive states to protect self and resist change in response to perceived threat.[8]

1. Jung (1965)

2. Freud (1949)

3. Jung (1965)

4. Assagioli (1965)

5. Perls (1968)

6. Kernberg (1975)

7. Masterson (1981)

8. Witt (2007)

43

Characterological, Neurotic, and Relational Defensive Structures: Discrete, Yet Interconnected

The difficulty in discussing these three levels of defensive structures is the same difficulty encountered in discussing any aspect of human functioning. We humans are holographic, multidimensional beings who exist simultaneously on many levels (possibly transtemporally[1]), and who constantly shift the emphases of our beings intentionally/reflexively. Each of us has some degree of characterological, neurotic, and relational defensive structures—predispositions to feel, think, believe, and act in certain ways when we feel threatened—that constellate uniquely in each person and manifest as idiosyncratic defensive states.

There are useful distinctions that can be drawn between these three kinds of defensive structures—distinctions which can help therapists cocreate healing cultures. Defensive states can be used in countless ways as tools to cultivate compassion and depth of consciousness.

CHARACTEROLOGICAL DEFENSIVE STRUCTURES THE DEEPEST AND DARKEST

A useful axiom in dealing with defensive states is that depth of regression co-varies with decreasing empathy, decreasing capacity for self-reflection, decreasing ability to self-regulate amplified emotion, increasing intensity of destructive impulses, and increasing license to do emotional and/or physical violence to self and/or another. Characterological defensive structures manifest as the most regressed defensive states that most psychotherapists are likely to routinely deal with: states that involve practically no empathy, miniscule capacity for healthy self-reflection, and frequent license to do emotional and/or physical violence to self and/or others.

If characterological defensive structures are pervasive in an individual and that individual has enormous difficulty being self-aware of them and little success in self-regulating the defensive states involved, that person can be diagnosed as having a personality disorder (an Axix II disorder as they are referred to in the DSM1V).

If such defensive structures are episodic and available to increasing self-awareness and self-regulation, they tend to constitute more character traits than pervasive character disorders.

Since frankly psychotic individuals such as schizophrenics, people lost in florid manic episodes, or catatonics, are more biochemically driven and often don't benefit all that much from traditional psychotherapy (they usually benefit more from treatments that emphasize an integration of biochemical and environmental interventions involving teams of psychiatrists, cognitive behavioral therapists, social workers, care facilities, work placements, and law enforcement), the character disorders/traits are the most regressed and disturbed defensive structures that most psychotherapists encounter in their work.

Not surprisingly, character disorders generate some of the most violent and destructive emotional/behavioral symptoms. Projective identification, dissociation, accelerated capacities for distorting reality, and irresistible impulses to do emotional and/or physical violence are common indicators of characterological defensive structures. The infantile feel of clients while they manifest characterological defensive states supports the general consensus that character disorders somehow involve Fulcrums 1 and 2 trauma and/or arrest. The combination of relentless egocentricism with almost no empathy and enthusiastic attack on self and/or others are signature qualities that can show up suddenly and unexpectedly under subjective stress. One hazard for therapists, under the onslaught of such defensive states, is that it can become easy to forget the excruciating emotional pain that arises suddenly in these clients and drives them towards emotional and/or physical violence.

An example of a characterological structure with accompanying defensive states is the following exchange where Tom and Anne are discussing their son Jake. Notice how quickly Anne decompensates when threatened, and how naturally Tom moves into a complementary defensive position that supports both of their regressions. His defenses are more neurotic (he has some capacity for insight, self-reflection, and emotional self-regulation), but nevertheless, they are still complementary in that he is collaborating with Anne in pretending that she is actually coming from an adult perspective, able to have rational conversation:

Tom: "We're trying to decide what school to send Jake to."

Anne: "It's an important decision. He's entering the sixth grade, and that's such an important time."

Keith: Knowing that there is an issue beneath this apparently innocuous topic. "I agree. Middle school is where the child identity transitions into the emergent adult identity. Kids become formal operational cognitively, sexually more mature, and physically very different. What are the choices?"

Anne: "The local public school is good, but I really like the Santa Barbara Middle School."

Tom: "I like it too, but twenty thousand dollars a year is a little steep for junior high school, don't you think?"

Keith: There is a sudden feeling of danger in the room. Anne is tensing up. Tom appears oblivious. I have the impulse to move delicately. I smile tentatively and look casually at first Tom, and then Anne.

Anne: Using a hostile tone and a hard stare at Tom. "All you care about is the money."

Tom: Defensively. "I didn't say I wouldn't do it. I just said it's a lot of money. Christ, it's more than I paid for college."

Anne: Venomously. "All you care about is yourself. You don't care about Jake. You don't care about me. You creep."

Tom: More defensively. "Hey, slow down. All I said was …"

Anne: Interrupting, leaning forward in her chair, index finger extended. "This is just like his Montana Camp. He loves horses, but not as much as you love money! You are such as worthless father."

Tom: Angry. "You can't say I'm a bad father. I've …"

Anne: Beginning to interrupt again, but I've seen enough to determine it won't serve them for her to continue. Anne's clearly at the beginning of what James Masterson calls an abandonment depression, an acute surge of distress in her chest, solar plexus, and stomach, combined with massively distorted beliefs and irresistible impulses to attack; a signature characterological defensive state[2]. I need to interrupt before it gathers any more momentum. Knowing Anne's unavailable for confrontation of her current sadistic impulses, I interrupt her, soothe her, and confront Tom, modeling for Anne how she can make her point without demonizing him."

Keith: "Excuse me, but stop."

Anne: She's on a roll and heatedly begins to talk. "He can't …"

Keith: Holding up my hands, subjectively extending my energy, my sense of self in a soothing fashion over both of them. "Stop. I need to make this point. What's happening now is exactly what brought you into therapy. Anne, I get it that you'd do anything to support Jake. Tom, I know you love Jake and Anne, and you've made many sacrifices and are willing to make more sacrifices for them, but when you get anxious about money it's harder for Anne to trust you."

Anne: Contemptuously. "Sacrifices, why he …"

Keith: She's talking to me now and I feel affection between us. I just validated one of her most sacred foundation principles, her dedication to her son. I'm drawn to confronting her. "Anne, you're doing what you often do when you're threatened. You're taking an irritating or alarming aspect of Tom and distorting it into him being a complete and utter jerk."

Anne: Less venomous. "He is a jerk."

Keith: "But not a complete and utter jerk." Both laugh.

Anne: Softer. "Maybe not a complete and utter jerk."

This episode could have accelerated into days of attacks, defenses, destructive states, and lots of suffering. When Anne is not absorbed in her defensive state, she has practically no conscious concern about her capacity to enter it. Subjectively, she attributes the defensive state, and the characterological defensive structure, entirely to Tom. She takes no responsibility (much less cultivates self-reflective insight) for the distortions and attacks and, when it passes, she believes it won't return if Tom just "stops being a jerk." It will be many months, possibly years, before she can effectively be aware of and self-regulate her amplified emotions, distorted beliefs and perceptions, and destructive impulses while in an abandonment depression. My job is to minimize the damage, and maximize the benefit for both of them in each episode.

Often, I'll recommend individual therapy for one or both partners in such a situation, but I choose my referral sources with care. A friend and colleague, Dr. Janet Loxley, once told me that a shorthand diagnostic evaluation of a borderline personality disorder was, "When you feel lousy after the session, and you fight with other people about them, they're probably a borderline." If other clinicians don't share this understanding, they run the risk of being sucked into the operatic dramas instead of deescalating the violent enactments.

Anne's example is just one of a number of defensive states that can arise out of different characterological defensive structures. Most character disorders are constellations of traits from different categories, with an emphasis in a particular area, but the distinctions are real and useful. Let's examine some of them. For brevity's sake, I'll exchange "a person suffering from a narcissistic (borderline, passive-aggressive, compulsive, or histrionic) character disorder," to simply, "narcissist," "borderline," "passive-aggressive," and so on.

Narcissists are absorbed in their sense of entitlement and endless hunger for the narcissistic supplies of other's validation, admiration, and accommodation. If narcissists are also depressed, this grandiosity is expressed in their distorted amplification of their own suffering and the ongoing entitlement they feel for special attention and consideration.

Histrionics often present as narcissists with dramatic, egocentric senses of entitlement (especially to attention and special consideration), and inflated opinions of their beauty/worth/importance. Unlike narcissists, they have some capacity for object relations, and less capacity for sadistic cruelty when caught up in regressed states.

Borderlines can present as self-aware and psychologically sophisticated until the abandonment depression constellates and projective identification drives them to cling and torture the perceived source of their injury. In individual therapy, the target often eventually becomes the therapist, creating significant dangers of the therapist being seduced into boundary violations of one form or another.

Compulsives are often contemptuous of therapy, skeptical about unconscious and intrapsychic processes, and dogged in their commitment to rigid points of view.

Dependents (or codependents if their dependence is expressed in neurotically serving others) organize their life around compulsive servitude to individuals lost in egocentric self-stimulation (such as alcoholism, drug addiction, or compulsive gambling), or compulsive care-taking of others where there is little or no discernment between healthy and unhealthy service.

Passive-aggressives are often dependent, but are usually aggressive in a different way from dependents, unconsciously organizing their lives to regularly express unacknowledged rage by indirectly attacking others. In therapy they consistently forget insights, rarely follow through over time on healing practices, and frequently complain about lack of progress.

Characterological defensive structures share core aspects.

All the above characterological defensive structures, when their defensive states are mobilized, share the core characteristics of having diminished empathy, little ability to effectively self-reflect, challenged capacity to self-regulate amplified or numbed emotions and distorted beliefs, and a felt license to do emotional and/or physical harm to self and/or others. All of them change slowly in therapy, and require much patience, self-awareness, and ability to self-regulate on the part of the therapist. It's always useful (often necessary) to have the ancillary support of other health practitioners and personal support systems when doing therapy with clients whose foundation defensive structures are characterological.

Diagnostic and treatment differences in characterological defensive structures.

Characterological defensive structures share many aspects, but there are also profound differences *between* characterological defensive structures, and differences *within* characterological defensive structures that have great relevance to prognosis and treatment.

There are significant differences between borderline, narcissistic, histrionic, dependent, passive aggressive, and compulsive defensive structures, the most common characterological defensive structures I have encountered in my practice (as I suspect is true for many psychotherapists). Even though individuals can, and often do, have defensive structures that borrow from several varieties, their deepest defenses will tend to lean towards one or the other. The differences most relevant to therapists are those that help indicate different treatment strategies, diagnoses, prognoses, and relative dangerousness to self, others, and therapist.

Borderlines: soothe their alarm and confront their distortions.

Borderlines, with their ability to have object relations, and their signature cling and torture defense, will stay in therapy, but are relatively dangerous clients. Treatment usually involves maintaining impeccable boundaries in the face of their regular efforts to have special treatment and create special relationships. The therapist establishes the holding environment, and then enters the (seemingly) endless dance of soothing the amplified emotions and confronting the distortions. When the therapist becomes the object of projective identifications, and the client seeks relief by clinging to and torturing the therapist, the therapist's tasks are to self-soothe, self-regulate, and engage in persistent and compassionate confrontation (reality testing in the Freudian language) of non-distorted perspectives, rather than retreat, attack, or defend. It's especially important when treating borderlines for the therapist to routinely access personal and professional support.

Narcissists: mirror their pain and interpret their wounds.

Narcissists, with less ability to have object relations, and with their signature defense of demean and withdraw, often flee therapy after initial relief, and are thus less dangerous to the therapist than borderlines. For example, they tend to engage in fewer intrusions into the therapist's personal life and are less likely to file licensing board complaints than borderlines. Treatment usually involves caressing their grandiose sense of self by acknowledging and admiring their very real strengths, while gradually reflecting back to them (mirroring) the deep wounds and accompanying pain they've organized their lives to avoid. Interpretation is the main road into their intrapsychic defenses, with cautious confrontation as the relationship slowly develops.

In spite of your best efforts, the therapeutic relationship frequently ends with your client experiencing a narcissistic wound of some sort, demeaning you in some particularly distressing way, and leaving therapy. This doesn't mean that you haven't helped them remediate their symptoms, enhance their health, or support their development. You've almost certainly helped them in those areas. It does mean that you've done your part in caring for this person, and now it's time to let them go to whoever their next healer and guide will be. My personal strategy is to support as much health and growth as I can.

Occasionally a narcissist takes conscious responsibility for his wounds and his healing, and disidentifies with (not dissociates from, where there is no effective self-awareness) and transcends his characterological defensive structures. It is a beautiful moment in therapy when your narcissistic client catches the defense, laughs at it, and chooses love instead.

Histrionic: borderline without the sadism, narcissistic without the flight.

Histrionics appear to have narcissistic self-aggrandizement and borderline instability in their relationships, but are not mindlessly sadistic like the borderline, or as quick to trash a relationship as a narcissist. Their operatic distortions and outbursts are less toxic and somehow more endearing than the narcissists they resemble, possibly because they have more genuine capacity for object relations; the capacity to care for other people. They tend to regress to childlike states when stressed, but are relatively easily soothed and confronted, and will listen with interest to interpretations of their defenses.

Dependents: a hallmark of addiction.

Dependents are often addicts and/or codependent with an addict, and their signature defense is to stay and suffer, but, unlike passive-aggressives, there is more innocence and less sadism in their suffering. Not surprisingly, they often stay in treatment (with the exception of practicing addicts who cling to denial, and can find therapy intolerably uncomfortable if the therapist stays focused on the dangers of their addiction), but the therapist will often feel subtle and powerful impulses to accommodate their symptoms rather than challenge them. Treatment involves maintaining the holding environment while regularly examining the pathologically dependent relationships (on substances, people, institutions, and/or activities) as areas that need scrutiny and change.

Passive-aggressives: deceptively hard to maintain positive change.

Being passive-aggressive is simply expressing anger indirectly. Most of us do this regularly throughout our lives to some extent, and when confronted, will often apologize, change, and move on. Clients with passive-aggressive character disorders create lives that are literally saturated with such activity, and, even though they give the appearance of receiving teaching, inspiration, confrontation, interpretation, and direction about their indirect hostility, will often forget, misinterpret, and otherwise avoid change. Passive-aggressives are more sadistic than dependents. They can unconsciously arrange their lives to create suffering for others, while self-flagellating and bemoaning their fate. They are often dependent, but less often addicted than dependents. Procrastination is a signature defensive symptom, creating vast anxiety in the client and infuriating frustrations for intimates.

Therapy with passive-aggressives benefits from patience, steadiness, and the therapist's ability to confront, with humor, the countless passive-aggressive maneuvers that arise in these clients' lives. A frequent hazard for the therapist is to become frustrated with passive-aggressive slow progress, and then surrender to defensive impulses to push the client to change faster than he or she can. This can create passive-aggressive negative transference activities in the client (such as forgetting appointments, bouncing checks, or whining and complaining) that can evoke resentful counter-transference in the therapist. These transference and countertransference issues can be useful in treatment, helped by the fact that, at least in the session, passive-aggressives are relatively more available to insight than other characterological disorders (although they tend to forget it after the session). It is an indication of significant progress when a passive-aggressive client finally gets the pervasive nature of their defenses, can recognize their defensive states, and consistently self-regulate outside of the session. This often translates into phenomenal successes, since the client has had to create whatever successes they have thus far had in their lives shackled to the ball-and-chain of one passive-aggressive self-sabotage after another.

Compulsives: often ORANGE and masculine.

Compulsives are often achievement oriented, competitive, hierarchical ORANGE and masculine. Their rigid belief structures resist change, and they are often contemptuous of psychotherapy, intrapsychic processes, and the unconscious in general. They are more likely to have numbed, or blunted, emotions, rather than amplified ones. I prefer to tolerate their contempt with good humor, and regularly confront them with the beneficial aspect of healthy perspectives and actions, emphasizing scientific data about externally observable aspects of their lives (for example, "Management studies show that a contemptuous attitude like yours results in less advancement and recognition than for an equally competent, but more friendly, employee in institutional cultures like your company's."). A hazard of working with compulsives is to not take some treasured rigid perspective (like a maniacal commitment to recycling) seriously enough, and thus alienate them to the point that they leave therapy.

Characterological defensive structures: mix and match, higher or lower functioning.

A client with characterological defenses can, and often does, have a variety of symptoms from any of the defensive systems explored above. There is usually a clustering, or emphasis towards one or the other, and this is what can alert therapists to adjust diagnosis and treatment strategies.

Also, a client with characterological defenses can be low functioning, moderately functioning, or high functioning. Low functioning reflects minimal insight, more negative drama, little ability to self-regulate amplified or numbed emotion or distorted thought, less tolerance of stress before decompensation begins, and more damage to self and/or other during defensive states. If the individual chooses a path towards health and development, they gradually improve on all these dimensions. Eventually, they can progress through moderately functioning to high functioning, in which there is more capacity for insight in defensive states, less negative drama, progressively more reliable abilities to self-regulate amplified and/or numbed emotions and distorted thought, a capacity to tolerate significantly higher levels of stress before decompensation begins, and progressively less damage to self and/or another during defensive states.

When a client becomes high functioning, the characterological defensive structures are still there, are still cued by a variety of inner experience and life conditions, but the client has grown to identify with a more healthy self that can be aware of, and better self-regulate, the defensive states that arise out of characterological defensive structures. In object relation's terms, the client now has developed an observing ego that they can turn to under stress to provide self-soothing and reality testing[3]. Essentially, they have passed through a developmental fulcrum and have, functionally, upleveled their characterological defensive structures to neurotic defensive structures, with corresponding reduced symptoms and enhanced health.

1. McTaggart (2007)

2. Masterson (1981)

3. *Ibid*

44

Neurotic Defensive Structures: Arising from Social Learning and Repression

All mammals are social beings with built in social learning systems. Human infants' nervous systems are literally taught how to grow with eye contact, holding, caressing, and vocalizations from caregivers[1]. At one year old, human infants begin to walk, feel emotionally separate from mother, and respond with shame emotions when disapproved of. One-year-olds are preconceptual, have practically no language, and have a very limited sense of past and future, so learning at this age is largely nervous system entrainment. Baby does something "wrong" by Mom's standards, Mom looks, acts, or sounds disapproving, and baby's nervous system shifts from pleasurable sympathetic buzz, to the painful parasympathetic collapse of a shame emotion. Baby's head drops, her neck and chest muscles weaken, she blushes, and she becomes immobilized. Her nervous system records this and she is likely to act differently in a similar situation in the future.[2] The evolutionary values of being able to immobilize a toddler at a distance with a disapproving glance or sound are obvious in a hunter-gatherer environment, where mothers can discern dangers more expertly and at greater distances than toddlers.

These entrainments take on new significance when baby grows to around two years old and can have an increasing sense of self in the past/present/future. A sense of self in the past/present/future combined with rapidly expanding language abilities results in *interior relationships* she has with herself that can involve approval/disapproval. Now she can *disapprove of herself* in the past/present/future with corresponding shame emotions. Toddlers don't have the neural capacity to self-regulate such emotions (as in, "I feel ashamed which means I've violated some interior value that I need to either honor of refine,"), so instead the child *reflexively avoids* the painful shame emotion by repressing, projecting, denying, scapegoating, or any of the other defensive activities that Freud observed and attributed to regulating anxiety. His developmental construct was thus partly accurate but also incomplete since he largely excluded the neurological shame dynamic. Yes, children avoid anxiety, but they largely avoid it in reflexively fleeing from shame emotions associated with forbidden thought, feeling, impulse, and behavior.[3]

Between one and four, as most of us successfully navigate our Fulcrum 2 emotional birth and integration into a coherent emotional sense of self, we enter the Fulcrum 3 world of the representational mind where we are more able to hold and manipulate images, symbols, and concepts. Our language development expands exponentially as does the conscious importance of relatedness to our families. The growing need for acceptance in our family culture is so intense that it eventually dominates our Fulcrum 4 conformist (BLUE) stage of development between around six and eleven. In Fulcrum 3, the combination of the ability to manipulate concepts, plus the growing need for family acceptance, plus the magic/mythic underpinnings of our emerging meaning-making, preoperational cognitive structures, leads to increasing capacities to repress, suppress, deny, project, introject, rationalize, distort, lie, and abreact in the face of real and/or imagined threat.[4] These capacities are unconsciously integrated with previous neural programming in response to attunement and approval/disapproval with caregivers and elaborated into emergent defensive intrapsychic structures that manifest as defensive states under perceived threat.

Of special importance during the first three fulcrums are the conflicting and emotionally charged messages we receive from our family and larger culture about our sexuality, our bodies, and socially inappropriate (depending on cultural context) feelings, thoughts, impulses, and behaviors. The way we make meaning out of such conflicting messages is to simultaneously grow in our natural drive towards healthy development, while avoiding threatening material by repressing and thus internalizing conflicts. Internalized conflicts stunt maturation in the threatening areas they protect us from, and, when evoked by internal or external cues, can manifest as neurotic defensive states where we have amplified or numbed emotions, distorted perceptions and thoughts, destructive impulses, and reduced empathy and self-reflection; all designed to protect us from the threatening truths (with their corresponding calls for changed perspectives and actions) we're avoiding. Defensive states arising from neurotic defensive structures can be distinguished from defensive states arising from characterological defensive structures by the presence, or relatively more easy availability of, an observing ego in neurotic states that has the capacity to disidentify from defensive states and self-regulate to healthy responses to the present moment.

Much of therapy is recognizing neurotic defensive states in our clients and ourselves, using them as guides to defensive structures, uncovering the truths that those structures were created to avoid and, (by bringing to bear the observing ego of our clients and ourselves) encouraging integration of these new truths into supporting more healthy (honest) perspectives and actions.[5] Neurotic defensive structures and states are far more common and omnipresent than characterological defensive structures and states. The main differences between defensive states generated by neurotic defensive structures and defensive states generated by characterological defensive structures is that, in states driven by neurotic defensive structures, there is relatively more empathy for others, more capacity for insight and self-reflection, and more ability to self-regulate emotion, thought, and impulse.

In therapy, the strategy for dealing with neurotic defensive states is to open them up as far as possible, relying on the client's mostly intact observing ego to evaluate the conflicted material with their subjective sense of truth. With clients burdened by characterological defensive structures, there is always the question of how much opening their more fragile ego-structure can tolerate before decompensating into inaccessible defensive states.

In the following exchange with Enid and Paul, there are a number of examples of neurotic defensive structures manifested as neurotic defensive states:

Enid: Demonstrating a defensive structure/state with a passive aggressive assertion. "I decided we could have sex once a week, and Paul could take it or leave it."

Paul: Angrily. "You decided. Don't I get a say in this?"

Enid: "You'll never be satisfied anyway, so why should I accommodate you?"

Paul: "Maybe I don't want to stick around and accommodate you."

Keith: Both are now in defensive states of consciousness. Enid is avoiding the guilt and shame she feels at not being sexually interested in Paul, and Paul is avoiding how threatening it is to him to feel dependent, unattractive, and sexually deprived. They're unconsciously cooperating to avoid this material by relating defense-to-defense (constellating a relational defensive structure) rather than truth-to-truth. I first want to interrupt their defensive states, then move them away from distorted certainty to more uncertain confusion, and then help them consider healthier perspectives. This is a common sequence in dealing with neurotic defensive structures. "You both are avoiding the real issues."

Enid: Confused. "What real issue? I don't see why ..."

Keith: Interrupting before the defensive state can gain momentum. "For you, Enid, the real issue is the shame and guilt you feel being rarely sexually interested in Paul, being unable to consciously inhabit the feminine side of your sexual polarity with him, and yet feeling sexual charge with images of inappropriate, abusive men."

Enid: "I want erotic polarity with Paul. I just can't feel it with him."

Keith: Confronting and praising the feminine. "You've felt it a number of times with Paul: You just can't consciously occupy it, you don't trust Paul to hold up his end, and you regularly feel angry, guilty, and ashamed."

Enid: "That's true. When I've felt it with you, Paul, I've really enjoyed it."

Paul: Angry, self-righteous, in a defensive state and so not having empathy for the fact that Enid has just become less angry and more loving. "Well, it doesn't help when you ..."

Keith: Interrupting. It's especially important to interrupt in conjoint work because a partner's defensive states accelerate more rapidly when in complementary reaction to a lover than they would in individual sessions. "Paul, you're avoiding the issue of feeling ashamed of not being consistently trustable to Enid."

Paul: Denying, rationalizing, trying to avoid this disturbing truth. "I'm a trustable man."

Keith: Confronting, challenging the masculine. "Not when you collapse into either infantile dependence or temper tantrums when Enid says 'no' to sex. Instead of caring for that part of you that feels dependent and abandoned, you're ashamed of that part and deny it by blaming and attacking Enid."

Paul: Sad and frustrated "I do feel so bad it's just shocking. And I am ashamed of that needy part of me. I don't want to hurt you, Enid."

Enid: Softening in response to his honesty and vulnerability. "I know you don't want to hurt me. I don't want to say 'no.' I just don't want to sell myself out."

Keith: Wanting to provoke self-reflection about her avoidance of embracing the feminine pole of their sexual polarity. "How are you selling yourself out?"

Enid: Invoking a second stage axiom of assertion and boundaries. She assumes it is always true, and will be surprised when I challenge it. "It's wrong to say 'yes' when you want to say 'no.'"

Keith: Smiling. "But don't you almost always initially want to say 'no' when Paul initiates sex?"

Enid: Ashamed. Surrendering to an impulse to attack herself. "Yes, I don't know what's wrong with me."

Keith: "You resist honoring and expressing your feminine erotic radiance. Last session I suggested sacred dance practices, sensual pleasure practices, and polarity practices. Did you do any of them?"

Enid: Interested in herself now. Entering a more healthy response to the present moment. Not currently guilty or ashamed. "I did the dancing once, the sensual pleasure practice twice, and I enjoyed them. I felt sexy. Then I just stopped."

Keith: "What stopped you from doing them more?"

Enid: "I guess I'm scared of opening that side of me with Paul."

Paul: Feeling more empathy. Touched by her vulnerability. "I want to make it safe for you to do that stuff."

Keith: They both are now open in healthy response to the present moment. I'm drawn to teach. "You make it safe for her when you can still love and cherish her even when she says 'no' to sex."

Paul: "That's so hard, but it feels right."

Keith: "To do this you need to love and cherish that needy, dependent, small child in you that gets so alarmed when she says 'no.' Never indulge impulses to trash that child. Take responsibility to love and care for him. Imagine that alarmed child on your lap right now. Can you feel him? Can you love and guide him to not attack you or Enid?"

Paul: "I can feel him a little. He relaxes when I hold him."

Enid: Touched by his work. "I love it when you care for that part of yourself, Paul."

Defensive states are blind spots that block truth and healthy change.

The above example reflects a central psychotherapeutic process of working with neurotic defenses. You get attuned to your client, elicit or reflect a goal they've consciously chosen, move towards that goal until defensive states are evoked. As defensive states arise, you relate, teach, inspire, confront, interpret, and direct the clients into disidentifying with and compassionately examining their defensive states. As this process helps them gradually constellate states of healthy response, you can support movement through the emerging confusion and distress and ultimately into the truths defensive structures conceal. As truths are uncovered and experienced in states of healthy response, the client tends to integrate them and act on them to remediate symptoms, enhance health, and support development.

This sequence happens endlessly with infinite variations, not only in therapy, but also throughout life. Defensive states constitute blind spots where we can literally not perceive that we are avoiding healthy perspectives and actions. The moment-to-moment awareness that therapy fosters helps clients notice blind spots and cultivate the will and skills to move into the confusion and distress, and through to the clarity of healthy perspectives and action.

The following exchange is from an individual session with Paul. Notice how, in individual therapy, there is less need to interrupt, and more opportunity for intrapsychic exploration:

Paul: "I don't know why I get so panicked when I'm angry with Enid."

Keith: "Describe the panic."

Paul: "Last night before I left, I just got freaked out. My heart was pounding. I was sweating, and I had to get out of there."

Keith: "Sounds like a panic attack."

Paul: "Yeah, I was panicked, but I was also really mad."

Keith: History is useful to the extent it liberates us in the present moment. When defensive states block us in the present moment, compassionate and deeper understanding can be cultivated (supporting compassion and depth of consciousness) by following sensations, feelings, thoughts, images, perspectives, judgments, or impulses back to early experiences that feel/taste/appear/sound/seem similar. This helps the client disidentify with current distortions, and bring to bear compassionate understanding onto historical aspects of the self frozen by defensive structures, thus cultivating intrapsychic integration, self-awareness and self-regulation of defensive states, and more freedom to have healthy responses to the present moment. "When have you felt this combination of amplified anger and panic before?"

Paul: Unconsciously resisting, wanting to make it about Enid. "It never happened in my first marriage."

Keith: "How about anytime, with anyone?"

Paul: "I felt it the first time I saw my brother with his arm around his girlfriend. I was sixteen. I just couldn't stand it. I was panicked, angry, and I had to get away."

Keith: Knowing Paul has a sturdy observing ego and primarily neurotic defensive structures, I'll open him as much as I can. I'll use Gestalt enactment techniques to maintain the emotional charge as we explore deeper. I would be much more cautious if his defense structures were primarily characterological. "Imagine yourself there, seeing your brother with his arm around his girlfriend. Describe what it's like as if it's happening right now."

Paul: "I hate it. I'm anxious and I want to get away."

Keith: Drawn to uncovering his conflicted parts hidden behind his angry panic. Using a variation of the redecision work that was pioneered by Transactional Analysis therapist/writers such as Mary and Bob Goulding[6]. "What's your opinion of yourself as you panic and want to get away?"

Paul: "I feel small, weak, and sick. I feel all alone."

Keith: Cultivating his observing ego. Checking if he's ready to bring compassionate understanding to bear on his defensive state. "What does this suggest to you?"

Paul: Relaxing and smiling as something clicks into place. "I need Enid to have sex with me or I'll feel small and weak and all alone. That's a lot of pressure to put on her, and it's not me taking responsibility for that young frightened self."

Keith: Feeling admiration. "Well said."

Clients and therapists feel and act in characteristic ways when the client enters specific defensive states.

When a client enters a neurotic defensive state, their demeanor, tone, and content shift in ways a therapist grows familiar with over time with each client. Equally importantly, the emotional, energetic processes in the therapist shift when a client enters neurotic defensive states. I often feel a tiny bit of tension/anxiety in my solar plexus accompanied by a subjective sense of interest at the point the neurotic defensive state begins to manifest. When a characterological defensive state begins to manifest, I'm more likely to feel a sense of dread, and the same sense of focus and danger in my torso that I used to feel as a martial artist fighting with a new opponent who has just revealed a desire to do me real damage. Every therapist has his own subjective and objective indicators of neurotic and characterological defenses in themselves and their clients. We are regularly immersed in intersubjective fields that are always communicating consciously and unconsciously. With training and practice we can cultivate our abilities to attend to these signals and use our selves as instruments to attune and intervene with clients.

Healing feedback loops: a signature characteristic of healthy living and good therapy.

The more we learn how to courageously attend to whether we, personally, are opening or closing ourselves and others in the moment, and the more resolutely we commit to opening ourselves and others, the more naturally we occupy the feedback loop of perceiving defensive states, following them to defensive structures, resolving those structures into the underlying lies, truths, and risks we have been avoiding, and then challenging those lies, embracing those truths and taking those risks in the service of health and love. Over the years, I've found that good therapists, regardless of orientation, tend to occupy these healing loops in themselves, and effectively support them in their clients.

1. Siegel (1999)

2. Schore (2003)

3. Witt (2007)

4. Wilber (2000)

5. *Ibid*

6. Goulding (1979)

45

Relational Defensive Structures

Each of our characterological or neurotic defensive structures has the tendency to constellate in patterned ways with other peoples' defensive states when experiencing certain combinations of intimacy and threat. These constellations constitute relational defensive structures that manifest as complementary defensive states and characteristic relational defensive patterns.

For example, in the following exchange with Tom and Anne, Tom is deescalating out of a jealous abandonment depression that was cued by Anne having an innocent meeting with a previous lover at her place of work. Tom's abandonment depressions typically involve overwhelming impulses to hate Anne and withdraw all positive attention from her. Tom indulging these impulses cues Anne's own fears of abandonment, which then result in her experiencing amplified anxiety, distorted beliefs about her own worthlessness, and impulses to seek validation from Tom. In complementary fashion, if Anne indulges these impulses, and pleads for validation, she cues Tom to experience further amplified doubt, distorted beliefs about her faithlessness, and sadistic impulses to demean and reject her. Notice how, even in conflict, they have a shared, though distorted, worldview:

> Keith: "I think it's clear that Anne was entirely innocent in her meeting with Jay."
>
> Tom: Talking to me, not Anne. "I can see that."
>
> Keith: Directing. "So, Tom, look at her."
>
> Tom: Looks at her, and Anne looks back with a hurt and concerned expression. He turns to me and complains. "She has that same 'I'm worried you're going crazy' look."
>
> Keith: Avoiding the defensive invitation to engage in nonproductive dialogue that maintains the distorted perspective. "Look at her again, and this

402

time, Anne, give him another expression." Anne makes a funny face and Tom laughs. Anne goes over and kisses him. He returns it. At this moment they are in a healthy response to the present moment. They have a healthy shared perspective that they are both loving and lovable.

Keith: "Doesn't this feel better?"

Anne: "Yes, it's so much better."

Tom: "I do love you, Anne."

Anne: Unconsciously indulging a defensive impulse. Still smarting a little from his previous rejection. Testing him, as the feminine is drawn to do, to see if he'll collapse. "You have to admit. I've been nothing but faithful for seven years."

Tom: Instantly outraged. Unconsciously falling back into the relational defensive structure in complementary fashion. Collapsing and becoming repulsive as a masculine partner. "What about those business trips to Boston? You expect me to believe you did nothing with all those guys at those parties?"

Anne: Beginning to cry. "You'll never believe me."

Tom: Angry, gathering momentum, and inviting further conflict, thus avoiding the more pleasurable, but also more threatening, waters of healthy intimacy that they previously had just entered. "Why should I?" They have now reentered the relational defensive structure. Each is caught up in a defensive state that is harmonizing with the other's to resist self-reflection and change. They share the perspective of their relationship not serving love, the other being at fault, and that further defense and attack is appropriate. Like most relational defensive structures, this one is complementary without being empathetic.

Keith: Confronting the relational defensive pattern first. This often paves the way into individual defensive states and structures. "You both were out of the pattern, loving each other, and then you, Anne, did what you tend to do when you're anxious, you tested Tom and asked for validation. Then you, Tom, did what you tend to do when you're coming down off of jealous alarm, you collapsed, took offense, and attacked Anne."

Anne: "I only …"

Tom: "She never …"

Keith: Interrupting. Feeling an urge to direct again, and show them what love is like outside of the relational defensive structure. Since I especially want Tom, who just collapsed, to cultivate masculine depth of consciousness and to better inhabit the masculine pole of their sexual polarity, I challenge him to lead in shifting perspectives. "Stop talking and look at each other. Come on Tom, you did it again. You collapsed and attacked her. So what? You'll never be perfect, she'll never stop testing you, and you'll never pass all the tests. Let it go and love her again. Where's your sense of humor?"

Tom: Cracks a smile. "Oops."

Anne: Smiles back.

Relational defensive structures are inevitable consequences of development.

Relational defensive structures are the inevitable consequence of our defensive structures and states expressed through our central drives to create meaning, relate intimately with others, and establish social position on subjectively important hierarchies. We are born with much of our temperament (shy, thrill-seeking, or risk-adverse for example) and type (masculine/feminine, introvert/extrovert) hard wired into our nervous systems. In the crucible of our family-of-origin, we have ongoing drives to love, defend, and establish social position. Our family-of-origin is a primordial soup in which we are constantly developing, loving, being loved, feeling secure, feeling threatened, trusting, distrusting, surrendering to change, and defending against change. Since development is include and transcend, we never lose our capacities for the most profound confluences of love, and most primitive compulsions to defend.

Heaven and hell in intimate relationships.

Tendencies and capacities to love and defend either mature in healthy ways or become arrested through trauma, neglect, ignorance, cultural pathology, or physiological disposition. As we age, we develop increasing capacities to develop deeper intimacies outside of our family-of-origin, though the family-of-origin always remains an unconscious standard for depth of intimacy. "I love him like a brother," "She is like a daughter to me," "He is like a father to me," all reveal the family-of-origin as a primary standard for depth of intimacy.

In early adolescence, as we move from conformist, ethnocentric Fulcrum 4 to competitive, merit based Fulcrum 5 (BLUE to ORANGE capacities and tendencies), we become sexually more mature and more able to enter states of romantic infatuation which catalyze depth of connection in the genetic imperatives to create new families-of-origin. Romantic infatuation is driven by dopamine and norepinephrine—excitement neurotransmitters—and tends to create states of romantic intoxication which can literally medicate defensive tendencies temporarily[1]. Eventually romantic infatuation matures into more intimate bonding mediated by oxytocin and vasopressin—bonding neurotransmitters. We feel familiar, intimate, and committed, but intoxication has faded, no longer protecting us biochemically from defensive states.

These intimacies rival and surpass the depths of connection of our early family experiences, and thus cue the capacities for deep love and defensive states we developed growing up, but now with the addition of much more mature bodies, minds, spirits, and depths of consciousness. The intimates we attract and are attracted to, being similar to historic figures in some ways, but also different in other ways, evoke our capacities to love and defend. The similarities to our families-of-origin attract in some ways ("I feel like we've known each other before"), and the differences attract us in some ways ("I would never tell my parents about this, but I can tell you"). In this confluence of factors reside our most profound potentials for inhabiting deep, abiding, transcendent love, and horrific, destructive, regressive defensive states. We can create Heaven in blissful love, or Hell in defensive regressions.

Healthy intimacy is complementary and empathetic, while relational defensive patterns are complementary and non-empathetic.

Healthy relational patterns always involve some level of empathy. Your lover feels injured by something you did or didn't do, and you feel concern and impulses to help him feel better, even if it means changing your behavior or perspective. For example, in this exchange between Paul an Enid, notice how naturally they adjust perspective and behavior to care for each other. This empathetic adjustment is characteristic of healthy responses to the present moment in intimacy, or healthy relational patterns:

> Enid: "I got angry when we had sex in Dallas. I pushed Paul away, and then I really wanted him to fuck me hard. It worries me."
>
> Paul: "I don't want her to have to be angry. I tried to not react badly."
>
> Keith: With minimal intervention. I just need to support this healthy process. "Did you both enjoy the sex?"
>
> Paul and Enid: Enthusiastically. "Yes!"

Keith: "Then it seems that you, Enid, finally feel safe enough to show your dark side sexually, and you, Paul, are strong enough to contain her and penetrate her energetically and physically with love when she's angry."

Paul: "You mean, it's a good thing?"

Keith: "Absolutely."

Enid: "Isn't it wrong to be so angry?"

Keith: "The masculine craves the full spectrum of feminine eroticism. I think it's beautiful that you can show him your angry, passionate side."

Enid: "That's good, because it was hot sex, and I do feel you were strong with me, Paul. I like that."

Paul: Smiles and glows.

When couples are open, rather than caught in defensive states, much of therapy is teaching and inspiring. The empathetic care they feel for each other tends to accelerate their learning and growth.

Defensive relational structures always involve diminished empathy, and resistance to insight and change. The perspectives the couple share in defensive states are complementary in that they can continue processing for hours without real change, but neither feels particularly empathetic towards, or responsible for, their partner's suffering. This is not surprising considering that defensive structures are first established during the most egocentric periods of development, Fulcrums 1, 2, and 3.

Therapists participating in such dialogues will often have impulses in themselves to complement the patterns. I'll often feel frustration, resentment, or impulses to attack or defend one or both partners. These feelings and impulses help guide me to identify the relational defensive structures and help my clients shift from defensive states to healthy responses to the present moment, and thus healthy relational patterns of relating with care, humor, and empathy. Notice the defensive resistance to new perspectives and actions in this exchange with Paul and Enid from an earlier session:

Enid: Attacking Paul with hostile analysis, a common defensive strategy with psychologically sophisticated clients. "You act like a little boy. I'm sure you learned that from your mother."

Paul: Collapsing, complementing her attack with his sarcasm. "There you go, if it's not about me and my first lover, it's about me and my mother."

Keith: Feeling mild irritation at Enid for her hostile analysis, and at Paul for his biting tone. I also feel compassion and a desire to help. "Enid, I know you're wanting something from Paul right now. What is it?"

Enid: "I want him to grow up."

Paul: Not getting the irony of his childish tone. You tend to lose your sense of humor in defensive states. "*You* grow up. A grown woman has a sex drive."

Enid: "Not for little boys she doesn't."

Keith: Feeling her acceleration of anger and complementary attacks. Paul feels more accessible than Enid at this moment. He is visibly more relaxed, and he receives help from me in inhabiting mature masculine power relatively easily. I'll confront the relational defense first to satisfy the Fulcrum 4, conformist, second stage need for fairness that regressive defensive states often require in relational defensive structures, and then focus on shifting Paul's perspective to pressure Enid's perspective. I smile ruefully. "You two are, once again, conspiring to avoid progress."

Paul: "What?"

Enid: "Huh?"

Keith: "You attack and defend so easily, but neither of you is really caring about the other's pain at this moment. Neither of you is looking for what's valid in the other's perspective. Look, Paul, Enid shouldn't analyze you, but you do appear like a child to her sometimes. What's valid about her perceptions?"

Paul: "Sometimes I feel like a little kid around her."

Enid: Pulling him back into the pattern, unconsciously resisting the dangerous change that is represented in this approach. "Who wants to have a little boy for a husband? Not me."

Keith: Interrupting and persisting with Paul. I can tell this is getting through to both him and Enid right now. "Of course she doesn't want to have sex when you're in that child state, but that's not what you need in that state anyway. You need to love that child yourself, hold him, support him, and show him how to handle an angry woman."

Paul: Laughing. "How do you handle an angry woman?" Both laugh.

Keith: "Just like that, with presence, humor, and love."

Relational defensive structures are revealed in complementary defensive states.

All human interaction is complementary by necessity. Two or more people need to cooperate to communicate. Content and states tend to evoke complementary content and states. Shortly after birth, infants mirror facial expressions and neural activation patterns of caregivers, who's brains incline them toward nurturing when gazing at, holding, hearing, and smelling infants. This reciprocal process, anchored in extensive resonance circuits that include mirror neurons in various parts of our brains that read other's intent and recapitulate their states of mind, continues to evolve until death[2].

Our drive to create meaning, which Robert Kegan believes is a primary engine of individual evolution[3], combined with our drive to affiliate results in a universal tendency to cocreate meaning with others in our interactions. If an interaction is not complementary, there is a subjective sense that communication is not happening, and the interaction tends to stop, which usually negatively reinforces whatever we were doing when it stopped. Thus, we learn throughout development to do whatever it takes to continue, or complement, interactions with others so there is a shared sense of communication happening.

Content evokes complementary content, process evokes complementary process.

Content evokes similar content. If I start talking about ducks to you, you'll have to discuss ducks to some extent or risk not feeling like we're communicating. If you talk about reading, I will feel an impulse to respond with content that has something to do with reading. Similarly, process evokes process. If I use a soothing tone, your response will tend to be more soothing. If I use a hostile tone, your response will tend to be more hostile. Inspirational speakers feel inspired, and thus evoke complementary states of inspiration in their audiences. Interested listeners evoke interest in their partner, and loving attention tends to evoke loving response. Finally, defensive states tend to evoke complementary defensive states, both in content and process.

When a defensive state manifests in one person in a relational context, everyone else in that context, whether one person or a group of people, will have some impulse (often an impulse they aren't consciously aware of) to enter complementary defensive states. If we indulge such impulses we are constellating complementary defensive states into relational defensive patterns.

"Complementary" does not mean pleasurable or satisfactory. To the contrary, these interactions are usually frustrating, painful, and often cycle to some sort of explosion. What makes them complementary is that all parties are unconsciously cooperating with a shared defensive agenda rather than working towards healthy responses to the present moment. The tendency will be to create meaning that normalizes our own amplified or numbed emotions, distorted beliefs/perceptions, and destructive impulses, while attacking and pathologizing our partner's reactions, which tends to reinforce and support their amplified or numbed emotions, distorted beliefs/perceptions, and destructive impulses, etc.

When two or more people constellate a relational defensive pattern, it requires some effort for any individual to consistently shift into a healthy state, and to relate from that healthy state to the other's defensive distortions. Such efforts, though, are exactly what's required when a relational defensive pattern is constellated. This is reflected in two of David Deida's principles for dealing with distressed lovers. The feminine partner offers deeper trust and devotional love than her masculine partner deserves ("deserves" from a second stage, 50/50 perspective), and the masculine partner offers more presence and depth of consciousness than the feminine partner deserves.[4]

Similarly, when couples are caught up in defensive relational patterns, I encourage either one to focus on telling their partner what's valid in their distorted perspectives, rather that surrendering to their natural tendencies to point out what's not valid.

Relating from a healthy state to a defensive state can paradoxically initially add extra stress to the system because it's frustrating to not have complementary communication. Refusing to join into the relational defense is, at least partly, refusing to have complementary communication, but it is exactly the right thing to do to influence another to shift states, stop surrendering to defensive impulses, and engage in healthy, intimate exchange.

Psychotherapists soothe and frustrate defensive states simultaneously

Cocreating a culture that cherishes the client and the client's universe, experiences each moment as a gift and an opportunity, and considers healthy perspectives and actions beautiful, good, and true means that the therapist is routinely evoking defenses, soothing the alarm associated with them, and challenging the distortions with compassionate reality testing. A useful device for accomplishing this is to look for the real suffering and authentic desire for healthy perspectives and actions that always reside within defenses, and to evoke, validate, and stroke these things to help the client (and the client's partner if it is a conjoint session) do the same.

The ethical stand the therapist usually occupies is compassionate concern for the client's suffering, utter confidence that healthy perspectives and actions exist and are accessible, and a relentless refusal to accept violence to the self and/or another as preferable solutions. This violence resides in all the destructive impulses associated with defensive structures. In relational defensive structures, emotional or physical violence evokes complementary violence in partners.

Violence can take the form of indulging impulses to make critical judgments about self and/or other, indulging impulses to injure self and/or other emotionally and/or physically, or indulging impulses to dissociate from self and/or other. Delicately optimizing the healing tension at the event horizon of soothing alarm while frustrating destructive defensive impulses is the art of therapy. In relational defenses, the added task is to educate and empower the partners to do the same with each other.

In the following exchange with James and Michelle you can observe the balance between soothing their pain and frustrating their destructive impulses. James is a successful businessman in his mid-forties, and Michelle left her medical practice to raise their two small children. This exchange illustrates the principle that content is almost always secondary to state of consciousness in therapy. In fact, often the best use of content is as a tool to create and support changes from defensive states to healthy responses to the present moment.

As I'm fond of telling clients in defensive states, traditional marriage counseling suggests that good communication leads to loving feelings and actions. This is true to a certain extent (especially in growing from first stage egocentricism to second stage safety and clean boundaries) until we can grow to the point that we can cultivate loving feelings and actions to create good communication:

Michelle: "James just doesn't want to participate in the family."

James: "Bullshit."

Michelle: On a roll, feeling the immediate relief that attacking someone you resent always delivers. "You never follow through. You always change plans and disappoint the kids. You always choose work over the kids and me, and you always come home late. You …"

James: Interrupting, complementing her attack with one of his own. "Why should I come home early? You're always angry and mean."

Keith: Interrupting, confronting, and interpreting the relational defensive structure. "If you two were at home, how would this end?"

Michelle: "I'd sleep in the other room." Glancing angrily at James. "I might sleep there tonight."

James: Disgusted tone. "It never ends."

Keith: "That's because you cooperate with each other to keep the conflict going."

Michelle: "We need to talk. We never talk."

Keith: "Non-productive talk is often worse than no talk. You need productive talk, and to do that you need to relate from more generous, less stingy states."

James: Confused. "I don't know what you mean."

Keith: James has now shifted his state of consciousness slightly by relating to me instead of Michelle, and by inhabiting confusion rather than angry certainty at her rejections. He's opening, but her defensive state could re-evoke his in an instant. I'm drawn to confronting him directly and her indirectly through him. "You refuse to validate Michelle's genuine suffering at not having enough of you for her and the kids. You're identifying her by her anger at you rather than by her yearning to feel more love *for* you and her yearning to feel more love *from* you for her and the kids."

James: "But she's so angry."

Keith: "That's where your suffering is. You yearn for her warmth and love, but you're too angry in complementary reaction to her to do what it takes to evoke it. Validate her suffering and love her. Change what you honorably can to answer her yearning, and she'll open like a flower to you."

Michelle: Softening as her suffering is validated and soothed, and her yearning is articulated. "Keith's right, James. I'd rather love you, but I've been let down so much."

James: Unconsciously resisting a changed perspective and the challenge to engage in healthy actions. "I can't help it if work is demanding."

Keith: Michelle is now more open. I'm drawn now to confronting James indirectly through confronting and interpreting Michelle's defenses, and teaching her feminine practice. "Michelle, you keep trying to get James to change by attacking him, and it never works. You do need to show him your suffering without attacking him when he lets you down, but more importantly, you need to show him your pleasure when he shows up to love you."

Michelle: Resisting. "When does he show up?"

Keith: Confronting. "He shows up regularly and that's my point. You're often too mad to feel pleasure, much less express pleasure, when he does. That's your work, to feel and express pleasure through your body when he's his best self."

James: "I could be at home more if it's a more friendly place."

Keith: Not letting Michelle step into a complementary hostile role. I want to model a healthy response to his criticism. "James, it's your job to become more reliable, and feel more responsibility to evoke Michelle's warmth. You know how to do this generously. You forget, and become stingy when you're angry. Then you just criticize."

Michelle: "It would be easier to be nice if you come home on time more."

Keith: "So, when he does, love him up. Show him your pleasure through your body. Your pleasure attracts him to your home, like honey attracts a bee."

James: Smiling. "You're my honey."

Michelle: Insecure. Caught in the endless feminine wheel of "I feel loved, I don't feel loved. Does he love me? Does he not love me?" "Sometimes I wonder if you love me."

James: Empathetic now. Concerned and generous. "Of course I love you. I love you more than I've ever loved anyone."

Michelle: Becoming radiant and generous. "It feels good to hear."

Keith: Teaching, inspiring. "This is where your power is, each of you. Deciding to reach out through your anger and validate what's true about your partner's concerns, and to make generous offerings. You especially need to do this when you feel the least like reaching out, the least like finding what's valid in the other's complaint. When you do, you're moving both of you towards love."

Relational defensive structures manifest as complementary defensive states that are enacted as relational defensive patterns in the therapy session. Understanding and working with these shifting defensive structures, states, and patterns to help people feel and honor their deepest masculine and feminine essences, and deepest needs for love and passion, is one of the mainstays of conjoint work.

Summary: states all over the place.

In this Section we examined states of consciousness starting from the three great states of gross (waking), subtle (dreaming), and causal/formless (deep dreamless sleep). We examined how to identify and work with these states in therapy, and moved on to healthy responses to the present moment, and defensive states generated by intrapsychic defensive structures. We explored the phylogenetic and ontogenetic inevitability of defensive structures and states, and a variety of psychotherapeutic options for working with these states in individual and conjoint therapy. Finally, we examined relational defensive structures and patterns, how they develop, and a few principles for working with them in the psychotherapeutic session.

In Section Seven we'll explore additional principles and techniques for working with couples at various levels of development, and, in Chapter Fifty-two, we'll follow one couple, Jerry and Kay, from intake to termination working with one model of sex therapy.

1. Carlin (2004)

2. Siegel (2007)

3. Kegan (1982)

4. Deida (2004)

Section Seven

Conjoint Therapy:
Working with Lovers

46

All Therapy Involves Relationships

All psychotherapy is about intrapsychic and/or interpsychic relationships of one sort or another. Since conjoint therapy involves working individually with each partner while also working with the couple, let's examine the importance of relationships in individual therapy first, and then work our way into conjoint therapy.

Interpersonal and intrapersonal relationships in individual therapy.

Most psychotherapists will acknowledge that they routinely process current and past relationships their clients have had or are having with people such as lovers, family members, friends, coworkers, and people in general. Seventy percent of human communication involves talking about other people. Individual therapy also involves clients discerning and working with aspects of themselves that are strong, resilient, injured, dissociated, or otherwise conflicted; all of which are in relationship with other aspects of themselves that are more or less healthy or wounded, mature or immature, in defensive states or states of healthy response.

Self-aware consciousness comes into being as memory and language skills come on line throughout the first two years of development. Because of our human capacities for grammar, symbolic communication, memory, and past/present/future orientations, human children encounter a potential infinity of perspectives—including a potential infinity of interior relationships between these perspectives—as language and memory develop. I believe that self-aware consciousness arises from within this infinity of internal relationships, that it is interior to these relationships.[1]

When we are in a state of healthy response to the present moment, our body/mind/spirit systems tend to automatically self-regulate. Painful emotion, if experienced in a state of healthy response, generally changes significantly within about ten minutes. The feminine practice of being a clear channel of emotion is describing an individual who doesn't unnecessarily repress or amplify emotion. Painful emotion is allowed by healthy aspects of self, which stay open in the face of pain and thus keep surrendering to and contributing to the moment rather than shutting the moment down. Pleasurable emotion is allowed and enjoyed as long as it naturally lasts. An open person in a state of healthy response doesn't grasp, pursue, or pathologize self or others as pleasurable and painful states ebb and flow.

Defensive states are another story. Emotion, if repressed in response to defensive fears and demands, can turn into symptoms such as physical illness, or chronic rage, shame, depression, or anxiety. Emotion, if amplified by distorted thoughts and perceptions, can cue destructive impulses and actions that create progressively more suffering in self and others. These are cases of emotional flow being directed from an unhealthy aspect of self—usually a self dominated by a defensive state, driven by a defensive structure—resulting in closure in the face of pain, and poisoning (or closing) the moment to some extent.

All the above processes reflect relationships between intrapsychic elements of self. Individual therapy seeks to mobilize wise and compassionate elements of self (cultivating compassion and depth of consciousness), and to bring those elements into accepting relationship with distressed parts of self to remediate symptoms, enhance health, and support development.

When I was twenty-five, Becky and I rented a house together in the foothills of Santa Barbara. It was 1975, and we were both wounded seekers, struggling with our desires to love and grow, and our characterological, neurotic, and relational defensive structures' tendencies to screw things up with ourselves and each other. We later called this house "The Fat House," because we seemed to lose ourselves in an overindulgence of destructive impulses. Not surprisingly, I began to have nightmares that became progressively more horrible. Finally I woke one morning from a dream of Keith suspended by a rope being tortured by sadistic, shadowy figures, and I decided I needed to do something. "Time to practice what you preach," I told myself (a relational dialog between the part of me that wanted to face the pain and the part of me that wanted to avoid it), and I sat in meditation and went into the dream, becoming all the figures, one by one. As I became the suspended, tortured Keith, all I could feel was one long unending scream. Becoming the current Keith, trained in the healing arts, I held the screaming figure as lovingly as I could, demanding nothing, asking nothing. I continued this meditation daily until the tormented hanging Keith transformed into the tortured adolescent I had been, and who was finally able to have dialogues with the more mature man I was becoming. In retrospect, I was providing the feminine holding that the tortured Keith had starved for in his development, was disidentifying with the agonized figure, and identifying with a deeper, more mature self who took responsibility for loving the conflicted part of me I had been running from with "Fat House" excesses.

The nightmares stopped the day I began the meditation practice. I went into intense physical and spiritual training, and Becky and I stopped getting more toxic with each other and started getting more loving. We sought support and guidance, both individually and conjointly, from therapists and spiritual teachers. My key to these positive shifts was taking responsibility for conflicted intrapsychic relationships that I had been avoiding.

Either we take responsibility for our suffering or we do not. Either we acknowledge and harmonize our myriad aspects of self or we do not. All this work involves intrapsychic relational activity. All individual therapy, on some level, promotes disidentifying with destructive aspects of self, identifying with more mature, more loving aspects of self, and committing to integrating and harmonizing the whole system from the most mature self we can access. As we do this, we grow.

As Robert Kegan has observed, the subject (I) of one developmental level becomes the object (he or she) of a new subject (I) on the next developmental level, who then becomes the object of another new subject, and so on.[2]

The irony of all this dualistic activity is that it promotes unity. A single system in harmony functions as a single entity in many ways. Multiple systems in harmony function as a single entity in many ways, and so on until we are one with Unity. Dissociated or conflicted parts of self obstruct and stunt this process. Pain influences us to separate, dissociate, and regress. Suffering distracts us from beauty, truth, and goodness.

Individual psychotherapy often seeks out dissociated or conflicted aspects of self, mobilizes wise and loving aspects of self, and relates, teaches, inspires, confronts, interprets, and directs each client to take on the responsibility to disidentify with defensive states, identify with their deepest heart, and commit to integrating their whole body/mind/relational/professional/spiritual systems so that they can be true to their most authentic nature and give their deepest gifts to the world.

Our deepest sense of self is profoundly influenced by our masculine and feminine aspects.

A third stage practitioner consistently mobilizes whatever aspects of self that are required to open the moment. If feminine aspects are required to open the moment, feminine aspects are mobilized, if masculine aspects are required to open the moment, masculine aspects are mobilized. A more masculine individual will naturally more often mobilize masculine aspects, and a more feminine individual will more often mobilize feminine aspects. This is especially true in relationship with others, and colossally true in relationship with lovers. When we are closed, conflicted, blocked, or constricted, we lose our capacity to open optimally from all parts of ourselves including our masculine and feminine aspects. The purpose of psychotherapy is to support opening, resolve conflicts, dissolve blocks, relax constrictions, and promote integration so that we can open to give our best gifts, and fully inhabit our best selves.

Lovers: the most wide-open relationship of all.

The lover aspect is what makes a couple's relationship unique. The potential to be wide open from the full spectrum of our masculine and feminine cores means we can go deeper into more dimensions with our lover than in any other relationship. More aspects of our self (young, old, healthy, defended, open, closed, masculine, feminine, light, dark, enraged, joyful, terrified, child, parent, friend, and lover) can be expressed in complementary patterns, both healthy and unhealthy, with our lover than in any other relationship.

One telling aspect of this I've noticed over the years is that when a husband or wife has a secret lover, they usually report feeling more wide open with their lover (more loving, generous, and passionate) than with their spouse. This illustrates how sexual polarity is at the core of the lover relationship, and naturally mobilizes the openness associated with satisfied lovers. If we don't feel fulfilled in that polarity, we'll yearn for it, and potentially seek it elsewhere, even if it means going outside our marriage, opening more deeply to a lover than to a spouse, and causing great suffering for people we love.

Sexual polarity and willingness to practice love at the same level: the main criteria for choosing a lover.

Two factors to carefully consider when choosing a lover are sexual polarity and whether that potential partner is willing to practice love at the same level as we are.[3] If there is little or no polarity, then a lover relationship is enormously difficult, since polarity is the engine that runs the lover relationship. If we choose a partner that wants to practice love at a much higher, or much lower, level than we do, we have a basic conflict of values that begins a relationship with huge systemic problems that can doom it to failure.

Sexual polarity runs off of the more feminine partner's willingness to open, shine as light, and offer devotional love, and the more masculine partner's willingness to inhabit deepest consciousness, commit to deep soul's purpose, and embrace the responsibility to be true to his principles, be a trustable presence, and do his best to open his feminine partner in ways that are best for her. Even though both partners will have both masculine and feminine aspects, each will usually be more fundamentally masculine or feminine in their sexual relationship. The energetic connection between these deepest masculine and feminine essences determines the state of the couple's polarity, and is always being expressed in numerous ways when lovers are in each other's presence.

The state of a couple's sexual polarity is a constant indicator of the health of their relationship. Supporting and enhancing their polarity is an ongoing dimension of conjoint work, just as supporting an individual in identifying and being true to his or her deepest masculine or feminine essence is an ongoing dimension of individual therapy.

The teaching aspect of psychotherapy is particularly important here, since these aspects and energies are often ignored, misinterpreted, or distorted in American culture.

Conjoint therapy is individual therapy plus ...

Both individual and systems' work combine in conjoint psychotherapy. Cultivating compassion and depth of consciousness to support healthy perspectives and action is what therapists do in all psychotherapeutic environments. Cocreating a culture that cherishes our client and our client's universe, experiences each moment as a gift and an opportunity, and considers healthy perspectives and actions beautiful, good, and true is what we strive for in all psychotherapeutic encounters.

In conjoint therapy, the added dimension of the couple creates opportunities to help each partner better love their spouse, better love their children, more effectively relate in social and professional environments, enhance health, support spiritual practice, solve problems, or better separate with a minimum of suffering (if that's what one partner resolves to do). Optimal health almost always involves relationships with others, and especially with significant others. Relational satisfaction figures hugely in physiological and social health, and our internal experiences of felt satisfaction, fulfillment, purpose, and moral clarity.

Conjoint and individual therapy simultaneously: sometimes with the same therapist, sometimes with different therapists.

There is a certain intimacy of the therapeutic relationship, and a certain depth of penetration of the client's defensive structures, that can be diminished in conjoint therapy. This is one reason it's often useful for one or both partners to have occasional or regular individual sessions to maximize progress or, especially the case of deeper pathology often generated by characterological defensive structures, to even make progress possible.

Occasional individual sessions are usually best done by the conjoint therapist with the provision that no secrets will be kept from the other spouse. Regular individual work with one partner by the conjoint therapist is sometimes appropriate if both partners are relatively healthy with almost exclusively neurotic defensive structures. Sometimes the added depth of having a spouse in individual work with the conjoint therapist supports the conjoint work.

In general, the more either partner's defenses are characterological and/or the more likely a couple is to separate, the more appropriate it is for the individual and conjoint therapy to be done by different therapists. The less functional and more pathological an individual is, the more crystal clear and rigid the boundaries of therapy need to be, and the more the therapist has to plan for decompensation and/or separation when doing conjoint work. An added advantage of using different therapists for individual and conjoint work is that clients sometimes feel more supported and cherished if they have an individual therapist/advocate whose primary psychotherapeutic responsibility is their care. Encouraging a conjoint client to do individual therapy with another therapist can simplify transference issues and provide a safety net to catch a client if they fall out of conjoint therapy.

1. Witt (2007)

2. Kegan (1982)

3. Deida (2004)

47

What is Required for Effective Conjoint Therapy?

I once read an article, clearly written by earnest, well meaning, well educated, GREEN, pluralistic psychologists on multiculturalism and diversity in therapy. When I got to the "recommendations" section, the authors used the word "must" thirteen times, betraying the signature GREEN position of "We support many points of view, as long as they agree with ours."

I believe each therapist develops a unique style that reflects personality, training, experience, and clientele. My doctoral research suggested that any clinician who is practicing a treatment style he or she believes in has about the same health enhancing effects on clients as another committed clinician practicing a different treatment style.[1] All this makes me cautious discussing what is "required" for effective conjoint treatment. On the other hand, I've discovered that for me to feel effective as a conjoint therapist, there are a variety of requirements I usually need to meet. The three that I've found to be essential are to be active, to be comfortable dealing with the masculine and feminine, and to cultivate multiple perspectives.

Researchers in the conjoint field (my favorite is John Gottman[2]) have generated data that support many of my personal requirements. As usual, I encourage you to evaluate these aspects with your own sense of what feels true, experiment with the material in your own practice, and decide for yourself what best serves you and your clients. Your personal style as a clinician will continue to develop throughout your career. The more effortlessly you discern and incorporate new or enhanced perspectives and techniques, the smoother your professional development is likely to be.

Be active; couples' relational defenses gather momentum quickly and often need to be interrupted.

John Gottman, in *The Marriage Clinic,* reports that all active (even somewhat active) conjoint therapy systems were superior to more passive systems in client satisfaction, dropout rate, and various other aspects.[3] Relational defensive patterns constellate quickly in a session. If they build up too much momentum, one or both partners can become so negatively aroused that they are effectively inaccessible to any intervention. This is especially true with characterological defensive structures and states. I've found that I need to interrupt such defensive patterns early, and direct the couple towards more healthy perspectives and actions.

It's useful to support the enactment of the relational defensive pattern until it is clear what defensive states are currently constellated, and what is the basic architecture of the relational defensive structure. As soon as these things become apparent to the therapist, and the couple is feeling some of the frustrated distress of being caught in the defensive states of a destructive pattern, it's usually time to interrupt and start relating, teaching, inspiring, confronting, interpreting, and directing. An example of this is the following exchange with Blake and Sadie. Both are in their early thirties, and conformist BLUE/achievement oriented ORANGE in their centers of gravity, with swooping regressions when in defensive states. Blake is dysthymic (chronically mildly depressed), with some dependent and compulsive traits. Sadie is anxious, phobic, and has some borderline traits on top of a narcissistic characterological defensive structure:

> Blake: "I need to talk about your trip to Reno. I know you were out partying every night."

> Sadie: Defensively. "I didn't have sex with anyone."

> Blake: "I heard you were getting pretty heavy on the dance floor, and doing shooters with different guys."

> Sadie: Angry now. "Who did you hear all this from?"

> Blake: Angry. "You were there with a bunch of people from your company, Sadie. They all saw it."

> Sadie: Turning away from Blake and me. Shrinking into the chair, scared of his anger and moral condemnation. Visibly beginning to dissociate and regress. "He's just mad because I wouldn't have sex with him when I got home."

Blake: Embarrassed, wanting to avoid his dependent needs for sex to reassure his anxieties, now talking to me. "You're supposed to be able to have sex with your wife aren't you?"

Sadie: Sinking deeper into the chair. Looking dramatically despairing. Sounding more dissociated. "I can't stand this."

Keith: This has accelerated far enough, maybe too far. Sadie is dissociating, and Blake is hot with anger. Each is provoking the other further with no empathy for the other's pain. Their relational defensive pattern is revealed in an interplay of defensive states generated by characterological and neurotic defensive structures. "Let me interrupt."

Blake tries to say something.

Keith: "No, excuse me, but I need to interrupt. This is turning into your typical pattern of attack, dissociation, and blame. Neither one of you is paying the slightest attention to what's valid about the other's point of view, or how much pain your partner is feeling right now."

Blake: Angry. He's a big man, and unconsciously uses his size and anger to try to dominate the moment. He leans forward and attempts to direct the session forcefully. I feel compassion for the vulnerability he's trying to protect. I have a vision of myself being a bouncer at bar with a big, intimidating guy who's just been publicly humiliated. "We need to discuss this!"

Keith: Concerned about Sadie's dissociation. Needing to bring her back into the room, while soothing Blake's extreme, though neurotic rather than characterological, defensive state. He's more accessible than she is right now, so I'll try to reach her by confronting him. "Of course you need to discuss the Reno trip, but look at Sadie. She's dissociated. She's staring out the window, lost in despair, and relating to you like those creeps who abused her when she was a kid."

Sadie: Engaged to come back into the room by my compassion, but still in her defense. "He *is* a creep."

Keith: Relieved. She just spoke directly to me. The spell is partially broken. I want to strengthen her tenuous adult consciousness and keep her present in the room, and confront him while engaging her. "I know how scared you get when Blake gets angry. He has no idea how intimidating he is when he's threatened. But Blake's a good man. He's not a creep. Look at him."

Sadie: Childish voice, pouty. Still defended but now relating to me, even though it's slightly flirtatious, and thus designed to torture Blake with the feminine erotic radiance that he's not getting from her. "No. I won't look at him."

Keith: Using our polarity to bring her further back into the session, and back to Blake. Smiling, modeling for Blake how to handle her in this defensive state. "There's your sense of humor. It's great to see. Now, look at Blake and tell me how you feel."

Sadie: Looking at Blake. Using the same flirtatious tone. "He's a dope."

Blake: Smiling in spite of himself. Softening. "OK. But I'm not a creep."

Keith: Wanting to keep them connected and to point out how they just changed states. If either can see and comment on a defensive state and/or structure, they've disidentified with it for the moment, and are inhabiting a more mature, healthy self. "Good distinction, Blake. Notice how you can stay connected if you hold on to that angry self and remember your sense of humor. Sadie's making an effort to connect, and your job is to help her feel safe."

Sadie: Adult tone. "I don't feel safe when you're mad, Blake."

Keith: Remembering that the feminine often grows best with praise. "Good job mobilizing your adult self, Sadie. When Blake gets mad, you often dissociate and check out. Dissociating and checking out was a great response when you were a kid at the mercy of abusive adult creeps. It's a terrible response with Blake because you lose your adult self and capacity for adult contact with him. It's so much better to do what you're doing right now; look at him, feel your body, stay adult, deal with this moment; and take a stand for love."

Blake: Getting that his job is to help her feel safe. "I want you to feel safe. I just need to talk about Reno."

Sadie: Cautiously. "OK. Just don't get so mad."

You can see the interface between their explosive defensive states and my active intervention. If I had been more non-directive and less active, they probably would have entered their complementary defensive states and continued to accelerate through the session until one of them collapsed or exploded in some fashion. Blake might have stormed out of the session, or Sadie might have become catatonic, both unconsciously minimizing the threat of changed perspectives and actions that they simultaneously yearn for and fear. In general, the more pathological the defenses and the less functional the partners, the more active I believe I need to be as a therapist.

Cultivate familiarity with, and be comfortable with, masculine and feminine essences, practices, and polarities.

Therapy is not value free. It's clear to me that couples with solid erotic polarity and individuals with knowledge of their deepest essences, and abilities to inhabit those essences, do much better. These perspectives often result in paradigm shifts as they are progressively understood on deepening levels.

I've demonstrated in many of this book's clinical examples how these perspectives, driven by the inescapable fact that we all are a sexual type of individual with a unique blend of masculine and feminine, form a metastructure that naturally underlies and supports other psychotherapeutic activities. This is especially vital material in conjoint therapy, since sexual polarity between lovers is always waxing and waning either consciously or unconsciously.

Cultivate multiple perspectives during each session.

I've learned to trust my felt sense of appreciation for different perspectives, and be curious about my critical judgments that arise during sessions. Critical judgments tend to block felt appreciation, which tends to block discerning what's good and useful in a perspective, action, person, or institution. Critical judgments, often signals of defensive states, arise naturally out of both clients and therapists during sessions, and have their own truths inherent in them. Discerning critical judgments and/or defensive states when they arise, and seeking the compassionate truths they both indicate by their presence and conceal by their nature support good psychotherapy.

When I have discerned, and felt in my body, the compassionate perspective beneath the critical judgment and/or defensive state, I trust myself much more to relate spontaneously and naturally from that spot. The subjective experience when I feel compassion during a session is of opening a channel into an ocean of truth and healing, and allowing material to flow through that channel, through me, to my client.

An example of these processes is the following exchange with Lorinda, a highly anxious fifty-eight-year-old woman with four grown children, and a second husband of five years, Herb, whom she generally adores. Both Lorinda and Herb are healthy, multi-cultural, egalitarian GREEN, with regular flashes of YELLOW compassion for all points of view. Lorinda, when cued by threats to important relationships, regresses into defensive states of obsessive anxiety. Since she generally has such a high center of gravity, it's easy for me to expect too much from her and to have little blooms of frustration when she regresses:

Lorinda: "My son is majoring in psychology at college, and he says I should take antidepressants for my anxiety."

Herb: "She's been really worried about it."

Keith: I feel a flash of irritation at both her son for doing what psychology students (including me when I was in school) have always done, and at Lorinda for her anxious impulsivity. I internally reach to anchor myself in compassionate understanding of her son's love, concern, and desire to help, and her current perspective. "It sounds like he's concerned about your anxiety, believes you need more help with it, and that part of you agrees."

Lorinda: "I don't know. I don't want the side effects, but after I talked to him I got worried that I might be making a mistake. I've been talking to Herb about it."

Herb: Laughing ruefully. "And talking and talking and talking."

Lorinda: Laughing back. "I know I obsess about things. That's why I wonder if I would benefit from the antidepressants."

Keith: Feeling more humor and compassion, and thus feeling safer to be more spontaneous. "So you got worried about being worried."

Lorinda: Laughing. "I guess so."

Keith: "Let's revisit medication as an option for your anxiety then. As we've discussed before, and as you've discussed with your doctor, there are plusses and minuses. You two can listen to the tape and talk at home and you can go back to your doctor together and discus it with him if you'd like. Either way, I think you should participate, Herb."

Herb: Knowing that sometimes he defers instead of offering her direction, but that she benefits from his opinions and participation. "Sounds fine to me."

As I felt irritation and critical judgment, I went inward and processed until I felt grounded in compassionate understanding. Anchored in compassionate understanding, I proceeded to offer my best help to Lorinda and Herb.

There are many other aspects of conjoint therapy that I find useful, and we will explore lots of them in the next five chapters. Being active, being familiar and comfortable with the masculine and feminine, and cultivating multiple perspectives are three components that I've found invaluable in working with couples.

1. Witt (1982)

2. Gottman (1999, 2001, 2005)

3. Gottman (1999)

48

Conducting a Conjoint Session

It is useful to cultivate the ability to begin a psychotherapeutic exchange with focusing alternately on content, healthy states, defensive states, or relational defensive structures, and be able to move back and forth between all of them.

How do you determine what to focus on in a session? Of course, we all ask our clients what they want to work on, and often they come in with issues, agendas, notes, or questions. Sometimes a client sits down in a session and says, "I don't know exactly what to work on today." Couples can instinctively protect each other from threatening areas by collaborating in maintaining that everything's fine, and sometimes everything really is fine. This Chapter will focus on determining an agenda, pursuing that agenda through encouraging each partner to do their personal work, typical clinical sequences in conjoint work, and a hierarchy of agendas (most urgent to less urgent) in a typical session.

The session's agenda usually constellates within the first twenty minutes.

In determining an agenda, I generally first probe with questions and reflections, looking for the optimal places to focus therapeutic attention. I feel for what's optimal while exploring externally observable data, historical data, and my internal reactions to what attracts, repels, or interests me, or what areas subjectively have emotional charge. My subjective moral sense informs me as to whether perspectives and/or actions fit within my client's, our community's, and my own moral standards, and my systems oriented knowledge helps me discern what actions/perspectives are likely to cause benefit or harm, and what are likely outcomes of different behavior patterns and treatment strategies.

We can use all the above sources of information to access our clients' universes through content issues such as "My wife and I can't agree on whether to buy a new car," or "I don't like how he looks at other women." We can also use healthy states such as "I want to learn to love my husband better," defensive states reflected in such statements as "All he cares about is himself," or relational defensive structures such as, "We keep getting in the same fight over and over." Therapy can start at any one of these access points, and flow to any other point, depending on the needs of the clients and the intuitions and inclinations of the therapist.

Certainly there are some sequences that appear more frequently. One frequent pattern is:

- sensation,
- to feeling,
- to distorted belief,
- to current blocks,
- to healthy perspectives and actions.

Another example of a common sequence with couples is:

- distressing episode,
- to defensive states,
- to relational defensive structures/patterns,
- to shifting into healthy states,
- to loving contact and resolving issues.

Sequences such as these often yield visible progress in self-regulation and adjusting from defensive states back to love, and also an ever-deepening understanding of defenses, relational patterns, levels of development on different lines, and idiosyncratic rates of progress. For example, in the following exchange with Paul and Enid, they initially present me with a deadline of sorts. My instinct when clients try to speed things up is to immediately slow things down and explore. The principle here it that the defensive impulse to speed things up (with deadlines or other means) is often best gently frustrated and explored more deeply, since it is likely to be a defensive attempt to avoid healthy insight or change:

Paul: "We had a fight Sunday."

Enid: "Just because I didn't want to hang out with him."

Keith: "A familiar fight."

Both: "Yes."

Paul: "Also, we're going to Japan this Thursday for three weeks."

Enid: "We were really looking forward to it. Now I don't know if I want to go."

Paul: "Great. My family has been so looking forward to seeing us. You not going would be a slap in their faces."

Psychotherapy occasionally involves a seemingly impossible situation dropped into the therapist's lap. This trip is a huge big deal in their relationship, and it *would* be a slap in Paul's very traditional parents' faces for Enid to summarily refuse to go. If we don't resolve the issue this session, she may self-destructively alienate a central part of Paul's universe, his family. It's helpful to breath, relax, and remember there is a whole session left to explore what's going on and how to help:

Keith: First normalizing the discussion in a non-alarmed fashion, which will tend to pull complementary states from both of them. "So we're dealing with three intervals here, now till Thursday, your trip, and when you get back."

Both: "Yes, OK."

Keith: Addressing the issue of Paul taking on the responsibility to self-regulate and be more trustable, which will have significant bearing on Enid's availability to process. "Paul, have you been practicing the self-soothing exercise we worked on last session; the one where you identify with your hurt child, feel the pain, identify with your loving adult self, and then hold and soothe the child?"

Paul: "No. I only feel that child when Enid's rejecting me. I don't feel him the rest of the time."

Keith: "You've done the exercise enough to have an opinion. Does it help? Would it benefit you to do it regularly?"

Paul: "Oh yes. It's just so much effort when I feel so bad."

Keith: Silence.

Paul: "I could do it more regularly."

Keith: "You don't sound resolved."

Paul: "I'll do it daily until our next session."

Enid: "I like your voice when you say it that way, Paul." Paul smiles.

Keith: "It feels good to hear and see you show Paul your pleasure when he's being present, Enid. That's excellent feminine practice. How about the other practices we discussed for you; the dance, breathing, and time for pleasure in your body?"

Enid: "I forgot about most of the exercises. On Sunday I took time just to focus on pleasure in my body and it made me cry."

Keith: Wanting to encourage her to self-reflect on the significance of the emotional charge. "It made you cry."

Enid: "It was like I wanted it so much and I didn't deserve it somehow. I imagine it's really good for me."

Paul: "And good for us too, I think. I want you to have lots of pleasure."

Enid: Smiling. "If you can do your thing, I can practice this more often."

Keith: "You are both in different states than when we started this conversation. On your trip, when it gets weird (and it will get weird, at least a couple of times) remember, when you focus on doing your own work, you support love with each other."

Content, defensive states, healthy states, relational defensive structures/patterns can all be doorways to productive agendas in a conjoint session.

The access points to conjoint work are often content, defensive states, healthy states, or relational defensive structures/patterns; all usually initiated by clients, but sometimes brought up by the therapist if clinical observation or intuition indicate, or if there is a technical reason of some sort (for instance, it's almost always a good idea to check with a recently recovering person on the status of their sobriety). Once engaged with an individual or couple, therapists can follow a variety of clinical paths towards remediating symptoms, enhancing health, and supporting development.

No therapist is expert in all perspectives and techniques, but almost all perspectives and techniques have validity, and each therapist will naturally lean towards their current favorites. This is great as long as we can discern when other approaches might be desirable or necessary, and make appropriate referrals. I am not a medical doctor, but I frequently refer clients to medical doctors. I am not a dance instructor, but I occasionally refer clients to dance classes, and so on.

Supporting individual resolve is often preferable to quid pro quo bargaining.

Processing an agenda with a couple involves lots of negotiation. There is a natural tendency in negotiation to operate from second stage 50/50 fair standards where one partner offers some form of shift or change with the expectation that the other will return with a corresponding shift or change. This form of negotiation is useful and sometimes necessary, especially when clients are in first stage moments where the dynamic focus of the interchange for the therapist is to encourage an egocentric individual to feel a sense of responsibility to care for another.

The above exchange with Paul and Enid is different from such quid pro quo bargaining ("I'll do something for you if you'll do something for me") that is characteristic of much traditional conjoint therapy, and one of the hallmarks of second stage relationships. The sense of fairness that quid pro quo bargaining creates is important, and I'll occasionally encourage such "deals." I've found, though, that deals with others are more rarely honored in defensive states than personal resolves with one's self to be different in healthy ways. A sense of fairness in conjoint sessions is often better served by an understanding that each partner has different work to do and different challenges to meet, and is personally responsible for how they engage in that work, *independent of whether their partner is changing or not*.

I believe an optimal way to influence our partners to change is to do our own work and not try to enforce deals or to coerce them in some fashion. Masculine and feminine partners usually have different work to do to support health and polarity. In the above exchange, my intent is to challenge Paul to resolve to do personal work that involves cultivating a difficult intrapsychic focus in the midst of his defensive states. I want him to remember that such work is also an offering of love to Enid. I want to support Enid in stretching energetically as a feminine person to be able to run more energy and pleasure through her body as a healing yoga and as her gift of love to Paul.

The fact that they both avoided most of my earlier suggestions paradoxically gives me more credibility in confronting them with resistance to change. Since none of my suggestions involve deals with each other or me, their resistance is less likely to be processed as betrayal or a broken promise by either, and more likely to be processed as a personal issue. On the other hand, the fact that I'm suggesting practices to both of them tends to satisfy the second stage itch for "fairness" and 50/50 egalitarianism. Developmentally, neither Enid nor Paul is ready to offer their deepest masculine or feminine gifts consistently in a third stage manner, so this perceived "fairness" relaxes and soothes both of them in the session and makes them more therapeutically accessible, while still emphasizing that their responsibility is to do their work independent of whether the other is following through or not.

The sequence of Paul and Enid's exchange developed from an incident (the fight Sunday), to a relational defensive structure ("a familiar fight"), to an intuitive curiosity on my part (asking about practices we discussed in the last session), to their individual defensive structures (forgetting, avoiding, or diminishing healthy practices, and blaming the other to avoid healthy changes in perspectives and actions), to shifting to states of healthy response to the present moment (both resolving to themselves to continue helpful practices, and considering how focusing on such material serves love in their relationship). This is an intimate, collaborative process that avoids supporting defensive impulses to enforce deals, and supports change through each partner's responsibility to self-regulate.

There is often a hierarchy of agendas in a conjoint session, with some agendas taking priority over others.

The hierarchy of agendas in a conjoint session (most urgent to less urgent) usually begins with the same responsibilities therapists have in individual sessions. Some agendas inevitably take precedence over others. Safety issues such as suicide risk and potential danger to others are first priority, as well as reporting issues mandated by law for child/elder abuse/neglect. Closely following these are current addictions, immediate crises, potential decompensation, and transference issues. In conjoint sessions, two issues that often demand immediate attention are:

- A partner's conscious decision to separate.
- A partner believing the other is currently lying.

A conscious decision by either partner to separate, or to not work at improving the relationship, generally demands immediate attention.

The basic contract of conjoint therapy is usually the current explicit intent of both partners to do their best to get healthier individually and to improve their relationship. Either partner can be ambivalent about their relationship, and partners often are. This doesn't interfere with the work if their conscious intent is to resolve the ambivalence by working to get healthier and relate better.

It is a therapist's responsibility to discern when a partner is consciously deciding not to work on relational improvement, and to set appropriate boundaries.

If either client explicitly states that they don't want to work on improving the relationship right now, the agenda shifts to addressing their position and resolving it into either recommitting to relational improvement or exploring the material, relational, and psychological dimensions of emotional and/or physical separation. It is the therapist's responsibility to discern when a partner shifts into consciously refusing to work on improving the relationship, and to set the boundary of confronting the refusal and processing it. This boundary protects everyone from the destructive pattern of either partner pretending to support relational improvement while consciously deciding that psychological and/or physical separation is a better course.

Ambivalence is inevitable.

It is a given that many people in conjoint therapy are ambivalent about deeper intimacy with their partner. This ambivalence is usually expressed at least partly through defensive structures and states. What makes this dynamic accessible and manageable psychotherapeutically is each partner's conscious commitment to better connection and deeper love. If one partner truly has reached a point where it feels wrong to work towards better connection and deeper love, then the session needs to shift into exploring how resolved that partner is to separate and, if they are firmly resolved, to support separation. An example of this is the following exchange between Sadie and Blake:

> Sadie: "I'm sick of being married to you."

> Blake: Alarmed. Wanting to argue rather than deal with this potential huge change. Using a sarcastic tone. "That's right, blame everything on me."

> Keith: Hearing a note of resolve in Sadie's voice. Noticing that she seems to be in an adult, possibly non-defensive, state of consciousness. "Sadie, what do you mean you're sick of being married to Blake?"

> Sadie: "I just don't want to do it anymore. I don't want to work on it. I don't want to live together."

Blake: Now very alarmed. Trying to coerce her back into staying through a sense of responsibility. "What about our son? You'd do this to him?"

Sadie: Angrily. "He already has to deal with your anger, and us fighting all the time."

Keith: "Wait a second. Blake, if Sadie is serious about separating, everything changes. Sadie, is this something that's just occurred to you, or something you've considered and talked about?"

Sadie: "I've talked to my individual therapist, and she agrees. I don't feel safe with Blake in the house. I like it when he leaves. I don't want to live with him."

Keith: Sadie is oriented in the present moment. She's discussed this with her individual therapist, and she's currently resolved. My responsibility is to shift the focus of the session onto exploring separation. "When one partner decides it's best to separate, the agenda of the session shifts instantly away from resolving issues, and towards exploring separation."

Blake: Now pleading, frightened at what this might mean. "Sadie, you don't want to do this to our family."

Sadie: Firmly. "It's better if we don't live together."

Keith: Being drawn to soothe Blake so he can participate in the difficult discussion that's constellating. Feeling a responsibility to teach and direct them into the most healthy and least painful ways of dealing with this. "I know it feels awful, Blake, but, if it doesn't feel right to Sadie to work on improving your marriage, or if she is resolved to separate, that takes precedence over everything else, and we need to explore the ramifications. Sadie, do you want to leave or do you want Blake to leave?"

Sadie: "I think it's best for our son if Blake finds another place."

Blake: Beginning to calm down and participate in a complementary fashion. "I could stay in Noel's guest house for awhile."

We'll explore the parameters of the separation session more extensively in Chapter Forty-eight. This exchange illustrates how one partner explicitly choosing separation cues the prioritization of respecting and exploring that choice.

A partner believing that the other is consciously lying takes priority.

Lying to another person is usually a form of violence. Most people lie regularly, even daily[1], but there are levels of lying that extend from moderate distortion for relatively innocent reasons (I can't go to your daughter's dance performance because I have a previous engagement) to devastating passive aggressive attacks (I am not having an affair).

Therapy suffers when the client consciously lies, and conscious lying is devastating to intimate relationships which are based on mutual trust. Believing that your partner is consciously lying to you during a session usually means one of two things about you. Either you believe he or she is currently untrustable and willing to commit acts of emotional violence to you and your therapist for egocentric reasons, and/or you are in a defensive state with distorted perceptions and beliefs, and a destructive impulse to attack your partner by believing they are consciously lying to you.

Either way, when there is an accusation of *current* lying (lying right now in the session), productive dialogue about the issue in question is virtually impossible, and the therapist's responsibility becomes shifting the agenda to exploring the assumption and confronting the couple with the reality that they can't talk productively if either is not believing the other's current, conscious commitment to telling the truth. The following example of this occurred during a session with Blake and Sadie about a month before our last exchange:

Blake: "Where did you go Friday night?"

Sadie: "I went to Linda's house."

Blake: "I don't believe you. I drove by and didn't see her car."

Sadie: Tone of righteous indignation. "You were checking up on me. We went to the store."

Keith: I don't know if Sadie is lying or not. I do know that Blake doesn't believe her right now, and so the agenda of the session needs to shift. "Blake, do you believe Sadie is consciously lying to you at this moment?"

Blake: "Yes, I do."

Keith: "Well, then we can't keep talking about Friday night. You can't discuss an issue if one of you believes the other is lying."

Sadie: Confused. "But I'm not lying."

Keith: Believing her, but also aware I have no way of knowing whether she's lying or not. We all three can observe that Blake is not believing her. "If Blake believes you're consciously lying, we can't talk about Friday night. When people are angry and think the other is deliberately lying, they tend to believe all the negative material they see and imagine, and think most of the positive material is lies."

Blake: Frustrated and wanting to discuss Friday night. Not as convinced as he was earlier that Sadie is lying, and a little embarrassed. This embarrassment is good because it indicates Blake is disidentifying from the angry state where he has amplified anxiety and anger, distorted (probably) beliefs that Sadie is currently consciously lying and cheating, and the destructive impulse to attack her about what he imagined she did Friday night. Meanwhile, Sadie is feeling the power of the therapeutic culture where telling the truth is necessary and lying or angrily accusing another of lying is compassionately and firmly challenged. "I'm sorry, Sadie, you didn't tell me you went to the store."

Sadie: Vindicated, triumphant. "We went for ice cream and a video."

Blake: "I believe you. It's just that you don't want to be with me. You'd rather do that stuff with Linda."

Keith: Observing the shifts from the defensive states to healthier, less distorted states. This creates the possibility of productive talk. "How do you feel looking at each other at this moment?"

Sadie: "Less angry."

Blake: "I believe you. I just wish you'd want to be with me on a Friday night."

There are lies of commission and lies of omission. A related issue is when one partner wants the therapist to share a major secret from their spouse, which essentially recruits the therapist into a lie of omission. Examples of such secrets are infidelity, personal history, financial problems, work problems, or secret decisions to separate. I've learned to tell clients that I won't lie by commission, and I usually tell clients that I can't do effective conjoint work with them while lying by omission to either of them about what I consider information necessary for progress. If a major secret comes out in an individual session, I'll encourage my client to share it with their spouse, and occasionally refuse to continue conjoint work until the secret is revealed.

1. Dike (2007)

49

General Principles of Conjoint Therapy

This chapter includes a variety of principles and techniques that I've found invaluable in work with couples. I'm sure you have favorite principles and techniques of your own that you've learned or developed from your own training and experience. It's useful to regularly examine, edit, and expand your operating principles for doing therapy. I've encountered so much great research and innovation throughout my career that I've come to believe that any perspective I hold is just the best I've discovered so far, and a better, deeper one will probably show up eventually.

It's always a little difficult for me to let go of a treasured perspective or technique when I discover ones that prove preferable in some situations. What makes the process mostly pleasurable is my recognition over the years that I don't lose previous perspectives or techniques as much as refine them as I develop personally and professionally, enfolding them in an include and transcend rhythm. The following is a partial list of guidelines that you might find useful to consider.

Speak about another person as if they are in the room with you, listening to the session.

Clients in defensive states have distorted beliefs and perceptions that they want you to complement and share. Imagining that someone you're discussing can hear your dialogue helps you maintain a compassionate perspective, which often subtly influences your client to shift from a defensive state to more a healthy response to the present moment. This is especially true when having an individual session with one member of a couple. Therapists are often wildly misquoted in couple's conflicts, and, when challenged in conjoint sessions, it's helpful to remember a compassionate perspective that you can articulate clearly and assertively. To do this often involves feeling and resisting subtle intersubjective pressures to impulsively acknowledge critical judgments ("My wife said you agreed with her that I was wrong" for example). Speaking about someone as if he or she is in the room organizes your body as an instrument of healing and helps insure that you have a compassionate perspective to draw on if you are challenged later about what you said. The following exchange is with Ted and Carol. Egalitarian, multi-cultural GREEN, in their early fifties, both have characterological and neurotic defensive structures; his more passive aggressive, and hers more borderline:

Ted: "Carol said that you said I was attacking her when I was late for the party. I had work to do. I couldn't help it."

Carol: "That's what you always say, and Keith agreed you were deliberately attacking me."

Keith: "What I said was I believed there was a passive-aggressive component to Ted being late. I don't believe he was consciously attacking you, but I do believe he was indirectly expressing anger."

Carol: Angrily. "Conscious, unconscious, it doesn't matter. He knows how much I hate it."

Ted: Passive-aggressively digging deeper. "I had a deadline."

Keith: "I could be wrong, Ted, but I know you were angry last Wednesday. In the past your anger has come out indirectly by inconveniencing or embarrassing Carol in ways very much like being late to this party."

Ted: "I was feeling a little self-righteous. I could have called."

Carol: "You never consider me."

Ted: Passive-aggressively attacking both of us. "Keith says you're just depressed."

Carol: "I know what I know. Anybody would be angry at what you did. I'm not just depressed."

Keith: "Carol, what I've told Ted is that I believe you often do have a depressed perspective on your self, your life, and your marriage. I encourage Ted to respect your opinions, but to not argue with you, or passive-aggressively agree with your depressed beliefs that you or he are worthless or that Ted has ruined your life."

If in either of my private communications with Ted or Carol I had expressed critical judgments of the other in response to the real injuries they've suffered, I'd likely be distracted by my own defensive impulses when later attacked or challenged. If I'm anchored in compassionate understanding, such attacks or challenges become opportunities to confront and interpret both their individual and relational defensive structures and to inspire them to reach for more compassionate perspectives themselves. Speaking about people outside the session as if they were in the room is a great device for cultivating compassionate understanding.

Psychotherapeutic attention in a session naturally flows toward the most resistance.

Clients usually come to each session with some resistance. This often takes the form of blaming the other for most of the relational problems. Partners tend to conceptualize more clearly and analytically (though rarely compassionately) about their spouse's problems and defenses than about their own. Individual defensive structures generate defensive states of consciousness where it's often the tendency to focus on another's weaknesses, faults, and failings, and avoid focusing on our own. In short, both partners can enter the session with resistance to perceiving, acknowledging, and changing their personal defensive structures and states, and with impulses to blame their spouse or someone else.

Resistance can take a variety of forms. Individuals can attack, be silent, become childish, distract, challenge the therapist, forget, project, deny, argue, or just walk out of the session. In general, the more pathological and regressed the defensive state, the more intense the resistance. Not surprisingly, characterological defensive states and structures will usually generate the strongest and fiercest resistance.

Resistance pulls psychotherapeutic attention. When I observe a client avoiding an obvious (to me) healthy perspective and/or action, I feel drawn to engage that defensive state, help resolve the resistance, and support insight and change. This engagement is a common access point in all forms of therapy to the ongoing balance point, the event horizon, of tension between maintaining the cherishing culture and challenging defenses.

In conjoint therapy, one partner's resistance can dominate a session, pulling most of the therapist's attention and interventions, and thus possibly neglecting useful work with the other partner. This is sometimes unconsciously (rarely consciously) supported by the less resistant partner with silence, offering their own hostile confrontations and/or interpretations of their partner's defenses, or with otherwise subtly (or obviously) provoking their partner into more robust defensive states. These maneuvers are often based in a genuine conscious desire to help, but are usually contaminated with the ongoing unconscious impulses to pathologize the other and avoid acknowledging and challenging one's own personal defensive states.

In the midst of these individual and relational defensive structures and states, the therapist's mission is to address all of them. A useful operating principle when one partner is more obviously resistant and pulling the bulk of the psychotherapeutic attention is to monitor the other partner's reactions to the work, and to weave in his or her contributions to the relational defensive structure. I often do this by confronting and interpreting complementary defensive states and structures while teaching and inspiring both to take responsibility for defenses and to change perspectives and behaviors in the service of truth, love and health. This process serves a variety of healing functions:

- Including and working with the less resistant partner helps heal their personal and relational defensive wounds that might otherwise be neglected while focusing on their more resistant spouse.

- Such work models insight and change for the more resistant partner.

- The more resistant partner can be indirectly related to, confronted, directed, taught, inspired, and interpreted through attributions and explanations while relating to, confronting, directing, teaching, inspiring, and interpreting the less resistant partner.

- As the less resistant partner is moved to inhabit healthy responses to the present moment, the more pressure he or she behaviorally and energetically puts on their spouse to inhabit complementary healthy states.

- The important intimate skill of empathetically checking in with our partner even in the most regressed states is modeled and practiced.

In the following exchange with Carol and Ted, Ted's resistance pulls the most energy, abetted by Carol making him the problem and directing therapeutic attention away from her and onto him. My job is to weave her defenses and her work into the session that is naturally constellating around Ted. Notice how masculine/feminine essence/practice again forms a subtext in the therapeutic process:

Ted: "I'm just ambivalent. Part of me wants an intimate relationship and love, and part of me wants freedom. I don't feel it towards Carol, and I know it hurts her, but maybe I'm not capable of love. Maybe ..."

Keith: Interrupting, noticing Ted look away and Carol's disgusted expression. "You seem disconnected from both Carol and me as you talk. You look away, and your voice gets a little singsong in it as if you're telling a story."

Ted: Continuing to resist passive-aggressively by attacking himself. "I don't want to cause her pain. I just have to be true to myself, and I can't lie. I'm not attracted. Maybe I can't commit and need to be celibate the rest of my life." Carol rolls her eyes. People are always communicating.

Keith: Observing and sensing that Carol is being marginalized, and not being related to by Ted as a real person in the room. "Carol, I notice you rolling your eyes."

Carol: "I've heard all this before. It's just blah blah blah to me."

Ted: Happy to keep attacking himself. "See what I mean? Maybe I'm not capable of ..."

Keith: Interrupting, again pulling Carol in, this time with confrontation and interpretation. Even though Ted's pulling the most therapeutic attention, it's beginning to look like Carol is the one who's the best candidate for actually changing the relational defensive structure. "Carol, you've stayed twelve years with a man who won't claim you emotionally or erotically. I imagine there is some defensive tendency in you that generates impulses to try to heal Ted so he can love, or to pretend to offer devotional love when you're actually repulsed. Both these things diminish masculine/feminine polarity."

Carol: Interested, more involved. "I must be weak or messed up somehow to put up with this. I've had other relationships end up this way."

Keith Confronting Ted through Carol. "What stops you from leaving a man who won't claim you?"

Carol: "I always hope he'll be different."

Ted: Resisting, pulling attention back to himself. Looking away and appearing weak and unresolved. "I can't claim someone when I'm so scared."

Keith: Sensing an opportunity to address the relational defensive structure by confronting and teaching. "I disagree, Ted. The only way you'll ever claim a woman is to be able to maintain your resolve through your terror and abandonment depression. Carol is becoming too healthy to stay with you in the absence of claiming her, and you're becoming too healthy to be at peace with surrendering to your fear of a woman you love."

Carol: Back to complaining to try to pressure him to heal and be able to love her. "He'll never be able. He can't claim me. He doesn't want to."

Ted: Back into the passive-aggressive smooth groove of the relational defensive structure. "Maybe you're right."

Keith: Knowing the probability is small for change in this relationship, but wanting to support the possibility of transformation. "You were able to sail to New Zealand by yourself. You have been struggling to love Carol better these last three months and, in our individual sessions, you've gone places you've never gone before. I believe you're kidding yourself if you think you can't face your terror and love more deeply."

Ted: "It's just so hard."

Keith: "That feels more honest. It's not impossible but it is so hard."

Ted: Appearing more resolved. "I'll have to think about this."

Carol: Relaxing and softening. "I like how this feels, but if you can't claim me I'll have to leave."

Keith: "That's great feminine practice, Carol. Show him your yums and yucks and, if love can't be served, take the risk of leaving."

It is my job in this session to interrupt Ted's passive-aggressive monologs and confront him with his masculine power, and to confront Carol with her power to stay or go, her defensive impulses to rescue Ted, and her responsibility to discern if love can be served in relationship to Ted. Ted's powerful resistance was pulling the bulk of therapeutic attention, and Carol was cooperating in constellating their relational defensive structure with complementary defensive states. Perceiving the relational defensive structure and noticing how Ted's resistance was pulling most of the therapeutic attention gave me the opportunity to disrupt their defenses by pulling Carol and her work into the mix.

Combining individual with conjoint therapy: when to do it and who should do it.

Individual therapy and conjoint therapy are complementary in most circumstances. The process of all therapy tends to be beneficial, and different combinations such as individual, conjoint, group, and family therapy provide different perspectives around the central themes of reducing symptoms, enhancing health, and supporting development. Many modern conjoint therapists including Susan

Johnson, John Gottman, and Dan Siegel are advocates of combining individual and conjoint therapy.[1]

Conjoint therapy is not a good idea when either partner is consistently too intimidated or conflicted to be honest about what they feel or think in the conjoint session. This is often true in abusive relationships that involve emotional or physical violence or intimidation, or when one partner simply will not address an important issue (such as an ongoing affair, an addiction, or a secret conviction that separation is the best course).

I'll recommend the combination of individual and conjoint therapy in a variety of situations. Sometimes I'll recommend myself as both individual and conjoint therapist, and sometimes I'll refer one role to another therapist.

If I'm working with an individual and a relationship—especially with a spouse or lover—is a primary focus of treatment, I'll usually recommend that my client invite their partner into a conjoint session. If my client or their partner is uncomfortable with me in both roles, I'll refer them as a couple to another therapist. I'll also suggest another therapist if my client has major secrets (a love affair, fear of abuse, or a profound desire for separation are common examples), or if either my client or their spouse has primarily characterological defensive structures, especially borderline or narcissistic.

If either partner seems stuck, especially over the course of several conjoint sessions, I'll often recommend individual sessions with me as a path to identifying and resolving blocks in the conjoint work. In rare cases where it seems that one partner is holding back for some reason, I'll invite one partner to sit in my waiting room while I spend ten to twenty minutes alone with their spouse. Second stage egalitarianism usually responds best if I then spend some time alone with the other partner, but not always. The following exchange is with Sadie after I invited Blake to sit in the other room for a few minutes. This was our third meeting, the session was feeling stuck, and I had an intuition that Sadie had some major information she was afraid to disclose:

Sadie: Visibly relaxing, but a little suspicious. "Why did you ask Blake to leave?"

Keith: "I had the sense that you were holding something back."

Sadie: Looking a little alarmed. "Like what?'

Keith: "Whenever the topic of being more intimate came up, you changed the subject or picked a fight."

Sadie: Angrily. "I don't want to be intimate with him."

Keith: Feeling that warm sense in my solar plexus that this is productive territory. "I completely understand that you don't want to be more intimate with him. Do you *want* to want to be more intimate?"

Sadie: Confused. I'm asking her to disidentify with the self that's angry and rejecting, and go deeper into a self that can observe the self that's angry and rejecting. She sits up straighter in the chair and begins speaking in a more mature voice. Clearly she's shifted into a different state. "I don't think so. It's confusing, but I don't think I want to get closer with him."

Keith: Exploring the depth of her resolve. "Does it feel more right to separate, or to stay and work towards deeper love with Blake?"

Sadie: Focused and thoughtful. "I really think it feels more right to separate, but I'm not sure."

Keith: Feeling a significantly increased probability that they will separate and wanting to help prepare her that probability. Observing that she seems to be passing from precontemplation of major change to contemplation of major change. "Two things. First, I think you need to be in individual therapy with someone, preferably a warm, understanding woman, to provide extra support and an advocate that is just for you. I know several great therapists and I'll give you their numbers. I don't think Blake would consider another therapist besides me and I want him to have individual support if you two separate, and you can't both have the same individual therapist during a separation. Second, let's bring Blake back into the session and discuss all this with him."

Sadie: Scared. "He'll get mad."

Keith: "Not telling your spouse the truth because you're scared is one of the definitions of an abusive relationship. Is Blake an abuser?"

Sadie: Challenged to discern between Blake, who's basically a good man, and the real abusers from her past. "No, he's not an abuser. But I still don't think I want to live with him. It feels so right to separate. Not divorce, but separate right now."

Keith: Directing. "I think you need to discuss this with him and I believe doing it in therapy maximizes both of your chances of not getting distracted into non-productive attacking and defending."

Sadie: Adult and resolved. "OK."

Keith: "I'll go bring him back into the session."

This last exchange with Sadie illustrates several reasons to advocate for individual therapy in addition to conjoint. Sadie allowed herself to explore perspectives alone with me that she was scared to explore with Blake present. This suggests that there might be whole realms of feelings, beliefs, and impulses that aren't showing up in the conjoint work. Also, Sadie has historically had the capacity to decompensate to non-functional states of distortion, withdrawal, impulsivity, and/or substance abuse. Individual therapy provides a safety net to catch her if she either decides to separate or if she decompensates and drops suddenly out of conjoint sessions. Finally, my insistence on individual therapy reflects how seriously she needs to address self-regulation issues at this critical time. It's often easy for clients to deny, rationalize, or diminish the power of defensive states and structures when they are not in them (and sometimes when they are in them). This is especially true for characterological defensive states where there is little or no observing ego, frequent black/white splitting and projective identification, negatively warped memory, overwhelming amplified emotion, and little or no insight and empathy.

When individual sessions are an episodic feature of conjoint work, I usually prefer to do them myself. This is also true if there is a series of sessions required for a particular purpose such as dealing with abusive memories, an acute onset of an anxiety disorder, or an abandonment depression. If the individual work looks to be ongoing and probably will involve a fair amount of intrapsychic exploration, I prefer to be either the conjoint therapist or the individual therapist but not both. Transference and counter transference issues can get fiendishly complex in some situations when a therapist occupies both roles.

1. Johnson (2005), Siegel (2005), Gottman (2005)

50

Separation sessions: Painful, but Necessary and Useful

In the last example in Chapter Forty-nine with Sadie and Blake, we observed how, when one partner suspects that the best course of action is to separate and/ or divorce, the focus of the conjoint session changes instantly. As it turns out, Sadie's resolve continued to grow in the subsequent months resulting in separation and eventual divorce. Each time separation was raised as a desire by her in a session, we explored separation as an option. It didn't matter strategically if she was truly wanting separation or indulging a distorted belief and destructive impulse. If her resolve to separate was primarily a defensive impulse to attack Blake (as it was in early sessions), taking it seriously quickly revealed both the lack of authentic resolve to separate, and the necessity of taking on the responsibility of working to improve a distressed relationship rather than indulge impulses to attack. If she deeply believed that separation was the right course of action (as was increasingly true as therapy progressed), but not yet ready to make the assertion to herself or Blake, me taking her expressed desire seriously and supporting her right to leave if she so decided helped prepare her for the difficult next step in decision making. A firm, expressed desire to separate is a cue for the therapist to confront both partners that their contract as a couple has—if only for the moment—changed dramatically and that the therapeutic contract is right now very different.

Separation sessions require firm direction from the therapist.

I become especially directive in a separation session. Initially I explain how conjoint therapy for couples who are separating is no longer about resolving issues but rather has become about facilitating separation with a minimum of pain for all involved, especially children. Pain is inevitable for everybody during separation/divorce, and it's important for each partner to explore his or her own responsibilities in dealing with each person's distress. I relentlessly interrupt any attempts to discuss issues during a separation session and keep confronting each spouse with the realities and practicalities of separation. Issues can often only be productively discussed when the conscious agenda is to stay in relationship and support enhanced intimacy. In a separation session there are a number of difficult questions that I need to help partners explore, and provide support and direction in helping each answer:

- Who is going to leave?

- Where will he or she go?

- How will money be handled?

- Are both willing to see a lawyer/mediator as soon as possible to hear what rights and responsibilities each have under the law?

- If children are involved, where, when, and with whom will the children stay in the immediate future?

- When and what do you tell the children, and who tells them what?

- What emotional support sources does each spouse have, and do they realize that, if they try to seek understanding and/or support from each other, they will almost certainly constellate a relational defensive pattern and create unnecessary suffering?

- Are they willing to have psychotherapeutic support in the form of individual therapy during the difficult transition from married to single, and how can I best serve them in this?

- Does their fidelity contract end when one partner leaves, or has it already ended for one or both partners?

- Do they realize that, after the above issues are clarified, regular conjoint therapy needs to stop unless both decide they are willing to spend time together as a couple and pursue reconciliation?

Often, when confronted with this deluge of issues and responsibilities associated with one partner's resolve to separate, one or both partners bring up a charged issue to discuss. This can be an unconscious attempt to avoid the overwhelming separation agenda in a familiar fight. The therapist's job here is to interrupt and redirect into the separation agenda. I tell couples that it only makes sense to discuss a charged intimacy issue if they both want to stay together. People always separate, at least partly, because they're unable to productively discuss charged intimacy issues. If they couldn't have such productive talk when the contract was to stay together and get closer, they certainly won't be able to have it when the contract is to separate.

The focus of discussion in a separation session is about material problem solving involving logistics, money, children, who to inform and how to inform them, and how to create a next level of problem solving when these issues are deadlocked. Since I'm not a lawyer, I refer couples to lawyer/mediators who meet with both partners to inform them of legal rights and responsibilities, and whose job it is to help solve financial/property/custody/legal problems and keep personal animosity to a minimum.

The following exchange is from a separation session that happened when Sadie finally resolved to live separately. In this segment she has already told Blake she wants him to live elsewhere, and both are struggling to deal with the consequences to them and their nine-year-old son, Caleb:

Keith: "Do either of you have a preference on who moves out?"

Blake: "It's my house. You want to separate, you move out."

Sadie: "Caleb would suffer if we had to move out."

Blake: Angry. "What's this 'we'? He's my son too."

Keith: "First of all, I think you both need to go see a lawyer to find out what your rights and responsibilities are under the law. I recommend you see a mediator who is a lawyer who will talk to you both at the same time, and try to help the process be more cooperative and less expensive. I'll give you names of mediators my clients have had good experiences with in the past."

Sadie: "It will be harder on our son if I move out."

Keith: "You need to find out what the legal ramifications are. I think it's best to find out together."

Blake: "What do we tell Caleb?"

Keith: "You need to agree on exactly what you're doing now; where, when, and who he's staying with for the immediate future. You're both loving parents with good relationships with Caleb. It's important that he not be presented with ambiguous messages, or feel he's part of the decision making process of your separating. That can lead to him feeling responsible."

Sadie: "That makes sense, but what about Blake's anger and Caleb?"

Blake: Angrily. "I've never laid a hand on him. I'm a good father."

Keith: Recognizing the unconscious impulse in both to reengage in familiar fighting rather than dealing with the separation issues. "Sadie, you've been the recipient of almost all of Blake's amplified anger and distorted beliefs, as has Blake been the recipient of most of yours. Blake and Caleb have always done well alone together."

Blake: "That's right."

Sadie "You two do get along well when I'm not around."

Keith: Refocusing on the separation session. "So, Blake, Sadie thinks it would be easier on Caleb if you—at least initially—moved out. What's valid about that, in your opinion?"

Blake: "She's probably right. I can stay with my brother for a while, and look for a place. That will probably feel more normal for Caleb since I'm away on business so much."

Sadie: Relaxing and grateful. "Thank you, Blake."

Blake: Feeling the loss acutely as she is warmer. "Do you really want to do this?"

Sadie: "I think it's best to separate right now. I don't want to divorce right away."

Keith: Knowing there are legal consequences of separation. "I want to emphasize that I believe it's best if you go see a mediator soon to find out your rights and responsibilities."

Blake: "I'll call the names you give us and set up an appointment."

Sadie: "That's good."

Sadie: "But what do we tell Caleb?"

Keith: "You tell him the truth in terms that make sense to his nine-year-old universe. If you blame each other, he will be inclined to make moral judgments about one or the other of you. I suggest you tell him that sometimes good people can care for each other but be unhappy living together. Tell him you asked for and received help but you still couldn't find a way to be happy living together, and so you needed to separate. Tell him your separation has absolutely nothing to do with him. Think about what you want him to remember hearing for the rest of his life. Think about supporting his impor-tant relationships with both of you."

Blake: Angry. "Sadie's the one who decided to do this."

Sadie: Angry. "Right, blame me as usual."

Keith: "You can tell him that you, Blake, wanted to keep trying in therapy, but it stopped feeling right in Sadie's heart to keep trying, and did feel right in her heart to separate. She couldn't pretend to work on the marriage so she had to be honest and tell you she wanted to separate."

Sadie: "That's exactly what's happening."

And so, one by one, we address all the questions I posed earlier until Blake and Sadie each has a sense of what their immediate responsibilities are to themselves, their son, and each other. It's often heartbreakingly sad to discuss this material with couples and families but, as I remind myself in separation sessions, it's usu-ally preferable to have these discussions in my office where I can give them the benefit of my knowledge and experience and protect them somewhat from caus-ing themselves, their children, and each other unnecessary pain.

Good signs and bad signs.

The following chart is by no means a comprehensive list of good signs and bad signs for the probable success of marriage or lover relationships. It does list a number of behaviors and characteristics which, taken individually, are clear indi-cators of increasing or decreasing probability of a couple being able to grow and love each other better with the help of therapy:

GOOD SIGNS AND BAD SIGNS FOR SUCCESSFUL RESOLUTION OF PROBLEMS BACK TO LOVE

GOOD SIGNS	BAD SIGNS
Honesty to self	Lying to self
Honesty to partner	Lying to partner
Honesty to others	Lying to others
Sobriety, or controlled use of euphorics	Uncontrolled and/or progressive use of euphorics
Financially secure	Financially self-destructive
Fidelity	Infidelity, especially chronic
Good relationships with family-of-origin	Conflicted family-of-origin relationships
Your friends like and respect your partner	Your friends fear, or have contempt for your partner
Caring for others	Egocentric, uncaring of others
Can self-regulate emotions and behaviors	Has difficulty self-regulating emotions and behaviors
Never physically abusive	Physically abusive
Rarely, if ever, verbally abusive	Verbally abusive
Reports "Satisfying sex"	Reports sexual dissatisfaction
Willing to do therapy	Unwilling to do therapy
Rarely depressed	Chronically depressed
Rarely obsessive or anxious	Often obsessive or anxious
Good relationship with children in spouse's opinion	Poor relationship with children in spouse's opinion
Frequent, mutually pleasurable, verbal and physical strokes	Infrequent verbal and physical strokes
Sense of humor	Little sense of humor
Self-reflective, enjoys insight, even about defensive states	Finds self-reflection irritating and/or repulsive
Allows self to do little damage when in defensive states	Allows massive damage in defensive states
Success in the world	Trouble with the law

I am usually straightforward in articulating many of these signs to individuals and couples in treatment. I do this for several reasons. First, clients hire me partly for my knowledge, experience, and discernment, and so I have a responsibility to provide these things. Second, me talking objectively about charged issues, and objectively balancing good signs and bad signs models for each partner how to do the same. Couples in conflict are always evaluating their relationship internally and often interpersonally with one another, other family members, and friends. I want to help them both acknowledge good and bad signs in themselves and their partner, and disidentify with those signs to the extent that they can consider and process them in nondefensive states. When one partner is considering separation it is useful to be candid about the good signs and bad signs in both partners to help him or her evaluate what areas to invest energy and attention.

Good signs and bad signs are also useful in most other aspects of conjoint treatment. For example, the following exchange between Tom and Anne is typical of the kind of feedback I give a couple at the end of their first or second conjoint session:

Anne: "Well, Keith, what do you think?"

Keith: "I think there are good signs and bad signs."

Tom: "What do you mean?"

Keith: "It's a good sign that you're both willing to work in therapy on loving each other. It's a good sign that, when you're not hurt and angry, you have hot sexual polarity. It's a good sign that you're both faithful, and that neither of you seems addicted to drugs or alcohol. It's a good sign that you're both dedicated parents. It's a bad sign that when you're hurt it's so easy for you, Anne, to get critical and condemning, and for you, Tom, to get cold and distant. It's a bad sign that when you have a fight you stay alienated sometimes for days instead of minutes. It's a bad sign that you, Anne, smoke pot and withdraw when you're hurt instead of finding a way to reach through to love. It's a bad sign that you, Tom, keep taking your anxiety to Anne in the same way that's guaranteed to alarm her."

Anne: "Are we messed up or what?"

Keith: Laughing. "We all have strengths and weaknesses. The difference is that some of us acknowledge our strengths, confront out weaknesses, and work towards being better men and women; healthier and more able to love."

Tom: "That's how I want us to be."

Anne: "Me too."

Keith: Laughing again. "That's another good sign. We're on a roll here."

Gradually, such frank discussion in non-defensive states of consciousness moves the conflicted issues from being considered and talked about almost exclusively in defensive states to being considered and talked about when Tom and Anne are more mature and compassionate in healthy responses to the present moment. As couples do this, situations and episodes that historically cue defensive states begin to cue more mature self-reflection, disidentification from defensive states, and expanded possibilities to move deeper into health and love.

One good sign/bad sign dimension that is especially important is the ratio of positive verbal and physical strokes to negative strokes.[1] In general, distressed couples have too few positive and too many negative strokes in their intimacy. Changing this ratio is often crucial to progress, and constitutes an ongoing agenda while doing any conjoint work. A central role of therapist is to model giving many positive strokes and framing criticisms as specific behavioral feedback designed to help people be stronger, more successful, and more beautiful. I teach this, inspire this, confront the presence or absence of this, interpret the resistance to this, and direct them to practice these skills themselves through suggestions, exercises, and assignments.

Divorce does not necessarily equal failure.

A relationship ending does not necessarily indicate complete failure. Individuals usually leave a marriage wiser and deeper in various ways than when they entered the marriage. Statistically, second marriages tend to be both shorter and more satisfying than first marriages. This makes sense from the perspective that, in second marriages, people tend to be somewhat wiser in choosing a partner, more able to love in a satisfying manner, and more discerning when love is not being served and separation is appropriate.

I've found that the more an individual works on growing and loving, the more satisfying and less toxic their relationships eventually become, regardless of whether they divorce or not. The concept that a relationship was successful in supporting health and growth, even though it ended in divorce, is comforting to individuals suffering the grueling pains of loss, discomfort, grief, change, and financial hardship that usually accompany separation and divorce.

1. Gottman (1999)

51

Tips

There are a variety of details in the practice of conjoint therapy that I've found to be useful over the years. The therapy environment is often one room that you spend much of your professional life in, and even small details can make a big difference to you and your clients. The following tips are aspects that have made this environment more comfortable and effective for me.

Tape your sessions and send the tapes home with your clients.

When clients listen to taped sessions, it almost always speeds up and facilitates the work. Some clients don't want to tape their sessions, which, of course, is fine. Often lawyers, judges, or other people in the legal profession don't want to tape; probably due to training and experience with people being hurt or judged by evidence of what they have said. When working with couples, I will not tape if either partner is uncomfortable with it and, if they both are comfortable with taping, I'll tell them the tape is just for the two of them and not for anyone else. If a couple intends to listen to a tape together I'll encourage each to avoid the tendency to confront and analyze their partner, and instead focus on noticing their own defensive states, distortions, and opportunities to have more compassionate perspectives and more healthy actions.

If one spouse tapes an individual session, I strongly recommend that he or she discuss the session in detail with his or her partner, but to not let their partner listen to the individual tape. I'll explain that it is often irritating and provocative to hear other people discussing you, even if what they're saying is mostly complimentary. On the other hand, listening to your own individual session, extracting insights and techniques that might help you be healthier and love better, and then discussing this material with your spouse, can create a variety of opportunities for pleasurable intimate exchanges.

Have moveable chairs so that you and your clients can adjust orientation and distance.

I will gently insist that each client can see and relate both to their partner and me during the session. Spouses will frequently orient themselves so they can easily look and relate to me, but have to turn to look at and relate to their partner. I let people know that this is probably a bad idea and ask them to turn their chairs accordingly. This helps set the stage for later in the session when I might insist that they look at each other while talking to or about each other. This simple intervention disrupts many defensive states that resist empathetic connection to enable attack. It's usually much harder to attack a lover while looking them in the eyes.

Keep scanning each partner's reactions during the work.

This is most difficult when doing an intense piece of intrapsychic work with one partner. I've learned to glance at the spouse every ten to twenty seconds while working with their partner. This is in order to maintain an information flow from his or her demeanor, breathing, and reactions. Often I'll interrupt an individual exchange to include the partner. The following is an example of this from a session with Ted and Carol. Ted is working on his passive-aggressive characterological defenses, learned in relation to his terrifying, physically and emotionally abusive father:

Ted: "I just get numb and confused and I don't know what to do."

Keith: Knowing confusion is usually a reliable guide to internalized conflicts. "When's the first time you felt the same sense—the same flavor—of numbness and confusion?"

Ted: "When my father was beating me with a stick when I was eight or nine."

Keith: I notice Carol looking exasperated and shifting positions. "Carol, you're reacting to this. I notice you looking exasperated."

Carol: "He blames everything on his family. It's no excuse!"

Keith: Noticing Ted recoil, but sticking with Carol's immediate distress. "You believe Ted talking about his physical abuse is part of an excuse for something."

Carol: Looking directly at me. "Yes; it doesn't matter what happened. He shouldn't neglect me."

Keith: I observe Ted looking at her with some compassion. "Look at Ted and tell him."

Carol: Looking at Ted. "You shouldn't neglect me."

Ted: "I don't want to. Sometimes it happens."

Keith: Weaving his individual work back into the session. "I imagine it happens often when you feel numb and confused."

Ted: "It does, and it does feel the same as when my Dad beat me."

Keith: Seeing Carol watch him with a little more interest and less hostility. "Imagine yourself being that child being beaten. What is your sense of yourself and your Dad?"

Ted: "I feel worthless, and I think he's a sadistic asshole."

Keith: Noticing Carol softening her expression. "Carol, tell Ted what you're thinking and feeling."

Carol: "I'm sorry he beat you. I don't want you to think I'm like that."

Conjoint sessions often progress like this, not as smoothly or directly as individual sessions, but rather more indirectly with both partners' defensive states ebbing and flowing. Staying attuned to both, even while focusing on one, helps the therapist weave the two patterns of growth together; always moving towards remediating symptoms, enhancing health, and supporting development and love.

Explore an extra one or two questions when you believe you have the theme of the session identified; sometimes there is a more immediate, important, or profound issue just a little deeper.

The theme of the session usually emerges in the first ten to twenty minutes. As we've discussed, it can come from a direct request, an unresolved conflict, a previous episode, a current enactment, or a defensive state in either client. Sometimes clients will unconsciously hide a more threatening agenda by leading with a less threatening one. I often like to take an extra one or two minutes to explore this possibility before diving into an agenda that will dominate the rest of the session.

In this exchange between Sally and Martin, the first issue wasn't what they most needed to address:

> Sally: "Martin was mean to our-fifteen-year old Jack and his girlfriend last week."

> Martin: "I did great with them. They needed to be talked to. They're almost having sex, for Christ's sake."

> Sally: Angry. "You had no business talking to them like that."

> Keith: Knowing this is a charged area, but also knowing that parenting issues often mask couple's issues. "I get it that you disagree about the episode with Jack and his girlfriend. Is there anything else that either of you want to cover today?"

> Martin: "We did have sex for the first time in four months yesterday."

> Sally: Embarrassed and angry. "I knew you'd bring that up!"

The significance of their sexual encounter is far more central to their work than the episode with Jack and his girlfriend. The extra exploration revealed it.

It is often better to openly acknowledge disagreement with clients' distorted perspectives, amplified or numbed emotions, and destructive impulses.

One reason clients come to therapists is for expert opinions, and therapists have a responsibility to share potentially useful perspectives and information with clients. It's often difficult to disagree with a client in a defensive state and, indeed, the more distorted the defensive perspectives are, the less disagreement the client can tolerate without feeling rejected, angry, and/or misunderstood. On the other hand, it's frequently soothing to a client to hear from a caring authority figure that amplified or numbed emotions, distorted perceptions and beliefs, or destructive impulses and actions don't meet some or all of the therapist's validity standards. Such confrontation by the therapist is especially useful modeling for a spouse who is likely to have a complementary defensive response to their partner's distortions. I tell clients my opinions but also freely acknowledge that I may be wrong and they may be right if we disagree. Sometimes this is exactly the case, but usually compassionate understanding is the most accurate understanding.

An illustration of this is the following exchange with Martin and Sally later on in the session from our last example. They are now discussing the lovemaking that took place the previous day:

Keith: "Did you both enjoy the lovemaking?"

Sally: "He did. All he cares about is his pleasure."

Martin: Unconsciously engaging in a complementary defense by beginning to make a case. "How about, after we started, when I …"

Keith: Interrupting Martin before he can passive-aggressively attack Sally by unnecessarily revealing a potentially embarrassing sexual act. Wanting to model for him how to meet her distortion. "I disagree. I know that Martin cares deeply about you feeling at peace and fulfilled sexually."

Sally: Defensive. "How do you know? I was there."

Keith: "I could be wrong but—from what he says and from what I've observed—that's what I believe. Besides, during lovemaking the more masculine partner often gets off more from his feminine partner's pleasure than from his own"

Martin: "Sure I had a good time. But I'm mostly glad we were able to break the ice and you were able to have some sexual fun with me."

Keith: Wanting to help Sally focus on pleasure in her body. "How about you Sally? Did you enjoy it?"

Sally: "It was fine. I just wish Martin could be more gentle."

Martin: "You're just trying to trash a good experience."

Keith: Noticing Sally's look of disappointment. "I disagree, Martin. Sally just gave you a gift in the form of valuable, specific feedback about how you could be a better lover, and you attacked her."

Sally: Vindicated. "Why should I tell you what I like if you just tell me I'm wrong?"

Martin: Getting it. "You're right, Sally. I like it that you told me. Tell me how you'd like me to be more gentle."

In this exchange I disagreed repeatedly with both Sally and Martin. Each time—even when Sally consciously found nothing valid in my perspective—the defensives deescalated and the relational defensive structure weakened.

Rarely pass up an opportunity to laugh.

Clients love their lives being fascinating and entertaining to their therapists. I laugh frequently at the bizarre twists, turns, and strangenesses that my client's lives and perspectives reveal. Usually they laugh along with me, which in itself reflects a change to a healthier state where they can disidentify from distressed perspectives and enjoy the spectacle of their own and other's human foibles. My clients seem rarely—if ever—offended by my laughter.

Deida maintains that a sense of humor is an essential ingredient in sexual polarity. The masculine partner anchors himself in resolute acceptance of death, and then does his best to serve the moment, knowing that what most delights his feminine partner is his presence, his shadow, and his humor. The feminine partner opens to the flow of life and love, and, if the moment becomes too tense, dark, or serious, opens it with her radiance, love, and humor.[1]

You evoke who you speak to.

Communication is complementary in variety of dimensions. Just as a defensive state in one partner tends to evoke a complementary defensive state in the other partner, a compassionate state in one partner tends to evoke compassion in the other partner.

In my therapy sessions I am usually speaking from compassionate understanding to my client's deepest, most compassionate self. To a certain extent I'm always addressing the ever-present witness that observes all objects and is itself not an object. Even while empathizing with and soothing a defensive state, I'm also talking to my client's deeper self who does not identify with that state. This is one foundation practice in cocreating a healing culture in the session. In the following exchange with Martin from an individual session, he is absorbed in his hurt, angry, sadistic defensive state. I continue to talk to his best self until that self is evoked:

> Martin: "She is such a bitch. I should just leave. Who stays with a wife who despises him and won't have sex?"

> Keith: "You have, and not just for neurotic dependency. You genuinely love her and want to serve her."

> Martin: "Nothing pleases her. She has nothing good to say to me or about me."

Keith: "That was almost all true in the beginning of therapy. Now she regularly has good things to say about you, as do you about her."

Martin: Beginning to shift. "It's just so slow and hard. I don't know if I can keep taking it."

Keith: "You might not, but today you're deciding to be married, and so your job is to stand unrecoiling and open her."

Martin: His face changes to more mature and thoughtful. "It doesn't help to bitch about her, does it?"

Keith: Laughing. "You tell me."

Think always of the healing and the loving

Miyamoto Musashi, in *A Book of Five Rings*, described the warrior as someone who, when he took a sword into his hand, focused solely on cutting his opponent. He advised warriors to learn all the martial arts, all the sword attitudes, and all the fencing techniques, but the bottom line was, think always of the cutting.[2]

The same principle applies to the healing arts. Whenever I have any professional encounter my job is to think always of the healing. Every moment of every therapy session is informed by the admonition to think always of the healing. With couples, as long as one member is not resolved to leave, this extends to thinking always of the loving. How does each moment support each partner giving and receiving love in healthier, more pleasurable, more passionate ways? Whatever the issues, whatever the defensive states or structures, the overriding agenda is to think always of the healing and the loving.

1. Dieda (2006)

2. Musashi (1974)

52

Sex Therapy: Jerry and Kay

Sex therapy exists as a discipline almost entirely because moral biases during the last century compartmentalized sexuality to some extent from conjoint psychotherapy. Conjoint therapy (or marriage counseling, or relationship therapy, or couples counseling) arose from the family systems theorists and clinicians who realized that therapy always involved intrapersonal and interpersonal systems.[1]

I remember being in a workshop with Virginia Satir in the mid-seventies when she simulated a family with volunteers from the audience and tied strings between the various members to externally represent the intersubjective fields that connected them. That web of strings was a powerful message to all the therapists in the audience that these connections are what we work with in therapy. Satir, Murray Bowen, Jay Haley, Cloe Madones, Salvadore Minuchin, Susan Johnson, John Gottman and many others have opened up psychotherapy to the reality of systems.[2] Everyone more or less agrees that the relationship between husband and wife is the heart of the family system. If that heart is beating happy and healthy, everything else tends to fall into place.

What most therapists were missing—particularly in the fifties and sixties—was the classic elephant in the living room, ignored and yet dominating: sexuality. Couples that could consistently have satisfying sex tended to have huge advantages and couples that could not tended to suffer badly in numerous ways.

Moral biases in puritan America and ascending traditions in general influenced science, art, and culture to avoid talking explicitly about sexuality, avoid looking explicitly at sexuality, avoid helping people explicitly enjoy and improve sex, or avoid explicitly integrating sexuality into spiritual practice (all these activities have generally been considered a form of sin in ascending traditions[3]). The human sexual response cycle was not adequately described until the mid-sixties with Master's and Johnson's groundbreaking work[4], and the anatomy of the Grafenberg area of the vagina (the G-spot) wasn't accurately studied until 1998.

Marriage counselors in the fifties and sixties had little success overcoming their own and their clients' moral biases consistently enough to address suffering in couples' sex lives. In classic conformist fashion, psychotherapy as a discipline compartmentalized sexuality as an entity somehow separate from marriage counseling, individual therapy, family therapy, systems theory, and human development.

Enter Masters and Johnson in the sixties. Not only did they bring scientific rigor to the study of sexuality, but they also created a treatment model that nuked the cultural bias against all things sexual. They insisted their clients look at sexuality from as many perspectives as they could generate, and they had phenomenal success. For years, marriage counselors all over the country sent couples to St. Louis to deal directly with sexual issues with their clients that they were too uncomfortable and unknowledgeable about to deal with themselves.

In the seventies the Masters and Johnson approach was popularized by researchers and clinicians like Lonnie Barbach[5] and Helen Singer Kaplan[6] and there was a boom in the sex therapy industry. Classes and systems proliferated. In California—where I was practicing and training at the time—wonderful teachers taught therapists how to apply these principles to treatment. I loved these classes and workshops. I went to a variety of them, incorporated the material into my work, and started teaching and leading workshops myself locally.

Meanwhile, most of us who were adults in the seventies remember what was happening with relationships and sexuality in the larger culture. Communes, open marriage, casual sex, free love, the sexual revolution, swapping, Penthouse magazine, and VCR's created a sexual shake-down where everything was examined and many experiments were conducted. In an American Humanistic Psychology conference in Santa Barbara in the early Seventies, the weekend began with a workshop in how to appropriately initiate casual sexual encounters with other participants. Predictably, most of these experiments led to disaster, but the genie was at least partially let out of the bottle.

In the early eighties, sex therapy somewhat fell off the map. The workshops and classes seemed to disappear, and many sex therapists seemed to go out of business. Like the Anasazi Indians in the Southwest, the movement came, flourished, and mysteriously vanished to a large extent, though there were still organizations, classes, books, and workshops being offered.

I attribute the de-escalation of the sex therapy movement to the fact that Western culture finally shifted moral biases sufficiently that sexuality could be more easily studied, talked about, and consciously experimented with by couples and therapists. This reconnected sexuality and conjoint therapy in many of the ways it had needed to be from the first. As a result, therapists were more able to help their clients articulate sexual yearning and suffering and bring compassion and depth of consciousness directly to bear on these issues, with the result that many exclusive "sex therapists" were out of business. Today even high profile clinicians in the field such as David Schnarch (author of *Passionate Marriage)* emphasize in their writing and workshops that they are presenting systems of conjoint therapy that emphasize enhanced sexual functioning, rather than offering a specific sex therapy.[7]

Still, sex therapy has existence. There are MDs and therapists that devote their lives to sexuality research and treatment.[8] Couples do enter treatment with specific sexual symptoms and concerns, and the focus of their work can revolve almost exclusively around this emphasis. Sex therapy therefore is an aspect of therapy. It is pervasive enough and important enough that this last chapter is devoted to one such couple, Jerry and Kay.

Sexual compulsivity

Currently there is a wealth of twelve step approaches to healing compulsive disorders in general, most of which are based on the Alcoholics Anonymous model developed by Bill Wilson and others in the recovery community.[9] Sexual compulsivity, like most eating disorders, is distinguished from substance abuse disorders because—almost without exception—complete abstinence from being sexual is not a realistic or desirable option as it is with drug or alcohol dependence. Twelve-step programs for sexual compulsivity (or sexual addiction as it is often referred to) therefore need to not only support stopping destructive behaviors and preventing relapse but also on promoting appropriate sexual expression in service of health and love. To individuals who literally have no control over sexual impulses to the extent that they compulsively cause suffering to themselves and/or others—up to sixteen percent of the population in some studies—these programs can be Godsends that provide necessary structure, information, and interventions to help them stop compulsively acting out, and learn to channel their sexuality to support love, joy, fun, and healthy intimacy. I've found programs of this type to be necessary adjuncts when working with sexual compulsivity with individuals and couples.

This chapter is not dealing specifically with issues of sexual compulsivity but rather with the wide array of non-compulsive sexual dysfunctions that commonly occur with couples.

Sex therapy

In this chapter we'll follow one couple, Jerry and Kay, from their first psychotherapeutic contact to their successful termination after eight months of conjoint therapy. Like most couples, Jerry and Kay are typical in many ways, and unique in many ways. The purpose of following their journey through this sequence of therapy is to transmit a flavor of a Waking Up approach applied over a course of treatment to a couple seeking help for primarily sexual problems.

The first call I received was from Jerry. He had been sued for sexual harassment by a waitress in one of his restaurants and was humiliated, angry, and highly anxious. At the urging of his wife and (mostly her) friends, he called me and we had an initial session. He had never been in therapy before and showed up anxious and defensive, but trying to follow the direction of the caring women who had referred him to me. Jerry was reserved, friendly, out of touch with his body, and embarrassed. He and his wife had both been raised in intact, middle-class, Roman Catholic, Anglo families.

Jerry's intake session was typical. He told me about the episode, the lawsuit, his family of origin (big family, reserved emotionally, practically autistic sexually), his physical health, use of euphorics/medications (both minimal), his relational history, sexual history, attitudes towards his profession, feelings about his wife and children (especially his wife), his spiritual orientation, and his fantasy life. We explored his life from multiple perspectives, with special emphasis on his development and defenses on his self, sexual, interpersonal, masculine, feminine, moral, and values lines. We explored healthy and defensive states he routinely inhabited, and what was the nature of his temperament and deepest sexual essence.

Jerry was conformist, achievement oriented BLUE/ORANGE, in good health, had no drug or alcohol problems, no history of trauma, loved his job, adored his wife and two teenage children (a boy and a girl), had no spiritual path, was inexperienced and inhibited sexually, had almost exclusively passive neurotic defensive structures and states, was extroverted, primarily masculine, non-assertive, and hadn't had sex with his wife in five years. He was emotionally down and anxious, but not enough to be diagnosed with either a depressive or an anxiety disorder. Like many couples, sex had slowed down after the birth of their children, continued to fade, and had then disappeared. He had no conscious knowledge of polarity, or masculine practice and responsibilities.

The following exchange stood out to me in our initial session in that Jerry simultaneously seemed interested in addressing sexual issues while hiding sexual material from himself and/or me:

Jerry: "The waitress who sued me said I made sexually suggestive remarks to her, and invited her to have sex with me. I didn't do any of that. I've been faithful to Kay all of our marriage."

Keith: "What do you think gave her the idea you were coming on to her?"

Jerry: "I kid with everybody. That's one of the great things about our restaurants."

Keith: "Was she attractive to you?"

Jerry: "No, she was an employee."

Keith: Feeling some tension in my chest, and experiencing this topic as emotionally charged. Jerry's voice is more animated. His body is more tense and he's making more movements with his hands and feet. "Would you have liked her to be attracted to you?"

Jerry: Pausing five seconds; a relatively long latency compared to previous silences of one or two seconds. "Well, no. Why should I want her to be attracted to me?"

Keith: Giving him permission to hunger sexually. "Because it feels good to have women attracted to you. Most men want that, don't you think?"

Jerry: Three seconds this time. "Yeah, sure, why not? That doesn't mean I was coming on to her."

Keith: "Of course not. Have any other women ever misinterpreted your kidding around for sexual harassment?"

Jerry: Looking uncomfortable. "Nobody's ever filed a lawsuit before."

Keith: Liking him, wanting to open him to new possibilities. "I think there's a connection between these women's misunderstandings and the fact that you and your wife haven't had sex in five years."

Jerry: Suspicious and interested. "What do you mean?"

Keith: "Five years of blocking and frustrating your impulses to open your wife to sexual bliss often reflects being shut down, blind, or insensitive to sexual signals. You can misread them, or give confusing messages to other people."

Jerry: "Kay and I just can't talk about that stuff. Besides, she thinks I really came on to Helen and seems mad at me."

Keith: "Of course, how could she not be mad? It looks to her like you gave another woman what you're not giving her."

Jerry: "She's not interested in sex."

Keith: Laughing. "I'll bet you ten to one you're wrong about that one."

Jerry: Laughs.

Keith: "Jerry, what was your longest relationship before Kay, and how did it end?"

Jerry: "I lived with a woman two years and then we broke up."

Keith: Noticing his resistance to relating details, but I feel a good connection at this point, and I'm comfortable pressing. "What were the circumstances of your break-up?"

Jerry: "She went off with another man."

Keith: "How was sex with her?"

Jerry: "Good in the beginning, but then she stopped being interested."

Keith: How previous relationships have progressed and ended are some of the best indicators of relational patterns and defensive structures. "You used the same reference for her that you did with Kay. You said she lost interest."

Jerry: Looking both intrigued and uncomfortable. "Yeah."

Keith: Feeling his passive-aggressive defensive resistance, and leaning into the defensive state that he's now constellating. "What does it suggest to you?"

Jerry: Confused. "I don't know."

Keith: Realizing he probably doesn't see a connection. He's avoided self-reflection all his life. "It looks like you have a pattern of affiliating with a woman, and then relating in such a way that you become alienated as lovers. This is probably at least partly due to strong inhibitions you have about dealing with sex and other difficult intimate issues directly. Inhibitions like these often arise in the kind of Roman Catholic family that you were raised in."

Jerry: Dawning realization and guilt on his face. "Why do I do that?"

Keith: "How openly were sex, emotion, vulnerability, and intimacy discussed in your family with your parents and your five sisters and brothers?"

Jerry: "We didn't."

Keith: "You probably have a family taboo against such discussions and a family definition of a good man as someone who doesn't pursue such discussions. It would have been rude or threatening to bring these issues up in your family, so you developed inhibitions to talk about such topics, or even consciously to pay attention to those areas."

Jerry: Relieved I haven't pathologized him. Instead, I've suggested he has bad habits as a result of trying to do right by his family standards. "That makes sense. I don't want it to hurt Kay."

Keith: "I suggest you go home and talk to Kay about all of this. You'd both probably benefit from coming in and having some marriage counseling."

Jerry went home, talked about some of this with Kay, and had two more individual sessions. I had strongly suggested that he bring her in for conjoint therapy but he seemed to have gotten enough immediate relief from our three individual sessions that I didn't hear from him again for six months. This is often the case. People frequently address issues in stages, and I've learned to be patient with and respect my clients' timing for when they want to deal with different material.

Six months later Jerry called, said he and Kay had uncharacteristically had a huge fight and that he wanted to schedule a series of conjoint sessions. They arrived looking very united. Kay was attractive, well dressed, verbal, and extroverted. She had a demanding job, did it effectively, and was well paid and highly respected by coworkers.

I've found it useful to gather initial individual intake information in conjoint sessions as well as in at least one individual session. If I have the slightest sense of one or the other holding back, I'll recommend additional, individual intake sessions. I had no sense of Kay holding back information, but I did have a sense of her holding back her yearning for emotional and sexual fulfillment, so I scheduled an individual session with her before our next conjoint session. In this session she opened up more about her yearning to be romantically fulfilled with

Jerry, her doubts about his masculine power, and her anger at his resistance to intimate talk of any kind.

Kay was achievement oriented, egalitarian ORANGE/GREEN, in good health, had no drug or alcohol problems, loved her job, was a dedicated mother, had no spiritual path, but had regularly happy and pleasurable contact with her women friends who had urged her to "stand up for herself," and press for marriage counseling. She was extroverted, had no history of trauma, but had been raised Roman Catholic with severe inhibitions around the expression and practice of sexual thoughts and behaviors. She was attractive, dressed in ways that enhanced her feminine radiance, related with warmth to everyone, and was almost completely out of touch with her eroticism. She blamed her marital problems almost entirely on Jerry's inhibitions and apparent lack of interest. The following exchange is from our second conjoint session where we are exploring what the purpose of the psychotherapeutic work will be:

Keith: "What do you want to accomplish in therapy?"

Kay: "I want to be normal. I want us to be normal."

Keith: "What does normal mean to you, Kay?"

Kay: "I want to have a sex life with my husband."

Keith: "What stops you?"

Kay: "We just stopped, and Jerry never talks about anything."

Keith: "What happens when you try to talk about difficult subjects?"

Kay: "He never says anything. I've tried. I bring things up. Nothing ever happens." She looks accusingly at Jerry, who looks abashed.

Keith: Modeling the reflex of compassionate understanding. Looking for validity in her comments and wanting to bring Jerry into the dialogue. "What's valid about what Kay says, Jerry?"

Jerry: "I don't know what to say. She brings things up and it goes nowhere."

Keith: "What's valid about what Jerry just said, Kay?"

Kay: Angry now. Entering a defensive state. Her breathing is up in her chest, her face is tightening, and her body is tensing. "It goes nowhere because Jerry won't talk about anything."

Keith: Feeling a good relational connection with her. Sensing that she needs to be aware of her own blocks to be able to do her part of the work. Opening her a little in the charged sexual area. Implying that Jerry isn't the only one who's inhibited. "Kay, do you masturbate?"

Kay: Clearly taken aback. Entering another flavor of defensive state, radiating helplessness. "No, I don't do that."

Keith: "You've never tried?"

Kay: "Uh, I guess I have."

Keith: With interest. Normalizing conversation about taboo topics. "What did you try?"

Kay: "I don't want to talk about it."

Keith: "So you have difficulty discussing some these topics also."

Jerry: Rescuing Kay. Inhabiting his part of the relational defensive structure that defends both of them from threatening sexual material. "It's all right, Kay."

Keith: Knowing he has strengths that she doesn't see. Happy to confront Kay that Jerry has less inhibitions than she does in some areas. "How about you, Jerry? Do you masturbate?"

Jerry: Uncomfortable. Trusting me enough to answer, and also wanting to open up the sexual Pandora's box that he's been secretly fascinated with all his life. "Yes."

Kay: Surprised, but also interested. "Really?"

Jerry: Looking her in the eye. Confronting her with the reality that he is a sexual being. "Yes, really."

Keith: "Kay, you don't know that Jerry masturbates?"

Kay: Beginning to get that this is a systemic problem. "I suppose neither of us has ever been comfortable talking about it."

Conjoint therapy, and especially sex therapy, is often directing clients to discuss what they haven't discussed. In this session I recommended to them that they take daily walks and have a couple of conversations about sex, initiated by Jerry, before our next session. I suggested that Kay read *For Yourself*, Lonnie Barbach's book on female masturbation, and *Mama Gena's School of the Womanly*

Arts, by Regena Thomashauer. Jerry was resistant to reading books, so I gave him some specific information about masculine practice. I taught them circular breathing and some holding exercises. I explained and demonstrated his responsibilities to notice whether Kay was opening or closing, and to adjust so she was opening. I pointed out his characteristic (mostly passive) forms of collapse and encouraged him to direct himself to notice his collapses and take responsibility for regaining presence. I confronted him with his ability to be present, unrecoiling, and attentive to Kay. I explained defensive states to both of them, gave them examples of their individual and relational defensive structures and states from the session, and cautioned them about how hard it is in a defensive state to be aware of the amplified or numbed emotions, distorted perceptions and beliefs, and destructive impulses. I encouraged them to cultivate awareness of the states and to try to do something different when they discovered themselves in defensive states.

Jerry and Kay came into the next session having experimented with a few of my suggestions. The following exchange illustrates how more conscious commitment to polarity leads to enhanced sexual charge:

Keith: "How did you like Mama Gena, Kay?"

Kay: Smiling. "She's pretty wild."

Keith: "Did anything stand out?"

Kay: "What she said about pleasure. I don't have that much that's just sensual pleasure to me."

Keith: "David Deida says that sensory pleasures nourish the feminine, and fills her up with life. Love through the body, through the body's pleasures, is a central feminine practice. Pleasure in the body to a woman is like sunlight and water to plants."

Kay: "I like having more of it."

Jerry: Smiling. "Kay seemed happier."

Keith: "How have you felt towards each other this week?"

Jerry: "Good, but we always like each other. We're best friends."

Keith: Recognizing his genuine appreciation, but also knowing "best friends" is a classic non-sexual reference. I again raise the taboo subject of erotic charge. "When were you most attracted to each other? When did you feel moved to be physically close?"

Kay: Defensive. "We feel close a lot."

Keith: "When did you want to touch or caress him, or want him to touch or caress you?"

Kay: Recoiling slightly. "I didn't."

Keith: Knowing, with her warm and affectionate nature, that there were moments she was drawn to him physically. "When did he look the most attractive to you; the most manly in an attractive way?"

Kay: "When he was telling the plumber that the sink in the bathroom wasn't fixed and he had to come back and do it right."

Keith: "Jerry's attractive to you when he's assertive and stands up to people?"

Kay: "Yes, it makes me feel protected."

Keith: "Did you show him your pleasure? Did you hug him, or kiss him, or caress him in any way?"

Kay: Uncomfortable. "No, but I felt like it."

Keith: "Jerry, do you see how, when you stand unrecoiling for what you believe is right, you're more attractive to Kay?"

Jerry: "It's news to me. I couldn't tell, Kay."

Kay: Warmly. "I might give you a hug next time."

Jerry: Feeling permission in the session to explicitly value physical caress. "I'd like that a lot."

Keith: "How about you, Jerry? When were you most attracted to Kay?"

Jerry: Embarrassed. "When I saw her get out of the shower."

Kay: "I've put on so much weight."

Keith: Noticing how Jerry looks frustrated and defensive. "Jerry, tell Kay how you're feeling."

Jerry: Reluctant. "I feel fine."

Keith: "You just told Kay you found her desirable naked, and she responded by dissing herself. You look frustrated."

Jerry: "You look good to me, Kay."

Kay: "I have gained too much weight."

Keith: "Part of this process is learning to love your body, and to enjoy Jerry loving your body whether you're heavy or light, old or young, wrinkled or smooth. When he finds you desirable, don't argue with him, receive his appreciation with pleasure."

Jerry: "I think you're beautiful, Kay."

Kay: Smiling. "Thank you."

Keith: "That's better. You, Jerry, offered loving praise, and you, Kay received it with pleasure. Now, if you could do that ten times a day, your relationship would automatically improve."

Kay: "But how do I just start loving my body? I hate it that I've gained weight. I don't feel attractive."

Keith: "Really good questions, Kay. You just did one of the most important practices by receiving Jerry's compliment with pleasure. When you receive a compliment and resist by not feeling pleasure, focus on the offering and the receiving until you feel pleasure in your body. Secondly, I suggest you stand naked in front of a mirror each day and focus on loving and praising your feminine body and beauty. Instead of looking at those parts you dislike, treat your body like a daughter whom you want to encourage to love and celebrate her femininity and sexuality independent of form. Besides, there is a lot to like about your physical being."

Jerry: "You can say that again." Both laugh.

The first several sessions were a lot of exchanges like this. I was finding out their strengths and vulnerabilities, their healthy states and defensive states. They were exploring themselves and each other, and getting to know and trust me. Teaching Jerry masculine practice and Kay feminine practice was an ongoing theme. At the end of this session, I reminded them about circular breathing, and suggested that Jerry arrange for them to hold each other three to five minutes every day with Jerry synchronizing his breathing with Kay's and imagining that he breathe her, deepening her breath. I suggested he do this for her sake. I suggested to her that she show him with sound and movement what was pleasurable during the exercise.

The reframing of intimate physical contact, from an imposition on her to a need of hers that he had a responsibility to fulfill with love, was a central part of my work with Jerry. The reframing of regular pleasure in the body, from a self-indulgence to a responsibility that she had to herself to be a better wellspring of love for Jerry and the kids was a central part of the work with Kay:

We processed the breathing/holding practice in the next session.

Keith: "How did the breathing/holding exercise go?"

Kay: Disappointed tone. "We only did it one time."

Jerry: Looking uncomfortable, a little guilty. "We were just swamped last week."

Keith: Exploring the positive to anchor them in the possibilities for change, rather than the disappointments of defensive states and collapse. "It's good you did it once. How did it feel?"

Jerry: Brightening a little. "I enjoyed holding her."

Kay: More cautious. "I liked it."

Keith: Evoking details until the next intervention suggests itself. It's clear to me at this point in the session that there are blocks to change. It's not clear yet where to focus therapeutic attention to move them forward. "Tell me the details. When and how did you initiate, Jerry? Did you practice the circular breathing, and were you able to feel yourself breathing Kay? What did it feel like to you, Kay? Was there pleasure in your body, and, if so, what kind of pleasure?"

Kay: Laughing. "That's a lot of questions."

Keith: Laughing. "We've got time."

Jerry: "I initiated it Tuesday night after our session. I asked Kay to do the breathing and we lay down. I spooned her and we did it."

Keith: Noticing how he describes the events without his emotional and physical experience. "Did you feel close, intimate, and/or turned on?"

Jerry: "All of those things."

Keith: "Tell Kay."

Jerry: With some effort. "I felt close and turned on."

Kay: Looks surprised. "You didn't tell me that."

Jerry: Plaintive. "Wasn't it obvious?"

Kay: Irritated. "No, you didn't say anything. You never say anything."

Keith: "So, two clear messages about this for you Jerry are that you have to be much more generous with telling Kay what you like, and that it is real effort to do so. How about you, Kay? What did you enjoy about the holding and breathing?"

Kay: "I felt cozy and safe in Jerry's arms. I felt like he loved me."

Keith: Normalizing her discussing pleasure. "Sounds pleasurable. Was it emotional pleasure, sensual pleasure, and/or erotic pleasure?"

Kay: Interested. "Certainly emotional pleasure, some sensual pleasure, and I didn't get turned on."

Keith: Modeling for Jerry how to provide safety and praise for the feminine. "That's fine. It's great that you did the exercise and felt emotional and sensual pleasure. What stopped you from doing the exercise more often?"

Kay: Accusingly. "Jerry just didn't ask after that."

Jerry: Defensively. "We were so busy, and I didn't think you had that good a time."

Kay: Angry now. "How can you know if you don't ask?"

Keith: Laughing. "I want you both to notice that you're arguing about a good time you had touching each other and loving better."

Jerry: Chagrined. "How am I supposed to know she liked it?"

Keith: Subtly confronting Kay through Jerry. "Didn't Kay show you she was enjoying it with "ah's" and movement like we discussed?"

Kay: Defensively. "I told you how hard it is for me to make sounds."

Keith: "Hard or impossible?"

Kay: More firmly. "I can do it."

Keith: Feeling a sense of charge in my heart and solar plexus, and wanting to go deeper into this area. "Try it now. Jerry, look at her with love and humor, and Kay, say 'ah' when you feel pleasure."

Jerry looks at her with a twinkle in his eyes and Kay forces out an "ah."

Keith: Smiling. "No, no, no. Relax into it, Kay. Don't constrict into it. Try it again."

They try it again and Kay relaxes into an "ah."

Keith: "How did that feel?"

Kay: "I felt a kind of rush of energy go through my body."

Jerry: "I like it."

Keith: Pressing him to be aware of his body. "Say what you felt in your body, Jerry."

Jerry: "I feel warm when Kay relaxes and says 'ah,' I feel happy."

The breathing exercise is just one of several practices that I suggested in the previous session. When I process such exercises in detail with clients, defenses are revealed. As this happens, my job is to uncover and normalize defensive states and structures, and help them self-regulate their defenses while growing in their abilities to inhabit healthy states where they can better love and be loved. One of the purest forms of fulfilling yearning to love and be loved is blissful sexual communion. In this sexual area a goal of the work is for both Jerry and Kay to move from the conformist level of sexuality where the goal is acceptance (lack of accepting sexuality in self and other has dominated their sexuality since childhood) to the psychoemotional level of sexuality where the goal is fulfillment. The next exchange is from later on in the same session:

Keith: "Kay, it's clear that when you're being caressed physically you tend to feel resistant to making sounds and movements of pleasure. This contributes to freezing up your body and inhibiting energy flows. I suggest you do five minutes of sexy dance in feminine clothes to irresistible music each day to open your body to movements of pleasure. While you move, focus on circular breathing to relax any blocked or closed areas, and making any sounds that naturally arise up out of your body. Also, when Jerry caresses you, you can allow your pleasure to flow into sound, just as you did in the session."

Kay: "That's hard. It's not my style to make sounds of pleasure."

Keith: Laughing. "It's a tough, dirty job, but somebody has to do it, and you're the one." Kay laughs.

Jerry: "It's great when I can tell what you like."

Keith: Challenging the masculine. "Your work is different, Jerry. Sometimes you just fade away from stuff that threatens you or Kay and go find other things to do. You forget the exercises, you don't ask Kay what she's feeling, and you don't tell her what you're feeling, wanting, or thinking. She reads all this as collapse, and then doesn't trust you. You need to step up, communicate your thoughts and feelings courageously, initiate the exercises, breathe yourself and then breathe her, feel your own pleasure, feel her pleasure, and support her moving and making sounds."

Jerry: "What if she rejects me?"

Kay: Vehement, unaware of the irony of her current rejecting tone, speaking to Jerry's obvious surprise. "Are you kidding? I've been dying to have you be more open with me."

Keith: Teaching. "As you do more of this work, you'll have regular moments of feeling loss at the years you've wasted not loving each other better in the ways you are now learning about. All you can do is accept that we get it when we get it, and do the best to love as best you can right now."

Over the next several sessions Jerry and Kay progressed into regular holding and caressing while lying naked together. Kay continued to focus on relaxing into her breath, body, sound, and movement, and accepting that Jerry found her beautiful and desirable, even though she felt unattractively heavy. Jerry continued to work on directing Kay into sensual caress while discerning and refusing to surrender to defensive impulses to avoid emotional and physical contact. Meanwhile they were having more disagreements with each other and more intimate talks as they took daily walks with each other in nature. Inevitably, Kay began to feel erotic tingles during their breathing and touching sessions. This next exchange occurred in a session where she'd felt several such tingles in the previous week:

Kay: "I really liked our touching this week."

Keith: "What did you really like?"

Kay: "I felt turned on a few times."

Keith: "What are the sensations of 'turned on'?"

Kay: A little embarrassed. "I feel tingly and warm in my pelvis and, you know, wet."

Keith: "Wet in your vagina?"

Kay: More embarrassed. "Yes."

Keith: "You seem embarrassed."

Kay: "I've just never talked about things like this before."

Keith: With humor, but also relentlessly normalizing the talk. "Things like you being turned on and getting wet in your vagina while Jerry caresses you?"

Kay: Laughing. "OK, OK. Yes. Getting turned on and wet, getting turned on and wet. I'm talking about it."

Keith: "Jerry, how do you feel when Kay talks like this?"

Jerry: Grinning. "I love it. But I know how she feels. We're both embarrassed talking about sex."

Keith: "You're lucky I'm not Mama Gena. She asks women all the time to listen to, talk to, and become their pussy. It's actually a great thing to do. You might try it, Kay."

Kay: "Maybe in private, at home. I like Mama Gena."

Keith: "You two are getting better at talking and touching. Jerry, did Kay let you know she was turned on?"

Jerry: "She did great. I could feel her being wet, feel her breath change, and hear some 'ah's.'"

Kay: "It's easier now that I trust Jerry to take care of initiating being close and not forgetting."

In this session I suggested that during the next week Jerry, using lubrication, begin gently penetrating Kay with his fingers and/or penis depending on what he felt was best for Kay and him in the moment. I encouraged each of them to ask the other if they were wondering what the other was feeling or thinking. I told them this was especially important if either had a negative assumption (such as the other being angry or having a bad time). Usually negative assumptions are partly or entirely inaccurate and, if they are accurate, the way to move back towards love is often to get it out and help each other. In this I was encouraging them to polish second stage communication skills. These skills are necessary to create the kind of safety that makes third stage relating possible. I further suggested to both to gently explore Kay's G-spot (Grafenberg's spot, about an inch interior and superior in most women's vaginas) with Kay giving Jerry ongoing "softer, harder, faster, slower" feedback.

Jerry and Kay were now moving into generating and enhancing erotic energy during their touching. Jerry, when he disciplined himself to initiate, was being more expressive and assertive, and this made him more trustable to Kay. Kay, in feeling and showing pleasure through her body, and talking explicitly about sex and pleasure, was appearing and feeling more sensually and erotically accessible to Jerry. They were discerning and interrupting defensive states in themselves more regularly, and engaging in more masculine/feminine practice. They were spending less time feeling separate and alienated sexually, and more time feeling connected as lovers. Often when this kind of progress is happening (and thus threatening systemic change) some event occurs that cues regression into defensive states. That's what happened in the week preceding our next session. This exchange is from that session:

Keith: "How are you doing?"

Kay: Irritated. "I always talk first. You talk first, Jerry."

Jerry: Looking anxious. I feel an empathetic tingle of fear in my chest and stomach. There's clearly a charged issue of some sort. "We had problems this week."

Keith: Feeling their tension, curious. "What problems?"

Jerry: "We had sex and it hurt Kay."

Kay: "That's not the main thing."

Jerry: "Well, we argued and then got busy with other things."

Kay: Angry. "You just disappeared. Talk about collapse. You wouldn't say word one."

Keith: "Slow down. First of all, tell be about the intercourse, and Kay, tell me exactly what kind of pain you felt."

Kay: "We were having a nice time. Jerry was touching me, stroking my G-spot and I was feeling turned on. The he put his penis inside me a little, and then pushed it in, and it felt like a burning in my vagina."

Keith: It's always good to get a lot of detail when dealing with pain. "Was it burning a lot or a little? Was it in one part of your vagina, or in your whole vagina? Did it get better or worse?"

Kay: "It only burned a little on my outer lips, and then it felt better when he began moving. I was just starting to enjoy it when 'bong,' it was over."

Jerry: Embarrassed. "I couldn't help it. It felt so good I just came."

Keith: "Did you use a lubricant?"

Jerry: "No, Kay was wet and I thought we didn't need it."

Keith: "First of all, always use a lubricant. Secondly, how did your vagina feel afterwards, Kay?"

Kay: "Fine, it was just so frustrating that he came right when I began having a good time. It used to be like that a lot when we had sex."

Keith: During our intake sessions, I had asked both of them about their previous sexual experiences in detail, and neither had mentioned premature ejaculation as a problem. Now, as they're beginning to reinhabit the sexual territory (what one woman client referred to once as "candy land"), new material is emerging, both pleasurable and painful. New material in the form of issues, memories, and associations, regularly emerges in all forms of psychotherapy. When it does, it's usually a good idea to embrace the new material and integrate it into the work. "Jerry, has coming too fast been a problem for you historically?"

Jerry: Reluctantly. "Once in awhile."

Kay: Indignant. "Tell the truth, Jerry. I remember it happening all the time in the beginning. We just had sex so much it didn't seem to matter."

Jerry: Somewhat helplessly. "I just got so turned on."

Keith: Laughing. "It's good you get so turned on. You want to find her sexy and desirable. You just need to learn how to tolerate more pleasure before you come. It's easy if you practice. I can teach you several ways."

Kay: Interested. "That sounds good."

Jerry: Hopeful. "What do I need to do?"

Keith: "First, you need to deal with things when they happen, Jerry. Kay was most angry about you falling into your old pattern of avoiding difficult topics and disappearing as an intimate partner."

Jerry: "OK. I admit it. I collapsed. I thought about it a lot and didn't say anything. I felt bad about coming too fast and didn't want to deal with it."

Kay: "It's nice to hear you just admit it."

At this point I explained the stop/start technique[10], and a yogic breathing technique that Deida details in his writing (there is also the famous "squeeze technique" but none of my clients have ever been interested in practicing it).

The stop/start technique involves the man, during penile stimulation and/or intercourse, focusing on the sensations and pleasure in his genitals, until he feels himself approaching his point of inevitability (men's orgasms have two stages, emission when there is a sense of the orgasm beginning internally, and ejaculation when there are a series of, usually, four to seven .8 second contractions and semen is pumped out). I directed Jerry, when he felt himself approaching emission, to slow down or stop his thrusting motions, all the time staying focused on the sensations in his genitals, and staying connected emotionally to Kay. When he felt himself more distant from his orgasm (it usually takes ten seconds to a minute of relative or complete stillness), he could begin slowly thrusting again, still focusing on his sensation and connection to Kay. I suggested he repeat this process at least three times each lovemaking session before he allowed himself to come.

The yogic breathing technique is taught by Deida in his books and lectures. When the man approaches his point of inevitability, he simultaneously exhales completely, draws his abdomen towards his spine, clenches his anal and perineal muscles with a feeling of pulling them up into his body, presses the tip of his tongue firmly against the roof of his mouth, and rolls his eyes up (either open or closed) as if he's looking straight above his head. When he is comfortably backed away from his orgasm, he uses circular breathing to recirculate his sexual energy down his front and up his back.[11]

Both the techniques can be practiced alone during masturbation, or with a partner.

The main significance of Jerry and Kay's conflict during the session was not Kay's burning sensation during the first part of intercourse or Jerry's premature ejaculation. Since Kay got more comfortable and turned on relatively fast, and the pain faded quickly, extra lubrication and more sensitive penetration by Jerry was probably the solution (which proved to be the case in later lovemaking). If this hadn't provided complete relief, there are a variety of behavioral, relational, hormonal, medical, and mechanical interventions that can be brought to bear to make intercourse less painful and more pleasurable. The Berman sisters' book, *For Women Only*, is an excellent, state-of-the-art, resource to guide psychotherapists and medical doctors for this and most other conditions that interfere with a woman's ability to enjoy sex.[12] Jerry's premature ejaculation was easily resolved by systematically using either of the techniques I just described. The main significance of their conflict was that when they encountered certain emotional and behavior cues both indulged defensive states. This resulted in deserting self and other, and then fading back into their old routines of avoiding intimacy.

People often tend to normalize suffering rather than challenge it, especially in forbidden, charged areas like sexuality. Couples will unconsciously enter relational defensive structures where they conspire to avoid threatening perspectives and practices until they can cultivate the depth of consciousness to understand the importance of addressing issues, and the compassion and love for self and other to keep moving back into uncomfortable areas without critical judgment. Kay (accurately) experienced Jerry's withdrawal after the tension of the episode as collapse and she felt correspondingly less trust and attraction for him and thus entitled to indulge her own avoidant defensive impulses. Jerry was uncomfortable and embarrassed by Kay's pain and his premature ejaculation and indulged his destructive defensive impulses to desert himself and Kay, thus falling back into the uncomfortable (but familiar and tolerable) rhythms of their previous life. After teaching them the technical information they needed, I confronted these issues:

Keith: "Are you willing to practice what I just described?"

Kay: "I know I am."

Jerry: "Sure."

Keith: "Do you trust the other to do their work? To not get threatened or distracted and disappear?"

Kay: "No, I don't. Jerry doesn't like to talk about these things if there's problems."

Jerry: "You weren't very encouraging when you were mad."

Keith: Noticing Kay's angry expression and wanting to interrupt repetitive attack and defense. "This is what I meant in our first session when I said that some of the work would be difficult. You see how easy it was to fall back into the old patterns."

Jerry: "I don't like her being mad."

Keith: Confronting, challenging. "Of course you don't. No man likes it when his woman gets mad at him. The problem is your defensive instinct to collapse and withdraw. What you need, and she needs, is for you to stand firm, unrecoiling in the face of her emotional storm and breath her in. That supports her in feeling safe enough to be an open channel of emotion that lets anger come and lets anger go."

Kay: "I like that."

Keith: "Try it right now, Jerry. Face her, relax, connect to your heart and her heart, and breathe in her emotion with love and humor."

Jerry: Sits up, turns to her, focuses, and breaths deeply. His face relaxes and becomes more beautiful as he does this.

Keith: "How does this attention feel, Kay?"

Kay: Smiling warmly. "Really nice."

Keith: "Feel her pleasure, Jerry. You are the masculine anchor of your polarity. You need to provide the depth of consciousness to think of what's best for you both, and then to courageously take whatever risk you believe is the right one. When Kay's upset, I suggest you breathe her in like this. I also suggest that you discern this week when it's best for Kay and talk intimately, touch intimately, and make overtures."

Jerry: "But I do that and sometimes she says 'no' and rejects me."

Keith: "Then you need to stand unrecoiling, love her anyway, and try again when it feels like a good time. That's what resolute acceptance is all about. You do your best and accept whatever happens with presence and humor."

Kay: Analyzing. "Jerry's family never deals with issues."

Keith: She's animating her masculine, and so I challenge that part of her. "What are you doing to evoke his overtures?"

Kay: Defensive. "What do you mean? I was swamped this week, and Jerry withdrew."

Keith: "Did you let your hurt show so he had to deal with it? Did you fill yourself with pleasure in the body? Did you show him your yearning and love with your smile, your touch, your voice, and your body?"

Kay: Uncomfortable. "No. I know I should."

Keith: Now speaking to her feminine heart. "Your work is to be wide open. If you're hurt, be hurt visibly until he has to respond. Otherwise, fill your body with pleasure and feminine radiance, which is magnetic. Do this especially when you resist. Can you feel how much you yearn for this in your heart and body?"

Kay: Tears in her eyes. "Yes, I feel it."

Keith: "You need to cherish these aspects of yourself. Last week you got angry and deserted yourself and Jerry."

Jerry: "I won't disappear no matter how busy we get."

Kay: "I love you, Jerry."

Keith: "This is good. Remember, don't strain to do more; relax into doing more. Relax into being open to pleasure in the body. Relax into shining as light. And you, Jerry, relax into presence and humor. Relax into breathing her in when she gets mad."

Two sessions later Jerry and Kay were having sex about twice a week, and Jerry was having some success controlling his orgasms. They cancelled a couple of sessions, and I didn't see them again for several months. When they came in, they were discouraged and depressed:

Keith: "It's good to see both of you. What brings us together today?"

Kay: Down. "It's the same old thing. We haven't had sex in three weeks, and Jerry won't talk to me."

Keith: "Jerry, what's valid about that?"

Jerry: Depressed tone. "Work got crazy. And our kids are on summer break. It's different with them around more."

Kay: "You're just making excuses."

Keith: Noticing how much easier he shares than when I first met him. Appreciative of their higher expectations for their sexuality and intimacy. "How is it different with the kids around more?"

Jerry: "It's just easy to fall back into being busy all the time."

Keith: "Exactly. When we first started, I suggested that it would take conscious effort for possibly years before you both were grounded in new habits. Development is like this. Glop and slop, forward and back. How about you, Kay? Have you fallen back into old habits?"

Kay: A little abashed. "It *is* different with the kids around so much more.

I don't feel as sexy."

Keith: Laughing. "The old mothering reflexes are taking hold?"

Kay: Laughing. "Now that you mention it. I cook them breakfast and lunch. They don't have jobs or sports so they are home for dinner a lot, though they are going out at night a fair amount." She looks significantly over at Jerry.

Jerry: "This might be their last summer they spend with us, and it's hard to get a job for only two or three months. But I get your point about them being out. We just watch T.V. or work. We could be making love once in awhile."

Keith: "It sounds like you know what to do, Jerry. You just haven't disciplined yourself to do it."

Jerry: Looking resolved. "You're right. I need to make overtures and make time for us to talk and be close."

Keith: "Are you going to make it happen?"

Jerry: Resolved. "Yes."

Kay: "I know I need to forget about the kids in the evenings, and focus on pleasure and time with Jerry."

Keith: "I'm noticing how much wiser and closer you are than the first time I saw you together." Both smile. "Why don't you change the things you need to change, and come back to see me in two weeks?"

Jerry: "All right."

Kay: "I just need to remember to make an effort."

Two weeks later they were sexually active (and experimental) again, and more intimately connected. I haven't seen them since, but they could call at any time if they encounter some kind of block. Couples I've worked with often call me when they feel stuck.

Jerry and Kay were a relatively uncomplicated couple to work with. Both were generally physically and psychologically healthy. Neither had major characterological defenses. Neither was particularly self-destructive, and both worked hard to make things better. Their arc of growth, though, is representative of what's possible when people decide to love better and be more true to their deepest essences.

My mission was to meet them where they were in their lives, and cocreate a culture where they and their universes were cherished, where each moment was considered a gift and an opportunity, and healthy perspectives and actions were considered beautiful, good, and true. My focus was cultivating compassion and depth of consciousness in myself and them to help them remediate symptoms, enhance health, and support development. The manner I did this was by relating, teaching, inspiring, confronting, interpreting, and directing.

Each client and each couple are unique. I'll never see a couple exactly like Jerry and Kay again, but the perspectives, principles, and practices I brought to bear in my work with them will be relevant to understanding and helping other clients.

Your clinical style is not mine, and you'll probably never see a couple *exactly* like Jerry and Kay either. What I hope is that you take the perspectives, principles, and practices that I've shared with you in this book, and integrate them into your own unique worldviews and forms of service to enhance your own natural healing style.

Waking up.

We can never learn all there is to know about healing, psychotherapy, or any of the disciplines I've discussed in this book. That being said, we have yearnings to grow and to serve others that can be enhanced by learning and living principles and techniques that seem beautiful, good, and true to us. Each new perspective is an awakening that expands us in different ways. This material has awakened me to deeper understandings of being a man, husband, father, friend, psychotherapist, and soul.

One major discovery I've made is that we can keep waking up all through our lives, regularly discovering new truths and capacities to love and heal. My favorite moment in Van Morission's exquisite song of ascending spirituality, *Enlightenment,* is when he exhorts us to "Wake up."

Namaste,
Keith Witt, Ph.D.

b. 1950

1. Nichols (2007)

2. *Ibid*

3. Wilber (2003)

4. Masters (1970)

5. Barbach (1976)

6. Kaplan (1974)

7. Schnarch (1997)

8. Berman (2001)

9. Carnes (2002)

10. Kaplan (1974)

11. Deida (2006)

12. Berman (2001)

Works Cited

Adler, A. (1956). *The Individual Psychology of Alfred Adler.* H. L. Ansbacher and R. R. Ansbacher (Eds.). New York: Harper Torchbooks

Ahrons, Constance R. (1994). *The Good Divorce: keeping your family together when your marriage comes apart.* New York: HarperCollins.

Alexander, Charles N., and Langer Ellen J. (1990). *Higher Stages of Human Development, Perspectives on Adult Growth.* New York: Oxford University Press.

Almaas, A. H. (1987). *Diamond Heart: Book One: Elements of the Real in Man.* Boston: Shambhala Publications.

_____. (2002). *Facets of Unity.* Boston: Shambhala Publications.

———. (2004). *The Inner Journey Home: Soul's Realization of the Unity of Reality.* Boston: Shambhala.

American Psychiatric Association. (1994). *Diagnostic and Statistical Manual of Mental Disorders DSM1V.* Washington, DC: American Psychiatric Association.

Anderson, Walter Truett. (1983). *The Upstart Spring: Esalen and the American Awakening.* Reading, Mass: Addison-Wesley Publishing Company.

Assagioli, Roberto. (1965). *Psychosynthesis.* New York: The Viking Press.

Barbach, Lonnie. (1976). *For Yourself: The Fulfillment of Female Sexuality.* Penguin

Baron-Cohen, Simon. (2003). *The Essential Difference: the truth about the male and female brain.* New York: Basic Books.

Beattie, Melody. (1987). *Codependent No More.* New York: Harper and Row.

Beck, Don Edward, and Cowan, Christopher C. (1996). *Spiral Dynamics: mastering values, leadership, and change.* Malden, MA: Blackwell Publishing.

Belliveau, Fred, and Richter, Lin. (1970). *Understanding Human Sexual Inadequacy.* New York: Bantam Books.

Bennett, Bruce E., Bricklin, Patricia M., Harris, Eric, Knapp, Samuel, Vander-Creek, Leon, Younggren, Jeffery N., (2006). *Assessing and managing Risk in Psychological Practice: An Individualized Approach.* The Trust: Rockville, MD.

Berman, Jennifer, and Berman, Laura. (2001). *For Women Only: Overcoming Sexual Dysfunction and Reclaiming Your Sex Life.* New York: Henry Holt and Company, LLC.

Berne, Eric. (1961). *Transactional Analysis in Psychotherapy.* New York: Grove Press, Inc.

Bloom, B. (Ed.). (1956). *Taxonomy of educational objectives: The classification of educational goals.* New York: Longman, Green.

Bodansky, Steve, and Vera. (2002). *The Illustrated Guide to Extended Massive Orgasm.* Berkeley, CA: Hunter House Publishers.

Bowlby, J. (1988). *A secure base: Parent-child attachment and healthy human development.* New York: Basic Books.

Bradshaw, John. (1988). *Bradshaw on The Family: a Revolutionary Way of Self-Discovery.* Deerfield Beach, Florida: Health Communications, Inc.

Brizendine, Louann. (2006). *The Female Brain.* New York: Morgan Road Books.

Brad J. Bushman, Ph.D.; Roy Baumeister, Ph.D; and Angela D. Stack, Ph.D. (1999). *Catharsis, Aggression and Persuasive Influence: Self-Fulfilling or Self-Defeating Prophecies? Journal of Personality and Social Psychology.* Vol. 76, No. 3

Campbell, Joseph. (1949). *The Hero With a Thousand Faces.* Princeton: Princeton University Press.

Carlin, Flora. (2004). *Cupid's Comeuppance,* Psychology Today: September/October.

Carnes, Patrick. (2002). *Out of the Shadows, Understanding Sexual Addiction.* Hazelden, Minn:

Centers for Disease Control and Prevention. (2005). *Youth Risk Behavior Studies.* U.S. Government Publications.

Childre, Doc, and Rozman, Deborah. (2005*). Transforming Stress: The Heart-Math Solution for Relieving Worry, Fatigue, and Tension.* Oakland, Ca: New Harbinger Publications, Inc.

Cloniger, Robert C. (2004). *Feeling Good, the Science of Well-Being.* Oxford University Press.

Csikszentmihalyi, Mihaly (1990*). Flow: The Psychology of Optimal Experience.* New York: Harper and Row.

Curran, Dolores. (1983). *Traits of a Healthy Family.* New York: Ballantine Books.

Danielou, Alain. (1994). *The Complete Kama Sutra: The First Unabridged Modern Translation of the Classic Indian Text.* Rochester, Vermont: Park Street Press.

Deida, David. (2005). *Blue Truth: A spiritual guide to life and death and love and sex.* Boulder, CO: Sounds True, Inc.

———. (2005). *Function, flow, and Glow.* Integral Institute: www.Integralinstitute.org

———. (2004). *Enlightened Sex.* (CD series). Boulder, Colorado: Sounds True.

———. (2004). *Enlightened Sex Manual: sexual skills for the superior lover.* Boulder, CO: Sounds True, Inc.

———. (2002). *Dear Lover.* Austin: Plexus.

———. (2003). Lecture in Los Angeles.

———. (1995). *Intimate Communion.* Deerfield Beach: Health Communications, Inc.

———. (1997). *The Way of the Superior Man.* Austin: Plexus.

———. (2006). *The Way of the Superior Man: The Teaching Sessions.* (CD series). Boulder, Colorado: Sounds True.

———. (2001). *Waiting To Love.* Austin: Plexus.

———. (2006). *David Deida, the complete recordings*: www.deida.info.

Dement, William C. and Vaughan, Christopher. (1999). *The Promise of Sleep.* New York: Dell Publishing.

Diagnostic and Statistical Manual: Fourth Edition. (1994). Washington DC: American Psychiatric Association.

Diener, Ed (1984). *Subjective well-being. Psychological Bulletin, 95,* 542–575.

Dike Charles C. (2007). *Pathological Lying.* Paradigm, Spring 2007.

Dixit, Jay. (2007). *Night School.* Psychology Today: November/December, 2007.

Druck, Andrew. (1989). *Four Therapeutic Approaches to the Borderline Patient.* Northvale, New Jersey: Jason Aronson Inc.

Dweck, Carol. (2006). *Mindset: The New Psychology of Success.* New York: Random House.

Enard, Wolfgang, and Paabo Svante. (2004). *Comparative Primate Genomics.* Annu. Rev. Genomics Hum. Gent.

Erik Erikson. (1998). *The Life Cycle Completed.* New York: Norton.

Fisher, Helen. (2004). *Why We Love: the Nature and Chemistry of Romantic Love.* New York: Henry Holt

Fisher, Helen. (2007). *The Laws of Chemistry.* Psychology Today, May/June.

Freud, Sigmund. (1949). *An Outline of Psycho-Analysis.* New York: W.W. Norton and Company, Inc.

———. (1952) *On Dreams.* New York: W.W. Norton and Company, Inc.

Friend, Tad: (2003) *Jumpers: The fatal grandeur of the Golden Gate Bridge*, The New Yorker, October 13, 2003 v79 i30 page 48

Gardner Howard, (2003). *"Multiple Intelligences after Twenty Years."* Invited Address, American Educational Research Association: April, 2003

Gilligan, Carol. (1993). *In a Different Voice: Psychological Theory and Women's Development.* Cambridge, Mass.: Harvard University Press.

Gottman, John. (1999). *The Marriage Clinic: A Scientifically Based Marital Therapy.* New York: Norton Professional Books.

Gottman, John, and DeClaire, Joan. (2001). *The Relationship Cure, a 5 Step Guide for Building Better Connections with Family, Friends, and Lovers.* New York: Crown Publishing.

Gottman, John. (1999). *The Marriage Clinic: A Scientifically Based Marital Therapy.* New York: Norton Professional Books.

Gottman, John. (2005). Presented at a conference, *The Anatomy of Intimacy.* Foundation for the Contemporary Family, UC Irvine, November 5 and 6.

Goulding, Mary McClure, Goulding, Robert L. (1979). *Changing Lives Through Redecision Therapy.* New York: Grove.

Graves, Clare W. (1970). *"Levels of Existence: An Open System Theory of Values".* Journal of Humanistic Psychology, November 1970.

Gray, John. (1992). *Men are from Mars, Women are from Venus.* New York: HarperCollins Publishers.

Haley, Jay. (1980). *Leaving Home: the therapy of disturbed young people.* New York: McGraw-Hill Book Company.

———. (1963). *Strategies of Psychotherapy.* New York: Grune and Stratton.

Hartmann, Thom. (2003). *The Edison Gene: ADHD and the Gift of the Hunter Child.* Rochester, Vermont: Park Street Press.

Harvard Mental Health Letter. (2005). *Meditation in Psychotherapy.* Harvard Medical School: Volume 21. Number 10, April, 2005

———. (2007). *Couple Therapy.* Harvard Medical School: Volume 23. Number 9. March, 2007.

Hayes, S.C., Strosahl, K., and Wilson, K. G. (1999). *Acceptance and Commitment Therapy: An Experimental Approach to Behavior Change.* New York: Guilford Press.

Hedaya, Robert J. 2000. *How to Beat the Side Effects and Enhance the Benefits of Your Medication: The Anti-depressant Survival Program.* New York: Crown Publishers.

Hite, Shere. (1976). *The Hite Report: A national Study of Female Sexuality.* New York: Kindle.

Hitti, Miranda, (reviewer). (2007). American Chemical Society's 223 National Meeting and Exposition, Chicago, March 25–29, 2007. News release, American Chemical Society. WebMD Medical News.

Johnson, Susan. (2005). Presented at a conference, *The Anatomy of Intimacy.* Foundation for the Contemporary Family, UC Irvine, November 5 and 6.

Jung, Carl Gustav (1965); *Memories, Dreams, Reflections.* Vintage Books: New York.

———. (1933). *Modern Man in Search of a Soul.* New York: Harcourt, Brace and World, Inc.

———. (1958). *Psyche and Symbol.* New York: Doubleday Anchor Books.

Kahneman, Daniel. (1999). *Well-Being: Foundations of Hedonic Psychology.* Portland, Oregon: Book News, Inc.

Kaplan, Helen Singer. (1974). *The New Sex Therapy: active treatment of sexual dysfunctions.* New York: Brunner/Mazel Publication.

Kaplan, Karen. *Study finds humans are still evolving—and quickly.* Los Angeles Times, January 12, 2008.

Kegan, Robert. (1982). *The Evolving Self: Problem and Process in Human Development.* Cambridge, Mass: Harvard University Press.

Kernberg, Otto. (1975). *Borderline Conditions and Pathological Narcissism.* Northvale, New Jersey: Jason Aronson Inc.

Kohlberg, Lawrence, Charles Levine, Alexandra Hewer (1983). *Moral stages: a current formulation and a response to critics.* Basel, NY: Karger.

Korzybski, Alfred. (1933). *Science and Sanity: An Introduction to Non-Aristotelian Systems and General Semantics.* Lakeville, Connecticut: The International Non-Aristotelian Library Publishing Company.

Lange, Arthur J. and Jakubowski, Patricia. (1976). *Responsible Assertive Behavior.* Champagne, Ill: Research Press.

Lazarus, Arnold. (1976). *The Practice of Multimodal Therapy.* Baltimore, MD: Johns Hopkins University Press.

Levine, Judith. (2002). *Harmful to Minors.* Minneapolis: University of Minnesota Press.

Levine, Peter. (1997). *Waking the Tiger: Healing Trauma.* Berkeley, CA: North Atlantic Books.

Liedloff, Jean. (1975). *The Continuum Concept.* Reading Mass: Addison-Wesley Publishing Company, Inc.

Linehan, Marsha M, Dimeff Linda. (2001). *Dialectical Behavior Therapy in a Nutshell.* The California Psychologist, 34, 10–13, 2001.

Lowen, Alexander. *Bioenergetics.* (1975). New York: Coward, McCann and Geoghegan, Inc.

———. (1967). *The Betrayal of the Body.* New York: Collier Books.

Madanes, Cloe. (1983). *Strategic Family Therapy.* San Francisco: Jossey-Bass Publishers.

Maslow, Abraham. (1962). *Toward a Psychology of Being.* Princeton, New Jersey: D. Van Nostrand Company, Inc.

Masterson, James F. (1981). *The Narcissistic and Borderline Disorders.* New York: Brunner/Mazel.

Masters, William H. and Johnson, Virginia E. (1970). *The Pleasure Bond: a new look at sexuality and commitment.* Boston: Little, Brown and Company.

McCarty, Wendy, Anne. (2004). *Welcoming Consciousness: Supporting Babies Wholeness from the Beginning of Life. An Integrated Model of Early Development.* Santa Barbara: WB Publishing.

McLean, J. A., (1994). *Dimensions in Spirituality.* Oxford: George Ronald.

McTaggart, Lynne. (2007). *The Intention Experiment: Using Your Thoughts to Change Your Life and the World.* New York: Free Press.

Minuchin, Salvador. (1974). *Families and Family Therapy.* Cambridge Massachusetts: Harvard University Press.

Musashi, Miyamoto. (1974). *A Book of Five Rings.* New York: The Overlook Press.

Nichols, Michael P. (2007). *The Essentials of Family Therapy.* Boston: Pearson Education Inc.

Prabhavananda, Swami, and Isherwood, Christopher. (1944). *The Song of God: Bhagavad-Gita.* New York: The New American Library.

Perls, Frederick. (1969). *In and Out of the Garbage Pail.* New York: Bantam Books, Inc.

———. (1968). *Gestalt Therapy Verbatim.* Gestalt Journal.

Phillips, Robert, D. (1975). *Structural Symbiotic Systems: Correlations With Ego-States, Behavior, and Physiology.* Chapel Hill, North Carolina: Robert Phillips, 100 Eastowne Drive, Chapel Hill.

Preston, John, and Johnson, James. (1990). *Clinical Psychopharmacology made ridiculously simple.* Miami, FL: MedMaster, Inc.

Ripley, Amanda. *Who Says a Woman Can't be Einstein?* (2005). New York: Time Magazine, March 7, 2005.

Riso, Don, Richard and Hudson, Russ. (1999). *The Wisdom of the Enneagram.* New York: Bantam Books.

Rodman, F. Robert (2003). *Winnicott: Life and work.* Perseus.

Roethke, Theodore. (1975). *The Collected Poems of Theodore Roethke.* New York: Anchor Books.

Rogers, Carl R. (1961). *On Becoming a Person.* Boston: Houghton Mifflin.

Sarno, John E. (1999). *The Mindbody Prescription: Healing the Body, Healing the Pain.* New York: Warner Books.

Satir, Virginia. *The New Peoplemaking.* Science and Behavior Books, Inc.

Schnarch, David. (1997). *Passionate Marriage.* New York: Henry Holt and Company.

———. (2002). *Resurrecting Sex.* New York: Harper Collins.

Schore, Allan. (2003). *Affect Regulation and the Repair of the Self.* New York: W.W. Norton and Company.

Schultz, Dutch. (1977). Personal communication.

Schwartz, Jeffrey M., & Sharon Begley. (2002). *The Mind and The Brain: Neuroplasticity and the Power of Mental Force.* New York: ReganBooks.

Seligman, M.E.P. (2002). *Authentic Happiness: Using the New Positive Psychology to Realize Your Potential for Lasting Fulfillment.* New York: Free Press/ Simon and Shuster.

Sheldon William. (1940). *The Varieties of Human Physique: An Introduction to Constitutional Psychology.* New York: Harper.

Shippen, Eugene, and Fryer, William. (1998). *The Testosterone Syndrome: The Critical Factor for Energy, Health, and Sexuality—Reversing the Male Menopause.* New York: M. Evans and Company, Inc.

Siegel, Daniel J. (1999). The Developing Mind, How Relationships and the Brain Interact to Shape Who We Are. New York: The Guilford Press.

Siegel, Daniel (2007). *The Mindful Brain: Reflection and Attunement in the Cultivation of Well-being.* New York: W.W. Norton & Company.

Siegel, Daniel J. and Hartzell, Mary. (2003). *Parenting from the Inside Out.* New York: Penguin

Siegel, Daniel J. (2005). *The Mindsight Lectures: cultivating insight and empathy in our internal and interpersonal lives.* Mind Your Brain, Inc.

Simonton, O. Carl. (1978). *Getting Well Again.* New York: St. Martin's Press.

Starr, Mirabai (translator). (2002). *Dark Night of the Soul: St. John of the Cross.* New York: Riverhead Books.

Stern, D. N. (2003). *The Present Moment in Psychotherapy and Everyday Life.* New York: W. W. Norton.

Taylor, Shelley, E. (2002). *The Tending Instinct: how nurturing is essential to who we are and how we live.* New York: Henry Holt and Co. LLC.

Tescher, Stacy A. (2005). *To Paddle or not to Paddle: it's still not clear in U.S. Schools.* Christian Science Monitor, March 17, 2005.

Thomashauer, Regena. (2002). *Mama Gena's School of Womanly Arts.* New York: Simon & Schuster.

———. (2003). *Mama Gena's Owner's and Operator's Guide to Men.* New York: Simon & Schuster.

Toffler, Alvin. (1970). *Future Shock.* New York: Random House.

Tzu, Lao. (1963). *Tao Te Ching.* Middlesex, England: Penguin Books Ltd.

US.: (2007). Corporal Punishment and Paddling Statistics by State and Race. U.S. Department of Education, Office for Civil Rights website on this page: http://vistademo.beyond2020.com/ocr2004rv30/xls/2004Projected.html

Wilber, Ken. (2000). *A Brief History of Everything.* Boston: Shambala.

———. (2001). *A Theory of Everything.* Boston: Shambala.

———. (2000). *A Brief History of Everything.* Boston: Shambala.

———. (2000). *Integral Psychology.* Boston: Shambala.

———. (2003). *Kosmic Consciousness.* Boulder: Sounds True (audio recording).

———. (1995). *Sex, Ecology, Spirituality.* Boston and London: Shambhala.

———. (2006). *Integral Spirituality.* Boston: Shambala

Witt, Becky. (2003). Personal communication about a Sophia Diaz led workshop.

Witt, Keith. (1982) *An Investigation of the Effectiveness of Treatment Involving Talking Plus Touching in Enhancing Health.* Santa Barbara, Ca: The Fielding Institute.

———. (2007). *The Attuned Family, How to be a Great Parent to Your Kids and a Great Lover to Your Spouse.* Santa Barbara Graduate Institute Publishing/iUniverse: Amazon.com

———. (2007). *The Gift of Shame: Why We Need Shame and How to Use it to Love and Grow.* Santa Barbara Graduate Institute Publishing/iUniverse: Amazon.com

———. (2006). *Sessions, All Therapy is About Relationships.* keithwitt@cox.net

Wolf, Anthony. (1991). *Get Out of My Life, but first could you drive me and Cheryl to the mall?* New York: The Noonday Press.

Wyckoff, James. (1975). *Franz Anton Mesmer: Between God and Devil.* Englewood Cliffs, New Jersey: Prentice-Hall, Inc.

978-0-595-51442-7
0-595-51442-1

Made in the USA
San Bernardino, CA
29 July 2014